197/a

HISTORY OF

INDONESIA

IN THE

TWENTIETH

CENTURY

BERNHARD DAHM
Translated by P. S. Falla

PRAEGER PUBLISHERS
London · New York · Washington

PRAEGER PUBLISHERS, INC.
111 Fourth Avenue, New York, N.Y. 10003, U.S.A.
5 Cromwell Place, London, S.W.7, England

Published in the United States of America in 1971
by Praeger Publishers, Inc.

© 1971 in London, England, by Bernhard Dahm
Translation © 1971 by Pall Mall Press Limited, London, England

Library of Congress Catalog Card Number: 71-95668

Printed in Great Britain

CONTENTS

To the memory of my mother
Grete Beisenherz (1906–1942)
born near Tarutung, Sumatra

PREFACE

For years past, the conflict in south-east Asia has been in the centre of world interest; and now, with its extension into Cambodia, the question of the stability of neighbouring states is again arising. Can these states prevent hostilities from spreading to their territories? How much popular support do their rulers have, and on which side of the world conflict do they stand?

Indonesia, with its territory of over three thousand islands and population of some 115 millions, is by far the biggest of Vietnam's neighbours. It has no common frontier with a Communist state, as have most of the countries of Indo-China, nor has it any special ties with the USA as have the neighbouring Philippines. As a result it has so far been able to afford the luxury of neutrality, though at times this has been of a very one-sided sort. Under Sukarno's régime, until his downfall in 1966, Indonesia leaned increasingly towards the socialist countries and formed part of the so-called Djakarta-Hanoi-Peking axis, but since then its neutrality has become equally biased in favour of the West. This change grew out of the estrangement between the new regime and the states of the former 'axis', itself the result of the harsh persecution of millions of members of the Indonesian Communist Party (PKI), which was banned after an attempted coup in 1965 that claimed several generals as its victims. For this reason it seems unlikely that the present efforts of the Indonesian government to mediate in the quarrel over Cambodia will have much success. Peking and Hanoi have denounced the present régime in Djakarta as a Fascist dictatorship and are giving all possible support to the Communist underground movement.

How stable is the new Indonesia? Anyone who travels through

Preface
===

Preface

the archipelago – a hazardous undertaking at times owing to poor communications, bad roads and precarious bridges – is impressed by the ubiquity and unquestioned authority of the armed forces in all parts of the country. From time to time a soldier will declare with pride that Indonesia is the only country in south-east Asia to have defeated the Communist threat without foreign help. But the traveller will also notice the tension that prevails between the soldiery and the peasants, who have lost in the PKI the one vigorous champion of their desire for a better lot, the redistribution of land and so on. He will hear of prisons full to bursting, arbitrary arrest and manhandling of suspects, and he will realize that this provides a fertile field for underground Communist activity – which in turn obliges the military to concentrate on security and prevents them from devoting their main energies to 'civic missions' such as road-building. As a result, the so-called 'new order' has not yet taken as firm root in the provinces as it appears to have done, since Sukarno's fall, in Djakarta and some other towns.

At first sight, the internal development of Indonesia has been similar to that of other young nations and may even be regarded as typical of their problems and reactions. The attainment of independence was accompanied by the highest hopes and expectations of a golden age, as promised by the leaders of the independence struggle. But disillusionment soon came when it was realized that the Western parliamentary system, which most such countries adopted at the outset, did not provide adequate means of solving the new problems. The optimism of the early years was quenched by petty regional jealousies, racial or religious strife and the lack of trained cadres for technical and economic development. The parties accused one another of mismanagement and corruption, and by so doing discredited the parliamentary system in the people's eyes. In addition, there was the problem of integrating the army into the State. The military did good service in the fight for independence, but the heroes of the revolution were loth to accept the control of party politicians; this state of affairs led to extra-parliamentary political activities and the formation of separate groups, and generally in the end to a take-over of State power by the military.

Similar as these problems and their immediate solutions arc from one country to another, the peoples and the leaders concerned are widely different. To take only the examples of Burma and Indonesia,

Preface

neighbouring countries which both underwent the development outlined above: it is hard to imagine that U Nu, with his concern for the revival of Buddhism, or Sukarno with his fondness for manipulating Javanese mysticism, would have had the same success in each other's country as they did among their own people. Although human beings in similar situations resemble one another in their expectations and reactions, the forces of indigenous tradition and culture maintain their influence even during periods of rapid external change and are only gradually superseded by new values.

This book describes the rise and development of modern Indonesia. Many aspects of its subject have already been analysed in detail by eminent scholars, while others, such as the dawn of Indonesian nationalism, still stand in need of special investigation to increase our understanding of them. To the best of my knowledge there has not yet been a comprehensive political history, beginning with the time when the Indonesian idea first took shape and continuing down to the present. Dutch scholars have dealt in greater detail with the role of the colonial power in the archipelago, and the author has thus been able to concentrate more on the Indonesian side. He is conscious that the present attempt has many shortcomings and limitations. Unfortunately, for lack of space, little attention could be given to developments in the field of culture, and other important aspects could only be treated in summary fashion.

The author thanks Indonesian statesmen, professors and students for the frank political discussions he was able to have with them when visiting Indonesia in 1966. He is indebted to the armed forces for the opportunity to travel widely throughout the archipelago, particularly in East Java, the islands of Lombok and Sumbawa, Sulawesi (Celebes) and North Sumatra, and for providing him with transport and drivers. He is also grateful for help rendered by the staff of the German embassy in Djakarta. He owes special thanks to the Department of Southeast Asia Studies at Yale University for inviting him to discuss his views with students and faculty members during two fruitful years.

London, 30 April, 1970

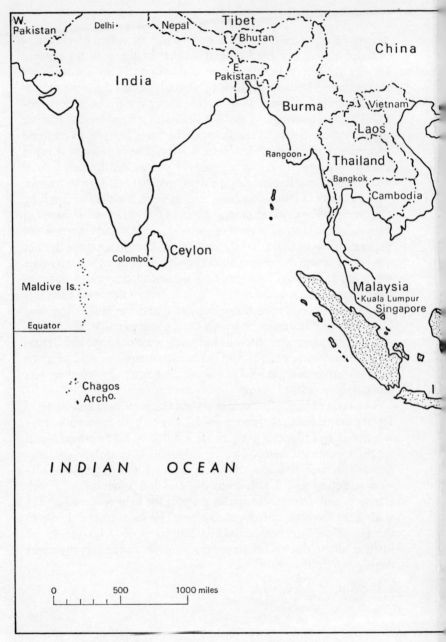

W.
Pakistan   Delhi·   Nepal   Tibet
                              Bhutan
                    E.
                  Pakistan.
        India   China

                        Burma   Vietnam
                                   Laos
                    Rangoon·   Thailand
                              Bangkok
                                   Cambodia

                Colombo· Ceylon

Maldive Is.:

Equator

        Chagos
        Arch°.   Malaysia
                              ·Kuala Lumpur
                              Singapore

INDIAN   OCEAN

0   500   1000 miles

Indonesia and her Neighbours

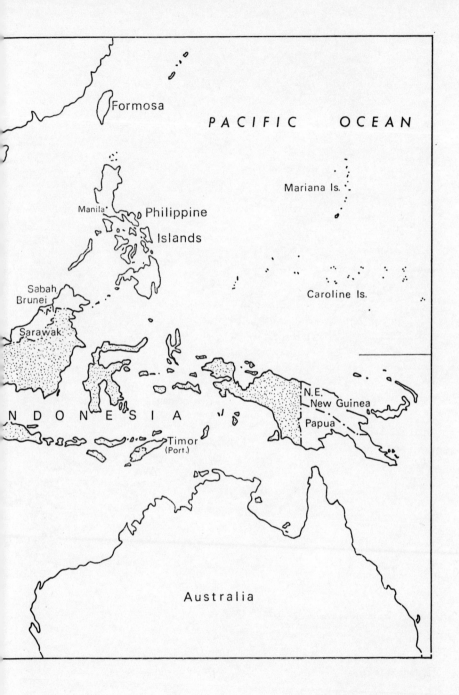

Formosa

PACIFIC OCEAN

Mariana Is.

Manila
Philippine
Islands

Caroline Is.

Sabah
Brunei

Sarawak

N.E.
New Guinea
Papua

INDONESIA

Timor
(Port.)

Australia

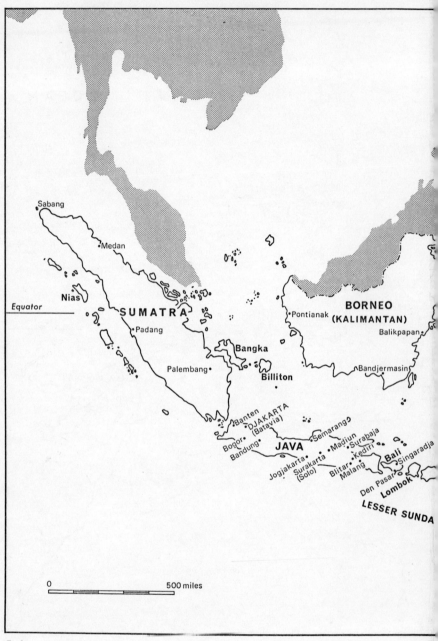

Sabang

Medan

Nias

Equator

SUMATRA

Padang

Palembang

Bangka

Billiton

Pontianak

BORNEO
(KALIMANTAN)

Balikpapan

Bandjermasin

Banten
DJAKARTA
(Batavia)

Bogor
Bandung

Semarang

Madiun

Surabaja

JAVA

Jogjakarta

Surakarta
(Solo)

Blitar
Malang

Kediri

Bali

Singaradja

Den Pasar

Lombok

LESSER SUNDA

0   500 miles

Indonesia in 1970

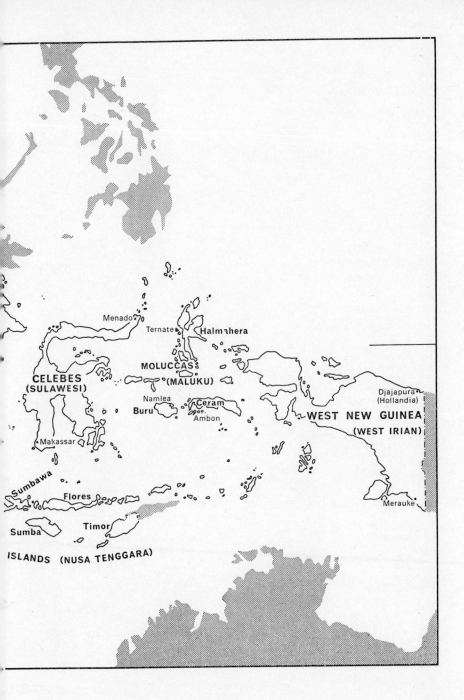

MENADO

Ternate● ●Halmahera

MOLUCCAS
(MALUKU)

CELEBES
(SULAWESI)

Namlea ●Ceram
Buru ● Ambon

Makassar

Djajapura●
(Hollandia)

WEST NEW GUINEA
(WEST IRIAN)

Sumbawa

Flores

Merauke

Sumba   Timor

ISLANDS (NUSA TENGGARA)

I

INDONESIA AT THE TURN
OF THE CENTURY

1 LACK OF A SENSE OF UNITY IN THE PAST

At the beginning of the twentieth century there was no Indonesia in
the present-day sense. There was a group of islands between the
Indian sub-continent and Australia, loosely united by the bond of
Dutch colonial sovereignty; and there were a number of tribes and
peoples with common notions of religion and customary laws, as well
as a common medium of communication in the Malay language,
which had been in use for centuries in the coastal areas of the archipelago, with its variety of native tongues. But the individual
peoples possessed no sense of belonging to a larger whole, and even the
inhabitants of a single island were often sharply divided from the
racial and cultural points of view, so that such designations as 'Javan'
or 'Sumatran' were of doubtful validity.

Sumatra, for instance, from north to south, was inhabited by the
Atjehnese, the Bataks, the Minangkabau and the Lampong; Java,
from west to east, by the Sundanese, the Javanese and a strong
Madurese element in the east; Celebes, from south to north, by the
Buginese, the Toradjas, the Menadonese, and so on. Often these
tribes and peoples were subdivided, as were the Bataks of Sumatra,
the Dayaks of Borneo or the Toradjas of Celebes, into groups
possessing their own languages and religious customs. It is questionable, therefore, whether one should use the term 'Indonesia' in
tracing the history of the Malayan archipelago. The name was first
used about 1850 by British scholars who proposed it as a geographical
designation, and appears in the title of the five-volume work on the
archipelago published in 1884 by the German ethnologist Adolf
Bastian.[1] But it does not follow that 'Indonesia' had any objective
existence at that time. It was not till some decades later, in 1924, that
Indonesian students in Holland first gave a political sense to the

term, which had meanwhile become increasingly common in academic use, and began to propagate the idea of an Indonesian unity transcending local differences.[2]

On several occasions during the history of the archipelago, kingdoms arose which succeeded in extending their rule beyond their original territory and even to several islands. The most important of these early 'Indonesian' empires were Srivijaya in Sumatra (sixth to thirteenth centuries) and Madjapahit in Java (fourteenth and fifteenth centuries). But their campaigns against neighbouring principalities and peoples can hardly be described as 'attempts to unite the whole archipelago into a single independent state', as was done by the Indonesian nationalists[3] who, at the time of the founding of the Republic of Indonesia in 1945, spoke proudly of a 'third Indonesian empire'.[4] Such bold claims require more to substantiate them than the sweeping interpretation of medieval chronicles, whose value as evidence is still disputed.[5] Such conceptions as the 'desire for unity' or an 'independent state' were completely unknown in the archipelago in earlier centuries, and the invocation of such modern ideas obscures the existence of factors which did in course of time contribute to the development of a sense of unity. We may here briefly indicate some of these.

First of all, it is noteworthy that, even before the archipelago was discovered by the Europeans, it was at times regarded by the outside world as forming a unity of its own. Indian, Chinese and Arabic sources sometimes denote the islands collectively as 'Java'. Marco Polo, who put in at Sumatra on his homeward voyage from China, distinguishes in his account between 'Java major' and 'Java minor', though it is not clear to which particular islands these refer.[6] The name 'Sumatra' seems not to have come into use until the fifteenth century, and further differentiation between the islands proceeded even more slowly. The *Itinerario* of the Dutch explorer Linschoten (end of the sixteenth century) uses 'Java minor' to denote the Lesser Sunda Islands of Bali, Lombok, Sumba, Flores, etc.[7]

In Indonesia itself, the collective designation of Java (*Djawa*) seems to have had some currency, also. The Buginese of Celebes for example, spoke of the inhabitants of the larger neighbouring islands —Java, Sumatra and Borneo—as 'Javanese', and named the smaller islands to the east *Djawa-Djawa*, or 'Java minor'.[8] The use of the global term 'Javanese' for inhabitants of the archipelago persisted longest at Mecca, where pilgrims from Indonesia were so named until well into the present century, as was the colony of students who remained at Mecca after completing the pilgrimage.[9] This uniform designation did much to foster a sense of solidarity among the Indonesian Muslims, who in the early twentieth century supplied much of the impetus behind the idea of Indonesian unity.

A second factor which helped to create a sense of unity, and which probably led to the term 'Javanese' being used by the outside world for the seafaring peoples of the archipelago, was the existence of lively trading relations between the various islands. By spreading the use of the Malay language, the traders from an early period laid the foundation for today's unified speech, the *bahasa Indonesia*. Moreover, the adventurous navigators who in early ages sailed as far as Persia, India and China brought back to their native islands political and religious ideas, especially from the Indian sub-continent, and thus prepared the way for the great Hindu and Buddhist eras of Indonesian history.[10] On the other hand, in some respects the trading spirit acted as an obstacle to the sense of unity, destroying in the coastal regions the spirit of *gotong rojong*, or 'mutual help', which is often extolled today as a cornerstone of Indonesian unity. In one of the earliest sources we read that, about A.D. 430, a Javanese king complained to the Chinese emperor Wen Ti that he was being incessantly attacked by his neighbours.[11]

During the heyday of the Hindu and Buddhist kingdoms there was occasional intermarriage between the Javanese and Sumatran princely houses, and negotiations for joint defence seem to have taken place at the end of the thirteenth century, when Kublai Khan was preparing an assault on the archipelago.[12] Such co-operation in defence actually took place after the Portuguese conquest of Malacca in 1511. During the previous century Malacca had become an important *entrepôt*, where Indonesian traders marketed spices from the Moluccas in the east of the archipelago. When the Portuguese began to interfere in this trade, a number of the coastal principalities of Java and Sumatra combined to fit out a fleet for the purpose of besieging Malacca. However, the fleet was destroyed by the Portuguese and the short-lived alliance disintegrated. The Indonesian peoples of that time had no sense of unity over and above common trading interests, although Islam had already gained a foothold in parts of the archipelago, its importance being enhanced by the persistent opposition of Atjeh in northern Sumatra and

Djapara on the north coast of central Java to the Europeans. This did not prevent other sultanates in Sumatra, Java and the Moluccas from seeking their own advantage in trade with the 'infidel'.[13]

True solidarity was not achieved even when, in the course of succeeding centuries, Islam gradually became the dominant religion of the archipelago. Although, after about 1620, the Dutch East India Company, and, after 1800, the colonial administration of the Netherlands Government, intervened from time to time in the affairs of one or other of the princely houses, the latter, when they rebelled against foreign suzerainty, received little or no help from their neighbours and co-religionists. From Sultan Agung's early attempt to 'drive the Dutch out of Djakarta' – in the words of a seventeenth-century chronicle[14] – to the Java rebellion of Diponegoro (1825–30), the many revolts in Celebes, Borneo and Sumatra, and finally the Atjeh war of 1873–1903, each successive rising against the colonial power was more or less thrown upon its own resources. For example, Snouck Hurgronje, who was subsequently an adviser on Islamic matters to the government of the Dutch East Indies describes how, during his stay in Mecca (1884–5), a south Sumatran sheikh living in the 'Java' colony was obliged to use threats and curses to dissuade a relative and compatriot of his from joining the Dutch colonial forces in a campaign against the Muslims of Atjeh.[15] This incident illustrates the lack of solidarity among Indonesians at the end of the nineteenth century, but at the same time shows how, in the loosely-knit archipelago, a new sense of common destiny might be called into being.

2   THE UNIFICATION OF THE ARCHIPELAGO

The penetration of Indonesia by Islam was a slow process, even after the latter's rejuvenation by the Wahhabi movement in the eighteenth century. The first Islamic wave reached Indonesia between the thirteenth and the fifteenth centuries, and the new religion found rapid acceptance in the coastal areas, but it took centuries for it to progress further inland. In some regions, such as central and eastern Java, it succumbed to syncretism and compromise, while in others – such as Bali, the Batak country, central and northern Celebes, Timor and Flores – its influence was superficial or non-existent.

The second Islamic wave, which took place in the nineteenth

4

century and was marked by greater missionary zeal, came up against the tenacity of the *adat* – the traditional religious and customary laws of the individual native peoples. In the Padri War in west Sumatra (1803–38), the native authorities finally appealed to the colonial power to help them defend themselves against the Islamic reformers known as *padri*. The latter's connection with the Wahhabis has been disputed,[16] but is probable in view of the close coincidence in time and the likelihood of contacts with the Arab world through Atjeh, which was still independent; moreover, the initiators of the Padri War came straight from Mecca and began at once zealously to combat the superstitions of the *adat*.[17]

The long drawn-out war was at last terminated by the intervention of the colonial government in favour of the *adat* party, and this marked the beginning of the extension of Dutch sovereignty over the whole archipelago. The Dutch, who had founded their first stronghold at Batavia in 1619 (formerly Jacatra and now Djakarta), had since then contented themselves with defending their trade interests, establishing bases on the coasts of certain islands, and carrying out the gradual penetration of Java. Their main rivals at the time were not the independent-minded Indonesians but the British, who were concerned to extend their own influence. From 1795 onwards the Batavian Republic, under French hegemony, was at war with Britain, as a result of which Java was occupied from 1811 to 1816 by the British and placed under the rule of Sir Stamford Raffles. In 1824 the Treaty of London delimited British and Dutch interests in the Straits of Malacca: Britain gave up Bengkulen in Sumatra and a few adjacent islands, while the Dutch renounced further influence in the Malayan peninsula and recognized Britain's annexation of Singapore.

The Dutch were now able to turn to measures of pacification. The war against Diponegoro, who took up arms because he was deprived of the Javanese throne, was followed by intervention in the Padri War and later by campaigns against the Balinese (1846, 1848 and 1849), fighting in Borneo (1850–4), Celebes (1858–60), and again Borneo (1859–63). In 1870 a rebellion broke out in Sumatra under the Batak priest-king Singa Mangaradja XII, and in 1894 a punitive expedition was sent against Lombok, where Balinese warriors had ambushed a Dutch force.

However, the most important military operation was the pacification of Atjeh from 1873 onwards. In accordance with the terms of the Treaty of London, the Dutch had undertaken to respect the independence of this area, but the obligation had been removed by a further agreement in 1871 concerning Sumatra. In order to escape the threat of colonization, the Atjehnese thereupon endeavoured to conclude assistance pacts with the Sultan of Turkey as Caliph of Islam, and also with Italy and even the United States. Foreign help was not forthcoming, but the world watched attentively[18] as the Dutch pursued efforts to subjugate the Atjehnese which continued for decades without leading to any decisive success. The struggle broke out with renewed violence in 1896 after the defection of Teuku Umar, who had from time to time collaborated with the Dutch, but from then on the latter gradually gained the upper hand. Their troops were commanded by General J. B. van Heutsz, who had repeatedly pressed for a military decision in lieu of fruitless negotiations. Victory was finally attained as a result of tactics recommended by Snouck Hurgronje which consisted of driving a wedge between the Atjehnese secular and spiritual leaders by concluding agreements with the former, the *uleebalangs*, while hunting down the latter, the *ulama* – or, as they were called by the Atjeh, the *teungkus*. By 1903 the pacification of Atjeh was complete.

Van Heutsz, who became Governor-General of the Dutch East Indies in the following year, regarded it as his main task to round off the acquisition of Dutch sovereignty. He obliged the rulers who had already submitted, and the other local authorities, to sign a so-called 'short declaration', in which they recognized Dutch suzerainty and promised to conduct no negotiations with foreign powers and to carry out all orders from the colonial government.[19] Further military [expeditions were undertaken to enforce these demands: to southern Celebes, southern Borneo and the Batak country, as well as Sumba, Ceram and Flores. The last campaign, 1906–8, was fought in the heart of Bali: after a hopeless resistance, whole princely families elected to commit suicide and stabbed one another to death in a ritual ecstasy rather than accept subjection to foreign masters.[20]

Thus, in the first decade of the twentieth century Dutch sovereignty was extended over the whole archipelago except for the British colonial territories in northern Borneo, and for the first time present-day Indonesia was united under a single administration. General van Heutsz may be regarded with some justice as the architect of the future state: by his drastic methods he had overthrown the autonomous structure of the traditional principalities, but by so doing he had paved the way for Indonesian unity.

3 SOCIAL STRUCTURE AND NATIVE AUTHORITIES

It would require a separate book to describe the social structure of the Indonesian peoples at the beginning of the twentieth century. The complexity was greatest in the 'outer provinces' – the general Dutch term for all the islands other than Java and Madura. Some tribal communities subsisted mainly on hunting and fishing, others on agriculture in areas cleared of jungle and known as *ladang*, while others again had become sedentary and cultivated irrigated rice-fields (*sawah*). Some villages were inhabited entirely by members of a single clan, others by three or four different tribes, and others still accepted outsiders as residents. There were territorial principalities based ultimately on the unity of a single tribe, patriarchal or matriarchal as the case might be; principalities based on the idea of a divine kingship; and sultanates in which an attempt was made, however superficially, to put into effect the precepts of Islam.

The religious[21] and legal[22] customs of all these peoples had suffered little change, since from time immemorial it was regarded as a supreme duty not to deviate from the *adat*, the 'ways of the ancestors'. Their contacts with the colonial power were limited; here and there a ruler might have refused submission, or the Dutch might have established trading bases or encouraged Christian missions as a check to Islam, as they did in the Batak country, Menado, or the Moluccas.

However, conditions were different in Java, which the Dutch had first used as a hinterland to protect their trading posts, but had systematically penetrated after they realized its value as a profitable area for plantations. In the course of the nineteenth century, Java became the core of the Dutch colonial empire of the East Indies. In 1900 it was the home of some 28 million, out of the total population of 36 million; it was in Java that the national independence movement was born and the foundations of the future republic were laid. We should therefore take a closer look at the Javanese social structure.

The *sawah* system of cultivation and the development of the territorial state had taken place in Java at an early stage, on the basis of village communities known as *desas* which were for a long time autonomous. Each *desa* comprised various sections of the population. Some groups, who traced their ancestry back to the founders of the village, possessed lands and other property; others owned only a house and a garden plot; and others still had no home or land of their own, but were quartered on their fellow-villagers. The village headman, who in Java was usually called the *lurah*, was the custodian of the *adat*, and as such little more than *primus inter pares*. The office was hereditary; the *lurah* was assisted by a council of elders, but he could be deposed for deviating from traditional ways.[23]

Although the institution of royalty began to make headway in the first centuries A.D., the *desas* remained largely autonomous. In theory the princes were the masters of both land and people; but their claim to rule was based on the welfare of the inhabitants as a reflection of heavenly favour, and it was thus in their interest to maintain steady and unbroken contact with the peoples of their territories. In return for protection, their subjects paid taxes in kind or in the form of labour, and this provided remuneration for the official class known as *prijajis* – the prince's 'younger brothers'. The prince, as a reincarnation of Vishnu or Buddha, generally remained secluded in his palace-city, or *kraton*, while the *prijajis* maintained contact between it and the village.

Members of the royal family and the nobility were entrusted with the administration of *kabupatens* (regencies). Their functions were to furnish revenue to the *kraton*, accompany the ruler to war, and pay homage at certain times. If they forfeited the ruler's confidence they could be dismissed and replaced at any time. The *bupatis* (regents) had under them officials belonging to the lesser nobility, who visited the *desas* to dispense justice, raise taxes and supervise the performance of labour duties. The peasants had the right to protest if they considered that their rights had been infringed, or that they were being exploited by the *prijajis*; there are many cases recorded of both individual and collective protests to the royal court.[24]

This system of administration was maintained by the East India Company when the native princes became subject to it. The Company appointed *bupatis* of its own choice, who were responsible to it for the payment of the revenues which had previously accrued to the prince. Where, as in central Java, the princes were allowed to continue in office, special arrangements and detailed treaties

8

were concluded, to be renewed whenever a new prince or sultan succeeded his father.[25]

The appointment of *bupatis* was a lucrative source of revenue for the colonial officials concerned, as the Javanese nobility were prepared to pay large sums for the privilege, which they then endeavoured to extract from the areas under their control. Consequently the Dutch were reluctant to agree to the regents' wish that their office be made hereditary. However, the Constitutional Regulation of 1854 contained a provision that, when a regency fell vacant, a son or near relative of the last *bupati* should if possible be appointed.[26]

At the turn of the century Java and Madura, which formed a single administrative unit, contained altogether 90 regencies, divided into districts (*kewedanaan*) and sub-districts (*ketjamatan*) administered by *wedanas* and *assistén-wedanas* respectively. The number of *desas* registered in Java was at this time something over 43,000,[27] so that each *bupati* was the ruler of about 500 villages, which he administered with the aid of about 5 *wedanas* and a number of *assistén-wedanas*. In addition, he was often assisted by a *patih* (chancellor), judicial officials (*djaksa*), secretaries and clerks (*djurutulis*), the last being the rank in which the *prijajis* generally started their career. By the end of the nineteenth century very few of the native officials could still trace their descent from princely families, except perhaps for the *bupatis*, who by degrees became known as 'higher *prijajis*', to distinguish them from the 'lesser *prijajis*' from the *wedana* downwards.

This native system of provincial administration was interlocked with the *bestuur* (government) of the Dutch colonial authorities. The Governor-General, with his residence at Batavia, represented the Crown, and was invested with full powers for the exercise of autocratic government. The Dutch Minister for the Colonies answered to Parliament for the Governor-General's acts. The latter was advised by a Council of the Indies (*Raad van Indië*), which was also appointed by the Crown, but he was not obliged to accept its recommendations. Under the Governor-General were governors, each possessing authority over several 'residencies': a residency, presided over by a resident, consisted in turn of several regencies. A Dutch assistant resident usually resided at the seat of government of each regency as the *bupati's* 'younger brother', while in the districts and sub-districts there were Dutch controllers, this being the lowest grade of the higher administration, a career reserved for Europeans.

The Dutch system of colonial government was thus in theory an indirect one, inasmuch as it did not destroy the indigenous social order, as the British did in Burma, and for this it has been authoritatively praised.[28] In practice, however, from the time of the East India Company onwards it was often of the most direct kind, ranging from contact with the *lurahs* at their level to interference, sometimes of a drastic nature, in the work of the *bupatis*. For a long time the Dutch were less interested in running a model colony than in extracting large revenues; this was especially marked at the time of the *Cultuurstelsel* (Cultivation System) of 1830–60, when the natives were compelled to use part of their land to grow crops in demand on the European market, such as sugar, tea, spices and tobacco. In this way, the *prijajis* and the village communities were, to an unprecedented extent, harnessed to the service of European prosperity. The consequences were far-reaching: the *prijajis* lost much of their traditional prestige, and the once-honoured role of the village headman also fell into disrepute, as men sought the office for their own benefit and so did not command the loyalty of the people.[29]

At the same time as the traditional authorities declined in public estimation, a new élite came into prominence with the 'second Islamic wave': the *hadjis* and *kijais* (religious scholars) – the teachers at the *pesantren* (village religous schools). At all periods, a certain number of the faithful had ventured on the journey to Mecca, despite the expense and hardships involved; but, after the Suez Canal was opened in 1869 and ships began to ply regularly through the Red Sea, thousands streamed annually from Java and the other islands to visit the Holy Land. As a result of the pilgrimage, they became aware of a general revival of Islam, linked with Mahdistic expectations and pan-Islamic ideas which they propagated on their return home. Whether the pilgrims or religious teachers correctly interpreted what was going on in the world of Islam is of minor importance; the main point is that as early as about 1887 there were, in the 43,000 *desas*, 49,819 *hadjis* and 21,500 religious teachers,[30] many of whom were prepared to call in question the authority, not only of the *prijajis*, but also of the colonial authorities.[31] From about 1890 onwards, the number of *hadjis* from the archipelago grew by over 10,000 a year.[32] It is not surprising, therefore, that the colonial power began to fear Islamic activities,[33] and that anti-

Muslim pamphlets began to circulate at the courts of the Javanese princes.[34]

At the turn of the century, ninety per cent of the population of Indonesia still lived on the land. Only a handful had found their way to the cities, where they earned a living as servants in European homes, small tradesmen or petty officials, or again as coolies or day labourers. They lived in *kampongs*, the poverty-stricken native quarters on the outskirts of the cities, and had no share in the wealth and luxury that was to be found in the larger trading centres such as Batavia, Surabaja or Semarang.

An important element in these cities, which had taken the place of the old pre-colonial trading and *entrepôt* centres on the coasts, were the settlements of Chinese, Arab and Indian traders dating from before the advent of the European colonists. Although the 'foreign Orientals', as the Dutch called them, obtained a firm foothold in rural trade, nevertheless Batavia, Surabaja and Semarang accounted for no less than half of the 277,000 Chinese and 18,000 Indians and Arabs who were registered as residents of Java. In the outer islands at this time there were 260,000 Chinese and 22,500 Indians, Arabs and other 'foreign orientals'.[35]

The Europeans, who at this time numbered 94,000, were similarly concentrated in the larger towns. Two-thirds of them (62,000) lived in Java, the majority of these in the three chief cities. Only a fifth were *totoks* – full-blooded Europeans who belonged to the administration or, especially after the 'liberal policy' was introduced about 1870, had come to seek their fortune in the colony as merchants, tradesmen or planters. By far the greater number of 'Europeans' – a term which soon came officially to include the Japanese, who were assimilated to them in law – were Eurasians. Although the law made no distinction between them and the *totoks*, their social status was ambiguous: they were often slighted by the Dutch, but felt superior to the *inlanders*, as the Indonesians were called. This led to many conflicts in the course of the nineteenth century, such as the 'Batavian May movement' of 1848,[36] and gave an important impetus to the twentieth-century independence movement: the first native organization to take shape was the *Indische Bond*, set up in October 1898 by Eurasians in Batavia to help their distressed co-racialists in the colony. The first nationalist who in 1912 openly demanded the independence of the archipelago from the Dutch was the Eurasian E. F. E. Douwes Dekker.

4 THE ETHICAL POLICY

From early times, voices were raised among the Dutch colonists in favour of paying more attention to native interests and not considering the colony exclusively as a means of filling the coffers of the motherland. Such voices were heard at the time of the Cultivation System, when the ordinances of the country's white masters began to transform the rhythm of village life. For example, an article in the *Tijdschrift van Nederlandsch-Indië* in 1852 argued that it was the duty of the mother country to 'develop and train the colonies and lead them to independence',[37] and elsewhere in the same periodical we read that a general desire for education had been fostered among the natives by contact with Europeans and the example of the mission schools in the outer provinces. If the government were to meet this desire with a consistent and intelligent education policy, it could attach the natives 'more and more closely to itself'.[38] In this way, opinion welcomed the government's soundings and first measures towards the establishment of a school system. But nothing materialized beyond the creation of a *dokter djawa* (a school set up in 1851 to train auxiliary medical personnel for the fight against epidemics) and the opening in subsequent years of a few training colleges to provide teachers for the projected educational system. It was a significantly long time before further steps were taken in this direction. Warnings heard at this time to the effect that 'native education . . . means the beginning of the end of our colonial rule'[39] were reinforced by reports of highly gifted pupils, and the advocates of a universal school system suffered a rebuff when their opponents reduced to five the number of training colleges, which had risen to nine. However, from 1880 onwards there were also three *hoofdenscholen*, one each in western, central and eastern Java, to train the sons of senior *prijajis* for an administrative career.[40]

Thinking members of the Javanese community observed that the colonial government had evidently not yet made up its mind as to the desirability of an educational system embracing wide sections of the population.[41] The question was not decided in the affirmative until the end of the century, when the second Islamic wave brought with it the danger of increasing estrangement between the colony and the mother country. The authorities realized suddenly that education was the crucial problem, and that they could not allow the teachers in the *pesantren* who preached hatred against the 'infidels' and their henchmen, the *prijajis*, to dominate the field. Revolts had repeatedly broken out in which the influence of the *pesantren* and *hadjis* had been clearly discernible, notably that at Banten in 1888, in which 47 people had been killed and a large number wounded.[42]

Note should also be taken of the Ratu Adil (Righteous Prince) movements inspired by belief in the advent, foretold in ancient times, of a Javanese Messiah who would bring the population, at the time when their need seemed greatest, good fortune, prosperity and freedom from taxes.[43] Movements of this type flared up repeatedly in the second half of the nineteenth century as an expression of social unrest and political discontent. In the same order of ideas, we may mention the Samin movement, a manifestation of social protest with a character of its own, which broke out near Blora in central Java towards 1900. Its leader, Surontiko Samin, was exiled in 1907 and died in 1914, but, instead of petering out like other Messianic revolts, the movement, with its elements of idealistic communism, continued to affect opinion up to and after the foundation of the Indonesian republic.[44]

These proto-nationalistic movements, accompanied as they often were by rural notions of miraculous help from heavenly powers and magic formulae for the creation of an earthly paradise, almost invariably took the same practical forms: refusal to pay taxes or perform labour services, hostility towards the foreign masters who had intruded into the life of the village, and contempt for the traditional authority of *prijajis*, *lurahs* and so forth. These were the 'signs of the times' to which attention was drawn by the 'ethical' school at the turn of the century, which called for a change in Dutch colonial policy. Its spokesman was C. Th. van Deventer, who, in an article in the spring of 1899 entitled 'A Debt of Honour', pleaded for the repayment of all the profits that had been drawn from the colony, to the value of several hundred million guilders. His well-documented case[45] was unshakeable, and his arguments gave rise to a discussion which led, in the ensuing years, to the adoption of the so-called 'ethical' course in colonial policy. By this was understood the moral obligation to remedy the 'low state of welfare' of the native population and to pay greater attention to its interests than in the past. As a friend of van Deventer's put it in a declaration of principles, the old policy had reached a dead end. After exploitation by means of compulsion under the cultivation system, the population had been exposed to capitalist exploitation as a result of economic liberalism, and was now being brought to ruin by starvation wages, high taxes, indebtedness and forced labour.[46]

The 'ethical' party put forward a wide range of demands for the restriction of arbitrary foreign rule, the safeguarding of legal rights and the abolition of unjust taxation and expropriation. This last was of frequent occurrence, despite the theoretical inalienability of native property, owing for instance to the activities of money-lenders and speculators using Indonesian 'men of straw'. The 'ethicals' also advocated the improvement of yields by better irrigation and a policy of encouraging migration within the colony, so as to relieve the pressure of population in Java and develop the more sparsely settled areas of Sumatra and Borneo. They also pressed for decentralization of the administration and the establishment of local councils, so that the population would gradually acquire a voice in their own affairs. The main emphasis, however, was laid on the systematic development of education, and opportunities, hitherto very restricted, for Indonesians to learn Dutch. In this way it was hoped to bring about an association, if not an assimiliation, of the two peoples.[47]

Most of these demands were fulfilled in the ensuing years. As the physical framework of the future state was being created by the unification of the archipelago, so the expansion of the educational system by the colonial power provided for the formation of a modern élite which might one day enter into possession. At the same time, arguments were advanced to justify it in doing so. Like their mid-century predecessors, the 'ethicals' of 1900 demanded that the mother country should prepare the colony for independence. As the Social Democrat politician van Kol put it, 'We must bring up the child in such a way that it can learn to dispense with our help.'[48] The 'ethicals' were agreed that 'by far the greatest part of the European colonial possessions in general and those of the Netherlands in particular were acquired by force against the will of those who possess more ancient rights than we, their present-day masters.'[49] However, van Deventer and those who thought like him did not infer from this that the Dutch should quit the colony at once. By so doing they would not repair the injustice of past centuries: for, by interfering in the natural course of development, they had placed the natives in a condition in which they could not at once dispense with the guidance of foreign masters. The 'ethical' policy might lead to a situation in which the colonies could develop into fully independent communities which would choose to dissolve the bond uniting them with the motherland. It must be hoped that this separation – 'perhaps a few centuries hence' – would not take place violently but on a basis of mutual respect and friendship. But, for these convinced democrats, there were no two ways of thinking as to the course which colonial policy should follow. The domination of one people over another was contrary to nature; 'the liberation of the subject people must come sooner or later, but it would be a misfortune for both sides if it were to do so prematurely or by violence.'[50]

Before many years passed, these 'ethical' arguments were being used as ammunition by the nationalists. The association with the motherland, which the ethical party and Snouck Hurgronje hoped to see as a result of the spread of education, did not come to pass. It might have done so had the policy been put into effect about 1850, when it was first mooted; but times had changed. The new educational policy was not a gift bestowed by the colonial power, but was wrung from it by the activities of Islam, increasing social discontent, and, as we shall see presently, the popular demand for schooling. Whereas in the past expediency had argued against a broadening of the educational system, the alternative now was to suffer further alienation from the people or to take the risk of emancipating it.

5   DEMAND FOR EDUCATION AND THE SCHOOL SYSTEM

By the turn of the century, the school system, which had begun with the creation of teachers' training colleges about 1850, had made little progress, especially in Java, where there were only 562 schools, more than half of which had been launched by private enterprise, for a population of some 28 million. The ratio of one school to 50,000 inhabitants appears especially low when the state of affairs in Java is compared with that in the outer islands, above all the mission territories such as the Batak country and Menado (cf. Table 1).

In 1893 the government schools (*inlandsche scholen*) in Java were divided into two classes. Those of the first class were intended to give the sons of *prijajis* a better education than the children of the common people, who in the opinion of the colonial power did not need more than a basic knowledge of the three R's, imparted in their mother tongue. The thirty-six first-class schools also taught natural history, geography, and the history of the area in question, but again the language of instruction was either the vernacular of the region or Malay.[52] The 'ethical' party proposed in the first instance that the number of second-class schools should be drastically increased. But General van Heutsz had a different plan: about 1906 he introduced a widespread system of low-cost village schools, the upkeep of which, together with the teachers' pay, had to be provided by the *desa* itself.[53]

Table 1   Elementary schools in the Dutch East Indies about 1900[51]

Territory	Government schools	Private schools	Mission schools	Total	Population in 1000s
Java and Madura	269	231	62	562	28,386
Sumatra (except Batak country)	77	17	4	98	2,862
Batak country	19	6	175	200	321
Borneo	12	3	21	36	1,076
Celebes (except Menado)	14	–	–	14	1,442 (1895)
Menado	115	14	237	366	423
Ternate	2	2	9	13	133
Ambon	74	75	17	166	271
Timur	15	10	16	41	306 (1905)
Bali and Lombok	4	1	–	5	1,039
Total	601	359	541	1,501	36,259

The Indonesians, however, in their more or less open demands for better education, were concerned not with quantitative but with qualitative improvement and with access to schooling at a higher level. This was possible only by way of the European primary schools known as ELS (*Europeesche Lagere School*), to which Indonesians were admitted on a limited basis provided they knew Dutch. In this respect the Indonesians of the outer islands, especially the mission areas, had an advantage over their Javanese compatriots, since the mission schools frequently taught in Dutch, whereas in Java, as late as the present century, it was necessary to engage a private teacher for this purpose. In some places there were opportunities of learning Dutch,[54] and there was also the exception that children who undertook to go on to the *dokter djawa* school were allowed to attend the ELS, even without a knowledge of Dutch;[55] but apart from this there was no relaxation of the rule. This being so, it is the more remarkable how Indonesians flocked into the ELS at the turn of the century.

Table II   Pupils in European primary schools (ELS) about 1900[56]

Year	Europeans	Foreign Orientals	Indonesians	Christians included in Indonesian figures	Number of schools
1890	11,421	148	808	338	144
1895	12,690	185	1,135	391	159
1900	13,592	325	1,545	557	169
1905	15,105	525	3,725	1,046	184

Thus each year saw a large increase in the number of Indonesians thirsting for education, who often acquired an elementary knowledge of Dutch at the cost of heavy financial sacrifice to their families. The relatively high percentage of Indonesian Christians, who only constituted one per cent of the total population about 1900,[57] is explained by the activity of the mission schools, whose importance for the formation of a modern Indonesian élite is thus not to be underrated.

The colonial authorities were alarmed by the steadily increasing flow of Indonesians into the ELS, and in 1906, in order to preserve the latter's character of a European primary school, they decided to include Dutch in the curriculum of the first-class government schools, and to extend the period of study from five to seven years. These reforms led in 1914 to the so-called *Hollandsch-Inlandsche Scholen* (HIS), by means of which the Indonesians were able to receive higher education without passing through the European school system.[58] In subsequent years, in addition to the HIS, they frequently also attended the MULO (*Meer uitgebreid lager onderwijs*: extended primary education), a type of junior high school which gave access to most forms of professional activity.

At the turn of the century, Indonesians who had attended the ELS had the following opportunities of further education. Firstly, the *dokter djawa* school, which had been reorganized several times since its foundation in 1851. By 1900 it was known as Stovia (*School tot opleiding van inlandsche artsen*: school for the training of native doctors), and provided three years of preparatory schooling followed by a six years' course of thorough professional training, which enabled graduates to practise on their own account. Secondly, the Osvia (*Opleidingsscholen van inlandsche ambtenaren*: training schools for native officials), of which there were six in Java and one in Menado in 1910: these provided a seven-year course which opened the way to the *prijaji* career up to the grade of *bupati*. Finally, there were five teachers' training colleges known as *Kweekscholen*, two of them in the outer islands, offering six-year courses by means of which teachers were recruited for the government schools. To become a teacher in the *desa* schools, it was sufficient to have attended the native elementary schools.[59]

In addition, Indonesians who had passed through the ELS might be admitted to one of the three *Hogere Burgerscholen* (HBS) in Batavia, Semarang and Surabaja, which offered a general five-year course leading to University matriculation. Up to 1900 only a few Indonesians attended these schools, but thereafter they took increasing advantage of the opportunity.

Table III   Composition of the HBS about 1900[60]

Year	Europeans	Foreign Orientals	Indonesians
1885	352	6	2
1890	354	–	5
1895	558	3	4
1900	549	4	13
1905	677	16	36

Even so, it will be observed (cf. Table II, p. 17) that only one per cent of ELS-leavers went on to the HBS. The reason was not only that the great majority could not afford the high fees, but had to start earning their living at once. It was an open secret at that time that Indonesians who had passed through the HBS did not find all doors open to them in the same way as did their European fellow-pupils. In particular, they could not hope to enter the higher ranks of the colonial administration – those of Controller, Assistant Resident, Resident and Governor. Until the 1920s, there was no university in the colony. Only the wealthier natives, generally the *bupatis*, could afford to send their sons to study in Europe, and even with them it was the exception rather than the rule. Consequently native pupils of the HBS usually had to accept jobs that bore no relation to the education they had received. One such, who in 1903 achieved the best examination results of all candidates from the three HBS, was refused a scholarship to study in Holland and had to earn his living as a translator and clerk in a coal-mining company. His subsequent career, during which he spent a few years as a secretary at the Dutch East Indies consulate at Jedda, made him a living refutation of the ethical party's hopes that education would bring about an association of the Indonesian intelligentsia with the Netherlands. The man in question was Agus Salim, one of the chief figures of the Indonesian independence movement.[61]

II

THE BEGINNINGS OF
INDONESIAN NATIONALISM

I EARLY MANIFESTATIONS

Rebellions against Dutch sovereignty in 'Insulinde' – as the region was sometimes poetically called – had never ceased to break out, from the time of the foundation of Batavia in 1619 to the final conquest of Bali in 1908. But, as already explained, the revolts of the native rulers were no more than isolated actions, and no basis existed for a permanent opposition embracing the whole archipelago. Even the second Islamic wave, strong as it was in the last decades of the nineteenth century, had not as yet brought about a sense of genuine solidarity. In many regions, this rejuvenated Islam found itself at grips with the traditional authorities, who often regarded themselves as true followers of the Prophet. In Atjeh, for instance, the conflict between the 'secular' *uleebalangs* and the 'spiritual' *teungkus* continued to rage during their common war against the colonial power, which was able to exploit the situation in the same way as it had done some decades earlier in the Padri War.

Accordingly, the comparatively late 'awakening of the sleeping beauty of Insulinde' (to use the phrase with which van Deventer welcomed the first beginnings of organization in Java in 1908) has been from time to time ascribed to other factors, such as the 'cannonade at Tsushima' in 1905 which signalized Japan's victory over the might of Russia – an event which later Indonesian nationalists often acclaimed as the prelude to their own struggle for independence.[1] However, important though the relationship is between the later independence movement and the general revolt of Asia against dominion from outside, the ideas to which the 'sleeping beauty' gave utterance when she was roused from slumber point in a different direction. The common bond which first united

20

the archipelago was the Western system of education, which abruptly called into question the traditional ways that had been so revered, and opened men's minds to new ideals. We may see this in the letters of Raden Adjeng Kartini, the daughter of the *bupati* of Djepara, who wrote to a European correspondent on 25 May 1899:

In my thoughts and sympathies, I do not belong to the world of the Indies but to that of my white sisters who are fighting for progress in the distant West ... Century-old, unbreakable traditions hold us today in a relentless grip. One day that grip will slacken and we shall be able to struggle against it, but it will not be for a long, a very long time. It will come about, I am sure, but perhaps not for another three or four generations. Oh, you cannot imagine what it is to love the new age with all one's heart and soul, yet to be bound hand and foot, chained to the laws and customs of our country. All our institutions are totally opposed to the progress for which I long in the interests of our people[2]

Raden Kartini, who was born in 1879, had attended an ELS, after which, at the age of twelve, she had been 'locked up' at home – the usual fate of daughters of the higher Javanese nobility until such time as a suitable marriage was arranged for them. However, her father, who was one of the more progressive Javanese regents, took the unusual step of giving his daughters a Western education, after which he allowed Dutch friends to persuade him to set Kartini free. For this she was grateful till the end of her days, both to her father and to the friends in question, who included members of the ethical party such as J. H. Abendanon, the Director of the Department of Education in the colonial Government from 1900 to 1905; the Social Democrat van Kol; the missionary to the Toradjas, N. Adriani; and several others. Her letters speak much of friendship with the Dutch people, who in her eyes had a great part to play in the emancipation of her fellow-countrymen. Yet here and there she displays indignation at colonial officials who mistreated the local population, spoke disparagingly of the Indies, or insisted on marks of respect to which, in her view, only the native princes and *bupatis* were entitled. Occasionally, too, she blames the Government outright for promoting the cultivation of opium in Java, which filled the coffers of the state but helped to reduced the people to misery, or for delaying the expansion of the educational system. She remarks that many Dutch people were against educating the

Javanese because they feared that this would put an end to the latter's state of subjection. But, she proclaims, 'we are on the march – they cannot stop the course of history';[3] and again: 'A transformation will take place in the whole of our native world. The change is predestined. It must come – but when? That is the great question! We cannot antedate the hour of revolution.'[4]

Such words as these show that Raden Kartini, who died in 1904 when giving birth to her first child at the age of twenty-five, is rightly looked on as a pioneer of Indonesian nationalism. She took a lively interest in the fortunes of the first Indonesian – not only Javanese – students in the Netherlands, and in 1903 did her best to get a scholarship that she did not herself need transferred to the Sumatran Agus Salim, so that he could study in Holland. But the cause to which she was devoted above all was that of the emancipation of Indonesian women. The publication of her letters to reach a wide circle of readers did much to help this cause, which was taken up by her sisters after her death.[5]

Some passages in her letters, especially those which criticize the colonial régime, have been thought to show the influence of her uncle, R. M. A. A. Hadiningrat, the *bupati* of Demak, who enjoyed much authority among his fellow-regents at the turn of the century. He was frequently consulted by the colonial Government, which in 1893 commissioned him to investigate the reasons for the decline in the regents' prestige among the population and to suggest how the situation might be remedied. In his report, published in 1899 – the same year as van Deventer's article on the 'debt of honour', Hadiningrat laid the blame principally on the lack of educational facilities provided for the Javanese. His own father had realized in 1850 that the way to overcome the backwardness of the Javanese people and open the way to progress was to provide access to Western culture;[6] and accordingly he had had his children educated in the Western manner at a time when this was still most unusual. It was in fact considered both unbefitting and pointless, since the coveted rank of regent was generally bestowed in accordance with the Government's preference rather than the individual's qualifications. In this way the Government was able to keep the *inlandsche hoofden* firmly under control, and the latter soon discovered that submissiveness was a better passport to promotion than insistence on rights and abilities.

Hadiningrat had vainly opposed this state of affairs as early as

1871, and in his report at the end of the century he pointed to it as the main reason for the regents' lack of prestige. He argued, further- more, that while Government circles had still not made up their minds as to the desirability of educating the Javanese, the cultural gap between the colonists and the local nobility had grown wider as a result of European progress. The Dutch authorities were no longer interested in discussion with the *bupatis*, who were regarded merely as instruments of the executive, a fact which had injured their prestige no less than the arbitrary method of appointing to high office and the obsequiousness of candidates. In future, he urged, the latter should receive a school education, be tested by an examina- tion, and thereafter enjoy opportunities of further schooling. This, he argued, was not only to the interest of his countrymen, but also to that of the colonial régime. New ideas and achievements would arouse fresh aspirations in the population at large, and if these were not to have untoward consequences, it was necessary to train up a body of trustworthy leaders. This might mean fewer marks of respect for the colonial régime and less toadying on the part of the native rulers; but such manifestations in any case served no purpose. They would diminish, whether the Javanese were educated or not; but civilized people knew what they owed to one another. The process of instilling culture would be a gradual one, and need therefore excite no alarm, especially if it were begun from the top as he advocated.[7]

In this way Hadiningrat discreetly indicated that he understood the authorities' anxiety, since the loss of prestige was as much a matter of concern to them as to the higher *prijajis*. The ethical party repeatedly invoked his views in support of their argument for a fresh policy. He had not advocated a 'gradual transition to self- government', or threatened, as has been claimed in Indonesia some years ago, that independence was certain to come one day, whether by peaceful or by violent means.[8] But his arguments were bound sooner or later, to lead in that direction. As a *bupati* he spoke of reform 'from the top', but he did not consider that the right to lead the nation should be confined to the nobility. 'How can a man help it', he asked, 'if he is born in a village hut, and not in a *kabupaten* [regent's dwelling]?'; and he continued:

I am therefore strongly in favour of showing the natives that it is right and proper to give non-nobles the opportunity to attain the highest ranks in the administration by dint of education, zeal and devotion to duty. But I do not think it desirable at this stage, when the people have not yet had the opportunity to become educated and to form clear ideas, to promote many non-nobles, since advancement of this kind is still contrary to native ideas of what is proper.[9]

Thus the *bupati* of Demak, whose views influenced not only his niece Kartini but also other progressive elements, especially among the lesser *prijajis*, stands at the source of two currents of opinion that were to develop in subsequent years. On the one hand were the champions of popular education and democratic ideals, and on the other those who, by reason of their birth and position, claimed special privileges of leadership for themselves and their class.

2   BUDI UTOMO, THE STUDENTS' 'HIGH ENDEAVOUR'

At the period when, under the influence of the 'ethicals', a change in colonial policy was taking shape, as evidenced for example by the appointment in 1902 of a commission to investigate the 'lack of welfare' of the native population,[10] the advocates of popular education were mainly to be found amongst the pupils of Stovia, the former *dokter djawa* school at Weltevreden, which is today the seat of the University of Indonesia. Of all the advanced schools in Indonesia, it was Stovia which did most to foster revolutionary ideas. Students met there from all parts of Java and also from Sumatra, Celebes and the Moluccas, so that the sense of kinship among all Indonesians was more lively than in the schools for the training of teachers or officials, which were scattered about the country and took only pupils from their respective provinces. A further important difference between Stovia and the Osvias was that the pupils at the latter were all sons of higher *prijajis* who could expect themselves to step into the better administrative offices, where they would enjoy good pay, good chances of promotion and high social standing.[11]

None of this was true of the Stovia pupils. For some decades past the higher *prijajis* had taken care to keep the 'vaccinators' at a social level well below their own: they ranked as lesser *prijajis*, received a salary of 70 guilders a month (half that of the Osvia graduates), and, when they travelled by rail at public expense, were allowed to use only third instead of second class, being thus equated with coolies and convicts.[12] Other slights of the same kind were put upon them, although the *dokter djawa* training took two years longer than that of the officials, and their work was far more exacting than the higher *prijajis'*.

The Stovia pupils were sons of lesser *prijajis*, such as teachers, secretaries and police superintendents; of the impoverished nobility, and, in exceptional cases, of the peasantry. Coming from the background of a society divided into nobles and commoners, the higher and lesser *prijajis* spent from five to nine years in a European atmosphere, and, having completed what was from 1900 onwards an arduous course of study, were expected to re-adapt themselves to the old system, in which superiority was claimed on grounds of birth by men who were often much less well educated than the *dokter djawas*. This naturally provoked rebellious tendencies, and discontent with the structure of native society frequently led to resentment against the colonial power which helped to keep that society in being.[13]

The existence of feelings of this kind in the *dokter djawa* school as early as the turn of the century is attested by A. Djajadiningrat, subsequently *bupati* of Serang, who at that time was attending the HBS at Batavia.[14] The principal spokesman for the pupils' discontent was Tjipto Mangunkusumo, who attended the Stovia from 1899 to 1905 and may be regarded as the father of the Indonesian independence movement.

Tjipto, the son of a teacher, was born in 1886 at Ambarawa near Semarang, the eldest of a family of nine. At the age of thirteen he entered the *dokter djawa* school, where he is said to have shown great ability but also a strong spirit of independence.[15] Given the strict regulations to which boarders were subjected, this led to friction, and he was eventually allowed to live in the *kampong*, the village-like settlement which the natives built for themselves in the area behind the city streets. The Stovia pupils in any case took their meals in the *kampong*, which aroused their awareness of social inequality in the cities and their desire to help the *wong tjilik*, the 'little man'.[16]

Tjipto, who liked to dress humbly, took part in occasional debates during his schooldays, but is not known to have played any specially important role at this time. After passing his examination he was sent for a year to Bandjermasin in Borneo, and from there to Demak, where he may or may not have met Hadiningrat.

25

His first significant rebellious utterance dates from this period (1907). In an article in the 'ethical' organ *De Lokomotief*, he criticized the privileges of the nobility and opposed a decree, issued at that time, which made the office of *bupati* hereditary. Since the *bupatis* had for centuries been tools of the Government, he argued, this measure was contrary to the latter's principle, or rather the ethicals' desire, that the people should govern themselves. Knowledge and ability, not birth, should be the decisive factor.[17]

Meanwhile other pupils of *dokter djawa* were coming to the fore. Abdul Rivai, a native of the west coast of Sumatra, who had finished school in 1895 and had set up a flourishing practice at Medan, went to Holland for further study in 1899. From 1902 onwards he and Clockener Brousson, an ex-officer of the colonial army, edited there a periodical entitled *Bintang Hindia* (Star of the Indies), the purpose of which, as announced in its prospectus, was to describe to Indonesians by word and picture their 'European motherland', to 'foster loyalty to the queen and the flag', and to combat superstition at home.[18] By order of Governor-General van Heutsz, all officials in the colony subscribed to his journal, whose chosen themes were so well adapted to the notion of 'association'. However, in Brousson's absence Abdul Rivai took the opportunity to raise political and social questions which went to the root of the colonial system. This was not welcome, and in 1907 the journal had to cease publication following an article of Abdul Rivai's on the rights of the Indonesian peoples.[19]

Another prominent figure was Wahidin Sudiro Husodo, who had practised in Jogjakarta since he graduated from the school in 1873. In 1906, when nearly fifty years of age, he began to travel throughout Java in order to raise money for a fund to enable gifted Indonesians to study in the Netherlands. The modest and even humble manner in which he presented his case, initially for the most part to the higher *prijajis*, belied a strong will which was not put off by failures at the outset. His method of waiting for days, if need be, to obtain a hearing won respect in quarters where the appearance of a 'little *dokter djawa*' was generally looked on as *kasar* (base or improper).[20] However, his main success was not with the *bupatis*, very few of whom showed solidarity with their poorer countrymen, but with a group of Stovia pupils who paid him a visit when he passed through Batavia in 1907. They praised his selfless devotion as a *budi utomo* (noble endeavour), and planned to foster the notion of solidarity

26

among their comrades. The leader of the group, who resolved to form a Budi Utomo Society, was Raden Sutomo, born in 1888, the son of an official who died in 1907 having attained the rank of *wedana*. As a child, Sutomo had been chiefly brought up by his grandfather, a respected village elder in central Java, who was determined that the boy should become a higher *prijaji*: when Sutomo entered the Stovia in 1903, the old man insisted that he should at least own a horse as a symbol of his exalted future rank.[21]

Sutomo canvassed other classes of the Stovia to gain support for the new organization, and contact was made with students at the Osvias and various institutions for the training of teachers, who sent representatives to Batavia for the inaugural assembly of Budi Utomo on 20 May 1908. The first Indonesian association thus came to birth in the great hall of the Stovia, and the day in question has since been regarded as marking the dawn of the Indonesian movement.

However, little was known of the origins of Budi Utomo and the early years of its development till recently. Some light has been thrown on them by the work of Akira Nagazumi, who challenges the view, commonly met with in literature on the Indonesian nationalist movement, that Budi Utomo was from the start nothing more than a Javanese cultural association. The earliest declarations of the Stovia pupils, in fact, make it clear that the association was conceived, in the spirit of Tjipto Mangunkusumo's ideas, as a movement of social protest against the position of the higher *prijajis* in Javanese society. The object was 'to stretch out a hand to the common people and free them from the darkness of ignorance, so that they are better armed in their struggle for existence and more able to stand up against interference by outsiders'. Experience having shown that no support could be expected from the higher *prijajis*, 'who always give way to pressure from above', an appeal had been made to the students as 'future counsellors of the common people', and they had responded to it with enthusiasim. The new organization provided a means of extending the appeal to the older generation, and it seemed now, two months after the foundation of the association, that some sympathy was to be met with among the *bupatis*. The young leaders declared themselves ready to hand over to more mature and experienced men, whose co-operation would, they hoped, strengthen the organization. But if their elders continued to hold back and did not wish or dare to lead the movement, the students, albeit reluctantly, would have to bear the responsibility themselves.[22]

In a second formal statement it was proclaimed that the purpose of Budi Utomo was to create a general Javanese union whose task would be to strive for the harmonious development of the land and peoples of the Dutch East Indies. On the basis of an association whose core was formed by the native element, it was hoped to create a national brotherhood irrespective of race, sex or religion. All should therefore join the movement who desired a happy future for the colony and its peoples. Budi Utomo was prepared to be merged in a wider union, since it would thereby be in a stronger position to achieve its demands for evolution, 'not only for itself, but also for the many racial groups and peoples of Netherlands India'.[23]

The two chief aspects of Budi Utomo's aspirations in its early days – the desire to help the common people and to create a movement embracing the whole archipelago – were soon lost to view when the 'elders' took over the association. Both objectives were native to the special atmosphere of the *dokter djawa* school, where students met from all over the archipelago – though the Javanese far outnumbered those from the outer islands – and the idea of community naturally flourished; moreover, the school was a meeting-place for the under-privileged members of Indonesian society, who acquired a sharper eye for social abuses and set themselves to promote the development of the lower classes.[24] Thus Budi Utomo was in its beginnings oriented towards social reform and towards the country as a whole, and may justly be regarded as the cradle of the Indonesian move-ment,[25] although, as will be seen, it did not maintain its original objectives for long.

3 SEDIO MULO, THE REGENTS' 'EXALTED PURPOSE'

By the foundation of Budi Utomo, the lesser *prijajis* of the future threw down the gauntlet to the higher *prijajis*. For the first time, an event of importance in Javanese social development had taken place over the heads of the *bupatis*, even the more progressive of whom felt challenged by the *dokter djawas*' initiative. As already mentioned, Hadiningrat, the latter's spokesman, had emphasized in his report that reform 'at this time' must come from the top, and the *dokter djawas* did not belong to the upper ranks of society.

Even *bupatis* who had received a Western education up to university entrance level, such as A. Djajadiningrat, the regent of Serang, were capable of treating the *dokter djawa* with the traditional arrogance of rank. Djajadiningrat himself relates how on one occasion a *dokter djawa* rebuked him for this.[26]

Since the turn of the century, the colonial government had pursued a policy of building up the regents' position: they had issued a circular (the *hormatcirculaire*) instructing officials to show proper respect to the *bupatis*, and had made their office hereditary. However, the *bupatis* for their part realized that, in a time of social unrest and revived Islamic activity, too close an alliance with the foreign overlords might in fact damage their prestige still further. Hadiningrat's report had drawn a line between popular wishes and Government interests, making it clear that these might be parallel but were not identical. He expressed himself still more clearly at a conference of regents in 1902, at which he declared that the people viewed with mistrust every measure that the Government took.[27]

In the next few years, more and more critical voices were raised among the *bupatis*. They gave 'unsought advice', as when the regent of Panarukan, in an article published in 1904 in the *Tijdschrift voor het Binnenlandsch-Bestuur*, complained that the natives were always the losing party: they were sometimes punished for planting without waiting for Government instructions, and at other times for awaiting instructions which did not come, so that they felt everything they did was wrong, and the sense of initiative was completely crushed.[28] Or again, the regent of Tuban in 1905 complained that the training of native officials at the Osvias was much too slow. Only ten out of 260 *prijajis* appointed to the residency of Rembang were Osvia graduates, and at this rate it would be 675 years before all officials of the administration had received adequate training.[29]

However, until the foundation of Budi Utomo there was only one case of a *bupati* taking the initiative. On 27 March 1905 Tjokroadikusumo, the regent of Temanggung, founded an association known as Sasanka Purnama, which may be translated as 'A Beginning'. The principles of this body, which he shortly afterwards recommended as a basis for the development of the Javanese people,[30] were that the *prijajis* were the leaders of society, and in order to develop the people it was necessary to develop them first. It was not enough to give a good education to a small number of future administrators; the work of training must go forward on a

29

wider basis. The *bupati* – who may thus claim credit for having founded the first modern Javanese association – describes in detail how he created first a library and then a place of assembly in which the *prijajis* of his regency met regularly to hear lectures and hold discussions. The subjects ranged from religious questions to village problems, and the *adat* was subjected to criticism as a hindrance to progress. Conditions as far afield as Minangkabau in western Sumatra came under review. A savings commission was set up to encourage the sense of economy, and there was a fund to help *prijajis* to undertake journeys that they might think necessary. Wahidin Sudiro Husodo, during his travels in Java, appealed to the Sasanka Purnama to support his scholarship fund and addressed it on the subject of Theosophy, a cult which had been active in Java since 1893, and had attracted much attention by its syncretistic approach to religion, thanks especially to the work of the Eurasian *kijai*, D. van Hinloopen Labberton.[31]

The ideas and initiative of the regent of Temanggung evidently made more impression on Wahidin than the Stovia pupils' demand for the education of the common people. Wahidin became president of Budi Utomo in August 1908, and at its first national congress at the beginning of October he made a speech urging priority for the education of *prijajis*. He argued that in the course of Javanese history two classes had taken shape: the peasantry, and the *prijajis* who formed the traditional élite; and that the latter were best qualified by nature to maintain the struggle for existence, in accordance with the principle of the 'survival of the fittest'. Other *dokter djawas* echoed Darwinian ideas in their speeches also, while some were sceptical of the value to the Javanese of Western education in general. Radjiman Wedioningrat, the court physician to the ruler of Solo, who had graduated from the *dokter djawa* school in 1899, and later had studied European philosophy, went so far as to warn against European learning altogether, declaring that it would only produce an educated proletariat, and would lead to the neglect of Javanese culture, which it was all-important to preserve.[32]

The reference to Javanese culture struck a note which was to be characteristic of Budi Utomo in the ensuing years. The Stovia pupils, who had come with high hopes to Jogjakarta to attend the first congress of the association they had founded, were bitterly disappointed. Their zeal for helping the common people was in danger of being stifled by the soothing talk of their elders, who were reconciled to the 'two-class structure' of society. However, Tjipto Mangunkusumo, who had first launched the idea of helping the common man, made a speech in which he had the courage to defy the Javanese élite in the very centre of their aristocratic society. He denied that men were different by nature, and insisted that they were products of upbringing. He rejected the notion that the association should devote itself to fostering Javanese culture, and rejected appeals to Javanese history; both history and culture, he declared, had for centuries been the private preserve of princes and their courts, while nobody cared about the common people. The urgent task now was to rescue the people from their spiritual and material destitution.[33]

Although Tjipto's appeal met with limited response at the congress, he had put it on record that the founders of the association protested against the distortion of their ideals. When the first committee came to be elected, it was plain to the representatives of the higher *prijajis* that their ideas of reform from above under their own leadership encountered little sympathy. True, the regent Tirtokusumo was elected chairman, but he had risen by ability from the lower into the higher ranks, while the rest of the committee consisted of lesser *prijajis*, as did the bulk of the association's membership, which then stood at about 1,200.[34]

In these circumstances, the *bupati* of Temanggung refused to merge his organization, the Sasanka Purnama, with the Budi Utomo.[35] Instead, three weeks later, he and an associate called for the foundation of an opposition league composed of regents.[36] The latter resented the leadership being taken out of their hands, and predicted that the education of 'peasants' sons' would mean an intellectual proletariat. They felt strong enough at this stage to take up the challenge of Tjipto Mangunkusumo and the lesser *prijajis*, who were their own direct subordinates and whom they hoped to intimidate by setting up a rival organization. In the course of 1909, a compromise was brought about by the efforts of Tirtokusumo, who occupied a middle position. The Budi Utomo leaders gave assurances that they sought the co-operation and protection of the *bupatis*, that room would be made for them on the committee, and that the opinions of those who were not committee members would be listened to before decisions were reached.[37]

The committee seats vacated in October 1909 were those of Tjipto Mangunkusumo and a colleague of similar views who refused to hold office after the 'surrender' to the *bupatis*. Tjipto's departure meant also the abandonment of the idea, which he had defended to the last, of representing the whole archipelago.[38] In this way Budi Utomo lost its original spirit, and became in later years an association wholly acceptable to the colonial power, having as its objects the 'harmonious' development of the Javanese people and the fostering of its culture.

The *bupatis* showed little appreciation of the large concessions that Budi Utomo had made to them. They still regarded the association as revolutionary, and in November 1909 a third of them founded the 'league of regents', which in 1911 acquired the title Sedio Mulo (Exalted Purpose). Its ideas were not much different from those of Budi Utomo, especially after the direction of the latter's 'high endeavour' had changed; but the *bupatis'* 'exalted purpose' included the aim of maintaining their claim to leadership for the future.

4 THE TRAINING OF THE RADICALS

Before Tjipto Mangunkusumo walked out of Budi Utomo in October 1909, he had made some mysterious allusions. He asked the committee whether they were ready for a 'great sacrifice', and smiled at their counter-question whether he meant that Budi Utomo should drive the Dutch out of Java. Soon afterwards, he puzzled the committee again by asking if a thorough study had been made of the condition of the Javanese people.[39]

The association, guided as it now was by the spirit of harmony and compromise, had become an encumbrance to the *dokter djawa* leaders, who thirsted for action, and regarded themselves as the champions of the common man. Their passionate defence of the people's interests caused them to be regarded in Budi Utomo circles as ambitious and self-righteous, a judgement echoed by some recent historians.[40] But Tjipto saw no way, other than open protest, of breaking loose from the 'chains' by which, as Kartini had complained, the progressives were bound hand and foot. His ideal was that of the *ksatria*, the warrior, who in the traditional Javanese shadow-theatre embodies the notions of chivalry and righteousness, and who, as Tjipto wrote about this time, 'is not afraid to risk his life, knowing that victory is his if he is only strong enough to follow his ideal unquestioningly'.[41] This devotion to the good cause led him to volunteer his services in combating a plague epidemic in Malang in 1911. For this he received a decoration from the colonial government, which in general took a hostile view of his activity and, indeed, obliged him to repay the grants he had received during his student years.

A no less radical and discontented figure was the then editor of the *Bataviaasch Nieuwsblad*, E. F. E. Douwes Dekker, a great-nephew of the Douwes Dekker who, in the mid-nineteenth century, had eloquently denounced the colonial abuses of the time in his novel *Max Havelaar*, written under the pseudonym Multatuli. The younger Douwes Dekker, or 'DD', as his friends called him, was born in eastern Java in 1879, the son of a Dutch father and a Javanese mother; he attended the HBS in Batavia and, after graduating in 1899, went to South Africa to help the Boers in their fight against the British. He was arrested and interned in Ceylon, after which he returned to Java in 1903 and became a journalist. He followed with lively interest the general awakening of the Asian world, and as early as 1907 was convinced that the Indonesians and Eurasians should join forces to liberate the archipelago from the Dutch.[42]

Douwes Dekker was a well-read man, and was the first to translate the arguments of the 'ethical' party into nationalist demands. He introduced Indonesia to the idea of 'capitalist exploitation', which, half a century later, still served as a magic formula to explain all difficulties. Capitalism was in his eyes the clue to the backwardness of the Eurasians and the subjugation of the Indonesians, in short to the whole phenomenon of colonialism.[43] To do away with the evil system, he endeavoured to unite the Eurasian organizations Indische Bond and Insulinde, founded in 1899 and 1907 respectively, into a joint opposition movement. Both these bodies, however, took the view that the best way to improve the economic and social position of the Eurasians lay in close association with the Netherlands, and they were not prepared to cut their ties with the mother-country.[44] Accordingly, DD formed the plan of creating a party of his own, and in 1910 he went to Europe to investigate sources of help and canvass support for his ideas. While there he wrote *Letters of a Barbarian from the Civilized World*, in which he sought to prove that oriental culture was superior to that of the West. He found ample material for this in works on the decline of Western civilization, but his 'false reasoning' and 'illogical assertions' provoked an outcry even from his friends, who judged the letters to be indeed those of a 'barbarian'.[45] This theme also became a slogan of the struggle for independence, and was later skilfully used by Sukarno among others.

Immediately after his return to Java, Douwes Dekker seems to have made contact with Tjipto Mangunkusumo, who had made a name for himself meanwhile, and promised DD his collaboration.[46] In a speech of December 1911 on co-operation between the white and brown races, and in the newspaper *De Expres* which he published in Bandung from March 1912, Douwes Dekker developed his ideas for an Indische Partij (Indies Party), whose programme was succinctly defined on 15 May 1912 in *Het Tijdschrift*, also published by Douwes Dekker, as 'Indië voor ons' – the Indies for us. Its aims included the legal equality of all races, equal pay for equal work and separation from the Netherlands. The Indies belonged to those who were born there and others who chose it for their permanent home – the Indonesians, Eurasians, Chinese and so on.

Douwes Dekker was afforded a further opportunity to proclaim his ideas when, in August 1912, the Dutch East Indies medical association expressed itself critically on the Government's plan to set up a second *dokter djawa* school, the Nias (Nederlandsch-Indische Artsen School), at Surabaja. The European doctors made scathing remarks about the sense of duty and morality of Eurasian and Indonesian practitioners who 'turned abortions into a source of revenue, and adultery into a pastime', and asked with factitious indignation: 'Can such people be made into doctors?' A storm of protest broke out, and Douwes Dekker wrote in an open letter to Idenburg, who had succeeded van Heutsz as Governor-General in 1909: 'If one day our fist should close upon a weapon, which may Destiny avert, it will not be our fault. It is you, the steward of the Netherlands Indies, and your friends who will have the burden on your conscience.[47]

After founding the Indische Partij at Bandung on 6 September 1912, Douwes Dekker embarked on a propaganda tour of Java which brought him much support. Party groups sprang into existence in numerous places, and their numbers were at once counted in hundreds. Indonesians, Eurasians and Chinese held endless joint celebrations even at places that Douwes Dekker had not visited, for example at Banten. The *bupati* of Serang, describing the events in his regency, spoke of a spontaneous general fraternization and a mood of excitement such as had not prevailed at the festivities he had arranged on the occasion of the birth of the Crown Princess of the Netherlands.[48]

The constituent assembly of the party, which by now numbered about 5,000 members, was held at Bandung at Christmas 1912. Douwes Dekker was elected president, with Tjipto Mangunkusumo as his deputy. The object of the association as laid down in its statutes was 'to awaken the love of all East Indians for the country that nourishes them; to bring them into co-operation on the basis of political equality; to enable our homeland to prosper; and to prepare it for independence.' Among the means listed to achieve these ends were the promotion of a spirit of nationalism embracing the whole country, emphasis on unity, and the equipment of the nation to defend its homeland against any aggressor. Everyone who felt himself to be an 'Indian' – the word 'Indonesian' did not become current till a decade later – was eligible to join the party, without distinction of class, race or origin.[49]

The party statutes were submitted for approval to the colonial government, which promptly rejected them. The same fate befell the 'alternative statutes' which the party had prepared in anticipation of the refusal of recognition: all political associations were in fact forbidden by Article 111 of the Constitutional Ordinance of 1854. The reasons for the refusal were explained to the party leaders by Governor-General Idenburg in an audience on 13 March 1913. Idenburg showed himself well informed on the subject of Douwes Dekker's radical utterances, and made it clear that, if he proposed there and then to declare war on the colonial régime, he could not expect the government's help in his endeavour. Dekker had himself declared that the alternative statutes would not detract from the radical spirit of the association, and it was this refractory spirit that the government could not tolerate. Idenburg – himself a convinced adherent of the 'ethical' policy, which he had helped to formulate during his tenure of the Colonial Ministry in 1902–5 and 1908–10 – made clear to the deputation that even after Article 111 was revoked, as he himself desired that it should be, the Indische Partij, by reason of its revolutionary character, would not qualify for recognition. In reply, Douwes Dekker reminded the Governor that the policy of the 'ethicals' was likewise to prepare the colony for self-government, and the ultimate consequence of this must be independence. To this Idenburg answered that Holland would never grant independence to the Indies.[50]

This exchange between Idenburg and Douwes Dekker reveals the whole dilemma of the 'ethical' policy, which had set in motion a development whose consequences were a source of alarm to its advocates themselves. Douwes Dekker, however, did not give up the argument. He pointed out to the Governor-General, who reputedly hoped to convert the archipelago to Christianity, that many Christian members of the Indische Partij would, if the latter was banned, probably join Muslim organizations, which were beginning to be active in Java. That could not be helped, replied Idenburg. He repeated the words twice. Douwes Dekker's point had gone home.[51] But his decision was unchanged. On 31 March 1913 the Indische Partij was declared an illegal association.

Douwes Dekker thereupon addressed a series of open letters to the Queen of the Netherlands, in which he ardently defended the viewpoint of the Indonesian nationalists. The last of these contained the passage: 'No, Your Majesty, this is not your country. It is our country, our homeland. One day it will be free, free for ever – we have sworn it!'[52] He also indicated that his movements were no longer free, and that he expected 'soon, under your laws and in your name, to be made an outlaw in my own country'.[53] The Governor-General had hinted at the audience that he had other weapons at his disposal besides making the party illegal, and Douwes Dekker may have hoped that, by assuming the role of a martyr, he would bring about an upsurge of support for his movement.

However, it was not his defiant words that finally provoked the colonial power to take action. Matters were brought to a head by two Indonesians: Tjipto Mangunkusumo, who as late as November 1912 had been critical of Douwes Dekker's occasional outbursts,[54] and Suardi Surjaningrat, who had also thrown in his lot with the Indische Partij.

Suardi was born in 1889, the son of a relative of the princely house of Paku-Alam at Jogjakarta. But his father was so poor that Suardi, who had entered the Stovia in 1903, had to abandon his studies in 1909. He had taken no part of any consequence in the foundation of Budi Utomo by his schoolmate Sutomo and Tjipto's brother, Gunawan Mangunkusumo. He became a teacher, and later came to Bandung as a member of a Muslim traders' association. There he met Tjipto, and became joint editor with him of the newspaper *Kaum Muda* (The Young Generation).[55] At the beginning of July 1913, learning that the government planned to celebrate in November the centenary of the liberation of Holland from French rule, and that money was being collected from the population for this purpose, Tjipto and Suardi founded in protest a *Comité Bumiputera* (Natives' Committee), which telegraphed to the Queen requesting that political parties be allowed and an Indonesian parliament set up. The Committee's motto was taken from the admonition to the hero in the *wajang* (puppet theatre): *Rawe-rawe rantas, malang-malang putung*—'Let nothing check you on your path; break all resistance.' Tjipto and Suardi were fond of using the *wajang* as a source of slogans, and this is still a common Indonesian custom. The same motto appeared at the head of a pamphlet published by Suardi in July 1913 with the title *Als Ik eens Nederlander was* (If I were a Dutchman,)[56] in which he drew a sarcastic parallel between the situation of Holland in 1813 and Indonesia in 1913. In his view, it was the height of indignity that the colonized Indonesians should be expected to celebrate the liberation of their masters.

The colonial government, on the other hand, considered that by setting up the Comité Bumiputera the malcontents had overstepped the mark. They feared that the rebellious spirit of Douwes Dekker, Tjipto and Suardi would infect ever wider circles at a time when, as we shall see, the Indonesian movement was in any case increasing like wildfire. Accordingly the government decided to make a drastic example. On the basis of Article 48 of the Constitutional Ordinance of 1854, which empowered the Governor-General, independently of the courts, to expel persons considered dangerous to the maintenance of law and order, or, if they were natives of the colony, to banish them to a specified place in the archipelago, the three radicals were condemned to exile in outlying islands. They were, however, given the alternative of leaving the colony altogether, and all three decided to go to Holland. On 6 September 1913, the anniversary of the foundation of the Indische Partij, the first victims who had dared to take the 'ethicals' at their word and demand independence for the Indies left their homeland as political exiles. But their fight was not yet at an end, and in the ensuing years they exercised significant influence. Suardi, taking leave of his friends, reminded them that in the *wajang* play the hero appears to be vanquished at midnight, but that good triumphs in the final encounter at sunrise. 'The sacred inheritance', he cried to them, 'will be ours at last.'[57]

37

III

THE STRENGTH AND WEAKNESS OF THE INDEPENDENCE MOVEMENT

I   SAREKAT ISLAM AND THE AWAKENING OF THE MASSES

Neither Budi Utomo nor the Indische Partij, welcomed as they were by the intellectuals, made any strong appeal to the mass of country-dwellers, who in 1912 still constituted over 95 per cent of the total population of the archipelago. At the time of its first congress in October 1908, Budi Utomo had 1,200 members, and in the ensuing years the figure rose to some 10,000, mainly from the ranks of the lower *prijajis*; but all chances of its becoming a mass movement were lost with the secession of those leaders who stood for the interests of the common people. Douwes Dekker's Indische Partji, which numbered 7,500 members when it was banned in March 1913, had equally little chance of mass support, since it was too much concerned about the Eurasians and Chinese, both communities who enjoyed special privileges in the administration and economy under the colonial régime. The Eurasians, despite their legal equality of rights, ranked below the pure whites in the social order, but for this very reason they sought to make up for the snubs they received by insisting on their privileges *vis-à-vis* the *inlanders*. The Chinese, thanks to their energy and extensive trading relations, had also developed into a middle class; legal equality was not yet theirs, but they had succeeded by their initiative in extracting concessions from the colonial power, such as the establishment in 1908 of Dutch-Chinese schools at which European languages were also taught. From 1901 onwards the Chinese possessed trading associations known as *Siang Hwee*, which did not confine themselves to promoting commerce but also worked hard to improve the social standing of the Chinese community.[1]

The activity of the Chinese had stimulated Arab and Indonesian traders to combine in similar fashion. An association of Arab and Sumatran traders known as Jam Yat Khair, formed in Batavia in 1905, stressed religious as well as economic interests.[2] Among those connected with it was R. M. Tirtoadisurjo, whose ambition it was to unite the native traders into a wider organization. Tirtoadisurjo had trained for an administrative career at the Osvia in central Java, but found himself more attracted towards journalism than towards the calling of a *prijaji*. He is said to have contributed to periodicals in the Malay and Javanese languages from the turn of the century onwards, and to have given attention to political themes, on the strength of which he has been called the 'father of the Indonesian press'.[3] But there is little definite information about this, and it seems doubtful whether he was active in politics before the period 1907–12, when he edited a loyal newspaper at Bandung called *Medan Prijaji* (The *Prijajis*' Forum).[4] He first attracted attention in 1909, when, in collaboration with the Arab-Sumatran traders' group in Batavia, he founded the Sarekat Dagang Islamijah (Association of Muslim Traders), clearly as a rival to the Siang Hwee. In 1911 he founded a branch association at Bogor (Buitenzorg) with the name Sarekat Dagang Islam. Although the Indonesian word 'Islam' was used instead of the Arabic form 'Islamijah', Arab merchants seem to have played a prominent part in the new association also.[5]

Tirtoadisurjo's activity aroused the interest of a rich Javanese batik dealer from Solo named Hadji Samanhudi, who with some of his fellow-Javanese had joined a Chinese trading association, but felt that their group was being exploited. He invited Tirtoadisurjo to come to Solo and set up an organization on similar lines to those in Batavia and Bogor. A branch of the Sarekat Dagang Islam was accordingly created, but friction arose between the two men, perhaps owing to Tirtoadisurjo's contacts with Arab traders.

In May 1912 Samanhudi resolved to find a new organizer for his association, and his choice fell on Umar Said Tjokroaminoto. This man, the son of a *we dana*, was born in 1882 near Madiun and was able, thanks to his father's position, to attend the Osvia at Magelang, whence he graduated in 1902. Like Tirtoadisurjo, whom he may have met there, he felt little inclination for an official's career. After spending three years as secretary to the Patih of Ngawi, he left the service and joined an itinerant *wajang* troupe. As we have seen in the case of Tjipto Mangunkusumo and Suardi Surjaningrat, the repertoire of the *wajang* players, based on Javanized Hindu mythology, was immensely popular among the natives. Later Tjokroaminoto was employed by a firm in Surabaja, where he attended extension classes in the evening, and was finally engaged as a chemist in a sugar factory.[6] Here he was contacted by representatives of Hadji Samanhudi.

Thanks to his years of study and travel, Tjokroaminoto was well informed for a Javanese at that time, and had a good knowledge of conditions in Java and especially the ideas and aspirations of the rural population. He had founded a branch of Budi Utomo at Surabaja, and when that organization became one of *prijajis* he had followed with interest the development of the Muslim traders' associations. He now went to Solo on Samanhudi's invitation to study the aims of the association there, and decided to co-operate with it. At this time, in August 1912, the association had organized a successful boycott of Chinese batik dealers, and consequently it was banned by the Dutch Resident for disturbance of law and order. On 10 September the association was re-founded under the name of Sarekat Islam (SI) or 'Muslim Association', with Tjok-roaminoto at its head and with a membership already reckoned at over 60,000. Its purposes, as set forth in its statutes, were (*a*) to promote commercial enterprise; (*b*) to aid members who had got into difficulties through no fault of their own; (*c*) to foster the spiritual and material interest of Indonesians; and (*d*) to further the cause of Islam by combating misconceptions, spreading knowledge of its true precepts etc. It was further declared that these objects would be pursued only by legal means, without breach of public order or offence to morals and decorum.[7]

During its first year or two of existence, the membership of SI grew at a rate without parallel in the history of modern independence movements:

Table IV   SI membership in Java, 1912–14[8]

April 1912 (Sarekat Dagang Islam)	4,500
August 1912	66,000
December 1912 (Sarekat Islam)	93,000
April 1913	150,000
April 1914	366,913

There has hitherto been no special study of the phenomenal rise of SI, and one or two of its causes may be indicated here in more

The Strength and Weakness of the Independence Movement

detail. In the initial phase support seems to have come mainly from members of the exiguous Javanese middle class, whose desire for union was stimulated by the successful boycott of the Chinese traders – *dokter djawas*, teachers, lesser *prijajis*, merchants, and traders who realized, as Tirtoadisurjo once put it, that the only way to give forceful expression to the desire for progress was to form a solid organization.[9] The successes of the Japanese, the Young Turks, and the Chinese revolutionaries inspired hopes of a like development for Java. Secondly, SI drew support from adherents of Islam: *hadjis*, *kijais* and *santris* of all kinds—that is to say all who came under the influence of the religious country schools known as *pesantren*. The revival of Muslim activity since the end of the last century, to which we have referred several times, had begun to deepen the already existing cleavage of the rural population into the *santri* and *abangan* civilizations, as described by Clifford Geertz. The latter term (from the Javanese *abang*, root) denotes the indigenous culture dominated by traditional elements such as animism and syncretism, and only affected superficially, if at all, by Islam.[10] The cleavage was further accentuated by the second Muslim wave, more especially the pilgrimage to Mecca and the steadily growing number of *hadjis*. As we have seen, in 1890 there was about one *hadji* to every *desa*. By 1905 this ratio had doubled, and before long it increased fourfold.

Table v Pilgrimages to Mecca, 1908–14[11]

Year	From Java	From Indonesia	World total
1908	6,814	10,300	69,077
1909	6,987	10,994	71,421
1910	8,198	14,234	90,051
1911	15,328	24,025	83,749
1912	10,902	18,353	83,295
1913	17,391	26,321	96,924
1914	19,784	28,427	56,855

The high figures for 1911 are due to the fact that it was a year of the *hadj akbar* (greater pilgrimage), which normally attracts larger numbers of the faithful. But the explosive rise, especially as regards Java, began just at the time when Sarekat Islam was recruiting members in great numbers (Table IV, p. 40). The two phenomena are clearly connected: the revival of Islam helped the SI to enlarge its membership, and the association, by propagating the Muslim faith, increased the numbers of those who conformed to its precepts of which the pilgrimage is one.

Besides the Javanese middle class and the *santri*, there was a third source of recruitment to SI, namely the belief of the rural population, as already mentioned, in the imminent appearance of a Javanese Messiah, the *ratu adil*. This belief, which was equally current in regions of *santri* and *abangan* civilization, was based on the concept of the reincarnated Buddha and expectations, connected therewith, of a new golden age. During the nineteenth century, and especially after the intervention of the colonial power made itself felt at the rural level, the messianic expectations had gained strength, and were strengthened by prophecies attributed to the medieval King Djajabaja of Kediri.[12] Muslim elements had gradually become interwoven with these prophecies, which thus reflect an epoch of Javanese cultural history. The *ratu adil*, or *heru tjokro* as he was also called, was to appear after a time of distress and oppression. Towards the end of the century he would live for a time un- recognized among the people, but, when he proclaimed himself, Allah would sweep all enemies from his path. The texts had been revised at various times by speculative minds to enhance credibility; historical events had been inserted as prophecies, and mystic significance ascribed to such phenomena as volcanic eruptions, floods, pestilence etc. In this way the 'signs' could at any time be related to the present day, and as the Messiah was to be unrecognized at first, anyone in practice could claim to be he. Such claims were frequent in the latter half of the century, and the belief sprang up again when Sarekat Islam began to canvass for the people's favour. The SI propagandists paid due observance to the text of the prophecies, using the 'forms of greeting the *ratu adil*' and con- forming to ritual practices such as the drinking of holy water; above all, they offered in Tjokroaminoto a charismatic personality in whom messianic hopes could be centred. It was soon learnt that he had been born in the year of the Krakatau eruption, the most fearful event of its kind in Indonesian memory. Was not even his name a broad intimation that the *heru tjokro* had come? Other revelations of the same kind were available for those who cared to seek them out. So the villagers thronged to enrol themselves among his followers, lest by hesitating they should forfeit the blessings of the new kingdom.[13]

The messianic expectations and the idea of a new kingdom gave cause for alarm to the colonial power and the native nobility alike. One of the texts described the time of the Messiah's advent as one in which 'the nobility is accursed and the people suffer tribulation'. It was made clear, too, that the Europeans were regarded as un-invited intruders who should be sent back to their own country. In a prophecy brought to light as long ago as 1816 it had been said that they would be driven from Java by another Asian power, the ruler of Kling in India.[14] Tjokroaminoto, who in general did not dis-sociate himself from the messianic belief but rather encouraged it, endeavoured to combat its xenophobic aspect. The fate of the Indische Partij was a clear lesson that his own movement would be banned if it came out openly against the colonial power. Officially, therefore, he proclaimed that he and his followers were content with Dutch rule, had no intention of driving the Europeans out of Java, and would confine themselves to legal means as laid down in the statutes. But the whole character of the movement in that turbulent period was anti-foreign: so was its secret propaganda, and such it was felt to be by the Europeans in Java.[15]

The colonial government hesitated for some time before approving the statutes. On 29 March 1913 Idenburg, the Governor-General, told a delegation headed by Tjokroaminoto that he proposed to wait till he was certain that the leaders were in a position to direct the movement in accordance with its statutes; meanwhile, he advised them to cease canvassing for recruits and concentrate on improving their organization.[16] However, the flow of new members continued unabated, and on 30 June Idenburg felt obliged to refuse his consent for a single organization, though he hinted that local SI groups might be sanctioned if permission were duly sought. In taking this line, he may have intended to spare the SI leaders responsibility for events that they might not be able to control.[17]

In the course of 1914, permission was given in this way for 56 local associations, mostly at regency level, and in the same year the movement spread to the outer islands of Sumatra, Borneo, Celebes etc. In 1915 a headquarters was set up to supervise the recognized branch associations and to control their leadership and activity. Such supervision had in fact been exercised from the beginning; but it became clear during that year that the Government was prepared to sanction a central control body, and it did so in March 1916. The central authority at SI headquarters consisted of Saman-hudi (honorary president), Tjokroaminoto (president), Raden Gunawan and Abdul Muis.

Raden Gunawan, like Tirtoadisurjo and Tjokroaminoto, had been educated at the Osvia, but he decided against an official career. He worked in Batavia as a journalist and hotel manager, and within a short time of the foundation of Budi Utomo his home became a meeting-place for those interested in politics. Abdul Muis had come from Sumatra to Java about 1900, and had been given lodging by Abendanon, then director of education for the colony. When the latter returned to Europe in 1905, Muis, who was fifteen years old, attended the Stovia, and later followed Suardi Surjaningrat to Bandung, where he worked on *Kaum Muda* and joined the Bumi-putera committee. When Tjipto and Suardi were banished for their share in the committee's activities, Muis was arrested for a short time and then released. He took a more cautious view of the move-ment's possibilities and had warned Tjipto and Suardi, when translating the latter's pamphlet *Als Ik eens Nederlander was* (If I were a Dutchman) into Malay, that its appearance might result in their being exiled.[18]

In 1915 the SI leaders were joined by another native of Sumatra, Hadji Agus Salim, who was to exercise a dominant influence in the movement. We have already mentioned that in 1903 Salim, whose home was in Minangkabau, obtained the best results of all can-didates in the HBS final examination. During his period of duty from 1906 to 1911 as secretary to the Dutch legation in Jedda, where he was responsible for looking after Indonesian pilgrims, he had studied the Islamic reform movement and become a convinced Muslim. Consequently, when he joined the governing committee of Sarekat Islam, he insisted that the organization should cut loose from the *ratu adil* aspects. He had in fact joined SI as a Government spy with instructions to find out whether it was plotting a rebellion; but he was soon convinced of the justice of its aims, and threw in his lot with it.[19] As a cool-headed Sumatran he had little feeling for the traditions and culture of Java, which exerted strong influence over Tjokroaminoto, as they did over Suardi Surjaningrat and Tjipto Mangunkusumo.

2   THE VOLKSRAAD AND GOVERNMENT PROMISES OF REFORM

The first national congress of Sarekat Islam was held at Bandung in mid-June 1916. Delegations appeared from over 80 local branches, representing a total of 357,000 members, more than 80,000 of whom belonged to the outer islands.[20] The growth in Javanese membership had been stemmed, and indeed some 100,000 members had left the association since 1914, disappointed at the failure to proclaim the messianic kingdom. But the movement had by no means lost its significance. As the messianic aspect dwindled, its political role increased, and the growing number of members in the outer islands showed that Sarekat Islam had become a country-wide movement.

On the eve of the congress G. A. J. Hazeu, the Government's Adviser on Native Affairs (Advizeur voor Inlandsche Zaken), approached Tjokroaminoto and indicated to him the concessions which the government was prepared to make to Sarekat Islam's desire for increased influence in political affairs. In the first place, non-Europeans were to be allowed to vote in elections to the municipal councils which had been set up since 1903, beginning with the larger towns, in accordance with the ethicals' policy of decentralization. The government also planned to revoke Article 111 of the ordinance of 1854 forbidding political associations. Finally, Hazeu described their plan to set up a colonial council, which would include Indonesian members.[21]

Next day, on 18 June, Tjokroaminoto made a speech to the congress in which he informed the delegates of these proposals. He welcomed the plan for a colonial council, but regretted that the Netherlands parliament was taking so long to pass the necessary legislation.[22] He may in fact have known for some years of the colonial government's plans for popular representation, since already in July 1913 Idenburg had spoken of 'expectations aroused' concerning a share in matters of government.[23] By 1916 the proposed Colonial Council – or *Volksraad*, as it was called after the debates in the Dutch second chamber at the end of the year – was a lively issue in colonial politics, but it is wrong to regard it as having been 'extorted' by the nationalists, as they themselves frequently claimed in later years.[24] The idea of a popular assembly for the Dutch East Indies had been discussed on many occasions since the middle or the last century, and in April 1891 the Governor-General, Pijnackef Hordijk, had drawn up a plan for an advisory body including private individuals as well as senior officials. In this plan, unlike most of its predecessors, Indonesians were not automatically debarred from membership of the advisory council, but Pijnacker Hordijk did not consider at the time that any suitable members could be found among the native or 'foreign Oriental' population.

Pijnacker Hordijk had two main objectives in drawing up his plan. He wished to check the Dutch government's tendency to interfere more and more in the colony's affairs, and also to improve relations between the colonial government and the resident Europeans by giving the latter a share in the conduct of affairs. He also advocated the creation of municipal councils; but his view was that if only one of the various reform projects – viz. local and provincial bodies and the colonial council – were to be undertaken, a start should be made with the last-named.[25] In the event, however, more and more importance was attached to the idea of municipal councils, and the 'Decentralization Law' was passed in 1903. The notion of a colonial council was revived indirectly as a result of the colony's attainment of financial independence in 1913. By allowing a popular assembly to debate the budget, the ever-critical daily press would be deprived of its monopoly as a mouthpiece of the opposition. In May 1909 Idenburg, then Colonial Minister and shortly to be Governor-General, had urged that the new body should also be given legislative duties; he also recommended – this being a year after the foundation of Budi Utomo – that Indonesians and foreign Orientals should be eligible to serve on the council. Of its membership of fifteen, five should be European officials, five European private individuals, three Indonesians and two foreign Orientals. He considered that, in the first instance, the council should be nominated by the Crown, and that later, when the colony was politically more mature, its membership could be supplemented by elections.[26]

Idenburg's ideas met with criticism. His proposal to associate the council with legislation was at first unacceptable both to The Hague and to the Raad van Indië which advised the Governor-General. The view in Holland was that the council should confine itself to discussing the budget, and in the relevant correspondence it came by degrees to be referred to as the Financial Council. But Idenburg, having meanwhile become acquainted at first hand with the demands and aspirations of Budi Utomo, Sarekat Islam and the Indische Partij, lost no opportunity of representing that a measure of co-responsibility was also urgently necessary in the legislative field. It was not enough, in his view, that the council was gradually conceded an advisory function. He warned his compatriots that the institution would fall far short of expectations, and once wrote in a private letter: 'Do the gentlemen at The Hague really know so much better than we do here?'[27]

The upshot, as expressed in the law of December 1916, was a compromise, in which the powers of the Volksraad were defined as follows. Its advice was to be sought by the Governor-General on any matter he wished. Further, he was to consult it in budgetary matters, and those concerning the equalization of financial burdens, or the imposition of military service on the native population. The Volksraad was empowered to represent the interests of the colony to the Sovereign, the Dutch parliament and the Governor-General (right of petition). It was to be composed of a chairman appointed by the Crown and thirty-eight deputies, half of whom were to be nominated by the Governor-General and half elected by the local councils.[28] The law further provided that ten of the elected deputies and five of the Governor's nominees were to be Indonesians. Accordingly, in 1917 the political associations set up a national committee to nominate candidates for the elections in the municipal councils. As, however, the latter still consisted almost entirely of Europeans and those enjoying legal equality with them, the so-called radicals – a group which included Tjokroaminoto, despite his protestations of loyalty, and Tjipto Mangunkusumo, who had returned from his exile in Holland in 1914 – had no chance of being elected to the Volksraad as people's representatives. They were, however, both nominated to the Council by Limburg Stirum, who had succeeded Idenburg as Governor-General in March 1916.

The candidates who stood the best chance of being elected were those of Budi Utomo; but the regents' league also saw in the new system an opportunity to assert its authority. At a conference at Solo in August 1917, A. Djajadiningrat, the *bupati* of Serang and the first of the regents to complete a Western secondary education, tried in vain to reconcile his fellow-regents with the democratic principle, urging that they should not regard themselves merely as transmitters of the colonial government's orders but also spokesmen for the desires of the population. But, as the meeting showed, the upsurge of the masses under the banner of Sarekat Islam had brought about no change in the regents' conception of themselves as an élite. As so often before, they showed more concern for their own position than for the people's welfare, and were anxious to avoid any conflict with the Government. Even a representative of the moderate Budi Utomo, which itself avoided friction with the government declared after this meeting: 'The regents must know what they are doing, but how can such a handful stand up against a movement of the whole people? How can those whose position is based almost entirely on hereditary privilege understand the spirit of the times? The people has now seen for itself what its regents amount to.'[29]

The Volksraad was opened by Governor-General van Limburg Stirum on 18 May 1918. Thanks to the right of nomination, all shades of the national movement were reflected in it. Kusumo Utojo and A. Djajadiningrat represented the conservative and progressive *bupatis* respectively, and there were two members of the princely houses of central Java, which still enjoyed a certain administrative autonomy. Budi Utomo provided five members, from Dr. Radjiman, who had pleaded for a renovation of Javanese culture at the first Budi Utomo congress ten years before, to Dwidjo Sewojo, who had continued to uphold the democratic principle after the 'radicals' abandoned the association. Sarekat Islam was represented by Abdul Muis and Tjokroaminoto; Tjipto Mangun-kusumo was nominated as a representative of the Insulinde association formed by adherents of the banned Indische Partij. Abdul Rivai, who had dared when in Holland to attack the foundations of colonialism in the columns of *Bintang Hindia*, also sat in the Volksraad as a member of Insulinde. Similarly, the European members included all shades of opinion, from the exponents of ruthless exploitation to those of gradual evolution and even to members of a socialist movement.[30] In his inaugural speech, the Governor-General welcomed the colony's first popular representatives and observed that the council's powers were as yet limited. It could only become a fully-fledged popular assembly when the general development of the colony was such as to justify this; but meanwhile there was much for it to do, and its influence would certainly extend far beyond the legal limits of its power.

In many ways this proved a true prediction. In the first place, the idea of national unity, which had so far found only occasional expression in individual parties, was now provided with a symbol and a forum under the direct notice of the colonial power, which was of great importance for the future of the Indonesian idea. Secondly, situations might arise which would cause the Governor-General to call on the council for advice. For instance, half a year after it was set up, a critical position arose in the colony in connection with the revolutionary events in Europe. In November 1918 rumours were rife in Indonesia that a revolution was brewing in Holland, and the Governor was for a time uncertain how the troops under his command would react to the slogans of a small group of socialists. On 18 November he instructed the Government spokesman in the Volksraad, Mr. Talma, to read a statement which declared *inter alia*: 'The new course which the latest world events have prescribed for the Netherlands will also determine the direction of our affairs here. With us, however, it is not so much a matter of changing course as of increasing speed. The government and the Volksraad are faced with a period of new relationships and changes of competence which cannot yet be foreseen.'[31]

This November Declaration, so frequently evoked by nationalists in future years, was used by the early radicals, who chafed at the restricted competence of the Volksraad, as a basis for demanding immediate and far-reaching reforms. A group led by Tjipto Mangunkusumo called for the appointment of a national council representing all the political organizations and reflecting the true state of popular support for each of them. This body would act as a 'preliminary parliament' to draw up a provisional constitution and frame a new electoral law as a basis for a truly representative assembly. In the so-called 'Tjokroaminoto motion' these demands were reduced to provide for the transformation of the Volksraad into a parliament elected from and by the people, with full legislative powers and an executive responsible to it.[32]

These proposals might be dismissed by the government as the utterances of 'extremists'; but it was given more cause for concern by a similar demand for the transformation of the Volksraad into a parliament in the full sense, put forward in the 'Djajadiningrat motion' by the regent of Serang and his group, which had hitherto been regarded as loyal.[33] Bowing to the unanimous wish not only of the Indonesians but of the resident Europeans, the Governor-General in December 1918 appointed a commission to draw up proposals for political reform.

In the Netherlands, where revolutionary stirrings had come to nothing, the reaction of the Volksraad was greeted with alarm. H.

Colijn, in particular, saw in the events at Batavia a confirmation of the view he had expressed at the beginning of the year, that the setting up of the Volksraad was a mistake that might have dangerous consequences. In a pamphlet on political reform he had argued that first local and then provincial councils should be created, so that the colony might one day be organized on a basis of federation. Weak as it was, the Volksraad, representing a unitary conception, stood firmly in the way of such plans.[34]

Idenburg, after his return to the Netherlands in 1916, had also fallen under the influence of Colijn – 'who runs everything and everybody here', to quote a letter addressed to Limburg Stirum from Holland in February 1919 by A. C. D. de Graeff, who was for many years president of the Raad van Indië and later himself Governor-General.[35] Idenburg became Minister for the Colonies for the third time in 1918, and viewed developments in the Volksraad with much misgiving. In full agreement with Colijn, he now advocated the creation of councils at regency level, and abruptly switched to opposition of the plans for associating the Volksraad with the legislature, for which he had pressed so insistently. He did not join in the chorus of criticism which broke out in Holland when Limburg Stirum's November Declaration became known, but he gave the latter clearly to understand that he 'would rather do away with the Volksraad as an unsuccessful experiment than be involved by it in a pernicious course of action.'[36]

Another prominent member of Colijn's circle, who was already preparing to step into Limburg Stirum's shoes as Governor-General, was the lawyer Dirk Fock. Fock had been Minister for the Colonies in 1905–8, when he had been regarded as an 'ethical' for advocating the expansion of the educational system. Whether or not he had been one at that time, he was certainly now a 'reactionary'. He denounced Limburg Stirum in the second chamber for having made promises without consulting parliament and for arousing expectations for which the time was not yet ripe. If the Volksraad were indeed given legislative functions, the result would be an 'oligarchy of intellectuals representing only themselves'.[37]

During his own term of office as Governor-General (1921–6), Fock succeeded in stemming the tide towards political co-responsibility. He used his legal ability to create a network of regulations whereby attempted strikes and offences in the domain of the press and public speaking were ruthlessly suppressed, while arrests and banishment were the reward of any action directed against *rust en ordre* (tranquillity and order) in the colony. This 'tranquillity and order' was in fact deceptive. Nationalism and the 'ethical policy' had taken root too deeply for the Indonesians to put up with the condition of permanent political inferiority which the reactionaries sought to impose upon them. Under Fock's régime the tenuous bond that still existed between the Indonesian movement and the Netherlands was broken, and the hope of association finally destroyed. It is idle to speculate whether fundamental reforms based on Limburg Stirum's November Declaration might have preserved the tie between the colony and the motherland. The advocates of such reforms, who were chiefly to be found in the Faculty of Indology at Leiden University, argued in vain for a policy of 'unity through separation'. Had this been followed in good time, it would at all events have opened up other possibilities for the Indonesian movement and its leaders than Fock's estranging policy of 'Je maintiendrai', or 'What I have I hold' – a maxim which, it is true, has deep roots in Netherlands history.

3   THE SPLIT IN THE MOVEMENT AND THE ATTEMPTED
COMMUNIST COUP

From an early stage, the mass recruitment of Sarekat Islam aroused the interest of Dutch socialists in the colony, whose leader, Hendrik Sneevliet, had come to Java in 1913. The Indische Sociaal-Democratische Vereeniging (ISDV), formed at Semarang in May 1914, attempted at first to co-operate with Douwes Dekker's adherents, most of whom had joined the Insulinde association after the banning of the Indische Partij. But the Socialist leaders – notably Sneevliet, A. Baars, P. Bergsma and J. H. Brandstedter – soon realized that the Eurasians were unsympathetic both to their ideas of the class struggle and to an appeal to the workers and peasants. Even Tjipto Mangunkusumo, who returned from exile in 1914 and who had championed the common people ever since he became active politically, was accused by Sneevliet of taking insufficient interest in the cause of the proletariat.[38] Accordingly the Socialists transferred their attention to Sarekat Islam, which they conceived to be first and foremost a movement of social protest: its nationalist and religious elements would, they hoped, gradually be outweighed by the notion of the class struggle. They found an apt pupil in

Semaun, who from 1916 headed the Semarang branch of Sarekat Islam; although only seventeen at the time, he already played an active part in the railwaymen's trade union, to which his father also belonged. In the next few years his branch became the centre of a left wing of Sarekat Islam, which steadily grew in strength and eventually split the movement in two.

At the first SI congress in June 1916, Tjokroaminoto had been able to say with some justification that he and he alone determined the course of the movement and that there was no question of influence from any other quarter. Semaun, who spoke at the congress and criticized the proposed creation of the Volksraad on the ground that it would have no real independence, received a schoolmasterly rebuke from Tjokroaminoto, who declared that they did not want to repeat the experience of the negro republic of Haiti, which had collapsed because its citizens knew nothing of the art of government. The Volksraad, on the other hand, would be an excellent school of politics.[39]

In later years Semarang's protests could not be fobbed off so easily, for Semaun began to threaten that he would turn the branch into an independent headquarters if his views were not met. Tjokroaminoto, whose paramount concern was to hold the movement together, was soon obliged to make real concessions. At the second congress, held in Batavia in October 1917, it was resolved to include in the SI programme the combating of 'sinful', that is to say foreign, capitalism. Although this was done in the name of 'Koran Socialism', the formula was clearly designed to meet the far more radical demands emanating from Semarang. However, the new ideas were not yet strong enough to prevail over the nationalistic element in SI. Abdul Muis emphasized in his speech that it was not necessary to become an internationalist in order to improve the state of the world, and that it behoved Indonesian nationalists to devote all their efforts to alleviating misery at home.

The position of the Semarang group became appreciably stronger after the victory of the October revolution in Russia. It had meanwhile been joined by Darsono, a member of a noble family in central Java, and enjoyed the sympathy of other influential figures such as Surjopranoto, the elder brother of Suardi Surjaningrat and head of the SI branch at Jogjakarta. To counteract the leftward slide of the movement, a right wing was formed at Jogjakarta by Hadji Agus Salim and Abdul Muis, whom the Semarang group promptly branded as tools of the government. As early as 1918 sharp accusations were bandied between the two groups and the cleavage within the movement was plainly visible. But Tjokroaminoto, who still hoped for a compromise, succeeded in reconciling the hostile factions at the third congress. Semaun and Darsono promised to cease their attacks, and in return were given seats on the governing body of SI. The social revolutionaries were thus in a position to exert strong influence. Their spiritual fathers were no longer present: Sneevliet and Brandstedter had been expelled from the colony at the end of 1918 for preaching rebellion,[40] while Baars had for a time left Java of his own free will. But the Socialist movement continued to grow, and the neophytes showed that they were well able to stand on their own feet. At the fourth SI congress in October 1919 they distributed leaflets calling on the delegates to join in the class struggle, and declared that it was the duty of SI to turn itself into a workers' and peasants' organization to free the Indonesian proletariat. This propaganda had its effect. The ISDV organ *Het Vrije Woord* noted with satisfaction after the congress that SI was now committed to fighting capitalism as such and not only 'sinful' capitalism, a notion due to misunderstanding of Socialism.[41]

Within a few years, the Semarang group were in fact successful in eliminating the nationalistic idea from Sarekat Islam. Tjokroaminoto's newspaper *Utusan Hindia* (The Indian Messenger) declared in July 1920: 'Our goal is freedom, not independence; we demand the liberty of man, the abolition of the difference between rich and poor.' Tjokroaminoto himself, who still stood for the messianic aspect of SI and had contended that the *ratu adil* principle would be realized in self-government, now proclaimed that the *ratu adil* would not come as a man but in the form of Socialism, to content human longing for a better future.[42]

The success of the Semarang group was due to their radicalism; and we may recall the hopes with which the masses flocked to SI in 1913–14 and their later disappointment at Tjokroaminoto's alliance with the colonial government, which seemed to spell the indefinite postponement of their hopes for the establishment of a new kingdom, the reign of paradise on earth, in which they would enjoy freedom from taxation, the distribution of land to the poor, houses built of stone and similar blessings. Such hopes revived when, as already mentioned, the revolutionary events in Europe in 1918 aroused an expectation of political reforms in the colony. The membership of SI, which in Java had fallen to 268,355 in 1917, again rose dramatically (389,410 in October 1918), and, as was declared in the Volksraad itself, the advent of the *ratu adil* was once more preached in the villages. In 1919 a revolutionary atmosphere prevailed throughout Java. In the eastern part of the island, one sugar-plantation after another was set ablaze, while in central Java the peasants put up a tenacious resistance, supported by all the Indonesian parties, against the forced labour service that was still required of them. In western Java, the investigation of disturbances near Garut brought to light the existence of a branch of SI ('Section B') which had set itself to achieve the overthrow of the colonial régime.

The Indonesian members of ISDV, who also constituted the left wing of SI, were prominent instigators of these activities; and the feeling gained ground among the population that the 'red SI', which numbered some *hadjis* among its members, was a more reliable champion of their interests than Tjokroaminoto with his desire for compromise, or the right wing led by Hadji Agus Salim and Abdul Muis. These latter stood closer to a group of moderate European Social Democrats who, believing that a revolution would be a misfortune for Indonesia at this stage, had split off from the ISDV and founded their own organization, the Indische Sociaal-Democratische Partij (ISPD). One of their spokesmen, D. M. G. Koch, wrote in 1919 that it was not as yet in the natives' interest to engage in a struggle against European capital, whose function was to bring them to a higher stage of development. The rapid development of native capital was 'the only way to put an end to Western domination in our country'.[43]

The ISDV, for its part, insisted on the need for revolution, and on 23 May 1920, in order to distinguish itself more clearly from the ISPD, adopted the name of Partai Komunis di Hindia (altered in June 1924 to Partai Komunis Indonesia: PKI),[44] and applied for recognition to the Comintern. At the second Comintern congress at Moscow in July 1920, the Indonesian Communists were represented by the exiled Sneevliet (known to the Comintern as Maring), who argued for co-operation between the Communists and Sarekat Islam, and declared that, although the latter still bore a religious name, it had in fact become a class movement: it was truly representative of the masses and had embarked on a struggle not only against the colonial régime but also against the Javanese nobility.

He urged that the Third International should not deny recognition to the movement, since only by mass action could capitalism be effectively opposed. Although Sneevliet's views were in line with those of Lenin, who at the same congress pleaded for co-operation between the Communist parties and national revolutionary organizations in Asia, he was unable to persuade the Comintern to approve joint action with a Muslim body. On the contrary, a resolution was passed to the effect that pan-Muslim or pan-Asiatic movements should be opposed, since they tended to strengthen Turkish or Japanese imperialism and to hinder the struggle against the imperialists of Europe and America.[45]

This resolution had far-reaching consequences, in particular for the Indonesian movement. There had, as we have seen, been constant friction between different viewpoints in SI, and especially between the followers of Semaun and Darsono on the one hand and Hadji Agus Salim and Abdul Muis on the other; but external unity had been preserved thanks to the efforts of Tjokroaminoto, whose personal position was respected and had not been called in question as a result of the dissensions. After the second Comintern congress, all this changed. Soon after the foundation of the PKI, and before the second Comintern congress, Tjokroaminoto, under the influence of Salim and others and to the annoyance of the Communists, set up a committee in Batavia in support of the Ottoman caliphate, thus intimating that the religious title of SI was of more significance than Sneevliet was shortly to argue in Moscow. In this way the pan-Muslim idea, which had hitherto had few champions, suddenly came to the forefront within SI. On this and other grounds Darsono in October 1920 launched a devastating attack on Tjokroaminoto in the Communist paper *Sinar Hindia* (Light of the Indies), impugning his moral integrity and qualities of leadership and even accusing him of embezzling party funds.[46] This was a severe blow to Tjokroaminoto's authority, which till then had been uncontested. He nevertheless survived politically, thanks to the fact that he was arrested soon afterwards in connection with the Section B affair, and thus became a martyr of the movement: the Communist charges that he was friendly to the colonial government were shown to be without foundation. His arrest was important for another reason: during his detention Hadji Agus Salim, on the occasion of the SI congress at Surabaja in October 1921, introduced party discipline, forbidding its members to belong to other parties, a step which Tjokroaminoto had refused to take in the interests of unity. Those members of the PKI who did not voluntarily leave the movement were now forced to do so.

The co-existence of the two organizations continued for some years in certain branches of SI, but in general the ways of the sister parties diverged more and more. The contention between the former Semarang and Jogjakarta wings was now brought into the open; SI began to take a stronger interest in the ideology of Islam and to regard its own 'socialist phase' as terminated except in so far as socialism could be reconciled with the Prophet's teaching. The PKI looked to Moscow as its Mecca and, at any rate during the first few years, conformed strictly to the directives it received from there. The breach was completed at the SI congress at Madiun in February 1923, when the Communists present, questioned as to their attitude towards religion, replied that it was 'neutral'; one of them went so far as to accuse the religious leaders of hypocrisy. This led to stormy scenes and a final walk-out by the Communists. Polemics broke out again within the movement, and their echoes persisted for several months.

The conflict between SI and the PKI also led to the early collapse of the Radical Concentration, an alliance of all Indonesian parties from Budi Utomo to the PKI, which was revived at the end of 1922, having originally been formed in 1918 to demand wider powers for the Volksraad. In 1922 the parties again took soundings of one another in consequence of discontent with the Fock régime. They agreed on demands for the cessation of the harsh policy of prosecution and exile, freedom of speech and assembly, the fulfilment of the promises of November 1918 and a broadening of political responsibility, failing which they threatened to boycott the new Volksraad to be elected in 1923. At the beginning of that year protest meetings were held in all the larger centres. The initiative was mainly taken by the nationalist veterans Douwes Dekker, Tjipto Mangunkusumo and Suardi Surjaningrat, who after returning from exile in 1918–19 had formed their old adherents into the Nationaal Indische Partij (NIP), and who hoped to reunite the national movement by stressing common interests *vis-à-vis* the colonial power. But reports of events at the SI congress, together with Tjokroaminoto's readiness to stand for re-election to the Volksraad, deepened the rift more than ever.

Hitherto the quarrel between Communists and Muslims had

mainly taken place at the upper levels, but it now spread to the countryside, where the Communists attempted to win over branches of SI or set up rival bodies known as Sarekat Rakjat (People's Associations). These steadily grew in influence, as the Communists took up the cudgels for the rural population, voiced their grievances more boldly than the Muslim leaders had done, and were not afraid to challenge the Indonesian landowners. The PKI showed skill in arousing the hopes of the *tanis*, or small cultivators, for the rapid improvement of their lot, and strove to clarify Communist aims by founding Sarekat Rakjat schools and distributing popular expositions of Marxism. But the Communists, like other parties, were helped less by theories than by the still lively expectation of a Messiah and the hope that poverty and wretchedness would one day change, as if by a miracle, into prosperity and luxury. Such hopes were shared by the *tanis* with shop-keepers, traders and coolies, whether proletarian or not.

The PKI leaders were aware that their popularity in the countryside rested on questionable foundations, and warnings were voiced all the way up to the Comintern by those who feared that the Sarekat Rakjats would undermine the proletarian character of the movement.[47] But the leaders saw no other way of achieving the mass support which they regarded as essential in order to give emphasis to their demands. All their other attempts, in particular the organization of strikes among railwaymen, dockers, plantation workers and even pawnshop employees, had ended in failure, giving the Fock régime an excuse to pass sentences of banishment on a massive scale. Among the better-known Communists who had followed Sneevliet and Brandstedter into exile from the colony were Baars, Bergsma, Tan Malaka, Semaun, Hadji Misbach, Zainuddin, Datuk, Darsono and Mardjohan; other leaders were jailed for months on end and newspaper editors were constantly under threat of arrest for violation of the press laws.

In the face of these severe measures, the PKI leaders resolved at the end of 1924 to organize a rising. It was decided to form cells and replace the rigidly centralized party organization by a system of 'federal centralism', which permitted local units to operate independently provided they conformed to party statutes. The plans for a coup were given a more definite shape twelve months later at the Prambanan conference (December 1925), though the time of outbreak and other details were not yet settled.[48] Former leaders of the PKI warned of the dangers of the undertaking and pointed out that it might be fatal to the party's future: among these were Semaun, who had been arrested and banished in May 1923 in connection with a planned rail strike and was now the PKI representative with the Comintern in Moscow, and Tan Malaka, at this time Comintern delegate for South-East Asia, with head-quarters at Singapore.

Tan Malaka was born in 1894 at Suliki, a small village in Minang-kabau, son of well-to-do parents. He attended first the ELS and then the teachers' training college at Fort de Kock (Bukit Tinggi), and afterwards he went to Holland on a scholarship and remained there from 1913 to 1919. In 1921 he joined the PKI in Java, in-fluenced, not by the revolution in central Europe, but by what he saw after his return to the colony, especially among the contract coolies whom he encountered when working as a teacher on a rubber plantation in Sumatra. Within a year he was among the ruling group of the PKI, and in February 1922 he was arrested and exiled for instigating a strike of pawnshop employees. Although he had thus himself been responsible for an active policy, he warned his comrades from Singapore that the population was insufficiently prepared for a rising at this juncture. In a series of messages he urged them instead to lay the foundations of a mass movement and to seek the co-operation of all anti-Dutch forces. He envisaged a war in the Pacific which might one day help Indonesia to achieve independence; meanwhile, it was best to wait. Even if the latest government measures meant fresh trouble for the party – a ban on public assembly in November 1925 had made it almost impossible for them to carry on propaganda – it would still be better in the long run for the present party structure to be destroyed by the govern-ment rather than commit suicide by a premature attempt at a coup.[49]

Despite these warnings, the PKI leaders decided, as Darsono later explained to the Comintern, that it was 'better to die fighting than let oneself be killed':[50] these, it seemed to them, were the only alternatives. Of the leaders in Java who voted strongly for a rising, the most important were Alimin and Musso. Both owed their early advancement to Professor Hazeu, who had for many years advised the colonial government on native affairs but had had to resign following the discovery of Section B. Both men had lived for a time in Tjokroaminoto's house and had joined SI, but were also members of the ISDV, and from 1920 onwards, they were increasingly influential in the Communist movement. Alimin later functioned occasionally as a liaison man between Tan Malaka and the PKI, and may have come to share Tan Malaka's opinion that a rising was inopportune. But Musso held fast to the view that it should be attempted, and when he and Alimin visited Moscow in the spring of 1926 to explain the intentions of the PKI, he was at pains to dispel misgivings which might have led to the plan being vetoed on the ground that it was inadequately prepared.[51]

In spite of the doubts expressed by Semaun, Tan Malaka and the Comintern, the PKI continued to develop its plans for a rising during the summer of 1926, and on 13 September a 'Committee of Adherents of the Republic of Indonesia' was set up in Batavia, its members consisting of those who favoured early action. Encouraged perhaps by the replacement, on 7 September, of Fock by A. C. D. de Graeff as Governor-General, they made their final preparations, and decided on 12 November as the date of the outbreak. Some days before this, the government learnt of their plans through detailed counter-espionage reports and decoded telegrams; they were thus able to prevent disturbances in central Java by the timely arrest of ringleaders, while the revolts that broke out at a few places in western Java were quickly suppressed. It soon became clear that the revolution had been exceedingly ill-planned, and the inefficiency of its execution was reminiscent of the traditional movements of social protest. The same was true of disturbances that broke out in western Sumatra at the beginning of 1927, and were originally intended to touch off the rising. The west Sumatra rebels were better armed than those of west Java, but their actions were poorly co-ordinated and collapsed after a few days.[52]

Tan Malaka's fears were now realized. The PKI had given the government its opportunity to ban Indonesian Communism for the ensuing decades. The new Governor-General, who on arrival had been disposed to tolerate a moderate degree of nationalism, felt obliged to take stringent measures, beginning with the arrest of 13,000 persons connected with the PKI. Some were hanged on conviction of conspiracy to murder; 4,500 were imprisoned, and 1,308 were exiled to a penal colony in the Boven Digul area of west New Guinea. Tjipto Mangunkusumo was among those arrested in connection with this, the first persecution of Communists in Indonesian history, and was exiled to the island of Banda in the east of the archipelago at the end of 1927. The charge against him was that he had provided Communist refugees with money and was looked up to by the Communists as a 'national revolutionary'. A further reason may have been that he was regarded as in part responsible for a new growth of radicalism among the Indonesian nationalists, who, after the banning of the PKI, made it their business to ensure that the independence movement did not wither away, but took on a new lease of life.

4 THE NATIONALIST BREAK-THROUGH

During the short period in which Communism had dominated the political scene, Indonesian nationalism, which had surged up vigorously in the early years of Sarekat Islam, had disappeared as a motive force. Douwes Dekker, Tjipto Mangunkusumo and Suardi Surjaningrat had tried in vain to revive their old ideals in the colony by means of the NIP after their return from Holland. They were shadowed by government spies, and their freedom of movement was restricted, Tjipto and Douwes Dekker being forbidden to leave their assigned place of residence at Bandung without special permission. Suardi Surjaningrat, who did not return to Java till 1919, drew the appropriate conclusions and, in July 1922, began to organize a school system which later became known as *taman siswa* (pupil garden), and which rapidly spread throughout the colony. At this time, according to Javanese custom, he took a new name – Ki Hadjar Dewantoro, 'Teacher who mediates among the Gods' – to signify that he was embarking on a new period of his life. The purpose of the schools was to provide further instruction but most of all to acquaint the pupils with their own culture and thus turn them into convinced nationalists. The teachers were not graduates of the government training colleges, but members of the nationalist movement, themselves often students or senior schoolboys.[53]

It was the students, in these years, who enabled Indonesian nationalism finally to assert itself. In the spring of 1920 a technical college had been set up at Bandung to help supply the need for experts; a law school was founded at Batavia in 1924, and the creation of other faculties eventually led to what is now the Universitas Indonesia. This enabled Indonesians to study in their own country, and provided a chance of academic training for many who would not have been able to afford the expensive journey to Europe. However, since the turn of the century there had always been some whose parents were prepared to send them to Holland, though originally this was confined to *bupati* families. For instance, Kartini's brother Kartono studied at Delft and Leiden, and Hussein Djajadiningrat, the brother of the regent of Serang, took his doctorate at the university of Leiden in 1913, the first Indonesian to do so. Gradually students came to be drawn from the families of the lesser *prijajis*; such were Gunawan Mangunkusumo, a brother of Tjipto's, and Raden Sutomo, who were both founder members of Budi Utomo and completed their medical studies in Holland. Others, such as Tan Malaka, came from well-to-do families in the outer islands.

Soon after the foundation of Budi Utomo, the Indonesian students then in Holland formed the Indische Vereeniging, this, however, played a modest part in the first few years of its existence, concentrating on promoting the 'common interests' of Indonesian students in the mother country.[54] It was not till the first political exiles arrived, as well as the founders of Budi Utomo, that the association began to take more interest in politics, especially after it was joined by Suardi Surjaningrat. In 1918 the Indische Vereeniging published a volume commemorating the tenth anniversary of Budi Utomo: this contained an undisguised expression of Indonesian nationalism, and in November of that year the students took up the demand of the parties in Indonesia for the transformation of the Volksraad into a full parliament.[55] In 1917 the Indonesisch Verbond van Studeerenden was founded at Leiden: in accordance with the principle of 'association' between the motherland and colony, its members included Dutch students who were training for service in the Indies. The term 'Indonesia', thus used for the first time in the title of a society, had a geographical rather than a political significance; the Verbond in fact took up so critical an attitude towards the independence movement that the latter's adherents withdrew in 1922 and founded their own Indonesische Vereeniging, which in 1925 adopted the Indonesian form of its title Perhimpunan Indonesia (PI). Through this association, the Indonesian students became the advance guard in Europe of the independence movement, advising their colleagues at home on tactics. The leader who came to the fore among them was Mohammed Hatta, born at Fort de Kock in west Sumatra in 1902, who came to

Batavia in 1920 to take the HBS leaving examination, and in 1922 enrolled at the college of political economy at Rotterdam.

In March 1924 the PI started publication of a militant journal entitled *Indonesia Merdeka* (Independent Indonesia), which openly discussed all questions relating to independence. The first number of the journal pointed out that the lack of a specific name for the home territory would make itself increasingly felt as the quest for international contacts developed. The name 'Indonesia' had been chosen to avoid confusion with British India; to call the colony 'Nederlandsch Indië' was as intolerable to its present-day inhabitants as the designation 'Spanish Netherlands' had once been to the Dutch. The association's purpose was summed up in the word Merdeka, 'independence', to be striven for in concert with the national movement in the homeland.

In this way the political concept of Indonesia was born, and it soon came to hold the field in the colony itself, where it was pointed out that the Indonesian idea had inspired the founders of Budi Utomo, had played an important part in Douwes Dekker's party, and had been adopted without question by Sarekat Islam. Meanwhile, the provinces also began to play a part in the political life of the archipelago. There were leagues of Sumatrans, Minahassans, Ambonese and Madurese, also Bataks, Batavians, Sundanese, and so on.[56] All these associations were located in Java, and most of them had their own youth organizations or Scout troops, so that one might discern many elements of a potential federal system; but before this could take root, it was swept away by the wave of 'Indonesian' sentiment.

The students who formed the membership of PI themselves came from all parts of the archipelago – Hatta, before leaving for Holland, had for some time played a leading part in the young Sumatran association – but from the outset they argued for unity among the parties, urging the formation of a single front which could attract mass support on a nationalist basis and thus wring concessions from the colonial government. The way to gain influence for the movement was to boycott the councils of the colonial overlords, follow the Indian example of non-cooperation, and in general rely on native strength and ability. When the students returned from Holland to Indonesia, they endeavoured to put these ideas into practice, and set up 'study clubs' to discuss problems with party leaders and intellectuals: the first of these was the

Indonesian Study Club at Surabaja founded by Randen Sutomo, who was now a qualified doctor. In this way, the erstwhile founder member of Budi Utomo once again gave the impulse for a new stage of development in the colony. To demonstrate his Indonesian outlook he withdrew in January 1925 from Budi Utomo, which had become more and more centred on Java. In March of that year he also resigned from the municipal council at Surabaja in protest at the neglect of native interests.[57] Following his example, more study clubs were set up in the next few years, the most active being the Allgemeene Studieclub founded at Bandung in 1926. Bandung was a centre for those who could not afford to study in Europe and was also, as already mentioned, the place of residence assigned by the government to Douwes Dekker and Tjipto Mangunkusumo.

The two veterans of the nationalist movement had been unsuccessful in propagating their views through the NIP, which was dissolved in May 1923, but they had continued to preach them to the students at a time when nationalism and the idea of an independendent Indonesian state was regarded as a chauvinistic deviation by both the PKI and Sarekat Islam. Their aptest pupil was Sukarno. Born at Surabaja in 1901, the son of an elementary schoolteacher who made great sacrifices to provide his son with the best possible education, Sukarno attended the ELS and then the HBS at Surabaja, and in 1921 passed the examination enabling him to attend the technical college at Bandung. During his schooldays he lived in Tjokroaminoto's house, and was thus well acquainted with the development and problems of the Indonesian movement when he came to Bandung in the autumn of 1921. He was a member of Sarekat Islam, but also sympathized with Communist views; he therefore regarded the split in the movement as a misfortune, and saw in nationalism a means of restoring unity. He became secretary of the Bandung study club formed by one Iskaq Tjokroadisurjo, who had just returned from Holland, and after graduating as an engineer in June 1926 devoted himself unreservedly to the task of reconciliation within the movement.[58]

Sutomo had already striven to close the ranks of the independence movement as urged by the PI in Holland, but he soon found himself at odds with both the PKI and the Muslim parties, as owing to his absence in Holland he was insufficiently informed of the background to their dissensions, and was accused by the Communists of ignorance of Marxism.[59] In this respect Sukarno

63

was better equipped. He knew personally most of the leaders of both parties, their arguments, and their sensitive points. In a series of articles, under the title 'Nationalism, Islam and Marxism', published from October 1926 onwards in *Indonesia Muda* (Young Indonesia), the organ of the Bandung study club, he tackled the problem in a cautious manner, emphasizing the common interests of all shades of opinion and trying to explain away their antagonisms as misunderstandings.[60] Since they all aspired to an independent Indonesia, nationalists, Muslims and Marxists were natural allies. The Marxists' chief enemy was capitalism and imperialism, but this meant first and foremost the colonial powers, who would be greatly weakened by the loss of their dependencies. As for the Muslims, they were the chief representatives of the spirit of freedom in Asia, and must desire independence in order to practise their religion without requiring the consent of alien masters. Both groups, therefore, must logically co-operate with the nationalists. But, over and above this, the factors uniting Islam and Marxism were stronger than those that divided them. Sukarno drew attention to the socialism of the Koran, the democratic spirit of the early Muslim community, the prohibition of usury and the equality of all men in the sight of Allah – arguments which Sarekat Islam had used in controversy with the Communists, and which figured in a pamphlet composed by Tjokroaminoto at this time.[61] In addition, Sukarno defended the Communists against the charge of wanting to do away with religion. The hostility between Marxism and the Church in Marx's time, he argued, was due to the particular circumstances of Europe, where the Church had supported the ruling classes; but in Asia the position was the other way round, since religion was on the side of the oppressed. Philosophical materialism was not Marxism, but empty speculation; true Marxism was historical materialism explaining social development. The Muslims should give up their old prejudices, and the Marxists should conform to the 'new tactics' of the Comintern, which called for closer co-operation between Communist parties and other organizations striving for independence. In conclusion he appealed to both sides to concede a little and put aside their differences, since only in this way could the movement become an irresistible stream, sweeping away obstacles to the independence which all desired.

In the following months Sukarno discussed these ideas – which are important for the understanding of his later career – with the various bodies concerned. At the time when his articles appeared, the PKI's unsuccessful attempt at a rebellion had just taken place, and the party was therefore excluded from political life, but Sukarno's efforts were effective with the other groups. December 1927 saw the first federation of Indonesian parties, including all political groups of consequence since the banning of the PKI: Budi Utomo, Sarekat Islam, Dr. Sutomo's study club, the Sumatran, Sundanese and Batavian organizations (the last two known respectively as Pasundan and Kaum Betavi), and finally Sukarno's own party, the Perserikatan Nasional Indonesia (PNI), founded on 4 July 1927. The federation was known as the Permufakatan Perhimpunan Politiek Kebangsaan Indonesia (PPPKI – Union of Indonesian Political Associations), and at the inaugural assembly Sukarno proudly called it 'a return to our own selves'. The federation was to conduct its business in the 'Indonesian way': that is to say, by unanimous decision (*mufakat*) following general consultation (*musjawarah*), as had been the ancient custom of the archipelago, for instance in the *desa* councils of elders. The 'Western system' of majority decision was rejected in order, as Sukarno explained, to prevent tyranny over minorities. Each association possessed a vote on the standing consultative committee (*madjelis pertimbangan*).[62]

The PPPKI was often extolled during his lifetime as a 'state within the State', and it reflected the growing urge towards unity more clearly than did the Volksraad; but it did not become a fighting force as Sukarno had hoped. Its weakness was shown up by Sukarno's own principle of discussing only such matters as did not threaten unanimity, and avoiding discord as far as possible. As a result, its existence soon became purely nominal; but it was a name and a symbol that served to transform 'Indonesia' from the concept of a few intellectuals into a living idea shared by a whole people. The fact that this was achieved was above all due to Sukarno's party, renamed in 1928 the Partai Nasional Indonesia (PNI), whose ranks included many who had studied in Holland. To this category belong the founder members Iskaq Tjokroadisurjo, Budiarto, Sunarjo, Sartono (these four all lawyers), and Dr. Samsi Sastrowidogdo, together with two influential recruits of a later date, Gatot Mangkupradja and Ali Sastroamidjojo.

Viewed with growing suspicion by the colonial authorities, who hoped to have restored 'law and order' by banning the PKI, the PNI, with much trumpeting in the press, proclaimed its ideal of an independent Indonesia throughout the country. The nationalists had their red-and-white flag and their 'national anthem', 'Indonesia Raja', the words of which were composed by W. R. Supratman, a poet who died young, for a youth congress held in October 1928 at Djakarta – this being the name by which the nationalists henceforth referred to Batavia, commemorating the town of Djakatra on the same site, which was destroyed in the seventeenth century. The congress, which marked a further step towards Indonesian unity, adopted the slogan: 'Indonesia, satu bangsa, satu bahasa, satu tanah-air' ('Indonesia, one people, one language, one mother land'). The young representatives showed greater tenacity of purpose than their seniors in the PPPKI, and in September 1930, following the example of Indonesian student groups, they formed a unitary association known as Indonesia Muda (Young Indonesia).[63]

The day of Indonesia had dawned. There were Indonesian party congresses, youth congresses and women's congresses. Sarekat Islam changed its name in 1929 to Partai Sarekat Islam Indonesia (PSII), and no association founded in the ensuing years omitted the magic word from its title. Even Budi Utomo, the oldest association in the field, dissolved itself in 1935 and merged with the Partai Bangsa Indonesia, the successor of Dr. Sutomo's study club, to form the Partai Indonesia Raja or Parindra (Party of Greater Indonesia). H. Colijn, who visited the colony after the attempted Communist coup, wrote in a pamphlet of 1928: 'The teim Indonesia, which is often used to give a name to the whole entity, is really void of content. The archipelago is a unity because it constitutes the Dutch East Indies, and for no other reason.'[64] But in speaking thus he was giving a better description of the epoch of Budi Utomo than that of the PNI. 'Indonesia' had become a term full of content, and the fact that it had come to stay was proved, despite all repressive measures, during the years from 1933 to 1937, when Colijn himself was Prime Minister and Minister for the Colonies.

5   THE QUEST FOR INDEPENDENCE IN THE 1930S

Although the Indonesian idea became a political reality in 1927–30, the nationalists had little success in forging an instrument of power in support of their demands for radical reform and a greater say in political and administrative matters. Even recruitment for the universally popular PNI was a slow business. At the end of 1929 it had only 10,000 members, a trifling number in comparison with Sareket Islam in its early days. The short shrift which the Communists had received had had its effect on the population, and although the masses ecstatically applauded the daring speeches that Sukarno and others made at PNI meetings, the nationalist leaders were dangerously in error if they thought themselves in a strong position *vis-à-vis* the government. The PNI's principle of non-cooperation served to mask, but not to nullify, the true balance of power. When rumours of imminent revolt accumulated at the end of 1929, the government showed with disconcerting ease that it was master in its own house. On 29 December the PNI leaders in various localities were arrested in a single purposeful action, and the movement was thrown into complete disarray.

The next few months should have afforded ample occasion for solidarity among the Indonesian parties, since Sukarno and three of his associates – Gatot Mangkupradja, Maskun and Supriadinata – were sentenced to prison after a lengthy trial, although they proved the charges that the PNI was plotting a rebellion to be completely groundless. But there was no reaction apart from the fact that some Volksraad deputies who sympathized with the movement joined the 'nationalist faction' in that body. On the contrary, the unity that had been so painfully achieved was once more jeopardized: the PPPKI – and, worse still, the PNI – was split by internal disagreement while Sukarno was serving his sentence, which Governor-General de Graeff reduced from four years to two. This state of affairs prompted some members of Perhimpunan Indonesia in Holland, who had welcomed the revival of the national movement under Sukarno's leadership, to explore the causes of the discouraging reaction of the Indonesian parties after his arrest. Among those who were thus moved were two West Sumatrans, Mohammed Hatta and Sutan Sjahrir.

Mohammed Hatta had himself been under arrest for half a year in 1927–8 on account of his activity as a representative of 'Indonesia' at international conferences, and of contacts between Perhimpunan Indonesia and exiled communists. Sjahrir, who was only twenty-two years old in 1931, returned in that year to Indonesia and was not long in finding fault with the party's strategy, particularly the fact that Sukarno had turned the independence movement into a holy war, instead of concentrating on educating the people and training leaders. He deplored that so much had been made of the nebulous concept of 'sacred unity', which had not led to any practical co-operation, although important questions which might have jeopardized it had been sedulously avoided. In his view, 'PPPKI politics' were a waste of time. If the independence movement was to become a real force, it must turn to the genuinely revolutionary elements of the people, namely the workers and peasants, and set about educating them systematically. In the meantime, it should avoid needlessly challenging the government with revolutionary speeches.[65] On this basis Sjahrir founded a 'new PNI', the initials standing this time for Pendidikan Nasional Indonesia (Indonesian National Education). The party included former members of the PNI and PI who were discontented with Sukarno's methods, among them Hatta, who returned to Indonesia in 1932.

It was true that Sukarno had done little to educate the masses. Like Tjokroaminoto, he enjoyed the aura of mass activity, but he had confined himself to depicting the past and present in a gloomy light and fixing all hopes on the millennium of Indonesia Merdeka. At his trial it was noticeable that hardly any of the many witnesses was capable of explaining the statutes of the PNI. He had hoped that the spirit of revolution as preached by him would spread like wildfire, and he rejected the co-operation proffered by de Graeff, who had tried to regain the nationalists' confidence after the destruction of the communists.

In setting about the task of building up cadres, Sjahrir and Hatta counted on enjoying the same degree of liberty as the old PNI, as long as they did not openly challenge the government. They adopted the principle of non-cooperation, but for some years kept very much in the background and were content with a mere thousand members or so. The adherents of the old PNI took a different line. The latter having been branded, in the verdict on Sukarno, as a quasi-illegal association, Sartono in 1931 founded as its successor the Partai Indonesia or Partindo, which differed only in name from the old PNI and was ready to carry on the fight in the old crusading style. Directly after his release in January 1932, Sukarno addressed a congress of Indonesia Raja at Surabaja and promised in ecstatic words that he would reunite the two national parties. But he soon saw that the new PNI had been founded in direct opposition to himself, and accordingly joined Partindo in August 1932. Unlike the 'new PNI' (PNI-Baru), which placed its hopes in the gradual mobilization of the proletariat and the impoverished peasants, Partindo tried to enlist the support of as many sections of the population as possible, using Sukarno's concept of the *marhaen* or 'little man' – not only workers and peasants, but craftsmen, traders, fishermen and even small industrialists and landowners, in short all who were in any way exploited by colonialism and imperialism. *Marhaen* – originally the name of a humble peasant living near Bandung, who could hardly feed his family on the yield of his rice-fields – came to denote any Indonesian who was against imperialism. In Partindo's propaganda, racial conflict took the place of the class struggle, and it was indicated that there would be no class differences in an independent Indonesia. National independence was described by Sukarno as a 'golden bridge', after crossing which it would be possible to erect a social order based on justice: to this he gave the name 'Social Democracy', since it was to guarantee the political and economic equality of all citizens.[66]

As in the time of the old PNI, congresses and mass meetings were organized to attract the population into the movement. As before, Sukarno depicted the blessings of an independent Indonesia and declared 'the fight that knows no peace' to turn his dream into a reality. But meanwhile Governor-General de Graeff had been succeeded by B. C. de Jonge (September 1931–September 1936), who was not disposed to make concessions to the nationalists as his predecessor had done, the more so as the world economic crisis of the early 1930s had left deep marks in the Netherlands Indies also. Soon after he arrived at Batavia, he had announced that he recognized no such thing as a nationalist movement, but only the movement representing the regents.[67] His appointment was in part due to his friendship with H. Colijn, whose arch-colonial (or 'colijnial') views were a byword in Indonesia. In May 1933 Colijn became Prime Minister and Minister for the Colonies, and on 1 August Sukarno was again arrested and soon afterwards banished to the island of Flores in the east of the archipelago.

The tactics adopted by Sjahrir and Hatta seemed at first to pay off. Sukarno was accused by Colijn of 'presumptuous and conspicuous behaviour', a charge that could not be levelled against the new PNI: its leaders, whose long stay in the Netherlands had accustomed them to the rule of law, hoped that their attempt to educate the people for independence would meet with sympathy rather than hostility from the authorities. These hopes, however, proved misplaced. Sjahrir and Hatta were regarded by De Jonge as more dangerous than Sukarno, who fought openly in the style of a *wajang* hero: they were arrested in February 1934 and banished to the notorious Boven Digul camp in west New Guinea.[68]

The drastic measures taken by Colijn and De Jonge seriously weakened the independence movement and called in question the value of the non-cooperation tactics which most parties had hitherto followed. The nationalists began increasingly to transfer their activity to the Volksraad, which they had previously scorned. Following the appointment of a reform commission in accordance with Limburg Stirum's proposals at the end of 1918, the Volksraad had been endowed in 1927 with 'joint legislative functions'; its membership had been increased to 60, and since 1931 the Indonesians enjoyed a majority, having 30 seats assigned to them as against 25 for Europeans and 5 for foreign Orientals. The phrase 'joint legislative functions' was a euphemism for the council's powers, which in practice remained circumscribed. Apart from the right to discuss the budget and present petitions, it possessed powers of initiative, amendment and interpellation – that is to say, it could draft proposals for government measures, suggest changes and obtain information from the Governor-General on specific matters.[69] But the latter was in no way bound to accept its recommendations, and there were many ways in which the government could take action without prior discussion in the Volksraad.[70] The Council of Delegates set up in 1927, a permanent body elected by the Volksraad and consisting of a third of its members, had no wider powers than its parent body. As sessions of the Volksraad were fairly short, it fell to the Council of Delegates to exercise its 'legislative functions'; but the council, whose membership was reduced in 1935 from 20 to 15 for reasons of economy, made only hesitant use of its powers.[71]

The distribution of seats in the Volksraad so as to represent all interest groups in the colony was maintained when its membership was raised to 60. Table VI on page 71 shows the picture for successive sessions in accordance with government estimates, the figures in brackets representing seats in the council of delegates.

In these estimates, members of the liberation movement were designated as 'left' or 'extremist', and those who might one day favour an independent Indonesia as 'moderate left'. It thus appears that despite the 'Indonesian majority' in the Volksraad, up to the end of colonial days there was a solid majority in that body for the preservation of a close connection with the Netherlands.

Table VI   Composition of the Volksraad, 1927–38[72]

Session	right	moderate right	moderate left	left	Total
1927–30	6(2)	36(12)	9(3)	9(3)	60(20)
1931–4	10(3)	24(8)	14(4)	12(5)	60(20)
1935–8	10(2)	27(7)	13(3)	10(3)	60(15)

The extremist spokesman in the Volksraad was Mohammed Husni Thamrin, born in 1894 and a co-founder of the Kaum Betavi (Batavian party), who had been given a seat in 1927 in recognition of his services on the Batavia municipal council, and was regarded by the Governor-General at that time as a moderate nationalist and a possible foil to the 'extremists' in the PNI;[73] however, from 1930 onwards he appeared as the undisputed leader of the 'national fraction' in the Volksraad and council of delegates, championing the cause of Indonesian independence. As a deputy he enjoyed the right of free speech in the Volksraad, and could therefore criticize colonial abuses more effectively than the nationalists, who refused to take part in the councils of the governing race but were constantly harassed by the police and their spies. De Jonge, who summed up Sukarno with his above-board tactics as 'dangerous but stupid', described Thamrin as 'dangerous and crafty', since, unlike the others, he offered no handle for attack.[74]

From time to time, Thamrin was able to enlist the support of the moderate left in the nationalist cause, for instance after the mutiny on board the *Zeven Provinciën*. This broke out at the beginning of February 1933 arising from reductions in pay, though the white press, without evidence, ascribed it to nationalist agitation.[75] On such occasions, as on that of De Jonge's Wilde Scholen Ordonnantie of 1932, which provided for government supervision of Ki Hadjar Dewantoro's Taman Siswa schools,[76] the Moderates rallied in solid support of Thamrin's eloquent protests; but for the rest this group, who consisted mainly of *prijajis*, as a rule adopted a neutral attitude. They realized that their influence among the people was being undermined by the radical nationalists, and, while sympathizing

71

with the idea of independence, were concerned to maintain their traditional claim to leadership. In 1929, led by R. A. A. Wirnata Kusuma, the *bupati* of Bandung, they founded the Perhimpunan Pegawai Bestuur Bumiputera (Association of Native Civil Servants), whose spokesman in the Volksraad and later president, was the *patih* of Gresik, Sutardjo Kartohadikusumo.

Whereas Thamrin worked for independence outside as well as inside the Volksraad – he was the head of the political section of Parindra, set up in 1935 – Sutardjo's group was active inside the council only. It first attracted wider attention by initiating the 'Sutardjo petition', addressed by the Volksraad to the Queen on October 1936; this requested the holding of an imperial conference, at which representatives of the Netherlands and the colony should have equal rights, and should be charged with drafting a programme of reform looking towards self-government for Indonesia within the Dutch commonwealth.[77] In order to gain a majority for this petition, Sutardjo abandoned his original demand that self-government should be attained within ten years. In this way he secured Eurasian support, and the voting was 26 to 20, in favour of the petition. Even in its moderate form, however, it was unacceptable to the Dutch government. Colijn had since 1918 opposed any extension of the powers of the Volksraad, and in a pamphlet of 1928 described this body as a 'tree rotten at the root' that should be removed: it was intolerable to the colonial power as a forum of unbridled criticism, and useless to Indonesians because it could not offer them genuine responsibility 'in any measurable time'.[78] In its place Colijn advocated the development of regency and provincial councils, and he had worked in this sense since becoming Colonial Minister in 1933. It was not to be expected, therefore, that he would view the Sutardjo petition with favour, and in fact he ignored it. But even his successor, Charles J. I. M. Welter, who became Minister for the Colonies in June 1937 and held the office almost without a break till the eve of the Pacific war, was at first entirely opposed to making any concessions to nationalism. In November 1938, two years after the petition, he wrote in a letter to the Queen that the desire for self-government was felt only by 'an extremely thin layer of the population', among whom there was no agreement as to further aims. This being so, there could be no question of granting the request or of taking any action in the sense urged by Sutardjo.[79]

The latter's speeches at this period reflect the tragedy of those Indonesians who hoped that in return for the loyalty which had impaired their credit with their own people, the Dutch government might grant them a sign that the course they had adopted was not a blind alley.[80] But no such sign was forthcoming. The colonial power felt strong – as Colijn put it in 1928, it felt its authority in the Indies to be as deeply rooted as Mont Blanc in the Alps. Its confidence was not diminished when, after the refusal of the Sutardjo petition became known, the Indonesian political associations formed a new union for the better co-ordination of their activities. The new body was known as Gabungan Politik Indonesia, or 'Gapi' for short – and the initiative in its formation was due to Thamrin. At a Parindra conference in March 1939, he had expressed the view that it was doubtful whether the Netherlands could remain neutral in the war that threatened Europe, and that the Indonesian parties should close their ranks so as to meet all eventualities. All those of any importance were in fact represented in Gapi, which was constituted in April 1939.[81]

Immediately after the outbreak of war in Europe Gapi launched an intensive campaign with the slogan 'Indonesia berparlamen' ('a parliament for Indonesia'). The colonial power remained unresponsive, despite the danger that Holland might be involved in war, and the fact that even such traditionally pro-Dutch organizations as the Ambonese and Minahassa leagues and the Indonesian Catholic party, who had abstained from joining the PPPKI, now openly supported the demand for a parliament. The first Indonesian people's congress, organized by Gapi and known as the Kongress Rakjat Indonesia Ke–1, met at Christmas 1939 and reiterated the demand for a parliament and preparation for self-government. Loyalty to the Indonesian flag, anthem, and language was proclaimed on all sides; yet at this time Welter circulated a note containing the words: 'It must be quite clear that we should adopt and maintain a completely negative attitude towards all such objectives.'[82] His remedy for Indonesian discontents – as he indicated in October 1939 to Starkenborgh-Stachouwer, who became Governor-General in September 1936 – was to encourage the provincial councils instead of, as previously, the regency councils. He was genuinely convinced that if a responsible system of government was created in the provinces, aspirations for centralized self-government could in this way be channelled off and made harmless.[3]

Such views testified not only to the rulers' arrogance but also to the impotence of the Indonesian political associations, who, for more than a quarter of a century, had been expressing the desire for more genuine consultation and ultimate self-government, without making any adequate impression on the authorities. This was partly due to the severe policies adopted by the latter since the onset of the world economic crisis after 1929. It was also due to dissensions among the organizations, which numbered over twenty at the outbreak of war, and were never wholly certain of their own tactics and objectives. As we saw, the 1920s were marked by divisions between the nationalist, Muslim and socialist currents of opinion – or *aliran*, to use the native term by which Clifford Geertz designated them in his studies of Javanese society in the fifties; and despite Sukarno's eirenic efforts, these divisions had become more pronounced in the following decade. Moreover, the three principal camps were themselves split internally. The opposition between PNI-Baru and Partindo, the two successors of the Partai Nasional Indonesia, has already been described. These parties lost importance after their leaders were exiled: Partindo dissolved itself in November 1936, while PNI-Baru, which was from the outset an association of intellectuals, continued to exist in name without influencing the course of the movement. The main forces on the nationalist side were the Parindra and Gerindo (Gerakan Rakjat Indonesia – Indonesian people's movement), founded in 1937 in succession to Partindo. Some former members of Partindo joined Parindra, such as Iskaq Tjokroadisurjo, but most of them considered it too far to the right and too little concerned with the common man and the social doctrines of marhaenism. Gerindo, on the other hand – under its leaders A. K. Gani, Amir Sjarifuddin and Muhammad Yamin – presented itself as a nationalist organization with Socialist overtones, whose programme included the combating of fascism. There are claims that the Gerindo was also in close contact with underground organizations of the outlawed Communist party, though the influence of the latter in this period is as yet not altogether clear. Besides Parindra and Gerindo there were several other nationalist bodies, mostly of a regional character, such as the Ambonese and Minahassa leagues, and Pasundan.

The picture was still more complicated in the Muslim camp, which had once been so decisively dominated by Sarekat Islam. After Tjokroaminoto's death in 1934, the PSII had lost much of its influence; it was now led by his brother Abikusno Tjokrosujoso, and adhered to the principle of non-cooperation even after this was abandoned by the nationalists. Many of its followers thought this a mistaken policy, and in 1938 a group headed by Wiwoho Purbohadijojo and Dr. Sukiman broke away and founded their own Partai Islam Indonesia (PII). This was the second secession from the PSII, as in 1937 Hadji Agus Salim had founded the Pergarakan Penjadar, or 'self-realization movement', after the style of Sjahrir's national education party, for the purpose of strengthening Islamic ideals.[84]

However, by far the strongest Muslim association was the Muhammadijah, a reform movement which was founded in 1912 by Kijai Ahmad Dahlan of central Java, but was not originally involved in politics. Dahlan, born in 1868, had made the pilgrimage to Mecca as a young man, and had later been influenced by the Egyptian reformer Muhammad Abduh. Like him, Dahlan wished, while preserving the Koran and the *sunnah* as the foundations of belief, to free the Prophet's teachings from superstitious accretions and local compromise with the *adat*. This aroused hostility in orthodox quarters, which Dahlan, however, succeeded eventually in overcoming. The Muhammadijah devoted itself primarily to teaching and social work, building schools, hospitals and mosques; its unobtrusive activities were supported by the colonial government, and it gradually spread over the whole archipelago.

A counterpart to the Muhammadijah was the Nahdatul Ulama, founded in January 1926 – an association of orthodox *kijais* and *ulamas*, the statutes of which emphasized strict adherence to the four Islamic schools of doctrine (*mazhabs*) whose authority the Muhammadijah called in question. Its influence was confined to Java, and it was not until after independence that the conflict between the orthodox and the reformists came to a head.[85] In 1937 Kijai Hadji Mas Mansur, then head of the Muhammadijah, founded the Council of Muslim parties of Indonesia (Madjlisul Islamil A'laa Indonesia: MIAI) with the object of co-ordinating the various Islamic associations. Its scope was originally confined to religious questions, but after the outbreak of war it became involved in politics, as several of its constituent bodies (such as PSII and PII) were members of Gapi, and Mansur himself was on the governing body of PII. In this way, a united political and religious front began to take shape for the first time towards the end of the colonial period; even so, the links between Gapi and MIAI were loose, and in supporting Gapi's efforts for an Indonesian parliament, MIAI insisted that it should be based on Islamic constitutional principles.[86]

However, a greater handicap for the leaders than all internal dissensions and ideological disputes was their failure to enlist the support of the masses. Since the initial success of Sarekat Islam, the parties had tried in vain to mobilize the population of the archipelago, which had meanwhile grown to 60 million. Of this number, more than 40 million were concentrated in Java, which was the main seat of activity of most of the organizations, so that the general apathy towards parties and programmes cannot be ascribed first and foremost to geographical dispersion. It was due rather to the essentially passive temperament of the people, who awaited major political and social changes without feeling called on to help bring them about. In March 1919 the Communist A. Baars complained that the only effect of much self-sacrificing work had been that 'the masses applaud, but don't want to do anything for themselves'.[87] Ten years later, Sukarno suffered the same disappointment in his propaganda campaign for the PNI. As a neutral observer remarked, 'when Sukarno makes a speech, the people turn up in thousands and shout themselves hoarse; but there the matter ends. When they are asked to enrol, they say they must have time to think, or they are frightened.'[88]

If things were like this in 1919 and 1929, they were still more so in 1939 after the draconic measures of Colijn and De Jonge. The ten associations represented in Gapi had less than 50,000 members all told. The PSII, the largest political organization, had only 12,000 left of its former membership of over 366,000. Parindra and Pasundan had 10,000 each, while the so-called 'mass parties' of Gerindo and the Catholics had only 5,000 each. The Muhammadijah counted 20,000, PII about 3,000 and Nahdatul Ulama only 1,000. Of the remaining organizations, the only one to reach a respectable figure (9,000) was the West Sumatran Muslim party Persatuan Tarbijahtul Islamijah, known for short as Perti, which concentrated on education and social questions. All the other parties or splinter groups lay around the thousand mark, such as the Ambonese and Minahassa leagues, or below it, like H. A. Salim's Partai Penjadar with 500 members. In 1940 it was estimated that the total number of politically organized Indonesians was 80,700, while about 200,000 were politically or socially conscious.[89] The latter figure is roughly equal to that of the Indonesians who could speak and read Dutch, which was put at 187,000 in 1930 and had probably risen by something like 100,000. The number of literate persons, which was 3,746,000 in 1930, had grown by 1940 to about 6 million.[90] It is not to be supposed that most of these, who had had some schooling in their own tongue or in Malay, knew anything about the programme and objectives of the Indonesian movement. But even if they did, they represented only a tenth of the total population of 60 million; the number of those politically conscious was less than half of one per cent of this, and little more than a third of them were organized. Figures like these tell more about the movement's 'strength' than do congress speeches and resolutions. At the outbreak of the Second World War, the Indonesian independence movement did not constitute a threat to the colonial government.

6   THE END OF DUTCH COLONIAL RULE

The German invasion of the Netherlands in May 1940 came as a shock to the colony. The fear, repeatedly expressed by some parties, that Indonesia might be involved in hostilities and become an object of Fascist colonial ambitions was now suddenly a real danger. In the first instance, expressions of sympathy with Holland's plight reached the colonial government from every side: for example Tjipto Mangunkusumo, who had been in exile in Banda since 1927, made a statement in this sense, and appealed to other exiles to join with him, such as Hatta and Sjahrir, whose place of banishment was near his own, or Sukarno who was now at Benkulen in south Sumatra. Immediately after these demonstrations of loyalty, demands were once more heard for political reform.[91]

Following the occupation of Holland, a state of emergency had been proclaimed in the colony; this circumscribed the activity of the Indonesian associations, and the nationalists turned increasingly to the Volksraad. Some months before, in February 1940, Wiwoho had brought in a motion proposing the early transformation of that body into a full parliament and the creation of an imperial council on which Holland, Indonesia, Surinam and Curaçao would be represented with equal rights. He now repeated these proposals, while emphasizing that he did not want to take unfair advantage of the state of duress in which Holland found itself. Requests in the same sense were made by Gapi to the Governor-General, and further suggestions were put forward: a new 'Sutardjo motion' for the introduction of 'Indies citizenship' – the moderates still shrank from the term 'Indonesia', which the government had frowned on for some time past – and the radicals' counter-proposal in the 'Thamrin motion' for the adoption of the name 'Indonesia' instead of 'Netherlands Indies', and 'Indonesian' for the natives instead of *inlander* and *inlandsch*.[92]

The Governor-General, Tjarda van Starkenborgh-Stachouwer, having in mind the ill-fated November Declaration by Limburg Stirum, made it known in the Volksraad on 23 August 1940 that he was not prepared to arouse expectations which the government could not promise to fulfil. He gave exhaustive reasons for rejecting the various proposals, his basic objection being that political reform was a matter for the home parliament, which could not assemble until after the occupation. At the same time, he did not shrink from repeating the decades-old formula that the Indonesians were not ripe for self-government. Finally, as had now become the usual practice, he announced the appointment of a commission to enquire into the attitude of all sections of the community towards reform.[93] The Indonesians rightly saw this as a temporizing manoeuvre, and Wiwoho withdrew the three motions on behalf of their sponsors, on the ground that there was clearly no prospect of agreement between them and the government. Gapi went further, and at first forbade the parties associated with it to have any dealings with the commission, which was set up under the chairmanship of Dr. F. H. Visman. However, Gapi was later invited to furnish the commission with an outline of its ideas for the future political organization of Indonesia, and did so in January 1941. Its proposals envisaged a federal union between Indonesia and the Netherlands. The head of the Indonesian state would have executive powers and be assisted by an advisory council; ministers would be appointed and dismissed in consultation with parliament, which would be bicameral and possess exclusive powers of legislation; all sections of society would be represented in the upper house, while members of the lower house would be elected by direct popular vote. These reforms were to be introduced within five years, and proposals were made for the progressive appointment, during the intervening period, of Indonesians to positions of responsibility, where they would in the first instance be associated with Europeans.[94]

MIAI supported Gapi's proposals, while demanding special rights for Islam: the president and two-thirds of the ministers should be Muslims, there should be a ministry of Muslim affairs etc. But the general atmosphere of progress was of short duration. When the Visman committee's report was published, it was clear that the plans of Gapi and MIAI, based on the Philippine model, had not been seriously considered. The report declared that neither the Philippines nor British India could serve as a model for Indonesia, and that special regard must be paid to the peculiar conditions of the archipelago.[95]

Meanwhile, discussions had begun in Java between the colonial government and a Japanese trade delegation which arrived in September 1940. The Japanese, led by their minister of trade Kobayashi, showed special interest in raw materials and expressed wishes which it was difficult for the Dutch authorities to satisfy.[96] The conversations were conducted on the Dutch side by J. H. van Mook, the deputy Governor-General and successor-designate to Starkenborgh-Stachouwer: their tone was friendly, but the Japanese also made contact with Indonesian nationalists, which excited much speculation among the public. The indifference of the Indonesian masses towards their political parties did not signify, as the Dutch often wrongly supposed, a widespread desire for the continuance of colonial rule, but merely an expectation that things would change without their help. The past few years had seen a revival of Djojobojo's prophecies, one version of which predicted that the whites would be driven out by an Asiatic power. This power might once have been identified with India, but since Japan had become a world power the role of prospective liberator had been transferred to it. Prophecies of this sort were current at the end of the twenties, and ten years later they were rife throughout the archipelago.[97] The colonial government had always been sensitive to such rumours, and when they now learnt that members of the Japanese delegation had had talks with Douwes Dekker (who had given less trouble in recent years, and was then head of a national school of Bandung) and the more active Thamrin, concerning a possible Indonesian government under Japan's 'new order', they arrested Dekker and Thamrin at the beginning of January 1941. A few days later, Thamrin died of a heart attack in the prison where he was detained for interrogation. Soon after this unhappy event, the government, alarmed at the situation, deported Douwes Dekker to Surinam.[98]

Other nationalists, especially in Parindra circles, had taken account in their calculations of a possible Japanese invasion, as became clear in June–July 1941 when discussions took place for the formation of a native militia. In the First World War a Comité Indië Weerbar (Committee for the Defence of the Indies) had been set up, and the parties led by Budi Utomo had pleaded for the institution of a militia to help defend the colony. Between the wars the idea fell into the background, but it was revived towards the end of the thirties. With the rising danger of war, the nationalists began to link the question of participation in defence with that of political reform. This had been Thamrin's attitude, and after his death the same line was taken by his fellow-member of Parindra and the Volksraad, Sukardjo Wirjopranoto. By this time the government itself was pressing for a militia. The nationalists were not disposed to sacrifice their last trump so easily, and devised all sorts of objections to the government's plan to call up five or six thousand men for a limited period.[99] Apart from the practical disadvantages of the plan which they themselves had once been so eager to see put into effect, they were moved by opportunism. The government eventually got its way – the proposal was approved by the Volksraad on 11 July – but the nationalists calculated that their protest would not go unnoticed in Japan.

During the last few months before the Pacific war, the rift between the Indonesians and the colonial government widened. Bitterness was aroused by the government's completely negative attitude towards all proposals, whether from extremists or moderates. True, the Queen of the Netherlands, now in exile in Britain, had indicated in a speech on the anniversary of the occupation, and again on 30 July, that she would agree to constitutional changes in the empire; but Welter, the Colonial Minister, who was in Indonesia from March to June 1941, once more declared in the Volksraad that nothing could be done about reform until the war was over and the Dutch parliament had been consulted.[100] In August, the government spokesman in the Volksraad even threatened that if the nationalists did not limit their demands and moderate their actions, the authorities would have to adopt a 'tougher attitude'.[101]

Meanwhile the Indonesians had been going their own way, and had announced the formation of an Indonesian national council (Madjelis Rakjat Indonesia). This body, set up in September 1941, comprised representatives of Gapi, MIAI and the trade unions of government employees. The *prijajis*' association (PPBB) had for the first time put forward in the Volksraad the demand for Indonesian self-government within the Dutch empire, and had formed a new parliamentary group of nationalists. When the Atlantic Charter was proclaimed in August, it fell to Sutardjo, hitherto regarded as a moderate leader, to ask the government whether it felt bound by the allies' pledge concerning the right of self-determination. The government showed itself unmoved by the new radical trend, and replied evasively to Sutardjo's question. The Charter, it declared, was a guide to international relations, and was not concerned with the internal policy of empires; however, the government believed in democratic principles and would apply them within its own sphere.[102] Some idea of what this meant as regards Indonesia may be gained from a plan of reform which was drawn up at that time but has only recently been published: the Governor-General was to be assisted by a 'government' – the quotation marks were in the plan itself – composed of a vice-president or chancellor and four ministers, all appointed by the Governor-General and responsible to him. There was thus not a vestige of the idea of transforming the Volksraad into a full parliament, representative of the people and with ministers responsible to it, as had been consistently demanded by almost all the Indonesian parties since 1918. On the contrary, the proposed new assembly was to enjoy powers scarcely wider than those of the Volksraad, and the plan contained 'no single element of the parliamentary system'.[103]

In this way the Dutch policy of standing fast, in the spirit of 'Je maintiendrai', was upheld without deviation until the colony was wrested from the Netherlands by a stronger power. Soon after the outbreak of the Pacific war, the colonial government, which associated itself with the Allies' declaration of war on Japan on 8 December was forced to lay down its arms, The Dutch fleet was decisively defeated in the Java Sea at the end of February 1942, and at the beginning of March the Japanese, who had already occupied large areas of Sumatra, landed at various points in Java. On 8 March the Dutch command signed an unconditional surrender. In Atjeh, an anti-Dutch resistance group under religious leadership, formed in 1939 and known as Persatuan Ulama Seluruh Atjeh (Pusa), did not wait for the Japanese before throwing off its allegiance. This area, which at the beginning of the century had been the apex of Dutch rule in the Indies, stood in open rebellion against its former masters from February 1942 onwards: in its history of many centuries, Dutch rule had been but a short interlude.[104]

IV

THE JAPANESE INTERREGNUM, 1942-45

I FROM 'LIBERATION' TO 'ANNEXATION'

Even before the Japanese began their southward drive, they had
revived Indonesian hopes that the Pacific War might lead to
independence for the archipelago. Broadcasts beamed to Indonesia
and accompanied by its national anthem spoke of imminent liberation from Dutch colonial rule. Aircraft dropped miniature Indonesian flags and pamphlets announcing that Djojobojo's prophecies
would shortly come true. When the Japanese landed in Java, it was
not surprising that large sections of the population greeted them
with enthusiasm as liberators.[1]

The high hopes that were raised are attested by the discussions
that appeared at the time in Indonesian newspapers concerning the
composition of the first national government. On 9 March, the day
after the Dutch surrender, a group of associations belonging to the
Madjelis Rakjat Indonesia presented the Japanese military government with a list containing a choice of three names for each cabinet
post.[2] Even Gerindo subscribed to the list, although in the previous
years and months it had issued repeated warnings against Japanese
Fascism. This was especially true of its president, Amir Sjarifuddin,
whose name did not figure on the suggested list of ministers, and
who attempted from the outset to build up an anti-Japanese
resistance movement. He was helped in doing so by the fact that the
'liberators' soon turned out to be new masters who had no intention
of allowing the Indonesian nationalists to interfere in their plans.
On the very day of the Dutch capitulation an order was published
forbidding all political assemblies and demonstrations. A week later
the display of the Indonesian flag was prohibited, and a further order
forbade 'any discussion, speculation or propaganda regarding the
political organization or administration of the country'.[3] Infringe-
ments of these decrees were drastically punished, and rumours of
decapitation for minor offences were soon circulating. Within

barely four weeks of the 'liberation', nothing was left of any illusion that the Japanese intended, as their propaganda had claimed, to restore the independence of Asian peoples. The Dutch, it is true, were put in internment camps, but there were signs in plenty that the Indonesians had jumped from the frying-pan into the fire.[4] The drastic suppression of all nationalist movements; the arrogant behaviour of the new masters, who did not shrink from using the degrading punishment of flogging to extort obedience to themselves and their orders; the enactment obliging the population to bow deeply in the direction of the imperial palace in Tokyo, which especially offended the Muslims, as Mecca was in the opposite quarter; the shaving of students' heads and the compulsory learning of Japanese – all these measures enhanced the new masters' unpopularity from day to day.

The nationalists, however, were alarmed most of all by the way in which the unity of the country was jeopardized by administrative measures. Java was occupied by the Sixteenth Army; Sumatra formed part of the command of the Twenty-Fifth Army, stationed at Singapore; while Borneo, Celebes and the whole eastern part of the archipelago were administered by the Japanese southern fleet, with its headquarters at Macassar. The division of the archipelago into areas of military and naval command had been decided before the outbreak of war. The Japanese main objective was to exploit the natural resources of the islands as quickly and fully as possible, and thus to reduce the burden which the war imposed on the homeland. Areas which were more sparsely populated and difficult of access were assigned to the navy, while the army took control of densely populated regions where it was necessary to recruit a labour force.

Accordingly, and on the basis of the most recent census (that of 1930), the picture of Indonesia under Japanese occupation was as shown in Table VII.

The Japanese had given less attention to the future political status of the territories they intended to occupy. In comparison with the detailed plans for economic exploitation, the political directive merely said that Japan's war aim was to work for a Greater East Asian Co-Prosperity Sphere under the aegis of Dai Nippon (Greater Japan). For the time being, it was left undecided which territories were to be permanently incorporated into the Japanese empire. Until Tokyo had made up its mind on this score, 'no

premature support' was to be given to local independence movements. Existing political structures were to be taken over as they
stood, and even trained colonial personnel, such as the Dutch in
Indonesia, might be retained if they showed themselves co-opera-
tive.[6]

Table VII   Indonesia under Japanese administration, 1942–5[5]

Territory	Administration	Area (km²)	Pop. (millions)	Pop. (per km²)
Java and Madura	16th army	132,174	40·8	315
Sumatra and surrounding islands	25th army	473,606	7·7	17
Borneo, Celebes, Moluccas, Lesser Sunda Islands etc.	2nd southern fleet	1,298,565	10·5	8

This general directive left a certain freedom of manoeuvre to the
respective area commanders, and advantage was taken of this by
Lieutenant-General Imamura, the commander of the Sixteenth
Army, who soon realized that the Indonesians' will to co-operate
had been choked off by the ferocious behaviour of the occupiers.
This could be seen in the failure of the Tiga A (Three A's) movement, which was planned shortly after the landing in Java by the
propaganda department of the military government, as a means
of winning popular support for Japan's war aims. Its title was
derived from the slogan: 'Japan, the light of Asia, the leader of
Asia, the protector of Asia'.

The leader of the movement in Indonesia was Raden Samsudin,
a lawyer from Bogor, who had offered his services to the Japanese.[7]
Samsudin did not belong to the élite of Indonesian nationalism;
he had been a member of Parindra, and in 1940 became a deputy
to the Volksraad elected in the preceding year. He was not on the
parties' list of 48 candidates for ministerial rank, and his appointment
testifies to the fact that the Japanese originally considered they
could do without the help of acknowledged Indonesian leaders.[8]

Tiga A initially spread widely with the aid of the Japanese propaganda machine under Shimizu Hitoshi, and from the end of April 1942 published an Indonesian daily, *Asia Raya*, with the Parindra leader Sukardjo Wirjopranoto as an important member of its staff. But its one-sided glorification of Dai Nippon prevented the movement from gaining any lasting ascendancy over the population.

However, the Japanese needed help from the natives if only to carry out their economic programme, and the military began to look round for other leaders. Since the deaths of Tjokroaminoto (1934), Sutomo (1938) and Thamrin (1941), the most notable of these were the exiled nationalists, in particular Tjipto Mangunkusumo, Sukarno, Hatta and Sjahrir, of whose existence the Japanese were aware. Tjipto had been released from banishment in 1940, on account of illness (he suffered from asthma) and in consideration of his appeal to the population to co-operate with the Dutch during the war. He returned from Banda to Java in 1941; but the veteran of the independence movement was no friend of the Japanese invaders, and he made his position unmistakably clear. His death in March 1943 was something of a relief to the Japanese, who did not think it politic to arrest so universally respected a leader, as they had done with Amir Sjarifuddin on discovering his underground activities.

Hatta and Sjahrir had been brought back to Java by the Dutch authorities on the outbreak of the Pacific War: they too had repeatedly denounced Japanese Fascism, and the Dutch hoped to secure their co-operation in building up an effective opposition to the enemy. These plans were frustrated by the rapid occupation of Java, and Hatta and Sjahrir were now wooed by the Japanese. Hatta had little freedom of action: at the beginning of 1942 he had written an article urging resistance to the Japanese, and if he now refused co-operation he could hope for no mercy. He therefore accepted the 'invitation' to assist the military as adviser on Indonesian affairs. Sjahrir pretended illness, and was able to avoid collaborating with the occupiers; unlike Hatta, he was little known in the country at large outside PNI-Baru circles.[9] In the next year or two, he began to carry on anti-Japanese activity, especially among students, and as he went about this more cautiously than Amir Sjarifuddin he was able by the end of the war to create a resistance movement which played a significant part in the achievement of independence.

There remained Sukarno, whom the Dutch had not allowed to return to Java. In 1938 he was moved from Flores to southern Sumatra, and shortly before the Japanese invasion the authorities, fearing untoward consequences if he were allowed to contact the Japanese, transferred him from Benkulen to Padang. In March 1942 he met the Japanese at Bukit Tinggi (Fort de Kock), the home of Hatta and Sjahrir. He accepted their proposal for collaboration, and went to Palembang to await permission to return to Java, which was not granted till July. The authorities of the Twenty-Fifth Army had warned the Sixteenth Army that he was a 'secessionist' and would give trouble; but Imamura, who had received many requests for Sukarno's return, was prepared to take the risk.[10]

Sukarno's arrival rekindled nationalist hopes. Despite his seven years' absence from Java, he had lost none of his popularity, and he became once again, as *Asia Raya* put it, the 'central figure and focus of interest of all Indonesian trends of opinion'. At a meeting with Hatta and Sjahrir he agreed that an attempt should be made to extract concessions from the Japanese in return for his co-operation with them. Unlike the other two, Sukarno was not anti-Japanese in principle. He regarded the Japanese as Fascists, but in the twenties he had already been prepared to collaborate with them in the event of a Pacific war, in order to expel the colonial powers who were Asia's chief enemies.[11] His decision to help the invaders was thus not a matter of bowing to *force majeure*, as in Hatta's case,[12] but of exploiting a sudden opportunity. This did not, however, mean that he embraced the Japanese war aims; a Japanese Indonesia was no more to his liking that the continuance of Dutch rule. His object was to bring about a partnership, and at his first interview with the Japanese commander he asked bluntly what his government's plans were for the future of Indonesia. Imamura replied in strict accordance with his directive; he did not know whether Indonesia was to be given autonomy within the Japanese empire, freedom within a system of alliances, or complete independence. The Emperor and the Japanese government would decide the question themselves, and the result might not be made known till after the war. However, Sukarno could be assured that care would be taken of the population's welfare, and that Indonesians would be allowed a voice in political and administrative matters.[13]

Sukarno found this a hopeful answer, and in the next few months devoted much effort to creating a new organization to reinforce

Indonesian aspirations. His first success was the appointment on 24 September 1942 of a commission to study Indonesian customary law. Its members consisted exclusively of Indonesian political and spiritual leaders – Sukarno, Hatta, Sutardjo, Abikusno, Mansur, Dr. (of medicine) Mulia, and Professors Supomo, Purbatjaraka and Hussein Djajadiningrat; and it acted as an advisory council to the military government, informing it of the population's wishes, rather than a body for studying the *adat*.[14]

Next came the institution of the Empat Serangkai – the 'four-leaved clover' of Sukarno, Hatta, Mansur and Ki Hadjar Dewantoro. In this body, Kijai Hadji Mas Mansur represented the Muslims: he was, as already mentioned, the head of the Muhammadijah, the great reform movement, a member of the committee of the Partai Islam Indonesia, and a leading member of MIAI. Ki Hadjar Dewantoro, formerly Suwardi Surjaningrat, had become an important figure in cultural policy, thanks to the Taman Siswa schools, and represented the national educational system; Hatta stood for the intellectuals, and Sukarno was the popular tribune, claiming to speak for all the various national tendencies or *aliran*. These four leading personalities were to form the directing body of a new unified movement which, unlike Tiga A, would enjoy real and widespread support among the population, and would thus also be of value to the Japanese.

The Japanese for their part realized that a popular movement of this kind could easily turn its thoughts towards independence. A hard tussle took place behind the scnees as regards the nature and functions of the organization and the powers of its leaders; this lasted from November 1942 to March 1943. Its name was decided upon at an early stage – Pusat Tenaga Rakjat (Centre of People's Power), abbreviated to 'Putera'. This conveniently indicated the new body's twofold character: the full title described its functions from the viewpoint of the Japanese, while to the Indonesians it was *Putera* (son), a native institution which would take filial care of the motherland. To emphasize this aspect, Sukarno and Hatta asked that 'Indonesia' be added to the name, and that the national flag and anthem should once more be allowed. Tokyo's reply to these requests, which had been expected in December 1942, the anniversary of the Pacific war, did not arrive till March 1943, shortly before the anniversary of the 'liberation' of Java: it was negative on all points. The 'Indonesian idea' was wholly eliminated, and the movement's functions were defined as 'collaboration in the service of Greater Japan so as to bring about final victory in the Great East Asian War and to ensure the smooth execution of the military government's orders, thus creating a new strong Java as a member of the Great East Asian Co-Prosperity Sphere.'[15]

The Indonesian nationalists had already noted with misgiving that Tojo, the Japanese prime minister, in a speech at the beginning of 1943 to the eighty-first session of the Diet, had envisaged independence for Burma and the Philippines, but had not mentioned Indonesia. Since that time, military government circles had spoken only of a 'new Java', and the suspicion grew that Japanese plans did not as yet provide for an independent Indonesia. However, with the official inauguration of Putera on 8 March it was hoped that the new organization would make it possible to spread the notion of independence throughout the country. The leaders' optimism seemed justified by the high hopes to which Putera gave rise among the population as a whole.

In the next few weeks and months branches of Putera were created in most provinces: Sukarno appeared at rallies, as in the days of the old PNI or Partindo, to mobilize opinion among the masses who were mistrustful of Japanese demands. He declared that the time was one of trial, and that the burdens imposed on the people had their favourable side. Thanks to the efforts now imposed, the nation would be hardened and ready to defend its independence in due time. He urged his hearers to support the occupying power, which had freed Indonesia from its 'centuries of slavery' under Dutch rule and was now engaged in a life-and-death struggle with the powers which refused to give up colonial sovereignty in Asia.

A central bureau for Putera was set up in Djakarta (the Japanese had adopted the native name for Batavia since the end of 1942), comprising departments for propaganda, organization, education and health matters. The new headquarters was opened on 16 April, but at this time Indonesian optimism suffered a setback. Yamamoto Moichiro, the new head of the Office for General Affairs (Somobutjo) who had arrived at the end of March, replied to Sukarno's plea for fruitful co-operation between Japan and Indonesia that Putera's plan to mobilize all the nation's forces was nothing but an attempt to secure the Japanese victory in the East Asian war. The only task of the Indonesian leaders would be to carry out the orders and plans of the military government.[16]

Such harsh and sobering words had not been heard from the Japanese side since Sukarno's offer of co-operation, and occupation policy had in fact entered on a new phase. Tojo's omission of Indonesia from his January speech had been deliberate: the strategically important and economically profitable archipelago was to be annexed to Japan. The Putera leaders appealed in vain to Aoki, the minister for Greater East Asian Affairs, who visited Java at the beginning of May, to persuade Tojo to hold out hope of Indonesian independence.[17] On 13 May a secret conference in Tokyo adopted a resolution for the incorporation of Indonesia into the Japanese empire.[18]

2 THE HARNESSING OF ALL FORCES TO THE WAR EFFORT

In this way, after a year of occupation, the die was cast as regards the future status of the archipelago. The consequences of the decision were most felt in Java, where the military régime had been under stronger pressure from the nationalists than elsewhere. Yamamoto Moichiro now began systematically to curb their activities. The press was called to order, Sukarno was obliged to submit his speeches to censorship, and Putera was not given the chance, as had been hoped, to set up branch organizations in the *desas*. Yamamoto later recalled that on his arrival in Java, Putera had been a kind of independence movement: he had 'altered its direction', much to its leaders' annoyance.[19]

However, the reports of officials returning from Java seem to have convinced Tokyo that a completely negative attitude towards Indonesian wishes might be dangerous to the occupying power at a time when the fortunes of war were beginning to shift from the Japanese to the allied side. Aoki, for example, reported Hatta's frank statement that 'it was perhaps necessary for strategic reasons to divide Indonesia into separate areas of military administration, but Indonesians will not give up the desire and determination they have shown over the past forty years to unite these territories into one glorious nation.' Or again: 'The future fate of Indonesia, and any plans that exist, therefore must be frankly made known.'[20] On 15 June 1943 Tojo finally informed the Diet that the peoples of the 'southern regions' (*to indos*) were henceforth to be given an opportunity to co-operate in government, especially in Java, where such was the wish of the population.

Indonesian hopes were once more raised, and even the Muslim leader K. H. Mansur, who was in general inclined to moderation, exclaimed ecstatically: 'I do not know how to express, in word or deed, my gratitude towards Greater Japan. The best way we can respond is to give Japan all we have. We will aid the imperial forces, even if it means further restricting our rations, and we will fight on to final victory.'[21] However, when it was discovered what the Japanese meant by co-operation in government, the disappointment was all the greater. A Central Advisory Committee (Tjuo Sangi-In) was set up at Djakarta and similar bodies (*sangi-kai*) in the provinces, with the function of 'providing information and making proposals to the government'; in addition, some responsible Javanese were to be appointed advisers in various military government offices.[22] The exclusive use of Japanese terminology made it clear that the policy was one of gradual Nipponization. The new commander, General Harada, who had arrived in May, declared that the recent measures should be used by the Javanese 'to become outwardly and inwardly one with Japan and its people'. These and similar statements were made on 1 August, on which day *Asia Raya* reported that Burma had become independent – a goal from which Java, let alone Indonesia as a whole, seemed further away than ever.

The period that ensued was a difficult one for Sukarno and his fellow-collaborators. They were allowed some influence on the composition of the Central Advisory Committee, most of whose 43 members were reputable nationalists of earlier days; but if the Volksraad in its time had been stigmatized as a caricature of a genuine popular assembly, the Tjuo Sangi-In appeared at first to be little better than a farce. At the opening of the first session in mid-October 1943, the deputies had been made to stand while the supreme commander's 'important question' had been read out to them: 'In what way can the population furnish practical help to the Japanese army?' – and had been given four days in which to provide the answer. The object of setting up the committee, it was made clear to them, was 'simply and solely to strengthen the military régime and make it more efficient': Japanese exploitation was to be sanctioned by the *mufakat*, or consensus, of respected Indonesians. However, subsequent sessions of the committee, which was summoned every three months to hear and answer questions similar to the above, showed that the deputies were more concerned to improve the lot of the population than to increase its burdens. In this way, the Japanese institution took on greater importance than the Volksraad. Whereas the latter body was composed of representatives of the most varied interests, among which the advocates of complete independence were in a hopeless minority right down to the end of the colonial period, the Tjuo Sangi-In consisted, apart from Japanese observers, exclusively of deputies who were of one mind in desiring independence. True, they were not allowed to criticize or present petitions or resolutions, but these rights had never been of any use to the Volksraad. If ever the course of the war should induce the Japanese to make genuine concessions to Indonesian nationalism, the identity of interest among the deputies meant that the Tjuo Sangi-In could be transformed promptly and smoothly into a working parliament.

That day was, however, still far distant at the end of 1943, when the Japanese bent all their efforts to enlist the various groups in the service of their own power. Unwilling to take the risk of permitting contact between Putera and the rural population, they looked round for other instruments of authority, and turned first of all to the Muslim community, whom they had from the outset treated with respect as the traditional opponents of colonialism. The PSII and PII, like other parties, had been dissolved at the beginning of the occupation, but the MIAI, as a federation of Muslim parties, had remained in existence alongside Tiga A.[23] Even after the foundation of Putera, it was not dissolved; Mansur was for a time appointed its vice-chairman, and thus acted as a link between the nationalists and Muslims. Like Putera, MIAI was not disposed to act as a one-way channel for the execution of army orders; and the Japanese had accordingly begun to circumvent it by setting up a special bureau for religious affairs at Djakarta, where *ulamas* and *kijais* were invited to attend courses of instruction in the task of furthering Japan's 'holy war'. This policy was intensified after the decision to annex Indonesia, and the MIAI was reduced to a shadowy existence, to which it put an end by dissolving itself at its first and last congress in October 1943.[24] This action was quietly encouraged by the Japanese, for the MIAI was not a suitable instrument with which to work on the masses; it was rather a microcosm of Indonesian Islam torn as it was between a multiplicity of official and unofficial organizations. Apart from PSII and PII, Salim's Partai Penjadar, the Muhammadijah and Nahdatul Ulama, there was an Indonesian branch of the Indian reform movement Ahmadijah,[25] a reform group named Persatuan Islam (Muslim unity) founded by A. Hasan in the late twenties at Bandung,[26] and several other associations which clung to their own independence and had been supported in this by the Dutch. The Japanese, however, needed a single organization which, instead of discussing religious problems, would influence the masses in their favour and win them to the idea of a holy war. The Dutch had been glad to see the Muslim associations keep out of politics for the most part; but the Japanese required to use Islam as a political force, and in November 1943 they created the Madjelis Sjuro Muslimin Indonesia (Indonesian Muslim Council) or Masjumi, a new organization which was designed to fulfil their ends and in which the existing bodies were forced to merge.

The unpopularity of this effort to harness Islam to the Japanese war chariot was not shown only by the protests of Muslim leaders, including K. H. Mansur. January 1944 saw the first organized revolt since the beginning of the occupation: near Tasikmalaja, a member of Nahdatul Ulama named Kijai Zainal Mustafa rebelled against the Japanese with 500 followers, and the situation was not brought under control for several days.[27] However, in the course of time the Muslims came to see the benefit of a unified organization comprising orthodox and reformists alike, and it remained in existence as an organ of Islamic interests for seven years after the Japanese occupation.

After bringing the Muslims to heel, the Japanese turned their attention to the *prijajis*. To begin with, they summoned to Djakarta representatives of the princely houses of central Java, who in the Dutch tradition had been allowed a certain independence in administering their areas, and 'advised' them to show greater concern in future for Japanese interests.[28] But the occupiers were still more interested in the lesser *prijajis* or, as they were now more often called, *pamong pradja* (administrative corps). These had enjoyed the favour of the colonial régime, and since the formation of mass organizations – whether Muslim, nationalist or socialist – they had, if anything, rallied even more closely round their Dutch masters, with whom their political future was linked. In spite of the risks involved, the Japanese now did not hesitate to endow the enemy's former servants with fresh authority, using for this purpose a new organization set up in February 1944 to replace Putera and known as Djawa Hokokai (Javanese People's Loyalty Movement). In this organization the *prijajis* were given authority over the *tonari gumi*, neighbourhood associations of a dozen or so families in towns or villages, which were created at this time and might be looked on as the nucleus of the Loyalty Movement.[29]

The Indonesian nationalists were incensed by the creation of the Djawa Hokokai, which deprived them of the organizational independence they had enjoyed in the time of Putera, and whose Japanese title, like that of the Tjuo Sangi-In, reflected only too clearly the occupiers' policy of Nipponization. They themselves retained key positions in the new movement, but they were sandwiched between the military and the *prijajis*, neither of whom were interested in encouraging ideas of independence among the masses. The military were interested only in greater Japan, while the *prijajis*, as popular discontent increased owing to the harsh exactions of the régime, found it easy to depict the advancing allies as liberators and to discredit Sukarno and his associates as henchmen of the Japanese.

Sutan Sjahrir was meanwhile taking a similar line, and his influence especially among students grew considerably at this time. The various opposition groups had an ally in Mohammed Hatta, who kept them informed of what was going on in Djakarta and of imminent raids by the Japanese authorities, who were giving short shrift to malcontents since the discovery of Amir Sjarifuddin's resistance movement early in 1943 and the Tasikmalaja rebellion. It was only thanks to the urgent pleading of Sukarno and Hatta that Amir Sjarifuddin survived the war.

In spring 1944 the Pacific War entered a decisive phase, the critical question being whether the Japanese could defeat the Americans' 'island-hopping'. Meanwhile the military régime in Java had succeeded in what the Indonesian leaders thus far were not able to achieve: they had mobilized the whole population. They had pressed the Muslims, nationalists, princely families and *prijajis* into their service. The methods they used were sometimes ruthless, it is true, but in disregarding the particularism of the various groups they helped the cause of unity, as in arousing opposition they helped the cause of revolution. And there was more which would prove of value for the future of Indonesia: to simplify the process of command they used the Indonesian language, which now for the first time became dominant over local idioms – Sundanese, Javanese and Madurese.

Finally, the most important of all, the military government had done what the Dutch had to the last refused, namely set up (in October 1943) an Indonesian volunteer army, the Sukarela Pembela Tanah Air (Voluntary Defenders of the Homeland), or Peta. From the end of 1942 onwards, young Indonesians had been able to receive military training in the Heiho, Keibodan or Seinendan, to mention only the chief of the Japanese youth organizations that were established in Java from time to time. In 1943, on the occasion of a visit of *prijajis* to Japan, Sutardjo suggested that compulsory military service should be introduced to help the Japanese forces in Indonesia, whereupon Gatot Mangkupradja made the counter-proposal that a volunteer army should be created. His reason may have been, as he now claims, that conscription was contrary to the democratic ideals of the Indonesian movement;[30] but it was more probably in order that the army should be composed wholly of convinced supporters of independence, who would fight the Dutch if and when they returned and not change sides as the *prijajis* were likely to do.

The kernel of Peta was constituted in the main by members of Muslim organizations; until the end of 1944 Masjumi received permission to raise military units of its own. As commissions were granted by preference to young men of 'strong will' and 'sound ideology' – that is to say, such as gave adequate proof of anti-Western sentiments – those who had had a Western education or belonged to Christian organizations generally dropped out of the running, in so far as they were interested in the first place. Indon-esians who had passed through the military academy of the KNIL (Dutch colonial forces) at Bandung – such as A. H. Nasution, T. B. Simatupang or Urip Sumohardjo, who had risen to the rank of major in the KNIL – were not allowed to join Peta till the end of the war, despite the advanced training they had received. At that time the volunteer units had swelled to 66 battalions comprising over 35,000 men. The highest attainable rank was that of battalion commander (*daidan-tjo*), of whom there were altogether 70; then came about 200 company commanders (*tjudan-tjo*), over 600 lieutenants (*shodan-tjo*) and 2,000 N.C.O.s (*bundan-tjo*). On its colours the army bore a crescent and a rising run; its first commander was Kasman Singodimedjo, a lawyer by profession and former leader of Muhammadijah.[31]

The true loosers of the Japanese harnessing for their war-effort were the forcibly recruited *romushas* – war 'volunteers' – who had to serve on the fronts in New Guinea and Burma, whence only a fraction returned to Java. Of the approximately 300,000 who were press-ganged in this way, ninety per cent disappeared in the jungles of south-east Asia, dying of exhaustion, disease or enemy action. The population at home, living on diminishing rations, was increasingly forced to work on building airfields, roads and in industries for war supply.

As Sukarno declared in speeches at this time, the hardships as well as the mobilization of all sections of the population would transform Java into a fortress that would resist all Allied attempts to capture it. This was true in the Dutch attempt at re-colonization. Moreover they led to changes in the social structure and the formation of new élite groups which decisively influenced post-war developments in Indonesia.

3   THE FIRST CONCESSIONS TO INDONESIAN NATIONALISM

A turning-point in Japanese policy, particularly as regards the making of concessions to the Indonesians in return for their collaboration, came with the fall of Saipan in the Marianas, an important link in communications between Indonesia and Japan, which was taken by the Americans in July 1944. This brought about Tojo's resignation and, in Java, the first concessions to the claims which the nationalists had been putting forward uninterruptedly since the 'annexation' in May 1943.

At the third session of the Tjuo Sangi-In in April 1944, this body had been asked to state how the inhabitants of Java could be made more conscious than before of their duty to take part in the 'holy war' and to show greater enthusiasm for the Japanese cause. This gave the committee a chance (thereby demonstrating its potential importance) to cast doubt on the co-operation of *prijajis* in the Djawa Hokokai, which had for some time been the object of criticism, and to recommend the appointment of genuine leaders. To this end they suggested 'the immediate formation of a *barisan pelopor* (pioneer troop) composed of young men of full age, conscious of their duty to fight for final victory, and prepared to give their lives in battle wherever the need might arise'.[32] Soon afterwards, on 19 May, *Asia Raya* explained the proposed functions of the *barisan pelopor* more fully. Its members were to set an example to

95

the people in every domain, fortifying their sense of responsibility, mingling with all classes including traders and peasants, and working actively for the creation of a new society in which individualism would be a thing of the past. These ideas had long been familiar to the Indonesian independence movement: they had been formulated by Sukarno in the early thirties, when he urged the formation of a *partai pelopor* with similar tasks. Under the strict régime of De Jonge this had remained a pious wish, but now it suddenly appeared close to fulfilment. The military government was faced with the unwelcome alternatives of either continuing to put up with popular apathy or using the suggested new stratagem, which seemed to offer some prospect of mobilizing the masses, though with unpredictable consequences for the occupying power itself. After the fall of Saipan it decided to take the risk; the *barisan pelopor* was sanctioned on 10 August and came into being five days later. Its leader was Sukarno, who had stood at the head of all important native bodies since his return to Java: he was *pemimpin besar* (supreme leader) of Putera, *san-jo* (counsellor) to the military régime, *honbu-tjo* (administrative chief) of Djawa Hokokai, *gi-tjo* (chairman) of the Tjuo Sangi-In, and many other things besides. What was more noteworthy was that all the senior and junior command posts in the *barisan pelopor* were held by Indonesians. Its advisory council consisted of Hatta, Mansur, Abikusno and a single Japanese, whose influence was negligible in the circumstances. Officially Sukarno was subject to the orders of the military, and provincial commanders had the last word; but the real power lay in the hands of Sukarno, who had already created the nucleus of the new body during his frequent propaganda tours of Java.[33]

On 7 September 1944 it was announced in Java that the new Japanese premier, Koiso, had declared to the eighty-fifth session of the Diet that Indonesia was to be independent.[34] This news, awaited for years with so much longing, came as a bombshell, and at one stroke restored the reputation of the collaborationist leaders, who since the 'annexation' had been increasingly stigmatized as lackeys of the Japanese. Ki Hadjar Dewantoro, who had resigned from Putera during the time of humiliation, exclaimed with relief: 'Now the people need no longer doubt its leaders, or refuse to trust us.'[35] Nationalist sentiment flared up on every hand. Permission was given to fly the red-and-white flag and to sing 'Indonesia Raya', and for days on end rallies and processions were held without number to celebrate Tokyo's promise. The nationalists of course realized that it was not an act of pure benevolence, and that the first object of the Japanese was to put fresh strength into their war effort. In proclaiming the news from Tokyo, the military had emphasized that without victory there would be no independent Indonesia. Moreover, the announcement remained unsubstantiated, and was not followed up by any concrete steps leading to independence.

Nevertheless, there was no choice at this time for Sukarno and the *barisan pelopor*, or for Masjumi and Peta, other than to stress their solidarity with the Japanese. They had no doubt that the Allied reconquest of Java would mean a fresh period of Dutch colonial rule: this had been made abundantly clear by the NICA (Netherlands Indies Civil Administration), stationed first in Australia and then in New Guinea. The slogan 'Life or death with Dai Nippon', which now began to be heard on all sides, was thus for many nationalists more than a piece of lip-service. At the sixth session of the Tjuo Sangi-In in November 1944, Sukarno secured the adoption of a resolution embodying the *pantja dharma* (five duties) of the Indonesian people. In the ensuing months these principles aroused violent controversy among the nationalists, and it is therefore of interest to quote them in full:[36]

1 Together with the other peoples of Greater East Asia, we stand in a single front with Dai Nippon in this life-and-death struggle, and are prepared for sacrifices in the war to defend justice and truth.

2 We shall found an independent, united, sovereign, just and prosperous Indonesian state, which will honour the achievements of Dai Nippon and live as a loyal member of the Greater East Asian family of nations.

3 We shall show genuine zeal in the pursuit of glory and greatness, protecting and respecting our own civilization and culture, promoting the culture of Asia and influencing that of the whole world.

4 In firm brotherhood with the peoples of Greater East Asia, we shall serve our own state and people with unswerving loyalty, responsible at all times in conscience to Almighty God.

5 We shall fight with a burning desire for perpetual peace in the world, based on the kinship of all races and peoples and thus conforming to the ideal of *hakko itjiu* ('brotherhood of peoples' – the Japanese war slogan).

After Tokyo's promises had thus been requited, it was some time before the Japanese made further concessions to Indonesian nationalism. The military in Java feared that, if they proceeded too quickly to set up a committee to discuss the problems of independence, they would no longer be able to hold the movement in check. As a first step, they began to make advances to the Muslims. In August 1944 they had appointed the much-respected Kijai Hasjim Asjari to be head of the *Shumubu* (office for religious affairs): its previous director, Professor Hussein Djajadiningrat, belonged to the Western-educated intelligentsia rather than to the *ummat Islam* or Muslim community. In November the authorities set up a committee to prepare the way for the foundation of a Muslim university, and in the following month they granted permission for Masjumi to form its own military organization, the Hizbullah (army of Allah). This was to form a reserve to Peta, but was at the same time concerned with spreading the Prophet's teaching, ensuring that the Muslim community fulfilled its religious obligations and defending Islam wherever it might be threatened.

The sanctioning of these missionary functions was a significant step, taken under the threat of invasion: on 20 October the Americans had landed at Leyte in the Philippines, Indonesia's immediately neighbouring territory. But it was most noticeable that the Japanese ignored the common wish of nationalists and Muslims that Djawa Hokokai and Masjumi should be merged into a single organization. This request was put forward in November by the Tjuo Sangi-In, and in February 1945 it was urged still more forcibly by the Masjumi and nationalist members of that body. But the Janapese did not respond, although in general they had insisted on the formation of unified groups. They hoped to gain time, and were reckoning on the probability that the nationalists and Muslims would quarrel among themselves, as had happened so often in the history of the independence movement.[37] But at this critical time, the policy of *divide et impera* failed to work. Nationalists and Muslims had a common interest in early independence, and continued to press their claims jointly. However, the decisive factor in bringing about the announcement that a committee would be set up to investigate the problems of independence – it was known as the Badan Penjelidikan Kemerdekaan Indonesia (BPKI) – was the incident at Blitar on 1 February when, for reasons that are still obscure, a whole Peta battalion, commanded by Lieutenant Suprijadi and equipped with modern weapons, mutinied against the occupying power.[38]

Even so, eight weeks elapsed from the date of the first announcement before the composition of the committee was made known, and a further month before it met for the first time at the end of May. Meanwhile, American victories followed thick and fast in the Philippines; the capture of Okinawa made possible direct bombing of the Japanese homeland, and the war in Europe had come to an end, thus freeing additional forces for south-east Asia. In these circumstances, the majority of Indonesians, noting the tardiness of Japanese concessions and the fact that BPKI was, after all this time, to do no more than discuss problems related to independence, came to the conclusion that they were being fooled, and that the Japanese had no intention of keeping their promise.

Meanwhile Java was in a ferment. The Blitar mutiny was not the only sign that unrest was growing, especially among the *pemudas* (maturer youths), and was spreading to the masses. Outside Peta and such paramilitary bodies as Heiho, Hizbullah, and Seinendan, there were at the beginning of 1945 four youth groups that displayed anti-Japanese feeling with increasing frankness. First, the intellectuals and students organized by Sutan Sjahrir, who opposed Fascism on ideological grounds, and who now ventured to come out of hiding. Secondly, the Menteng 31 group (this being the name of their headquarters), an offshoot of the Asrama Angkatan Baru Indonesia (school of the young Indonesian generation) founded by the Japanese propaganda department; its leaders were Muhammad Yamin, B. M. Diah, Adam Malik and Sukarni. Subsequent leaders of the PKI, such as D. N. Aidit and M. Lukman, also belonged to this group, though they were already trying to split off from it a left wing composed of the more revolutionary spirits.

A third group, Persatuan Mahasiswa (students' union), consisted of students and pupils of technical colleges, with its centre of gravity in the old Djalan Salemba medical school, the core of the present University of Indonesia: it was in touch with the other groups through its spokesman Chairul Saleh. Finally, there was a group centred round the Asrama Indonesia Merdeka (school of Indonesian independence), an institution founded in Java at the end of 1944 by Vice-Admiral Maeda, the naval liaison officer with the Sixteenth Army. Maeda had for some time been in touch with the Indonesian nationalists, and had lent an ear to their troubles before there had been any question of independence or of recognizing Indonesia as such. He had on occasion, without the knowledge of the Sixteenth Army, addressed proposals to Tokyo with the object of securing a decision in favour of independence, and this had led to friction between him and the military in Java.[39] As soon as Tokyo promised independence, he believed that he was acting in accordance with the Emperor's wishes in founding the Asrama. His chief Indonesian confidant was Subardjo, a shrewd diplomatist and former member of Perhimpunan Indonesia. Another prominent personality in touch with naval circles was Wikana, who, like Sukarni and Adam Malik, had formerly belonged to Gerindo, but had also maintained contact with the illegal PKI.[40]

Members of these youth organizations met at Bandung on 16–18 May in the Angkatan Muda (young generation) conference, at which forceful expression was given to the pent-up indignation at Japan's temporizing measures. The spirit of rebellion burst the bounds of the meeting: for the first time, the participants dared to sing 'Indonesia Raya' without the Japanese anthem, and to display the red-and-white banner without the Rising Sun, which was expressly forbidden by military regulations. The delegates discussed whether they wanted, after all, to receive independence as a gift from Dai Nippon, or whether it would not be better to fight for it. Finally they declared for the unification of all political organizations, immediate independence and the slogan 'Merdeka atau Mati' ('Freedom or Death').[41] Sukarno, who was staying near Bandung at the time, was informed of these resolutions by way of bringing home to him the explosiveness of the situation. He for his part had continued to preach the *pantja dharma*, and had held meetings at which those present were called on to stand and repeat the pro-Japanese creed, unpopular as it had now become. Sukarno's faithfulness to the idea of partnership, his identification with Japan's war and the slogan 'Life or death with Dai Nippon', gave rise to a crisis of confidence between him and his youthful opponents, which had yet to reach its peak. He who had so often complained that the Indonesians were lacking in revolutionary élan was now thrown on the defensive.

4 PREPARATION FOR INDEPENDENCE

During this time, when the *pemudas* (youth groups) were showing increasing discontent both with the occupying power and with the 'elder leaders' – Sukarno and his comrades of the twenties and thirties, who for the most part belonged to the *barisan pelopor* –

the BPKI (Committee for the Investigation of Independence) held its first meeting. It consisted of 63 nominated members from all classes of the population, including four Chinese, one Arab and one Eurasian, and leaders of all shades of opinion representing the nationalist movement.[42] The eldest of these and a founder member of Budi Utomo, Dr. Radjiman Wedioningrat, was elected chairman of the committee, thus leaving Sukarno and Hatta free to take part in the debates. As regards the *prijajis*, there were representatives of the princely houses of central Java from Solo and Jogjakarta; Wirnata Kusuma, the regent of Bandung, spoke for the *bupatis*, and Sutardjo for the main body of junior and ...ddie-rank officials, as he had done in the Volksraad. Among the nationalists already mentioned in this study, besides Sukarno and Hatta, were Ki Hadjar Dewantoro, Sartono, Oto Iskandar Dinata, Muhammad Yamin, Sukardjo Wirjopranoto, Samsudin and Subardjo. To this group also belong Professors Supomo and Hussein Djajadiningrat, though the latter also had links with the Muslim community. The actual representatives of Islam were Hadji Agus Salim, Abikusno, Dr. Sukiman, Mas Mansur, Ki Bagus Hadikusumo, Abdul Halim, A. Kahar Muzakkir, Sanusi, and Wachid Hasjim, son of Hasjim Asjari, whom he assisted as head of the office for religious affairs.

Despite this impressive roll of names, the Muslim representatives were in a minority on the committee. This was probably because of their lack of outstanding leaders rather than because the Japanese wished to limit Muslim influence in the constituent body. They hoped to gain time by setting up the BPKI, and that there would be endless argument over the place of religion in the future state.[43] For this reason they would certainly have welcomed a larger representation of Islam, had sufficient candidates been available.[4] However, at the first session (28 May–1 June) the various groups showed remarkable unanimity and a genuine desire to co-operate with the nationalists. This was as true of the racial minorities as of the Muslims. In this atmosphere of agreement the meeting adopted the *pantja sila* (five principles) as the basic ideology of the future state. These principles, which retain their special significance for Indonesia to this day, were formulated in Sukarno's speech of 1 June, shortly before the end of the session. In words which became celebrated, he invited the delegates to approve, as the basic Indonesian ideology, the five principles of nationalism, humanity, popular sovereignty, social justice and faith in one God.[45]

Nationalism, he explained, must not be understood in a narrow or chauvinistic sense: there was no question of 'Indonesia right or wrong'. It must be taken in its widest sense – as wide and free as the air by which all creatures live. Account must be taken of the diversity of all races and peoples of the archipelago: all of them must find a home in the new state.

Humanity was to be the rule of international dealings. The ideas of Marxism and Islam, which transcended national boundaries and by which Sukarno himself had been influenced in equal measure, inspired the choice of this principle; nor should the Japanese doctrine of *hakko itjiu* go unmentioned.

Popular sovereignty, as explained by Sukarno, was the antithesis of Western democracy. Indonesian democracy, as had been shown when the first federation was created in 1927, recognized only unanimous resolutions and rejected the Western system of decision by majority vote. True popular sovereignty required that all groups be represented and that general discussion (*musjawarah*) should led to a solution satisfactory to all (*mufakat*). In this way the objections of important minorities would not be lost to view, and only so could effect be given to the old Indonesian ideal of mutual help (*gotong rojong*).

Social justice was the reward which, Sukarno believed, would accrue especially from obedience to the last-named principle. As he had declared of old when advocating *marhaenism*, there were to be no more privileged groups: political and economic equality must be the goal of all state endeavour.

Finally, belief in God was common to all Indonesians, though they worshipped Him in different ways: some according to the Prophet's teaching, some in obedience to Christ, Buddha or other founders of religions. All religious scriptures spoke eloquently of tolerance, and in the new state tolerance would be duly safeguarded.

In the remainder of his speech, which was received with much applause, Sukarno argued with force that these principles were not contrary but complementary to one another. The first and second might be summed up as humanitarian nationalism, the third and fourth as social democracy. Together with belief in God, these constituted the three cornerstones of his philosophy: nationalism, Socialism and theism. That these three were closely related he had, he believed, shown as long before as 1926, and since then, as far as he was concerned, they had come to form a single whole. In

1941, while in exile, he had referred to himself as an embodiment of nationalism, Islam and Marxism, and had described this as a mighty synthesis.[46] Today, in the presence of his fellow-delegates, he again felt moved to demonstrate the inner unity of the several principles. Some might disagree with the three he had mentioned, and hanker after an *ekasila*, a single principle. Very well. This existed too, and he referred once again to *gotong rojong* (mutual help), in which all the other principles were contained.

The *pantja sila* were thus accepted as the national philosophy of Indonesia, where many greeted as a revelation Sukarno's fusion of ideologies, finding a solution to problems by means of syncretism in the ancient Javanese tradition. Others, however, were reluctant to sacrifice essential elements of their beliefs, which was a *sine qua non* for the acceptance of the *pantja sila*, and used the freedom of action guaranteed to them in the name of tolerance in such a way as to widen the rift between the various schools of thought which, as the history of the movement had shown, were in fact irreconcilable. Hitherto the groups had never united except for transitory and tactical reasons, as they now did when the Japanese occupation was nearing its end and independence appeared as a possibility.

As we saw, in November 1944 and February 1945 the Tjuo Sangi-In expressed a wish for the merger of Djawa Hokokai and Masjumi, but the Japanese turned a deaf ear. When this demand was repeated at the eighth session in mid-June, the Japanese gave their consent, alarmed at the public agitation in youth circles: the *pemudas* throughout Java were organizing mass demonstrations at which they were not afraid to speak out. Not only were the 'elder leaders' criticized for adopting a pliant attitude towards the occupying power, but speakers declared that the fight for independence need not necessarily be directed against the approaching allies. They made it plain that they regarded the Japanese as the main obstacle in their path. While Hatta sympathized with their views and openly commended this change of front, Sukarno viewed it with anxiety. He still regarded the allies as the chief enemy, and during the period of open revolt he continued to proclaim the *pantja dharma* which linked Indonesia to Japan. At the beginning of July he was given the task, together with Hatta, Wachid Hasjim and Wirnata Kusuma, of creating the *gerakan rakjat jang baru* (new people's movement) based on the 'five duties', unpopular as they were. It was agreed to appoint a number of the younger leaders to the committee which launched the new movement, such as Sukarni, Chairul Saleh, Adam Malik, Wikana and B. M. Diah. According to Sukarno the association, unlike its predecessors, was not to be under the aegis of the military; but when, at the opening session on 6 July, a Japanese officer intervened in the debate and expressed objections, the *pemudas* left the hall in protest.[47]

A few days later, on 10 July, the BPKI assembled for its second session, with an agenda comprising the nature and territory of the future state and the draft of a constitution. The question whether Indonesia should be a republic or a monarchy (the latter suggestion came from central Java) was settled without much argument on the first day by a majority of 55 to 6, with 3 invalid votes, in favour of a republic.[48] As regards territory, opinions were more divided. Hatta thought it should be limited to the former Dutch East Indies, excluding New Guinea, which was racially not a part of Indonesia but of Melanesia. The Papuans, he argued, had a right to freedom too, and in the next few decades it would be beyond Indonesia's powers to educate them for independence. On the other hand, Hatta saw no objection in principle to including Malaya, a notion advocated by some Malays at this time. He would welcome the Malays with open arms, he declared, if it was clear that they wanted to join Indonesia.

The majority of the committee, however, used the occasion to put forward exorbitant territorial claims. Muhammad Yamin, with the impetuosity that had more than once isolated him within the movement, and with arguments that were often confused, demanded the whole of New Guinea, Portuguese Timor, the British possessions in Borneo, and Malaya as far as the frontier with Thailand. Sukarno supported these demands, and added that he had formerly thought of including the Philippines also, but as these had now gained their independence he would be content with the area suggested by Yamin. Even Hadji Agus Salim and Sutardjo were among those who favoured a Greater Indonesia, while a third group, mostly former civil servants, wanted the territory of the Dutch East Indies as it stood. When the question was finally put, this group scored 19 votes, Hatta's proposal (to include Malaya, but not West New Guinea) 6, while Yamin's party were victorious with 39.[49]

Next came the difficult task of drafting a constitution. A sub-committee was set up under Sukarno's chairmanship, and, thanks mainly to the preparatory work of Professor Supomo, it was able to submit a draft only two days later. The sub-committee had set itself the task of realizing Indonesian democracy and the *musjawarah* system on the political plane, and had decided by ten votes to nine that the executive power should be confided to a president. As the constitution evolved at this time is in force at the time of writing, we may here outline its main principles.

Sovereignty was to reside in the Madjelis Rakjat Indonesia (Indonesian People's Congress), meeting at least once every five years, and consisting of the Dewan Perwakilan Rakjat – a parliament chosen by direct popular vote – together with additional deputies representing provinces and groups in proportion to their population and size. The congress was to elect the President and Vice-President by simple majority for a five-year term; it also determined the main lines of policy, and alone was empowered to amend the constitution. During his term of office, the President could appoint and dismiss ministers and was responsible to no one except congress during its infrequent sessions. He was assisted by the Vice-President, who replaced him in case of incapacity, and by a Dewan Pertimbangan Agung (council of state), which could make proposals, but whose advice the president was not bound to follow.

The council of state, which was also to embody the ideas of *musjawarah* and *mufakat*, was a clear descendant of the Raad van Indië which had advised the Dutch Governor-General; indeed, the whole constitution faithfully reflected the authoritarian principles of Dutch and Japanese rule which had hitherto been so violently criticized. Parliament had a share in legislation, but it could not call ministers to account and had no more power during the President's term of office than the Volksraad before it, although it formed the nucleus of the People's Congress. The President – who, as Supomo emphasized, must be thoroughly imbued with the nation's will – enjoyed a wide prerogative, which it was hoped would enable rapid decisions to be taken during the coming tussle with the Allies.

The sub-committee deliberately abstained from drafting a declaration of human rights. Explaining this to the main committee, Sukarno argued, as he had in the twenties and thirties, that individualism and liberalism had only led to exploitation and oppression, wars, class-hatred, and the rule of the stronger. Rather than individual freedom, Indonesia should promote collectivism, *musjawarah*, and *gotong rojong*.[50] In reply to these arguments, only

Hatta struck a note of warning; he, too, was against encouraging individualism, but the present constitution could lead to a régime of servile obedience. He urged that a clause be introduced guaranteeing certain fundamental civil rights, such as those of assembly and the formation of parties, and privacy of correspondence, so as to guard against the abuse of popular sovereignty that had occurred in Germany and Russia, where arbitrary rule was exercised in the people's name. For similar reasons, some check should be placed on the application of collectivism.[51]

Hatta's prophetic words were equally applicable fourteen years later, when matters came full circle with the reintroduction of the 1945 constitution; but they met with no support in the BPKI. The draft constitution, however, almost broke down on the question of the position of Islam. The nationalists had all along feared that the Muslims might give trouble on the ground that their interests were insufficiently recognized. To avoid this, they had conferred with Muslim leaders such as Abikusno, Wachid Hasjim, Kijai A. K. Muzakkir and Hadji Agus Salim, and on 22 June reached a compromise which Yamin termed the 'Djakarta charter'. This document, drafted as a preamble to the constitution, defined the Indonesian people's right to independence and its philosophy and aspirations, as set out in the *pantja sila*. In order to win over the Muslims without declaring Islam to be the state religion, the formula adopted was that the state was founded on belief in God and that the Muslims were obliged, by virtue of their citizenship, to follow the precepts of Islam.[52]

At the plenary meeting of the BPKI, some *kijais* objected that this was a vague and discriminatory provision. Ninety-five per cent of the population was Muslim, and this fact should be clearly acknowledged. The nationalists opposed further concessions, arguing that the matter was settled by the Djakarta charter; whereupon the aged Kijai Muzakkir, who had helped to draft the charter, thumped the table and demanded that all references to Allah should be struck out of the constitution and preamble. The state should either be secular or Muslim, with all that this entailed, but there was no place for lip-service. On the night of 15–16 July the nationalists and Muslims conferred once more to avert the danger that the *ulamas* would at the last moment quit the committee in a body, and it was agreed to add a provision to the constitution that the President must be a Muslim. Next day Sukarno begged the delegates with tears in his eyes to accept this new compromise, and the *mufakat* so deeply desired in this sphere was in fact achieved.[53]

A compromise was also reached in the matter of citizenship. The representatives of the racial minorities had pleaded for their automatic recognition as Indonesian nationals; the constitution, however, laid down (in Article 27) that the conditions of citizenship for other ethnic groups were to be determined by law.

Not all sections of opinion, either in or outside the committee, were satisfied with the ultimate form of the draft constitution. But speed was necessary, for the draft had to be submitted to Tokyo for approval before any concrete steps could be taken towards independence. On 17 July the military commanders received orders to expedite the procedure for independence; this had nothing to do with the committee's work, but was, like previous decisions, motivated chiefly by the critical development of the war, which had now reached the outlying parts of Indonesia. In accordance with Tokyo's instructions, the chiefs of staff of the Sixteenth and Twenty-Fifth Armies and the second southern fleet met at Singapore and agreed to set up an Indonesian Independence Preparatory Committee: this body, established on 7 August, was to begin its work a week later so that independence could be announced on 7 September, the anniversary of Koiso's promise. The territory of the future state was confined to the former Dutch East Indies, thus excluding Malaya, East New Guinea, Portuguese Timor and British Borneo. The new committee was to consist of 20 members, including for the first time representatives of the outer provinces.[54]

In the present study of events under the Japanese occupation, attention has necessarily been confined to Java, the scene of organized movements and steady pressure on the military authorities by nationalists, religious communities and young people's groups. But the lack of such organizations in the outer provinces did not mean that the population of Sumatra or the navy-administered areas accepted the occupation with goodwill. There were frequent rebellions against Japanese rule, which were often hard to suppress in the thinly populated areas, with their many opportunities for cover.[55] The military commanders in Sumatra and the navy area, like those in Java, had been ordered to allow the population to 'take part in government' in accordance with Tojo's announcement in June 1943; they had, however, not set up a central body like the Tjuo Sangi-In, but had begun with provincial councils. Only in

March 1945 was a single council for Sumatra set up at Bukit Tinggi, consisting of Atjehnese and representatives of west, east and south Sumatra.[56] The navy proceeded more cautiously still, beginning with municipal councils at Menado, Macassar, Bandjermasin, Pontianak and Ambon; provincial councils for Macassar and Menado followed in March 1944. In preference to using native leaders of pre-war organizations, as was done, for instance, in Atjeh, the navy relied on local chiefs. Dr. Ratu Langie, who was head of the Minahassa league for many years and a prominent member of the Volksraad from 1927 to 1937 – and who, along with Thamrin and Douwes Dekker, was arrested for a time in 1941 on the charge of being pro-Japanese – was summoned to Macassar as an adviser to the occupation authorities, as was Tadjuddin Noor, who represented southern Borneo in the Volksraad. But as their duties were never clearly defined, there was ground for suspicion that the object was simply to part them from their traditional areas of influence in northern Celebes and southern Borneo.[57]

When the composition of the preparatory committee was made known on 7 August 1945, it included three Sumatran representatives: Abdul Abbas from the Batak country, Dr. Mohammed Amir from west Sumatra, and Mohammed Hasan from Atjeh. Five represented the navy-ruled area: Dr. Ratu Langie, Andi Pangeran (southern Celebes), A. Hamidhan (Borneo), I. Gusti Ketut Pudja (Bali), and Latuharhary (Ambon), a lawyer who had spent the occupation period in Java and was a member of the Tjuo Sangi-In and BPKI. The nominees from Java were Sukarno and Hatta as chairman and vice-chairman of the new committee; Dr. Radjiman Wedioningrat and Professor Supomo, representing the BPKI; Wachid Hasjim and Ki Bagus Hadikusumo for the Muslims; Oto Iskandar Dinata and Abdul Kadir representing Barisan Pelopor and Peta; R. Pandji Suroso and Sutardjo for the *prijajis*; and Purubojo and Surjohamidjojo representing the princely houses of Jogjakarta and Solo. Subardjo served as an 'adviser', while Yap Tjwan Bing represented the Chinese minority.[58]

On 8 August Sukarno, Hatta and Radjiman were flown to Dalat near Saigon, where they were received by Marshal Terauchi, the Japanese commander for the southern areas, and informed that the committee was to begin its work on 18 August. Terauchi did not name a date for the proclamation of independence, but Sukarno later said that the date envisaged was 24 August. The original deadline of 7 September may have been advanced on account of the dropping of atomic bombs on Hiroshima (6 August) and Nagasaki (9 August), and Russia's entry into the war against Japan (7 August). But further developments took no heed of the Japanese timetable. The Indonesian revolution had begun, and was henceforth to go its own way.

V

THE INDONESIAN REVOLUTION

I THE PROCLAMATION OF INDEPENDENCE

On 14 August the Indonesian leaders returned from discussions with Terauchi to Java. Here they found that the news of the dropping of atomic bombs and the first Japanese peace feelers had filtered through, and the revolutionary spirit of the *pemudas* had risen to fever-pitch. Sutan Sjahrir, in particular, was convinced that the cause of independence could only be saved by means of a revolt against the Japanese. Before Hatta left for Saigon, he had urged him to put the nationalist case to Terauchi so strongly as to force an open conflict with the occupying power. The day after the delegation returned, Sjahrir tried to persuade Hatta to issue the proclamation on his own account.[1] Hatta refused, pointing out that a proclamation of independence in which Sukarno did not join would make no impression on the population. He then tried with Sjahrir to convince Sukarno of the need for an immediate proclamation. Sukarno, however, did not believe the rumours of Japan's capitulation that were going round on 15 August, and tried to ascertain the facts from Admiral Maeda. The Admiral, who had shown himself for the previous few years a true friend of the nationalists, promised to let Sukarno know what he could find out. Sukarno thereupon told the *pemudas* that the proclamation of independence was postponed till the next day. The *pemudas*, who had already armed in preparation for a rising, were furious. They wanted to issue the proclamation without Sukarno and Hatta, but Sjahrir would not have this, since 'it would place us in opposition to our own people, which must on no account happen'.[2]

The *pemudas*, nevertheless, decided to go ahead under their own leaders, the chief of whom were Chairul Saleh, Sukarni, Adam Malik, Wikana and B. M. Diah. On the evening of the 15th a deputation headed by Wikana visited Sukarno at his home (Pegang-saan Timur 56), and tried to force him to issue the proclamation.

Hatta was summoned, and the atmosphere became tense. When Wikana finally declared that if Sukarno did not proclaim independence there would be bloodshed and a general massacre next day, Sukarno lost his temper, and shouted in Wikana's face that there was no need to wait till tomorrow – if he wanted to kill him, he could do so at once.[3] The *pemudas*, who had not expected such a reaction, withdrew to consult at their headquarters, which had been transferred from Menteng 31 to Djalan Tjikini 71, and decided to kidnap Sukarno and Hatta. What precisely they expected to achieve by this is not clear, but they felt that the explosive situation called for some extraordinary action. In the small hours of the 16th, Sukarno and Hatta were removed to the Peta barracks at Rengasdengklok, about 50 miles from Djakarta, where they were held throughout the day without any decisive step being taken. Meanwhile they were being sought feverishly in the capital, and Maeda eventually discovered their whereabouts from Wikana, who had been attached to his office for some time. The delicate task of bringing them back to Djakarta was entrusted to Subardjo, who was in Maeda's confidence and was a friend of Sukarno's. When Subardjo reached Rengasdengklok, he was able to give Sukarno and Hatta definite news of the Japanese surrender and to assure Sukarni, who was responsible for their safety, that all preparations had been made in Djakarta for the proclamation of independence. Several pamphlets reporting these events also speak of a Rengasdengklok Agreement (*persetudjuan Rengasdengklok*), in which Sukarno and Hatta allegedly promised to issue the proclamation as soon as they returned to Djakarta.

Sukarno and Hatta had meanwhile doubtless made up their minds that a proclamation must be issued at once. Immediately on their return, in the middle of the night, they went with Maeda to military headquarters to assure themselves of the neutrality of the Japanese army and seek consent for the proclamation. But General Nishimura, who had only recently come to Java, refused to meet their wishes, and was not impressed by warnings of possible unrest; the *pemudas*, he said, should be told that the Japanese army was on the watch and would suppress any attempted coup. Finally, Hatta put forward an argument that was more calculated to win the general's assent. The *pemudas*' agitation, he declared, should be understood in the light of their psychology. The Allies might land any day and the *pemudas* were resolved to fight, but only if they knew that their death would be of service to the motherland. 'They must have a country to die for.' Nishimura had no reply to this, but he again refused officially to advance the date fixed for the meeting of the preparatory committee, most of whose members had by this time assembled in Maeda's house. He hinted, however, that he would have no objection to a 'tea-party'.[4]

Accordingly, well after midnight, the declaration of independence was drafted at Maeda's house by a group including fourteen of the twenty-one members of the committee (the Muslim representatives and those of the princely houses of central Java were absent), several *pemudas* and some Japanese observers, who took no part in the discussion. Sjahrir did not appear; he regarded the drafting of the proclamation in a Japanese officer's house as a betrayal of the Indonesian revolution.

Several drafts were presented. The version on which agreement was finally reached about 4 a.m. contained no pro-Japanese phrases, nor any of the anti-Japanese ones that had been suggested. It ran simply: 'We, the Indonesian people, hereby proclaim the independence of Indonesia. The formalities for the transfer of power, etc., will be settled in an orderly manner and as soon as possible.'

The document was signed 'For the Indonesian people: Sukarno–Hatta.' The *pemudas* thus after all abstained from signing, as did the representatives of the preparatory committee. Six hours later, at 10 a.m. on 17 August, the text was read out once more at an improvised ceremony at Sukarno's house in Pegangsaan Timur, the red-and-white flag was hoisted on a bamboo mast, and the assembled leaders sang 'Indonesia Raya'. On the same day, Adam Malik was able to broadcast the proclamation over the Japanese short-wave transmitter, while other *pemudas* in Maeda's office printed thousands of leaflets with its text, which were distributed with lightning speed throughout the archipelago and brought the news of independence to the remotest *desas*.

The great moment, for which long and painful sacrifices had been made, had arrived at last. It was forty years since Wahidin Sudirohusodo, the old *dokter djawa*, had toured the island to gain support for a union of all Javanese, and a little over thirty years since Douwes Dekker, Tjipto Mangunkusumo and Suardi Surjaningrat had first demanded independence for the archipelago. Barely twenty years before, the Communists had first staged a major revolt to put an end to colonial rule. Yet independence had seemed immeasurably far off as recently as ten years back, when the principal leaders were in exile on remote islands, or even in 1940, when the colonial power was still refusing each and every concession.

As everyone knew on that sultry Friday morning, to proclaim independence was not the same thing as to gain it. But the years of occupation had done one thing: the Japanese, with their organization, their propaganda machine, and their ever-increasing demands for increased production, labour and war volunteers, had mobilized the population and shaken it out of its previous indifference. The next few years were to show that, even with the pressure of military government removed, the nation was determined to defend the independence for which it had striven so long.

2 THE EARLY DAYS OF THE REPUBLIC

On the day after the proclamation of independence, the preparatory committee was summoned to complete the draft of the constitution and elect the President and Vice-President. The committee had enlarged itself by six members: Hadjar Dewantoro and Subardjo, of whom we have already heard; Kasman Singodimedjo, a devout Muslim who commanded the Peta garrison at Djakarta; Iwa Kusuma Sumantri, who with Hatta had once played a prominent part in Perhimpunan Indonesia, had acted as a contact man for the exiled Communists and was therefore banished from Java when he returned to the Indies; Sayuti Melik, a friend of Sukarno's who had been chosen to lead a new party; and Wirnata Kusuma, the regent of Bandung and a man of high standing among the higher *prijajis*. After some discussion, representatives of the *pemudas* were also invited, but they left the committee in protest when Hatta declared that its members still felt 'responsible' to the Japanese.[5]

By the terms of their surrender on 15 August, the Japanese were themselves responsible to the Allies for the maintenance of the political *status quo*, and they refused to meet the demands of the Indonesian nationalists in any way. However, Sukarno and Hatta managed to negotiate with them what was called a 'gentlemen's agreement', whereby the Japanese refrained from interfering in Indonesian affairs and undertook to maintain law and order till the Allies arrived. As the first Allied units did not land in Java till the end of September, the nationalists on the island had a chance to establish themselves as a more or less properly functioning government. But no one could know this on 18 August, and the first operations of government were carried out in frantic haste. The constitution was once more gone through point by point. The pro-Japanese phrases in the preamble were struck out, as were the concessions made to the Muslims at the last session of the BPKI, that the President must belong to their faith and that adherents of Islam must conform to its laws. In view of the coming struggle with the Allies, exceptional powers were conferred on the President for a term of six months, and it was resolved, until such time as the parliament (Dewan Perwakilan Rakjat) and people's congress (Madjelis Permusjawaratan Rakjat) could be elected, to establish a national committee, whose provisional composition should be decided by the President and Vice-President.

At this stage Sukarno was chosen President by acclamation, and Hatta Vice-President. The proposal to elect Sukarno may have come from Oto Iskandar Dinata, his comrade in arms since the first Indonesian federation (PPPKI) was founded in 1927.[6] The 'duumvirate' (*dwitunggal*), as Sukarno and Hatta were often called, had stood the test of the occupation period, in spite of their well-known disagreements dating back to the thirties, so that the delegates felt confident they were placing the fate of the young republic in good hands. In the next few days Sukarno and Hatta nominated the first 135 members of the Komite Nasional Indonesia Pusat (KNIP: National Central Committee of Indonesia), which, true to ancient ideals, represented all sections of the population. At its first session, held on 29 August, KNIP adopted a resolution declaring that the Indonesian people was determined to defend its independence by every means and that each Indonesian was obliged to co-operate for this purpose in his or her own sphere.[7] The provinces were called on to set up at once their own republican governments. They were eight in number: West, Central and East Java, Sumatra, Kalimantan (Borneo), Sulawesi (Celebes), the Moluccas and the Lesser Sunda Islands. Sukarno appointed a governor for each province, and the KNIP appointed a delegate to assist each governor. Local national committees were to be established everywhere, so that, in case of need, they could function independently of the central government. In his first broadcast as president on 23 August, Sukarno called on *prijajis, ulamas, pemudas,* nationalists, and all classes of the population to join forces in the local committees in order to:

1 give expression to the people's desire for independence;
2 create lasting unity among all sections of the people;
3 provide for national security; and
4 support their leaders' attempts to give reality to the ancient ideals.

At the same time, Sukarno announced the formation of a single party which would be the mainspring of the struggle in every sphere, defend the republic, and promote economic and social measures to bring about social justice as guaranteed by the constitution.[8] The new party, bearing the old name Partai Nasional Indonesia, was established on 27 August: its leaders included Sajuti Melik, Iwa Kusuma Sumantri and Wikana, and it was announced that it would be based on the organization of Djawa Hokokai. But within a few days it was dissolved, as it appeared to compete with the local committees, and was looked at askance by the former parties because it set out to include all schools of thought, in accordance with Sukarno's old desire for a united front. This did not suit the Mulims or the Socialists, let alone the Communists, who reappeared on the scene immediately after the Japanese surrender, and sought to use the revolution for their own ends.

Soon after the proclamation, clashes took place between the Japanese and Peta units, whereupon the military government ordered that all Peta and Heiho troops should be disarmed and disbanded. Sukarno and Hatta found a remedy for this in the creation of local security groups (Badan Keamanan Rakjat – BKR). The disbanded military and paramilitary units, numbering some 60,000 men, together with over 200,000 members of other bodies, such as Barisan Pelopor, Hizbullah, etc., were organized by the 3,000-odd officers and N.C.O.s who returned from the garrisons into Laskar or local battle units, loosely associated with one another.[9] Arms were obtained by raiding Japanese stores; in only a few places was there a regular hand-over, as at Banjumas, where Sudirman, the local Peta commander, obtained equipment from the Japanese provincial command through the intermediary of Iskaq Tjokroadisurjo.[10] Even after the Allies arrived, the self-help system persisted. A story was told at the time of the official Japanese surrender to the British outside Surabaja. Thousands had assembled to watch the event, and, when the Japanese laid down their arms and prepared for inspection, the Indonesians rushed upon the weapons and made off with them as if it were the most natural procedure in the world.[11]

In this way, the Indonesians in central and east Java obtained, as appeared from a check of Japanese stocks after the Allies' arrival:[12]

26,000 rifles with 27 million rounds of ammunition.
1,300 automatic small arms with 4·5 million rounds.
600 machine guns with 12 million rounds.
700 mortars with 23,000 rounds.
40 anti-tank guns with 8,000 shells.
16 howitzers with 10,000 shells.
30 flame-throwers and 9,500 hand grenades.

It does not follow, however, that all these arms were immediately serviceable or fell into qualified hands, and it was shown later in battle that traditional weapons such as swords, daggers and bamboo spears still played an important part. But a still more difficult problem than that of armament was that of co-ordinating the Laskar units. On 5 October a decree was passed setting up a national defence force (Tentara Keamanan Rakjat), whose name was changed at the beginning of 1946 to Army of the Indonesian Republic (Tentara Republik Indonesia: TRI). The former Peta and Heiho units and other paramilitary bodies were called on to report for registration at local security bureaux. A Ministry of National Security was created, and the first commander-in-chief of the new forces was Suprijadi, who had disappeared since the Blitar revolt and was regarded by the people as a hero. His chief of staff was Urip Sumohardjo, who had risen to be a major in the Dutch colonial army (KNIL) and later endeavoured to give the Indonesian army a hierarchical structure on the KNIL pattern.[13] For the present, however, this was out of the question. Local commanders were not amenable to unity and subordination; General Nasution, recalling this period in later years, even spoke of 'warlords'.[14] This was the origin of the system sometimes known later as 'bapakism', whereby the local military leader acted as a *bapak* (father) to his men, who in return were devoted to him and made him more or less independent of any superior officer. The youth organizations too, showed little readiness to submit to a single military command: towards the end of 1945 they united to form the Pesindo (Pemuda Sosialis Indonesia), which preserved an independent status. There was also the problem of relations between the Peta officers and those of KNIL, who had been trained at the Bandung military academy and regarded themselves as professionally superior, but were mistrusted on account of their links with the colonial power. Cases even occurred of KNIL officers being kidnapped.[15]

This rivalry also made itself felt at the first meeting of commanders at Jogjakarta on 12 November, held in order to choose a new supreme commander (*panglima besar*) in Suprijadi's absence. Passing over Urip Sumohardjo, who was senior in rank and length of service, the meeting elected Sudirman, the former Muhammadijah teacher and commander of the Peta battalion at Banjumas. Sudirman who shortly afterwards became a general, had gained a reputation by distributing ex-Japanese arms equitably and had recently expelled British troops from Ambarawa; moreover, he was to show on many future occasions that he had a flair for the morale of his own forces. He did not share the view of officers of the old school that the army was merely an executive organ of the government: like the Laskar commanders in general, he believed in the army's right to assume a political role in the defence of the nation's independence and interests.[16]

The idea of the army's share in political responsibility, which has played an important part in Indonesian history down to the present time, thus came to the forefront in the earliest days of the republic. The commanders at their meeting also elected a Minister of Defence, who was neither Sutan Sjahrir, then already responsible for policy, nor his nominee Amir Sjarifuddin, but Sultan Hamengkubuwono IX, who was present at their invitation. Sjahrir, however, ignored them, and appointed Amir Sjarifuddin. These events occurred at the end of a development which, only a few weeks after the proclamation of independence, was to deflect Indonesian policy into other channels than those envisaged by the committees which sat during the last months of the occupation. According to their proposals, the President was to determine policy and appoint ministers who would be responsible to none but himself. On 31 August Sukarno had formed his first cabinet, with Subardjo as Minister for Foreign Affairs, the *bupati* Wirnata Kusuma for Home Affairs, Professor Supomo for Justice and Ki Hadjar Dewantoro for Education. Other ministers were Iwa Kusuma Sumantri (Social Welfare), Abikusno Tjokrosujoso (Communications and State Enterprises), Amir Sjarifuddin (Information), Dr. Samsi Sastrawidagda

(Finance), Surachman Tjokroadisurjo (Economy), Dr. Buntaran Martoatmodjo (Health) and, without portfolio, Dr. Amir, Sartono, Maramis, Wachid Hasjim and Oto Iskandar Dinata.[17] Except for Amir Sjarifuddin, who was under arrest till after the Japanese surrender, all the newly-appointed ministers had in one way or another collaborated with the Japanese at least since the establishment of the BPKI. However, their collaboration was in most cases limited to working for Indonesian independence, and there was thus little justification for the campaign which the *pemudas* soon unleashed against the 'Japanese cabinet', especially as many of the youth leaders themselves had served under the Japanese: this was true of Adam Malik, Sukarni and B. M. Diah, who had worked for a considerable time in the propaganda department, and Wikana, who had served with Subardjo in Maeda's naval intelligence bureau. The real reason for the *pemudas'* indignation was in fact a different one, namely that the 'older leaders' – a term which usually denoted Sukarno and Hatta – had not only stood in the way of revolution, but were still evidently conforming to Japanese wishes.

The *pemudas* were encouraged in their hostility to the régime by Tan Malaka, the Communist leader of the early twenties, who after more than two decades' absence returned to Indonesia at this critical juncture. After being banished in 1922 he had become the Comintern's agent for south-east Asia, living first in Singapore and then in Manila, Tokyo, Canton and Bangkok. He had evolved an ideal which he called 'Aslia' – viz., a co-ordinated proletarian movement comprising south-east Asia and Australia – which was probably one of the main reasons that caused him to be looked on as a Trotskyist. After the failure of the PKI coup, executed against his advice, he had founded in Bangkok the Partai Republik Indonesia (Pari) to carry on underground work in the colony. Towards the end of the Dutch period, Sukarni and Adam Malik had belonged to this group.[18] During the occupation he returned incognito, and worked in a coal mine in west Java. Some hold that the Japanese knew of his return, but he did not appear publicly until just before the proclamation of independence.[19]

In the next few months he became the idol of the *pemudas* who were dissatisfied with Sukarno's leadership. Free of the taint of collaborationism and extolled by Yamin, in a swiftly-written biographical sketch, as the 'father of the Indonesian Republic' and a political philosopher superior to Plato,[20] the veteran revolutionary set out to foment anti-Japanese sentiment, provoke a clash with the occupying power, place himself at the head of the Republic, and oust Sukarno and Hatta, the 'servants of Japan'. A mass demonstration was arranged for 19 September at Djakarta, in order to denounce Japanese attempts to meddle in Indonesian affairs and oppress the population. This, the *pemudas* reckoned, would make a clash inevitable. From the early hours of the 19th, units mobilized by the Menteng 31 Group began marching to what is today Merdeka (Freedom) Square, and the Japanese brought well-armed troops to the scene so as to be ready for any eventuality. In this tense situation, Sukarno once more gave proof of his extraordinary influence over the masses. Addressing the crowd of about 200,000, he swore that the government would defend the Republic to its last breath: the people must trust it, and should show their trust at once by dispersing quietly to their homes. Sure enough, the crowd did so. As at the time of the proclamation, Sukarno had shown that he had gained for himself a position in the people's hearts far surpassing anything the young revolutionaries could command. Some of the latter, including Aidit and Adam Malik, who described these events in detail,[21] were arrested next day. The showdown with the Japanese failed to take place, and Tan Malaka had lost the first round in his struggle for power.

The backing that Sukarno enjoyed among the people had also become evident to Sutan Sjahrir, who had gone on a reconnaissance trip round Java after the proclamation of independence to study the masses' reaction to it. He found that Sukarno's popularity had not suffered during the occuation, even though his name figured on the hated orders compelling the people to increased war service, and that he was still the cynosure of popular hopes. Accordingly, in these weeks Sjahrir refused a suggestion by Tan Malaka that they should make common cause to overthrow Sukarno, and advised the other to tour Java and see Sukarno's popularity for himself.

When the Allies finally landed in Java on 29 September, they announced that 'the Indonesian government will not be deprived of power, but will be expected to maintain civil administration outside the areas occupied by British troops'; they also expressed the hope that the Dutch and Indonesians could be brought to negotiate.[22] This decided Sjahrir to support the Republican cause, on condition that the authoritarian system of government which offended his ideals was modified. The presidential constitution was also criticized as 'Fascist' by Tan Malaka's *pemudas* and other members of the National Committee, and at the beginning of October a large group in the KNIP presented a petition asking that the Committee, which had only advisory functions, should be turned into a legislative body responsible to the government. Sukarno, who only a few months before had fought tooth and nail for the present system of government and against the introduction of parliamentary democracy, had to give way. He knew that the Dutch would refuse to negotiate with him and would never forgive him for his collaboration with the Japanese, and even that his life was in danger from various quarters. He also knew that Sjahrir was a far better choice than himself for the necessary negotiations, not only because he had not been a collaborator, but also because he had had a Western education and knew the Dutch well. Consequently he abandoned the reins of government without a struggle to his old rival of the thirties, and accepted the role of a 'representative' head of state. The one thing that mattered for the time being was to preserve the Republic.

At the second session of KNIP on 16 October, a decree was issued by Hatta providing that, until the people's congress and parliament were constituted, KNIP should be vested with legislative powers and take part in shaping the main lines of policy. A working committee (*badan pekerdja*), responsible to KNIP, should be set up to carry on its day-to-day work. On 20 October Sutan Sjahrir was elected chairman of this committee, which at the beginning of November called for the formation of parties and the introduction of ministerial responsibility to KNIP. Thus in a few weeks the centralized state had been transformed into a parliamentary democracy. On 14 November the first Indonesian cabinet resigned, and Sjahrir announced the composition of his government.[23]

3   INTERNAL STRIFE AND NEGOTIATIONS UNDER SJAHRIR

Meanwhile relations between the Republic and the Allies had taken a turn for the worse. Together with the British forces, mainly Gurkhas, an increasing number of troops of the NICA (Netherlands Indies Civil Administration) had filtered back into Java. Whereas the British were chiefly concerned with evacuating internees and disarming and repatriating Japanese, the Dutch units began to engage in street fighting with the Indonesians, in which British troops occasionally became involved. At the end of October a tense situation arose at Surabaja, where a brigade under General Mallaby was encircled, and the British had Sukarno flown to the spot to arrange an armistice. He was successful, but a few hours later the general was ambushed and shot. Holding the Indonesians responsible the British surrounded Surabaja with large forces, and on 8 November issued an ultimatum ordering all military units to assemble next day at a specified place within the town to surrender unconditionally and hand over all weapons. If a subsequent search led to the discovery of any arms, the possessors would be liable to the death penalty.[24] The Indonesians rejected these humiliating terms, and the 'battle of Surabaja' was accordingly launched on 10 November with the aid of British bombers and warships. The fighting lasted for over fourteen days, and the stubborn resistance of the Indonesians, especially the Pemberontokan corps under the young Sutomo ('Bung Tomo'), made the world aware of their cause for the first time. Clearly the republic was not merely the chimerical invention of a few leaders, but enjoyed the deep-seated loyalty of the population.

While the fighting at Surabaja was at its height, Sutan Sjahrir was forming his new government. Sjahrir had always had a masterly insight into the minds of his European opponents, foreseeing their lines of argument and taking account of their likely reactions in formulating his own plans.[25] The present was no exception. He knew that the Dutch would do their best to affix the stigma 'made in Tokyo' to the young Republic, and therefore made a point of discarding all members of the previous cabinet who had collaborated in any way with the Japanese, even by merely serving on committees. At the same time he wrote a pamphlet entitled *Perdjuangan Kita* (Our Struggle), taking to task the collaborationists who had served the Japanese for private ends while the people were being exploited.[26]

These actions brought Sjahrir much unpopularity. Some of the ousted ministers hastened to join Tan Malaka, for instance Dr. Buntaran, Abikusno and Iwa Kusuma Sumantri, who claimed that they had defended the people's interests while Sjahrir held himself aloof. The military too were offended when Sjahrir, as already mentioned, overrode their choice of the Sultan of Jogjakarta as Defence Minister and appointed Amir Sjarifuddin, the only minister who survived the former cabinet.[27] Sjahrir's following consisted of members of the Socialist youth organizations, which united at the end of the year to form Pesindo, and of the Partai Sosialis, created by the merger in December 1945 of two Socialist parties founded by Sjahrir and Sjarifuddin. He also enjoyed some support in the Masjumi organization, revived in November, which like its namesake under the occupation included all Muslim groups, together with a party of 'religious Socialists' which had advocated reforms before the war but had remained in obscurity during the occupation.[28] A member of this group, Mohammed Natsir, became Minister of Information in January 1946. The PNI, which had likewise been revived, for the time being adopted a waiting policy *vis-à-vis* Sjahrir, as did the PKI, which was now openly active for the first time in twenty years, but was chary of contact with Tan Malaka, suspected as he was of Trotskyism. The former PKI leaders, such as Alimin and Musso, did not return to Indonesia for a further year or two.

While Sjahrir was in Djakarta preparing for negotiations with the Dutch, and while skirmishes between Indonesian and NICA troops continued and gradually spread from Java to Sumatra and Celebes, Tan Malaka tried to unite the opposition groups under his own leadership. Sukarno and Hatta, whose safety was increasingly threatened in Djakarta, took refuge at the beginning of 1946 at Jogjakarta, which became the republic's headquarters for the next few years. Tan Malaka too transferred his activities to central Java, where on 15 January he founded the Persatuan Perdjuangan (PP), or 'Fighting Front'. This body put forward as a 'minimum programme' that negotiations should not begin until the last foreign and enemy troops had left Indonesia, that they must be based on the principle of absolute independence, and that for this purpose all internal differences must be shelved and leadership entrusted to those who would stir up the population to battle.[29]

Tan Malaka's demands met with general acclamation. Nearly all parties, and the senior officers of the army, gave their adherence to the PP. The army's open support for Tan Malaka's views was based on the belief that the republican leadership could and should take a tougher line with the Allied troops, which at the end of 1945 numbered only some 60,000 British and 20,000 of the NICA, whereas the Indonesians had about three times this number ready for battle.[30]

At the beginning of February 1946, the Dutch let it be known that they would only negotiate on the basis of a commonwealth in which Indonesia would enjoy dominion status but would remain under the Dutch crown.[31] This isolated Sjahrir, who resigned when it became clear in the course of February that 85 per cent of the KNIP supported Tan Malaka's demands. Sukarno thereupon invited the PP to form a cabinet, but it proved unable to do so owing to the motley character of the opposition, scattered as it was through all parties. Sjahrir was accordingly once more given the opportunity to form a government, and with the help of Amir Sjarifuddin he was able to secure a majority of the KNIP, especially as it became clear that Tan Malaka's aim was to overthrow not only Sjahrir but Sukarno as well. Neither KNIP nor the army wanted to see Sukarno ousted, and the deadlock was resolved for the time being by the inclusion in the new government of members of PNI, Masjumi and the new Partai Kristen Indonesia (Parkindo): this gave Sjahrir his majority, although the key ministries were retained by their former holders.

Sjahrir's main tasks were to negotiate with the Dutch on the basis of recognition of the Republic, to unify the defence system, and to organize the maximum production of food and its equitable distribution. Tan Malaka, whose minimum demands had not been met in any respect, held a congress at Madiun on 17 March, during which he proclaimed the hostility of PP to the new government. The latter thereupon had him arrested by Pesindo troops and thrown into prison together with his principal followers, who included such well-known figures as Abikusno, Muhammad Yamin, Chairul Saleh, Sukarni and Adam Malik.[32] This drastic step brought about a transitory and apparent calm in the Republican camp, but the opposition remained active although deprived of its leaders. In particular it sought support in the army, which was still critical of Sjahrir and suspected him of planning, as part of his anti-collaborationist campaign, to appoint KNIL officers to replace those belonging to Peta, including Sudirman, the commander-in-chief, who had been made a general in December. The army watched mistrustfully as Sjahrir proceeded to create the élite Siliwangi division and a mobile police brigade in west Java, while increasing the influence of paramilitary bodies such as Pesindo and Hizbullah. In April he had the leaders of a PP group arrested for compelling the ruler (Sunan) of Solo to renounce his privileges and submit to the

Republic, whereupon Sudirman on his own account had the men released.

The main crisis was, however, yet to come. On 27 June Tan Malaka, Yamin and the others were set free, and on the same night Sjahrir was kidnapped at Solo (Surakarta). When this became known, Sukarno at once declared a state of emergency and himself took over the government. Pesindo forces moved in from east Java to rescue Sjahrir, and the Siliwangi division hastened from the west. Sudirman adopted a waiting policy, for there were parts of the army which sided with the PP. There was, for instance, Major-General Sudarsono, who commanded the Third Division, which was responsible for central Java.

On 3 July, Muhammed Yamin and Sudarsono visited Sukarno and demanded that he sign decrees dismissing the Sjahrir government, appointing a supreme political council headed by Tan Malaka, and relinquishing his own powers as commander-in-chief in favour of Sudirman. Sukarno refused these demands, and instead had the PP emissaries arrested. An attempt at this time to kidnap Amir Sjarifuddin, the Minister of Defence, miscarried, and Sjahrir was found and liberated by loyal troops.[33] Sudirman now came off the fence and declared his support for the Republic. In this way the most serious crisis since independence was resolved in the political leaders' favour, and Tan Malaka once more thwarted in his bid for power. He and his followers were re-arrested and were not released till two years later, during the crisis of September 1948.

The state of emergency being over, Sjahrir set about forming a government for the third time. Negotiations with the Dutch, which had been going on sporadically since March, had reached the point where a treaty was about to be signed, and Sjahrir was anxious to include all the main groups and parties in his new government so as to secure the maximum parliamentary backing. The cabinet, which was formed in October 1946 and held office till the following June, included representatives of the PNI, Masjumi, Partai Sosialis and Parkindo, PKI sympathizers and other personalities who commanded wide popular influence, such as Sultan Hamengkubuwono IX and Hadji Agus Salim.

The negotiations between Sjahrir, representing the Republic, and J. H. van Mook, the Governor-General designate, had up to this time led to only partial agreement.[34] Sjahrir had insisted on recognition of the Republic, while letting it be understood that if this was accepted there would be room for talks about closer co-operation. After violent debates, the Dutch parliament had accepted that the Republic (whose cause was pleaded by the far-seeing J. A. H. Logemans) might form part of an Indonesian Union under the Crown. Sjahrir's counter-proposal was that *de facto* recognition should be extended to cover Sumatra, and that the Republic as a sovereign state should form an alliance with the Netherlands. At this stage, a pause occurred in the negotiations owing to the crisis in Indonesia and a change of government in Holland. Van Mook used the interval to discuss the idea of a confederation with representatives of Kalimantan (Borneo), Sulawesi (Celebes), the Moluccas and the Lesser Sundas. These talks, held at Malino near Macassar in July 1946, led to the adoption of a resolution calling for a federation of the United States of Indonesia (USI), comprising four member territories with equal rights: Java, Sumatra, Borneo and the eastern part of the archipelago.

After the formation of Sjahrir's new government, a negotiating commission led by Professor Schermerhorn, a former Prime Minister and the leader of the Dutch Labour party, arrived in Java for the purpose of reaching an agreement with the Republic. All proposals and counter-proposals were discussed anew, and a compromise was reached on 12 November at Linggadjati near Cheribon. The main points of the Linggadjati agreement were as follows:[35]

1 The Netherlands government recognized the Republic as the *de facto* authority in Java and Sumatra.

2 The two governments would co-operate to form a sovereign democratic federal state consisting of three members – the Republic of Java and Sumatra, Borneo and the 'Great East' – to be known as the United States of Indonesia.

3 The governments of the Netherlands and the Republic would co-operate to form a Netherlands-Indonesian union under the Dutch crown.

4 The Netherlands-Indonesian Union and the USI were to come into existence not later than 1 January 1949. The Union would create its own agencies for the settlement of matters of common interest to the member states, especially foreign affairs, defence, and economic and financial questions.

5 Both sides would reduce the numbers of their troops, and the Dutch forces would evacuate Republican territory, subject to the need to

maintain law and order. The rights of foreign nationals to their property in the area controlled by the Republic were to be recognized.

Neither side was happy over this agreement, which was not signed till March 1947. The Dutch continued to pursue their 'Malino policy', and in December 1946, without regard to the promised 'co-operation', they proceeded at Bali to set up an East Indonesian state in accordance with their own wishes. The Republicans regarded this as proof that the Dutch did not take their engagements seriously, and violent opposition spread within the KNIP, particularly to the plan for a Dutch-Indonesian union. Even though all parties were represented in the cabinet, there was a danger that the KNIP would refuse to ratify the Linggadjati agreement. For this reason, Sukarno in December increased its membership from 200 to 514: this method of softening up old antagonisms by means of wholesale dilution is one which has frequently recurred in Indonesian politics. When the original members of KNIP expressed their objection to its being enlarged in this way, Hatta (the Vice-President) threatened that if they persisted in their attitude, he and the President would resign. The Republican leaders regarded the first agreement with the Dutch as a success, the credit for which they were unwilling to concede to the opposition, which called itself *benteng republik* (the fortress of the Republic) and, since Tan Malaka's arrest, mainly centred around the PNI.

The Republican *sajap kiri* (left wing) – composed of the Partai Sosialis, a labour party named Partai Buruh, the PKI, the left wing of Masjumi and the Pesindo units – found itself richly rewarded for its support of the government, as it was the main beneficiary of the enlargement of the KNIP which finally took place, after lively debate, in March 1947, (cf. Table VIII).

The new KNIP, which henceforth assumed the functions of a parliment to which ministers were responsible, began its sessions on 2 March and shortly afterwards approved the negotiations with the Dutch, so that the Linggadjati agreement was signed on 25 March. At this time also, the permanent Working Committee of the KNIP was enlarged from 23 to 47 members, reflecting the composition of the parent body.[37] It seemed as if the most difficult phase of the struggle for stability and sovereignty had been surmounted; but the real testing time for the Republic was still to come.

Table VIII   Composition of the KNIP (Central
Indonesian National Committee) in March 1947[36]
(*Pre-enlargement figures in brackets*)

Parties:		
PNI	45	(45)
Masjumi	60	(35)
Partai Sosialis	35	(35)
Partai Buruh	35	(6)
PKI	35	(2)
Parkindo	8	(4)
Partai Katolik	4	(2)
Occupational:		
Workers	40	(0)
Peasants	40	(0)
Regions (other than Java):		
Sumatra	50	(1)
Kalimantan	8	(4)
Sulawesi	10	(5)
Moluccas	5	(2)
Lesser Sundas	5	(2)
Racial minorities:		
Chinese	7	(5)
Arabs	3	(2)
Dutch	3	(1)
Miscellaneous:		
individuals, minor parties etc.	121	(49)
Total	514	(200)

4   WAR AND THE COMMUNIST REBELLION

Even before the signature of the Linggadjati agreement, its provisions had given rise to diverse interpretations, especially as
regards 'co-operation' and the proposed federal union. The Indonesians took the view that they were to be co-equal partners with the
Dutch in the joint tasks such as that of creating the other new states,
and that since Java and Sumatra contained 85 per cent of the
population of Indonesia, they were entitled to a leading role in the
federation. The Dutch, on the other hand, considered that they
themselves, being the *de jure* authority, had the right to determine
the course of events up to the formation of the union, and also that

the members of the proposed federation should enjoy equal rights. Taking this view, as early as May 1947 they unilaterally created a state of West Borneo under Sultan Hamid II of Pontianak, without seeking the consent of the Republican government. Still more offensive to the latter was the proclamation by the Dutch of an independent state of Sunda: this took place on 4 May at Bandung, on the very territory of the Republic whose *de facto* authority had just been acknowledged. The Dutch, moreover, failed to reduce or withdraw their troops; on the contrary, at the time of signing the agreement they occupied Modjokerto in east Java on the pretext of repairing a breached dam.

The Dutch, for their part, levelled charges of bad faith at the Indonesians, and complained in particular that the latter were conducting an independent foreign policy. Sjahrir had gone to India and had spoken on behalf of Indonesia at the New Delhi Inter-Asian conference in March 1947; Hadji Agus Salim, the Vice-Minister of Foreign Affairs, had visited the Middle East and was canvassing for recognition of the Republic by the Arab states. The Republicans, moreover, were accused of interfering in the affairs of 'other Indonesian states' and infiltrating 'terrorists' in order to cause unrest.

In this way it soon became clear that the 'spirit of Linggadjati' was a dead letter. The Dutch were increasingly desirous of settling the whole dispute by force of arms. They missed the annual tribute from the plantations and were burdened by the need to supply the army of more than 100,000, which they had meanwhile transported to Indonesia. At the end of May Sjahrir received the 'final proposals' of the Dutch negotiating commission, which were to all intents and purposes an ultimatum. They provided for the formation of a joint interim government composed of representatives of the different Indonesian territories and of the Dutch crown, the latter having the last word in case of any dispute. A foreign affairs council was to be set up, with two Republican members, one each for the 'states' of East Indonesia and Borneo, and one for the Netherlands, who again was to have the deciding voice. Finally, there was to be a Directorate of Internal Security responsible, with the aid of a Dutch-Indonesian gendarmerie, for law and order throughout the country.

The joint government and foreign affairs council were themselves unacceptable to the Republic, but the gendarmerie proposal was regarded as a barefaced attempt to reconquer the whole of Republican territory under the guise of maintaining law and order. Not only the *benteng republik*, but also the *sajap kiri* refused to accept the new proposals. Sjahrir, who knew that rejection of the proposals would mean war, sought in vain for a way out. Finally, he offered, as his maximum concession, agreement to the interim government and foreign affairs council, while insisting on the Republic's right to ensure law and order in its own territory.[38] This offer provoked violent criticism, and on 27 June the third Sjahrir government resigned. The *sajap kiri*, having further considered the consequences that might ensue, joined with Sukarno and Hatta to plead with Sjahrir to carry on the government; but he refused, although the US government addressed a note to the Indonesians urging them to co-operate with the Dutch, this making Sjahrir's concessions of greater value in the event of further negotiations. Sjahrir, however, knowing that the Dutch were bent on war, preferred to serve the Republic abroad as its diplomatic representative.

The task of forming a government now fell to Amir Sjarifuddin. Himself a Christian, he was obliged to seek Muslim support, and as the Masjumi refused to co-operate he persuaded some dissident Muslims to re-found the Partai Sarekat Islam Indonesia. Some ministerial posts were promised to the PSII in return for its help, and the cabinet also included members of the Partai Sosialis, PNI and Partai Buruh.[39] The new government, following Sjahrir's policy, agreed to the Dutch demands with the reservation of the police power in Republican territory; but the Dutch, resolved on war, insisted on this point also. To avoid a direct snub to the Americans, who on 27 June had urged that negotiations should be continued, they waited a week or two before commencing military operations. On 21 July, Dutch troops with armoured units and air support spread out from their bases – Djakarta, Bandung, Semarang and Surabaja in Java; Medan, Padang and Palembang in Sumatra – deep into Republican territory, and had attained their chief objectives before the United Nations intervened and an armistice was concluded, on 1 and 4 August respectively. The Dutch held the main ports on which the Republic depended for supplies, as well as the plantations in east Java and on the east coast of Sumatra, the territory under the Republic's *de facto* control was reduced to one-third of Java, including the central area round Jogjakarta and Surakarta with over 1,300 inhabitants to the square mile, and the province of Bantam at the western end of the island.

In the United Nations Security Council a deadlock was reached between the powers friendly to the Republic – Australia, Colombia, the USSR and Poland – and its adversaries – Britain, France, Belgium and, as the Indonesians believed, the USA. The first group supported the Republic's demand that the Dutch troops should withdraw to their bases, while the colonial powers were reluctant to create a precedent and the Americans were also not yet disposed to put pressure on the Dutch. The latter were thus able to continue the process of 'frontier adjustment' and at the end of August proclaimed the 'Van Mook line', cutting off the Republic from the ports and the east Java provinces with their valuable food supplies. Since the armistice, they also held Madura and the areas their troops had passed through during the hostilities. The Republic, whose life was now threatened by an economic blockade, once more appealed to the Security Council, and in October a Committee of Good Offices (CGO) was set up, under whose auspices a meeting of the parties was held in December 1947 on board the U.S.S. *Renville*.

The Committee, composed of representatives of the USA, Australia and Belgium, proposed that the Van Mook line should be accepted as a provisional military boundary on condition that the Dutch withdrew to their bases within three months, allowing the Republican civil administration to return to the evacuated areas. The Republic agreed to this suggestion, but the Dutch countered it with proposals designed to consolidate the *status quo*, threatening to resume military operations if the Republic refused to comply. On 29 December, during an interval in the negotiations, Van Mook actually proclaimed the establishment of a 'state' of East Sumatra, whose territory formed part of the area in dispute. On 9 January 1948 the Dutch issued an ultimatum, in the light of which the CGO announced six additional proposals. The chief of these was that, after an interval of at least six but not more than twelve months, a free plebiscite should be held in former Republican territory to determine whether the inhabitants wished to belong to the Republic or to another state of the USI.[40] The Republicans had no choice but to accept the Committee's proposals, and on 19 January signed the Renville Agreement, placing their hopes in the assurance of the US member of the CGO, Dr. Frank Graham, that his government would use its influence to ensure that the agreements were kept and especially that the plebiscite was held.[41]

Despite these assurances, the agreement brought about the fall of Sjarifuddin's government, and, in view of the state of emergency, Sukarno charged Hatta with the formation of a Presidential cabinet. This body, which was not responsible to the KNIP, was based chiefly on the Masjumi and PNI; the *sajap kiri* were unrepresented for the first time since 1945, as it was impossible to meet their demands for key positions in the cabinet. They accordingly went into opposition, and demanded that the Presidential régime should be transformed into a parliamentary one. This led to a split in the Partai Sosialis, which had been formed from adherents of Sjahrir and Sjarifuddin. Sjahrir, who had come to view with mistrust Sjarifuddin's evolution towards the left, now formed with his own followers the Partai Sosialis Indonesia (PSI) supported Hatta, while Sjarifuddin, to whom a majority of the Socialists remained faithful, became the focus of the opposition. On 26 February, a Democratic People's Front (Front Demokrasi Rakjat – FDR) was established, consisting of the PKI, the Labour party, Sjarifuddin and his Socialists, Pesindo and the trade union federation, Sentral Organisasi Buruh Seluruh Indonesia (SOBSI), which already claimed a membership of a round million.

The FDR, led by Amir Sjarifuddin, soon formulated aims which contrasted flagrantly with the policy he had pursued as Prime Minister. Its demands included the breaking off of negotiations with the Dutch, the abrogation of the Renville Agreement, which Sjarifuddin had himself signed, and the nationalization of Dutch enterprises in the territory that remained to the Republic.[42] The FDR's influence rapidly increased, as had that of the Persatuan Perdjuangan with its similar programme, especially when it became clear that the plebiscite was not taking place, and that new 'states' such as Madura and Pasundan were being created on former Republican territory.

The government, however, was at pains to carry out even the unpopular provisions of the Renville Agreement, such as the withdrawal of troops from the Dutch-occupied areas, loth as the men were to abandon their guerrilla strongholds. Having been Minister of Defence since November 1945, Sjarifuddin had many friends in the army (now called Tentara Negara Indonesia – TNI), which he had helped to build up, and they now welcomed his swing towards the radicals. The army had never altogether given up its opposition to the policy of negotiations with the Dutch, and the course of events now seemed to these circles to justify their advocacy of a firmer policy from the outset. Meanwhile Hatta, viewing as an economist the food situation which was made still more serious by the flow of refugees from the occupied areas, began to talk of demobilizing the army and using the resulting manpower in agriculture and road-building.

The idea of streamlining the army was probably attractive rather than otherwise to such strategists and influential officers as Colonels A. H. Nasution and T. B. Simatupang, who had been trained at the Dutch military academy at Bandung, and who may have had some part in the proposal to reduce the TNI to 150,000 well-armed, mobile, and efficient troops. However, the FDR found ready hearers and willing recruits among the prospective 'victims' of this cut in the armed forces, which had swollen to a strength of something like 400,000 ill-armed men, in many cases undisciplined and affected by 'bapakism'. This was recognized above all by the PKI, which had kept in the background since it was re-founded in October 1945 and had on the whole supported the government's negotiation policy. During 1946 the Dutch government had at its own expense transported to Java the Indonesian Communists who were still living in Holland, partly in the hope of strengthening the *sajap kiri*, which was in favour of negotiations, and partly in order to foment dissension in the Republican ranks. For similar reasons the remaining inmates of the Boven Digul camp had been transferred to Java, including Sardjono, the last PKI leader before the attempted coup of 1926. In April 1946 Sardjono became chairman of the new PKI, but the real power was wielded by Alimin, who returned shortly afterwards from Russia and had spent some time at Yenan with Mao Tse-Tung.

Rejecting Tan Malaka's 'Trotskyist' policy, the PKI had supported negotiations with the Dutch up to the Renville Agreement; but its attitude had changed after the establishment of the Cominform at Warsaw in September 1947 with its division of the world into the mutually hostile camps of imperialism and democracy, Indonesia being counted by Zhdanov a member of the latter.[43] From now on, the PKI began to lay increasing stress on the world-wide conflict between capitalist and Socialist states. The sudden leftward swing of Sjarifuddin's Partai Sosialis may also have been connected with the new strategy. The FDR was afforded much ammunition by the attitude of the US government, which in the opinion of Indonesians of all persuasions could have prevented the Dutch military intervention and, moreover, bore its share of responsibility for the humiliating outcome of the Renville Agreement.

Hatta's government, which was endeavouring to carry out the Agreement, thus soon came under fire as 'imperialistic'. The charge was strengthened in FDR eyes by his negative attitude towards a consular treaty with the USSR, negotiated in Prague by Suripno, a diplomatic agent and member of the PKI. The Soviet Union ratified the treaty in May 1948, but, instead of following suit, the Republican government recalled Suripno to Jogjakarta. With him, and ostensibly as his secretary, came Musso, the planner of the 1926 *Putsch*, who had since been in Moscow, where in 1935 he founded an illegal PKI, and was well informed through intermediaries of the situation in Indonesia. He arrived at Jogjakarta on 10 August 1948, and at once became extremely active, denouncing Sukarno and Hatta as traitors to the national revolution, and proclaiming a 'new course' for the Republic at a PKI conference on 25 August. His plan was for the formation of a 'national front', and he called on the parties which accepted Marxism-Leninism to unite in a single party of the working class. This appeal was answered on 27 August by the Labour party led by Setiadjit, and on 30 August by Sjarifuddin's Socialists.[44]

Immediately before this, Sjarifuddin made the dramatic announcement that he himself had been a member of Musso's illegal PKI since 1935, and had founded Gerindo as a cover for Communist activities. At the same time he avowed that it had been a mistake to collaborate with the colonial power: this had been done on Comintern orders at the time of the struggle against Fascism, but the days of collaboration were over. Sjarifuddin's disclosure had the effect of a bombshell in political circles, but it was met with scepticism: no one could believe that the devout Christian from the Batak country was telling the truth about his past. Some put his statement down to opportunism, and surmised that, having till now been the acknowledged leader of the left wing, he had panicked on Musso's arrival through fear of losing his influence. Others, such as Tan Malaka's followers – who with their leader, received a pardon on 17 August 1948, the third anniversary of independence – denounced him as an agent of the Dutch, who had sought to undermine the Republic by his policy of compromise and his later part in the attempted coup at Madiun. Another possibility was that the failure of negotiations had convinced Sjarifuddin that there was in the last resort no salvation for Indonesia except by joining in the battle on the side of the Socialist camp.

As a result of the fusion of parties, a new *politburo* of the PKI was formed on 1 September. Alimin and Sardjono were deposed from the leadership by Musso and relegated to the propaganda department, headed by Lukman, aged 28, Suripno was given the secretariat for foreign affairs, Sjarifuddin that for defence, Wikana of Pesindo that for youth, Sudisman that for organization, and Njoto that for 'representation', while Aidit, aged 25, became a member of the labour secretariat.[45] It was clear from the start that the new leadership was determined to bring matters to a head. On 2 September Hatta informed the Working Committee of the KNIP that the government, in case of need, would deal ruthlessly with anarchistic excesses. He had received declarations of loyalty from General Sudirman and the principal divisional commanders, and was certain of the support of Masjumi and the PNI, which had both firmly rejected the PKI's proposal for a united front. As for Tan Malaka's group, they had formed a new party, the Gerakan Revolusi Rakjat (People's Revolutionary Movement), in opposition to the 'new left', which was now accusing them of Titoism.

Musso, realizing that in these ·circumstances it was too soon to think of a coup, set out on 7 September, accompanied by other PKI leaders, to tour the Republic and sound popular opinion. He played up to the disaffection of units which were to be demobilized under Hatta's rationalization scheme, contacted officers of the Fourth (Senopati) division at Solo (Surakarta), which was regarded as a PKI stronghold within the army, and held mass meetings at which he attacked the 'distortion of the revolution' by Hatta's government, which had become a plaything of the imperialists. In this way, he sought to foment dissatisfaction to a point where the government could be overthrown without resistance. However, the propaganda of revolution bore fruit more rapidly than he had wished or expected. For weeks past, the Senopati division had resisted demobilization. Its commander had been murdered in August, and, when others of its officers disappeared on 7–9 September, Lieutenant-Colonel Suadi issued an ultimatum to the pro-government troops of the Siliwangi division, then at Solo, to set the missing officers free. When the ultimatum expired on the 13th, fighting broke out which continued for several days and spread to neighbouring areas. On the 18th, pro-Communist units at Madiun occupied the government offices, telephone exchange and army headquarters, and called on other PKI units to follow their example.

On hearing this news Musso, Sjarifuddin and other PKI leaders hurried to Madiun, where they arrived next day. They had no choice but to endorse the Communist action, and on the same day – the 19th – Sukarno broadcast a speech in which he linked the events at Solo and Madiun and declared that the PKI was clearly making a bid for power throughout the country. He called on the population to choose between Musso and the PKI, who if they had their way would transform the country's hard-won independence into a new dependence on Moscow, and Sukarno and Hatta, who would spare no effort to ensure independence for all time. An hour and a half later, Musso broadcast a reply calling on the people to overthrow Sukarno and Hatta without further ado. Under the Japanese occupation, they had traded with the lives of *romushas* and widowed two million Indonesian women, and now they were trying to sell the Indonesian people into the hands of the American imperialists. The events at Madiun and elsewhere were a signal for the people of the whole country to take power into their own hands. That was the only way by which they could free themselves from the puppets of imperialism and safeguard their own sovereignty. Sukarno had called for a choice between himself and Hatta on the one hand, and Musso on the other. Let the people give its answer – death to the traitors Sukarno and Hatta, the slaves of Japan and America.[46]

In the next few days, as the hoped-for general rising against the leaders in Jogjakarta failed to take place, and government troops neared the Madiun area, the Communist radio station broadcast repeated assurances that it was not the party's aim to overthrow the Republic, but merely to reform it. But Hatta had promised to deal ruthlessly with rebels, and now he intended to give no quarter. The insurgents retreated into the mountains of central Java, with the result that fighting continued for weeks. The government did not dare to use the troops stationed on the border with Dutch-occupied territory, and left the pursuit of the rebels to the Siliwangi division and troops of the mobile police brigade. On 28 October the last major unit was captured, thus putting an end to organized resistance. Three days later Musso was killed in a skirmish, and at the end of November Sjarifuddin and Suripno, the last leaders of importance, were arrested.

Such was the outcome of the Communist revolt, which threw long shadows over Indonesian political development for years to come. While the army and the rightist parties never forgot that the Communists had taken advantage of the Republic's hour of need in order to stage a coup, the PKI later evolved the story that the events at Madiun were a put-up job by the 'reactionary Hatta government', who used the 'appointment of a Communist mayor' as a pretext to crush the Indonesian left-wing movement 'with an iron hand', so that the party had had no choice but to defend itself.[47] These charges are conclusively refuted by documents dating from the time of the coup. The outbreak of the rebellion was certainly a surprise and premature from the PKI's point of view, but it had been included in the party's programme from the moment when it became clear that power was not to be achieved by parliamentary means.[48]

5   FROM THE 'END OF THE REPUBLIC' TO
FULL SOVEREIGNTY

During the internal crisis in the Republic, the US government put pressure on the Netherlands not to intervene.[49] The Hatta government for its part declined an offer by the Dutch to help put down the rebellion. The negotiations for the settlement of the 'main conflict' were suspended until the 'lesser conflict' was resolved at the beginning of November 1948. Discussion was then resumed on the question of an interim government pending the transfer of sovereignty. The Indonesians were prepared to acknowledge formal Dutch sovereignty during the transitional phase and to integrate their military forces and diplomatic relations into the proposed federation. But they remained firmly opposed to allowing the Dutch representative, who was to have the right of decision during this time, to introduce Dutch troops to 'pacify' areas where, in his opinion, it was necessary to restore law and order.

By 11 December the atmosphere had again grown so tense that the Dutch authorities informed the Committee of Good Offices that, the negotiations with the Republic having broken down, they intended to set up an interim government without Republican representatives. Hatta, who meanwhile, like Sjahrir or Sjarifuddin before him, had been the target of criticism by nearly all parties for his readiiness to make concessions, tried once more to meet the

Dutch and declared that he would recognize their representative's power of veto during the interim period provided some standards could be laid down beforehand as to the limits within which this power would be used.[50] The Dutch, however, met this advance with a fresh ultimatum, declaring that hostilities would be resumed unless the Indonesians accepted the proposals whereby they would enjoy identical status with the new 'states' that had been created meanwhile. The Republic was not even given time formally to reject this demand. In the early hours of 19 December, Jogjakarta was surrounded by Dutch parachute troops, and the government was virtually forced to surrender. At an emergency cabinet meeting Sjafruddin Prawiranegara, the Minister for Finance and a prominent member of Masjumi, who was at the time visiting Sumatra with a parliamentary group, was empowered to take over the government.[51] Senior officers who attended the meeting, including General Sudirman, who was in bad health, and Colonel Simatupang, the acting chief of staff since the death of Urip Sumohardjo, tried to persuade Sukarno to follow the troops into the mountains and direct guerrilla warfare from there. After some hesitation, Sukarno rejected their advice, influenced in part by the views of Hatta, who expected immediate intervention by the United Nations.

On the same day, 19 December, Sukarno and Hatta; the Foreign Minister, H. A. Salim; the Ministers for Information and Education, M. Natsir and A. Sastroamidjojo; and Sjahrir, who was present as an adviser, were all arrested by the Dutch. A few days later they were flown to new places of exile: Sukarno, Salim and Sjahrir to Prapat on Lake Toba in northern Sumatra, and the rest to the island of Bangka off Sumatra's east coast. Shortly before the government building was occupied, Simatupang had sought and obtained Hatta's agreement that the troops should fight on, whatever happened to the political leaders.[52] For this purpose, the units which had been placed under restraint in connection with the Madiun incident were set at liberty; they numbered about 35,000 men. The arrested PKI leaders, on the other hand, including Amir Sjarifuddin, who had done such service to the Republic, were shot on the night following the Dutch attack, to prevent a fresh Communist revolt being organized during the ensuing period of confusion.[53]

In this situation, Tan Malaka saw his chance to make a fresh bid for power. He had been released from arrest shortly before the

Madiun affair, and, after the revolt was suppressed and the left wing deprived of its leaders, he tried to re-form it by organizing the Partai Murba. 'Murba' was a term of his own coinage, analogous to Sukarno's *marhaen* in the thirties: Tan Malaka, like Sukarno and the PNI regarded 'proletarian' as too narrow a conception to fit Indonesian conditions. He argued, as he had already done in the twenties (and not without influence on Sukarno in those days), that the Indonesian people, including its middle class, had been turned by the long period of colonial rule into a race of 'have-nots', and that the first thing for them to do was to fight for their independence. Murba was the party of those who had no possessions except their body and brains; its historical task was to mobilize all the revolutionary forces of society to fight imperialist aggression, and lay the foundations for a Socialist order in Indonesia.[54]

On 21 December, after the surrender of the government at Jogjakarta, Tan Malaka broadcast from the radio station at Kediri a statement that he intended to continue fighting the aggressor. He pointed to the results of the policy of compromise that he had attacked since 1945 – Linggadjati, Renville, and now the 'end of the Republic' – and accused the PKI of sharing in that policy and also stabbing the Republic in the back, while he, Tan Malaka, had all along defended the views which he held today. This appeal was increasingly effective in wide circles of the population and among the guerrilla bands, recruited from Jogjakarta, which were now springing up in all areas.[55] For the time being, Tan Malaka's activity could only be welcome to the political and military leaders of the Republic. The Security Council was unable to enforce its call, issued on 24 December, for an immediate armistice and the release of the arrested politicians. The Dutch occupied the other cities in what was left of Republican territory, and continued their 'pacification measures', even after the Security Council repeated its demands on 28 December. They hoped that the 'end of the Republic' would in time come to be accepted, as the 'first police action' in 1947 had been; meanwhile they continued at discretion to form new 'states'. Pasundan was followed at the end of 1948 by east Java and early in 1949 by South Sumatra – all parts of former Republican territory.

This time, however, world public opinion did not accept the *fait accompli*. The Indonesian people offered tough and lasting resistance. Sultan Hamengkubuwono IX declared publicly that the

Dutch assertion that he was co-operating with them was a lie; he had granted their commander-in-chief, Spoor, a ten-minute audience for the sole purpose of discussing the withdrawal of Dutch troops. Sjafruddin's emergency government was able to make contact with India and testify to the population's spirit of resistance. At the United Nations, an Indonesian observer delegation led by L. N. Palar, a native of Menado and a diplomat schooled in the Dutch parliament, reinforced the reports of the CGO, and made sure that the Indonesian question was not pigeon-holed. But the decisive factor in ensuring that it remained a live issue was the activity of the Indonesian guerrillas in Java and Sumatra, which, after uncertain beginnings, gradually increased in effectiveness and in several places forced the Dutch on to the defensive.[56]

On 28 January 1949 the Security Council passed a new, more sharply worded resolution calling for the immediate cessation of hostilities, the return of the political detainees and the reinstatement of the Republic in its former rights. The Council also called for the resumption of negotiations, free elections to a constituent assembly, and the transfer of sovereignty to the proposed USI before 1 July 1950. At the same time, the functions of the CGO were enlarged from those of an observer body, to enable it to offer advice to the parties and the Security Council.[57] Even so, there was no indication of sanctions in the event of the resolution being disregarded. But more and more voices were heard in the USA urging that Marshall Aid to the Netherlands be cut off, and this question was openly discussed in the Senate. To demonstrate their obedience to the Security Council, the Indonesians began to damp down guerrilla activity and disarm units other than those of the TNI. In February Tan Malaka complained that TNI divisional commanders had issued orders for military action against groups that disobeyed the UN resolution. He contended that if Hatta and Nasution (the commander of the forces in Java) were given a chance to resume their policy of compromise, it would mean the end of the Republic in earnest; to prevent this, all parties and guerrilla units must continue the fight to final victory.[58]

At this point, however, fortune deserted Tan Malaka, as it had often done after brief periods of success in his varied career. The military leaders issued stricter orders for obedience to the cease-fire, although Nasution at this time complained in writing to Hatta that the armistice was contrary to republican interests.[59] Instead of becoming a public hero for demanding that the fight go on, Tan Malaka became an outlaw, and was finally shot by government troops near Blitar (East Java) on 16 April 1949.[60]

Meanwhile the Dutch had put forward a new plan for a Round-Table Conference, to be held in March at The Hague to discuss the early transfer of sovereignty with the Republic and the newly created states, or 'BFO states', as they were called following the session of a 'Federal Consultative Assembly' at Bandung in July 1948.[61] Louis Beel, the Dutch minister for overseas territories, hoped by this means to avoid the restoration of the Republic. Its leaders, however – now assembled at Bangka except for Sjahrir, who had returned to Djakarta – rejected the proposal and declared through their spokesman Muhammed Rum that they stood by the UN demands. Then an event took place which was to be repeated next year in a still more striking fashion: the BFO governments, which had agreed to the conference, suddenly changed their position, and demanded that the Republic should first be reinstated.[62] This volte-face by the states, which had been so carefully built up as a counterweight to the Republic, did much to destroy the credibility of the Dutch government's assertions that it was only concerned to protect Indonesian interests. The BFO states had begun to realize that the future of Indonesia lay with the Republic and not the Dutch, and they were anxious to avoid challenging the former.

In April, therefore, negotiations took place between a Dutch and a Republican delegation, and on 7 May, after each point had been stubbornly contested, they reached what was known (from the names of the respective leaders) as the Rum–Van Roijen Agreement.[63] This provided for the return of the Republican leaders to Jopjakarta, but not for the relinquishing by the Dutch of the territory they had occupied since 19 December, nor for the plebiscite which, according to the Renville Agreement, was to be held in the areas conquered by them in 1947. The Republican leaders had to agree to stop guerrilla activity by their troops, and to a proviso that the Republic should furnish only a third of the deputies to the proposed representative assembly of the USI. Once again the revolution seemed to have been betrayed. Tan Malaka's Murba Party, despite the death of its founder, was swelled by a large number of the discontented, while Chairul Saleh and other *pemudas* of 1945 carried on the struggle regardless of the political leaders' commands.

Sjafruddin's emergency government let it be known that it would only support the agreement on condition that the Indonesian troops remained in their present positions, and that the Dutch evacuated the occupied territory and acknowledged Republican sovereignty over Java and Sumatra, as agreed at Linggadjati.

On 30 June, the last Dutch units withdrew from Jogjakarta, and six days later the Republican authorities resumed control. Sjafruddin Prawiranegara resigned the mandate under which he had formed the emergency government, and the Working Committee of the KNIP approved his conditions for the acceptance of the Rum-Van Roijen Agreement. Hatta re-formed his cabinet, and conferred the portfolio of defence on the sultan of Jogjakarta, in recognition of his loyalty to the Republic during the occupation, which the Dutch had represented as an action to 'liberate the sultan'. In July talks took place between Republican and BFO representatives, who in a surprisingly short time reached agreement on the principles of a future federal constitution. The Republicans were concerned to safeguard their independence within the federation, but they had no objection to the creation of a senate, in which the individual states, numbering sixteen altogether, would have equal representation.

The long-awaited Round-Table Conference opened at The Hague on 23 August, and continued till 2 November.[64] During this time, final agreement was reached between Indonesia as a whole and the Netherlands. The Indonesian leaders were Hatta, for the Republic, and Sultan Hamid II, for the BFO states. The UN commission also took part, consisting as before of an American, an Australian, and a Belgian representative. Thanks to US pressure, agreement was reached for the outright transfer of sovereignty without the institution of an interim government headed by the Netherlands. The Dutch-Indonesian union also emerged from the conference in a different form from that planned by the Dutch. Its statute spoke of co-operation on the basis of absolute equality of rights, and it was declared that the union did not prejudice the status of either partner as an independent and sovereign state. A permanent secretariat was created, and it was agreed that ministerial delegations from either country should meet for discussions twice a year. The Dutch promised to disband the colonial army by July 1950, and the USI undertook to respect the rights, concessions and licences granted during the period of Dutch rule and to renew them if the beneficiaries so desired. Measures of expropriation, nationalization etc., were only to be taken in the interests of public welfare, and the value of the property involved in each case was to be fixed by judicial decision. The Netherlands were to be treated as 'most favoured nation' in Indonesia: this, however, was something of a courtesy formula, since elsewhere in the agreement it was expressly stated that all nations were to enjoy equal rights in trade with Indonesia and in its industrial development.

Two points gave rise to a tough struggle at The Hague: firstly, the question of Indonesian sovereignty over West Irian (West New Guinea), and, secondly, the amount of Indonesia's debt to the Netherlands. The Dutch assessed this at 6,100 million guilders, whereas the Indonesians claimed that they themselves were creditors to the tune of 540 million. They were well aware that they could not expect to receive this sum, but hoped in this way to secure a substantial reduction of the Dutch claim. Through the mediation of H. Merle Cochran, the US representative on the CGO, the debt was finally valued at 4,300 million guilders, a figure which still seemed exorbitant in Indonesian eyes.

No agreement was reached over West Irian. The Dutch stood on the position which they had taken up only in recent years, that it was a completely separate territory from Indonesia, whereas the Indonesians, as will be recalled, had designed to include it in their state since the constitutional discussions of 1945. Differences of race and language, and the cultural gap between themselves and the backward Papuans, weighed less with them than the fact that West Irian had been the place of exile of many Indonesian freedom fighters. It was finally agreed that negotiations to determine the future status of the territory should be held by October 1950; but in fact more than a dozen years elapsed before this question, which increasingly bedevilled Dutch-Indonesian relations, was provisionally settled in August 1962.

The Hague agreements were ratified by the governments concerned within a few weeks, and on 27 December 1949 the ex-colonial power formally transferred sovereignty to the new United States of Indonesia. A hundred years since the name of 'Indonesia' had first been mooted for academic purposes, and fifty years after the pacification of the archipelago by General Van Heutsz, what had been a loose conglomeration of islands now took its place in the international community as an independent state, and shortly afterwards became the sixtieth member of the United Nations.

VI

THE ERA OF
PARLIAMENTARY DEMOCRACY, 1949-57

I THE UNITARY STATE

To the Indonesian nationalists, the United States of Indonesia to
which the Netherlands had transferred sovereignty at the end of
1949 was not more than a half-way house. Their constitutional
discussions of 1945 had been expressly based on the idea of a
unitary state; federation had not even been mentioned. They were,
of course, aware of the great diversity of the archipelago, but they
believed that both Java and the outer provinces stood to gain from
close association with each other. Over-populated Java depended
on the natural wealth of the outer islands, while the latter relied for
expertise mainly on Java, where the modern schools were. Accordingly the nationalists invoked the saying, ascribed to the medieval
sage Tantular: '*Bhinneka tunggal ika*' ('Unity in diversity'), which
was brought out towards the end of the Japanese occupation,[1] and
was now adopted as the official motto of the new sovereign state.

By the end of the revolutionary period, the idea of national
unity was already some two decades old, its birth being usually
reckoned from the *pemudas*' oath of October 1928, when the youth
organizations solemnly adopted the slogan: 'Indonesia, one motherland, one nation and one language.' But the origins of the idea are
much older still. In the first place, the bulk of the population was
Muslim, and it was therefore natural that Sarekat Islam spread to
the outer islands as soon as it had become a movement of some
consequence in Java. Secondly, the coast dwellers at least had for
centuries possessed a means of communication in the Malay
language, which was later adopted by the colonial power for school
and administration purposes. But the main factor encouraging the
growth of a sense of unity was that the Dutch had treated the East
Indies as a single entity. The system of government was centralized

and plans for de-centralization were not seriously mooted until a late stage, when they appeared in nationalist eyes to be part of a 'divide and rule' policy. Batavia was the centre of the colonial empire from its first beginnings down to the Japanese invasion. It was the seat of the Governor-General (representing the Crown), the Raad van Indië, the supreme court and central administration, the government departments dealing with trade, finance, education, religion, and so on. The institution of municipal councils at the turn of the century, and the later plans for regency and provincial councils, could not divert the attention of the developing élite from events in Batavia. This was especially true after the creation of the Volksraad, whose real importance lay, not in the measure of legislative authority conferred on it in 1927, but in the fact that it constituted a symbol of unity.

One consequence of centralization was that the schools providing higher education were almost all concentrated in Java, so that pupils who wished to complete their training had to come there from the outer islands. As a result, the nationalist movement soon acquired an 'Indonesian' character, and associations on a regional basis were unable to stem the development of an Indonesian national consciousness. One illustration of this is the number of Sumatrans who were prominent in the independence movement and the revolution. The list is a long one: Hadji Agus Salim, Mohammed Hatta, Sutan Sjahrir, Tan Malaka, Mohammed Natsir, Amir Sjarifuddin, Mohammad Yamin, Iwa Kusuma Sumantri, Adam Malik, and Colonels A. H. Nasution and T. B. Simatupang. In the various branches of the movement, in the nationalist, religious and Socialist parties, and in the creation of the Indonesian army, these men played a role fully as important as that of the Javanese. They naturally did not have the same influence over the population of Java as did Sukarno, Tjokroaminoto and others; but they surpassed their Javanese compatriots in organizing ability and, at times, in sober-mindedness.

What was true of the Sumatrans was also true, in proportion, of the students of the other islands. All in all, Java became a centre of the Indonesian intelligentsia representing the whole archipelago – a fact recognized by the Japanese when, in September 1944, they announced the grant of independence not only to Java but to Indonesia as a whole. The Dutch, when they returned after the war, tried with their 'Malino policy' to reverse the development they had themselves instigated, and in doing so they followed the same method as when, in the Padri War a hundred years earlier, they had played off the local authorities and custodians of the *adat* against the Islamic reformers who were the innovators of that time.

At the middle of the twentieth century, the power of the *adat* or customary law in the outer provinces was to a large extent still intact. The members of the intelligentsia who had migrated to Java had lost touch with their home territory and had little influence on the local population. Thus the Indonesian idea penetrated only slowly to the remoter areas, which were less exposed to the impact of nationalist and Socialist maxims. In Atjeh, for instance – the traditionally independence-loving province in northern Sumatra – the opposition movement had little or nothing to do with the desire for an independent Indonesia. As in the past, the main theme of dispute was that between the *uleebalangs* and the *ulamas*, the local and the spiritual rulers of the community;[2] and this persisted into the era of political independence, since the ulama party were offended by the neutrality of the Indonesian state in religious matters.

In these circumstances, support for the local authorities in Atjeh was a two-edged weapon from the Dutch point of view, and it is significant that they did not attempt to create an Atjeh 'state'. In Borneo and the 'Great East' the situation was easier. The Japanese naval authorities, as we saw, followed the principle of backing local authorities, and the Dutch were thus able to resume their old policy when they began, after 1945, to grant autonomy to individual *daerahs* (provinces).[3] Their relative success in this field misled them into creating separate 'states' also in Java in opposition to the Republic, and this seriously diminished the prospects of survival of the federal system. The open adoption by the Dutch of a 'divide and rule' policy in order to curtail the Republic's influence had no chance of success except under a Dutch-dominated interim government. As it was, the federal system was ripe for collapse from the moment when sovereignty was transferred to it.

On 29 October 1949, shortly before the end of The Hague conference, an agreement embodying a draft constitution for the USI was signed at Scheveningen by representatives of the Republic and the fifteen other members of the federation. There was to be a senate and a chamber of deputies, the former consisting of two members for each of the sixteen states and the latter of 150 deputies, including 50 from the Republic. These two bodies comprised the legislative power. The executive consisted of the commander-in-chief of the armed forces and a cabinet, to be formed from time to time by an appointee of the President. The cabinet was not responsible to Parliament (article 122), but the senate could require explanations from it (article 123). Either house had a veto on laws. The draft comprised 197 paragraphs and, unlike the 1945 constitution, contained a long list of human rights and freedoms (43 paragraphs); the preamble also invoked the *pantja sila* as the philosophy of Indonesia. Elections were to be held at an early date, both to the chamber of deputies and to a new assembly which was to give the constitution its final form.[4]

Apart from article 122 the most important provision of the draft was article 139, which empowered the government, should it deem that a state of emergency existed, to pass laws that would be binding on all states of the federation. Such laws must thereupon be laid before the chamber of deputies for approval: if this were refused, they lost their validity, and the individual states could take their own counter-measures. Nevertheless, the latitude afforded by this provision was such that within six months the USI was transformed from a federal into a unitary state.

On 16 December, Sukarno was elected President of the USI, and on the 27th, the day after the transfer of sovereignty, he made a triumphal entry into Djakarta after an absence of four years. The constitution provided for the appointment of a committee of three cabinet *formateurs*, from among whom the President was to select the Prime Minister. Sukarno appointed four; namely, Hatta and Sultan Hamengkubuwono IX, for the Republic; Sultan Hamid II of West Borneo and Sultan Anak Agung Gde Agung of South Celebes, representing the BFO states. Hatta became Prime Minister and Minister of Foreign Affairs; Sultan Hamengkubuwono, Defence Minister; Sultan Anak Agung Gde Agung, Prime Minister of the state of East Indonesia, became federal Minister of the Interior; and Sultan Hamid II, minister without portfolio. The last-named was viewed with some suspicion in Republican circles, and events were to show that this was not unfounded. The other main cabinet posts went almost exclusively to Republicans, including Professor Supomo (Justice), Wachid Hasjim (Religious Affairs), and Sjafruddin Prawiranegara (Finance). The Ministry of Economic Affairs went to Djuanda, who had belonged to many cabinets, and was popularly known as a 'professional minister'. Dr. Leimena, another politician of wide experience, became Minister of Health. The Minister of Information, Arnold Mononutu, belonged to the state of East Indonesia, but stood close to the Republic. In addition to the federal cabinet, a Republican government functioned in Jogjakarta under Dr. A. Halim; it was regarded as a 'cabinet of experts'.[5]

Many of the federal states were jealous of the Republic's dominant influence in the first cabinet of the USI, which, as it turned out, was also the last. Their dissatisfaction inspired the adventurer Westerling, who had served as a captain in the KNIL till his demobilization a year before, to an attempt at 'making history'. He had originally come with the British to Medan in the autumn of 1945, and had set about clearing northern Sumatra of 'bandits and terrorists', as he called the Republicans. He had then been in charge of the pacification of south Celebes and, as he declared in his illuminating autobiography, pacified the area 'with astonishing rapidity'.[6] The casualties involved in this operation, according to Westerling, were six hundred terrorists and three of his own men; Republican sources put them at over 20,000. Having retired to West Java, he set about forming a private army during the last days of Dutch rule, under the title Angkatan Perang Ratu Adil (Forces of the Ratu Adil); rumours of the advent of the Javanese Messiah were still rife, even after the coming of the Republic. This force, according to 'Turk' Westerling (so called because he was born in Constantinople), was to be the salvation of the USI. At the beginning of 1950 he addressed an ultimatum in due form to the Hatta government, calling on it to put a stop to 'anti-federal propaganda' and the 'terroristic activity' of the Republican troops in Pasundan and other states, and to acknowledge the right of his own forces to police West Java.

By posing as the patron of Pasundan, he hoped to secure himself against attacks from Djakarta; but he was not accepted in this role even by the Dutch-appointed government under the Regent of Bandung, Wirnata Kusuma, one of the few leaders to secede from the Republic, which he had served as Minister of the Interior at the time of its foundation in 1945. Finding no allies in any quarter, Westerling went into action on his own account, and on 22 January captured Bandung for a brief period, at a cost of 60 lives. A few days afterwards, he attempted a coup to depose the government in Djakarta. His plans were detected, and investigation pointed to the responsibility of Sultan Hamid II of West Borneo – or 'handsome Max', as Westerling called him – who thereupon exchanged his seat in Hatta's cabinet for a prison cell. Westerling escaped to Malaya, where he was arrested by the British authorities and deported to Europe; he later adopted the career of an opera singer in the Netherlands.

On the strength of the Westerling incident, the USI government intervened in West Java and on 8 February demanded that the government of Pasundan hand over its affairs to a state commissioner. This was done on the following day, and on the 10th the state of South Sumatra made known its desire to merge into the USI. East Java, Madura and the tiny state of Central Java applied to join the Republic, to which agreement was given under article 139, and other states followed suit. By the end of April 1950 the only independent states left in the union were East Indonesia, East Sumatra and the Republic.

In East Indonesia, armed disturbances broke out in Celebes when Soumokil, the Minister of Justice, had a number of pro-Republican leaders arrested. The USI government sent troops from Java to restore order, whereupon Soukomil repaired to Ambon and in April proclaimed there the Republik Maluku Selatan (RMS – Republic of the South Moluccas). Attempts at reconciliation failed, and fighting continued until November between the government forces and Soumokil's troops, which were joined by many ex-members of KNIL. When this was over, the RMS adherents withdrew to Holland, where they formed a 'government in exile' and in the early sixties were still hoping to 'liberate the Moluccas' with Dutch help.

The East Indonesian government had immediately dissociated itself from the resistance in Celebes and, along with the government of East Sumatra, declared its acceptance of a unitary Indonesian state. Negotiations between the Republic and these two states as the last representatives of the federal system led to agreement on 19 May. The senate was to be abolished and a new Parliament formed, its members including the working committee of the KNIP and the 150 members of the federal house of representatives. The members of this body were to draw up a new provisional constitution, and a constituent assembly was to be elected as soon as possible to frame the final constitution. Sukarno was to remain President, and the cabinet would in future be responsible to

Parliament. Such was the basis of the 'provisional constitution of the Republic of Indonesia', which was drawn up at this time and remained in force until the 1945 constitution was restored in 1959. Its true originator, Professor Supomo, later drew up a point-by-point comparison between it and the federal constitution.[7] Apart from the abolition of the senate and the introduction of ministerial responsibility to Parliament (article 83), the new instrument contained a provision (article 84) empowering the President to dissolve Parliament, after which new elections must be held within 30 days. In other respects the President's powers were much reduced. As in the federal constitution, all his decrees, including those issued by him as commander-in-chief of the armed forces, must be countersigned by the competent minister (article 85). In addition to appointing cabinet *formateurs* as before, he could now also choose his own Vice-President. The subsequent procedure for the election of the President and Vice-President was to be determined by law (article 45).

On 14 August the new constitution was endorsed by the USI senate and house of representatives, and the Indonesian federation thus ceased to be. Three days later, on the fifth anniversary of independence, the unitary state was solemnly proclaimed by Sukarno, and the cardinal aim of the revolution was accomplished. Sukarno, however, was not yet content. 'Let no one think', he declared, 'that all problems are solved now that we have a unitary state, or that this is a magic key to the welfare of our people. The unitary state is only a means of facilitating the union of all our forces. Only with united forces and tireless energy can we remove the obstacles to our people's welfare.'[8] To the hundreds of thousands who assembled in Merdeka (Freedom) Square to hear him speak in that memorable hour, Sukarno held out no promise except the continuation of the fight for prosperity and for the liberation of West Irian from the Dutch grasp. He addressed them, not as a statesman seeking to consolidate what had been achieved, but as a revolutionary who knew that he had still a long way to go before reaching his goal and that the state was 'only a means' to this end. Back in the early thirties, in his pamphlet *For an Independent Indonesia*, he had described independence as the 'golden bridge' at the other end of which his people's fate would be decided, and had called on the *marhaen* – peasants, traders, clerks, labourers, fisherfolk, craftsmen, pedicab drivers and 'little men' of all kinds – to see to it that the Indonesian state did not become a tool of capitalism. The aim of the revolution was to achieve both independence and social justice: it must guarantee economic as well as political equality, a democratic social order based, not on individualism and liberalism, but on Indonesian collectivism and the spirit of *gotong rojong*.[9]

These ideas had found their reflection in the 1945 constitution, the drafters of which had deliberately omitted any reference to the liberal conception of human rights and freedoms or to a multi-party system, and had instead emphasized the Indonesian tradition of all-round representation, *musjawarah* and *mufakat*. Since then, advocates of the Western parliamentary system who had come to the fore criticized the presidential constitution as tending towards Fascism, and the new instrument reflected their preference for parliamentary democracy. Sukarno's appeal for unity in the same speech was partly due to concern lest, now that independence had been wrested from the Dutch, there should be a recrudescence of party strife which was all too familiar in the annals of the nationalist movement and which, even at the height of the revolution, had only with difficulty been subdued to the common interest. The preamble to the new constitution invoked the *pantja sila* and the spirit of tolerance, but it remained to be seen how far the parties would respect this spirit in the pursuit of their aims. Before long, it became clear that their acceptance of the *pantja sila* was lip-service only.

Two main political trends became discernible. One was represented by Hatta, who was again appointed Vice-President in October 1950, and who held that the achievement of sovereignty marked the end of the revolutionary era; and the other by Sukarno, who maintained that the revolution was still incomplete, and that the state was a means and not an end.

2 PARTIES AND PROGRAMMES

Since November 1945, more than twenty parties had responded to Sjahrir's call for the establishment of political groups. Seventeen of these were represented in the new Parliament, consisting of the Working Committee of the KNIP and the members of both houses of the old USI parliament – all of them nominees, as general elections had not yet been held. The following table shows the composition of Parliament by parties in the early days of the unitary state.

Table IX   Distribution of seats in the Indonesian Parliament, March 1951[10]

Party	No. of seats	Date of (re-) foundation
Madjelis Sjuro Muslimin Indonesia (Masjumi)	49	1943 (Nov. 1945)
Partai Nasional Indonesia (PNI)	36	1927 (Jan. 1946)
Partai Sosialis Indonesia (PSI)	17	Feb. 1948
Persatuan Indonesia Raya (PIR)	17	Dec. 1948
Partai Komunis Indonesia (PKI)	13	1920 (Nov. 1945)
Fraksi Democrat (BFO leaders)	13	
Partai Rakjat Nasional (PRN)	10	July 1950
Partai Katolik	9	1925 (Nov. 1945)
Partai Indonesia Raya (Parindra)	8	1935 (Nov. 1945)
Partai Buruh	7	Dec. 1949
Partai Sarekat Islam Indonesia (PSII)	5	1912 (July 1947)
Partai Kristen Indonesia (Parkindo)	5	1930 (Nov. 1945)
Partai Murba	4	Nov. 1948
Others	39	
Total	232	

The Muslim parties

The Masjumi, which ranked as the strongest of all parties in the early fifties, had been founded, it will be remembered, by the Japanese in November 1943 as a means of conveying their wishes and requirements to the Muslim community as a whole. It included the reformers belonging to the widespread Muhammadijah organization, as well as the orthodox Muslims of the Nahdatul Ulama; in addition, political organs of Islam such as the PSII and Dr. Sukiman's Partai Islam Indonesia threw in their lot with Masjumi after they themselves were banned, and took an active part in re-founding it in 1945. In the long run, however, the strongest influence in the new Masjumi was that of the 'religious socialists' led by Mohammed Natsir, the pre-war headmaster of an Islamic reform school at Bandung. Natsir's writings show him to be a man of wide reading, well-informed even outside the Islamic sphere.[11] His breadth of culture suggests comparison with Sjahrir and Hatta, who also came from West Sumatra; but unlike them, he was concerned for the renewal of Muslim life in a changing world. Reform, he contended, should be such as did not affect the foundations of belief in the Koran and Sunna; reinterpretations of holy writ should be governed by piety and a responsible desire to fathom the Divine will. When in 1940 Sukarno, from his exile at Benkulen, proposed that Islam should be renovated, 'without poring over every letter' but in accordance with its own spirit, which according to him could be summed up as 'progress', Natsir had protested vigorously at this form of 'freethinker's religion'.[12] He had no sympathy with Sukarno's syncretism, and regarded it as a blasphemy when the latter called himself 'a Muslim and a Marxist': ideas, he felt, should be respected and not used as counters for opportunistic purposes. Marxism was a challenge that it behoved Islam to meet, but it was neither a substitute for traditional religion nor a completion of it.

From the political point of view, the Natsir wing of Masjumi adhered firmly to Hatta's view that the revolution ended with the transfer of sovereignty: in Feith's classification they are termed 'administrators', as opposed to the continuers of the revolution whom he styles 'solidarity-makers'.[13] We shall not follow him in using the latter term, as it does not do justice to the fact that the group in question regarded themselves – limited as their opportunities might be – as custodians of the old ideals of the revolution. Instead we shall refer to them henceforth as the 'ideologists', since they often neglected practical politics for the sake of their ideology, which, be it repeated once more, taught that the revolution would not be complete until the ideals of social justice had become a reality. Their enemies were imperialism, capitalism, liberalism, and individualism: salvation, in their view, lay in traditional collectivism, *gotong rojong*, and the Socialist order which it was their task to build while warding off incessant attacks from outside. Their political 'style' was egalitarian, based as it was on the premise that their cause was that of the whole people.

The 'administrators', on the other hand, were liberals who believed in working towards their ends on a pragmatic basis. The Masjumi, for example, expected to be able gradually to create a Muslim state of a modernized type, even in a context of religious freedom.[14] Their economic policy was once described by Sjafruddin Prawiranegara on the following lines. The form of socialism suited to Indonesian society was not a Marxist but a religious one, stressing the initiative and responsibility of the individual. Class hatred and the class struggle were foreign to Islam, but there was everything to be said for healthy competition which would increase production and improve its quality. The only proper occasion for state intervention was when the working of the profit motive in a liberal economic order led to the restriction of production. Theories should not be applied blindly, but in the light of circumstances and experience.[15] By this formulation, Sjafruddin gave the Indonesian middle class the assurance that it was doing more for social welfare than were the advocates of the class struggle. Masjumi in fact found its chief support in the middle class of the cities and larger rural centres, the promotion of whose interests figured expressly in the Masjumi statutes.[16]

While the 'religious Socialists' and Muslim reformers led by Natsir and Dr. Sukiman – the latter representing the 'Javanese element' in the Islamic reform movement – played a more and more dominant part in the Masjumi, dissatisfaction grew among the *kijais* and *ulamas* who, in days gone by, had united against the reformers in the Nahdatul Ulama. That was in 1926, but in 1946, having gained in influence during the occupation, they expected to form the backbone of the new party of Muslim unity. Finding themselves relegated to second place, they urged the formation of a Muslim federation instead of a single party. The Masjumi leaders refused to agree, and in August 1952 the Nahdatul Ulama withdrew to form an independent organization, based expressly on the validity of the four *mazhabs*, or schools of religious thought – the Shafiite, Malikite, Hanbalite, and Hanafite – which the reformers had called in question.[17] However, it was not only their conception of Muslim orthodoxy that divided the *kijais* and *ulamas* from the reformers. The former, whose main support was among the Javanese rural population belonging to the *santri* civilization, continued to appreciate the value of Javanese mysticism and syncretism. Despite the sharp differentiation between the *abangan* and *santri* civilizations in Java,[18] the latter had preserved traditional elements which the reformers could not ignore. Apart from this, the critical attitude of the *kijais* and *ulamas* towards the reformers facilitated their contacts with the latter's other opponents, the 'ideologists'.

As early as 1947, when the Sjarifuddin cabinet was formed, the old PSII had split off from the Masjumi, partly from political opportunism and partly because it had always looked askance at the liberal philosophy which was gaining ground in that body. However, the influence of the PSII remained limited, as its Islamic interests were more effectively represented by the orthodox and the re-formists, and its political ones by the 'ideologists' or the egalitarians. Thus, the time was past when Sarekat Islam was a deciding factor in Indonesian politics. Apart from the Masjumi, Nahdatul Ulama, and PSII, the only group requiring mention is the Pergerakan Tarbijah Islamijah (Perti), a body which became prominent in Sumatra in colonial times for its work in the social and educational fields and the standardization of Muslim schools, and which retained its separate existence in the new Indonesia.

The nationalist parties

The split between Masjumi and Nahdatul Ulama (NU) left the PNI as the largest Indonesian party. Its membership was drawn from adherents of Sukarno's old PNI and Partindo, many of whom now occupied important positions: e.g. Sartono, Sunarjo, Ali Sastroamidjojo, and Iskaq Tjokroadisurjo. As the successor to the first nationalist party, PNI enjoyed great prestige, and during the revolution as well as after the transfer of sovereignty it attracted many 'new' nationalists seeking an entry into political life. Originally a party of the progressive urban intelligentsia, the emphasis it laid on the 'Indonesian way' had enabled it to penetrate the *abangan* civilization of the countryside, which distinguished itself from the *santri* culture, because in the former, Islam had not succeeded in ousting traditional Javanese animism, Hinduism and Buddhism. As a result, the PNI found many adherents among the class of government officials, formerly known as *prijajis* and now as *pamong pradja*, who in colonial times had been forbidden to engage in politics.

The ideology of the PNI was Sukarno's 'marhaenism', which aimed to bring about a socialist order without resorting to class warfare, through the co-operation of peasants, labourers, craftsmen, small traders etc., and on the basis of *musjawarah* and *mufakat* – i.e., widespread discussion ending in a consensus. The PNI statutes therefore provided for the establishment of provincial economic councils composed of representatives of the workers, employers and government, which would debate and decide on necessary measures. The party also called for the nationalization of vital enterprises, the expropriation of big landowners and a just distribution of land, so that all sections of society might benefit from the achievement of prosperity.[19] However, what appeared in theory to be a clear-cut system admitted in practice a variety of interpretations, in the same way as the *mufakat* principle depended more on persuasion than conviction. This had become clear in the first nationalist federation, the PPPKI, in the late twenties, and equally so in the constitutional discussions of 1945. The formulae on which agreement was reached generally left ample room for differences of interpretation, and so now did the PNI conception of 'vital enterprises' or 'just distribution'. Clarity was sacrificed in a desire to accommodate every view, and the resulting internal tensions were relieved in the PNI, as in former times, by the safety-valve of anti-imperialism. The law, it was agreed, must protect national concerns against foreign competition; foreign capital must not be allowed to harm national interests, the concessions of foreign landowners must be reviewed, and so on. When it was found that such fresh ambiguities led to corruption rather than stabilization, imperialism was again used as a scapegoat, as it had always been for dissensions in the nationalist movement.

The effect of this on the PNI leadership was to ensure the predominance of the 'ideologists', if only to relieve the tensions that appeared on every side. The 'administrators', who were by far the strongest group in the Masjumi, were here in a minority: their chief leaders were Wilopo and Susanto Tirtoprodjo, who had been cabinet ministers during the revolutionary period, and Sartono, who had been Speaker of the Parliament. Among the dominant ideologists, those of the earlier period included Iskaq, Surachman, Ali Sastroamidjojo, Sunarjo, and Gatot Mangkupradja; others who later became prominent were Dr. A. K. Gani and Sidik Djojosukarto who was party chairman in the early fifties.

Other nationalist parties were grouped around local personalities, such as the Parindra, headed by R. P. Suroso, who had sat for many years in the Volksraad as a representative of Budi Utomo and, after 1935, of the pre-war Parindra; or the Partai Rakjat Indonesia (Indonesian People's Party), headed by Sutomo, the hero of the battle of Surabaja. Yet other parties sought to amalgamate smaller groups representing outer island territories, such as the Partai

Kedaulatan Rakjat (Sovereign People's Party), of southern Celebes, or the Serikat Kerakjatan Indonesia (Indonesian People's Association) of South Borneo; deputies belonging to these combined with others to form the 'Democratic Fraction'. The Partai Rakjat Nasional (National People's Party) broke away in 1950 from the PNI, which it regarded as 'too capitalistic' under the chairmanship of Sidik Djojosukarto, although the new party itself declared in its statutes that it would support capitalist enterprises. The initial rapidity with which it gained recruits may have been due to the fact that it advocated the integration of Eurasians.[20]

However, the only one of the smaller nationalist parties to achieve any importance in Parliament before the general election of 1955 was the Persatuan Indonesia Raya (Greater Indonesian Union – PIR), founded in December 1948 shortly before the capture of Jogjakarta, and affording a home to those nationalists who considered the PNI 'too far to the left'. The motto enshrined in its statutes was 'the right man in the right place'. Led by Wongsonegoro, the PIR was supported by many of the senior *prijajis*, who hoped for an early stabilization of society and the retention of their old influence. Representatives of the nobility from the BFO states also belonged to the PIR, as did such personalities as Professor Supomo, Sutardjo Kartohadikusumo and Latuharhary.[21]

The Socialist parties

The smallest of all Indonesian parties – at its first congress in 1952 it was not ashamed to reckon its membership at 3,049, while the Masjumi and PNI counted theirs in millions – was the Partai Sosialis Indonesia, in which Sjahrir sought to pursue the policy of élite-formation which had inspired the pre-war 'New PNI'. Those who had followed him in those days preferred his sober analyses to Sukarno's diatribes against colonialism; and now that the new state was in process of development, many felt drawn even more strongly to support the Fabian Socialist, with his thorough grasp of theory and abhorrence of dogma. Sjahrir and his associates despised empty slogans and rhetoric, opposed sentimentalism in politics, and, as they had done twenty years before, tried to use social analysis to discover the causes of setbacks, instead of blaming everything on the 'imperialists'. They believed in Socialism based on personal freedom and the dignity of the individual, and opposed all totalitarianism, Fascist or Communist, with its party dictatorship and secret police methods. They had no objection to foreign capital investment as a stimulus to the economy, and favoured private initiative alongside co-operatives and state enterprises, production being co-ordinated by a system of limited planning under democratic control.[22] Sjahrir's Socialists, the 'administrators' *par excellence*, included outstanding specialists such as Dr. Sumitro Djojohadi-kusumo, the finance and economic expert; another figure who stood close to them was Sultan Hamengkubuwono.

The two other parties professing Socialism, the Murba and the PKI, were sharply opposed to the PSI. Tan Malaka, the leading spirit of Murba, had been Sjahrir's irreconcilable adversary since the time of the Persatuan Perdjuangan, when he called for a fight *à outrance* against capitalism, and refused to parley with the imperialists. With his death, Murba lost the support of the head of the national Communist movement, but it continued to take an aggressive line, and was more consistent than the PNI in demanding the nationalization of all foreign-owned factories and plantations, state control of all vital enterprises and the rejection of foreign capital. But Murba's heyday was over. With its classification of the people into machine *murbas*, country *murbas*, town *murbas*, trade, brain, and transport *murbas*, it was regarded even by the other revolutionary movements as a curiosity rather than the leading Socialist party. Much of its importance was lost when, in 1952, the re-organized PKI made itself the advocate of national interests, for doing which it had till then pilloried the Murba as an agent of Titoism.[23]

The PKI, for its part, had taken some time to re-form its ranks after the Madiun fiasco.[24] Besides the odium of having stabbed the Republic in the back, it was handicapped by the memory of its volte-face after the Renville Agreement. Moreover, it had lost several of its major leaders, and the struggle for power among the survivors continued into 1953. However, at the beginning of 1951 a group of young Communists, notably D. N. Aidit, M. H. Lukman, Njoto and Sudisman, had succeeded in ousting the veteran leaders Alimin and Tan Ling Djie from key positions in the party organization. In August 1951, when PKI members were arrested *en masse* in connection with disturbances in the port of Djakarta, Aidit, Lukman and Njoto succeeded in going underground. During the months which elapsed before their return to public view, they worked out a new strategy for the party.

The past careers of these three men are as follows. Aidit was born in Bangka in 1923, and attended a school of economics at Bandung from the end of the thirties; he belonged to the 'Menteng 31' group during the Japanese occupation; he was a member of PKI in 1945; and in 1948 member of the politburo with responsibility for labour. He travelled in China and Vietnam after outbreak of the Madiun rebellion. Lukman was born in central Java in 1920, and was a member of the 'Menteng 31' group; PKI member 1946; in 1948, he became member of the politburo (agitprop department); 1949–50, he accompanied Aidit on his travels. Njoto was born in east Java in 1925; in 1945, he was chairman of the PKI at Djanber and, in 1947, PKI representative on the Working Committee of KNIP; 1948, he was member of the politburo (department of representation).

The tactics on which they agreed were to aim, first of all, for a rapid increase in membership (which was achieved: between the beginning and middle of 1952, the party grew from 7,910 to 126,000 members), in order to appeal for the creation of a national front of all anti-imperialist parties which would complete the 'bourgeois-democratic phase' of the revolution. The party leaders argued as follows. Indonesia was a semi-colonial and semi-feudal country, and the PKI had set its face against the imperialists and big landowners. It was necessary to fight the imperialists because they would not surrender West Irian and were attempting to continue the exploitation of Indonesia by the more subtle means of capital investment, in which they were helped by the *compradors* of the wealthy native bourgeoisie. The fight against the big land-owners was necessary because they stood in the way of a just distribution of land to the peasants, whom they sought to continue exploiting, as in medieval times. While thus emphasizing their hostility to the 'wealthier bourgeoisie' and 'big landowners', the PKI leaders indicated that the way was open for an understanding with the 'national bourgeoisie' and the poor and 'middle' peasants, whom they hoped to include in their united front. Their advances were mainly directed towards the PNI and other nationalistic groups; from this time on, the Masjumi and PSI were incessantly attacked by the Communists as 'henchmen of imperialism'. Hatta, too, was branded by them as an enemy of the people, and the legend of his 'provocative action' at Madiun was very soon put about. Sukarno, on the other hand, who in 1951 was still a 'social imperialist' and a 'falsifier of Marxism', was now suddenly extolled as a 'rallying-point for anti-imperialist forces', and was never again openly attacked by the PKI. Well before Stalin spoke, at the nineteenth congress of the Soviet Communist party in October 1952, of the 'patriotic duty' of Communists, and thus introduced a new phase of international Communism, the young party leaders in Indonesia executed a 'swing to the right' on their own responsibility in the hope – which events showed to be justified – of turning their proscribed party into a political force of attraction.

The Christian parties[25]

The two Christian parties – the Partai Katolik and the Protestant Parkindo – had a small but stable following. Since its foundation in 1925, the Partai Katolik had supported the nationalist movement. I. J. Kasimo, who became its chairman after the war, had signed the Sutardjo petition on behalf of Indonesia's Catholics, and in 1939 led the party into the Gapi federation, which called for an Indonesian parliament. Apart from central Java, the main areas of Catholicism were in the Lesser Sundas – Flores, Timor and Sumba; but it had also gained a foothold in some provinces of Kalimantan (Borneo) and Sulawesi (Celebes), the traditional domain of Islam. In December 1949 the Catholic associations in all these regions decided to merge with the Republican Partai Katolik, and this decision was carried out in the following August.

The Protestant groups, which were less homogeneous than the Catholics, formed their own associations from 1930 onwards. They, too, desired to see the Volksraad transformed by degrees into a full parliament, with eventual independence for Indonesia, but they were in general less concerned with political affairs than the Catholics, perhaps because their main areas of support – the Moluccas, Menado and the Batak country – had traditionally enjoyed preferential treatment by the colonial power. After independence their pro-Dutch attitude altered, and from the time Parkindo was founded in November 1945 it actively supported the Republic. In August 1947 the Batak Christians joined Parkindo, thus restoring the unity of the Protestant organizations.

From 1945 onwards, Republican cabinets included several members of both Christian parties: Dr. Leimena, a subsequent chairman of Parkindo, held ministerial office more frequently than any other politician during the first twenty years of independence.

The chief concern of the Christian parties was naturally to ensure the preservation of religious freedom in a predominantly Muslim society. Ideologically, they stood between the PNI, with its adherence to the *pantja sila*, and Sjahrir's liberal PSI.

3 PROBLEMS AND GROUPINGS UP TO THE GENERAL ELECTION (1955)

The new unitary state was beset from the start with a multiplicity of problems, with the result that the parliamentary period might be described as an unbroken series of cabinet crises. We cannot here pursue in detail the history of the successive coalition cabinets; these may be tabulated as follows.[26]

Table x   Governments in the time of Parliamentary democracy
up to 1956

Main Parties	Prime Minister	Dates
Masjumi, PSI	Natsir	Sept. 1950–March 1951
Masjumi, PNI	Sukiman	Apr. 1951–Feb. 1952
PNI ('Administrators'), Masjumi, PSI	Wilopo	Apr. 1952–June 1953
PNI ('Ideologists'), Nahdatul Ulama, PSII	Ali Sastro-amidjojo	July 1953–July 1955
Masjumi *et al.*	Burhanuddin Harahap	Aug. 1955–March 1956

It is, however, of interest to note the reasons for the fall of the respective governments, since they constitute a list of the problems which stood in the way of internal stability. Thus, Natsir's government came to grief owing to its neglect of the West Irian question; Sukiman's, over the conclusion of a security pact with the USA; Wilopo's, over the dispossession of squatters on plantations in east Sumatra; Ali Sastroamidjojo's, because the army refused to accept a government nominee as chief of staff; and Burhanuddin's, over the unilateral dissolution of the Dutch-Indonesian union on account of the West Irian problem, which remained unsolved. From beginning to end of this period, the Republic was burdened with a complex of problems arising out of the legacy of Dutch colonial rule, the orientation of foreign policy, army-state relations, and the ever-acute issue of internal security.

The colonial legacy

As we have noted more than once, the unitary state itself is essentially the outcome of Dutch colonial policy in the early years of this century. When the Dutch attempted, during the revolutionary period, to mould the new state into a federal form, it was already too late for success. Apart from municipal and regency councils there was no parliamentary tradition in the outer provinces for the BFO states to build on – no council for Sumatra, Celebes or the rest, such as Colijn had advocated ever since the Volksraad was set up. The Dutch had not considered the establishment of provincial councils till the late thirties, and the war had forestalled any action in this sense. Meanwhile the nationalist movement had long been imbued with the idea of Indonesian unity, and all its efforts were directed towards the creation of a unitary state based on Java, from which regional differences would as far as possible be eliminated.

When this state came into being, it suffered from an almost total lack of skilled personnel to replace the Dutch in such fields as administration, finance, economics and transport. Although the educational system had been considerably expanded since the beginning of the century, the Dutch had at no time foreseen such an early end to their power, and had not geared their policy to a native take-over of the administration at any specific date. Towards the end of the colonial period, about 81,000 Indonesians were attending schools or colleges at which the language of instruction was Dutch: of these, 5,997 were receiving extended primary education (MULO), 1,205 secondary education (AMS or HBS), while 591 were at university.[27] Thus only some 10 per cent of those young Indonesians who knew Dutch were receiving modern training, in a country whose total population had passed the 60-million mark in 1930. During the occupation and revolution, their numbers did not increase but declined, as in most cases their education was interrupted. Thus, after the transfer of sovereignty, the Indonesians had no choice but to keep on the Dutch experts who manned the various ministries, though this frequently led to tension, owing to the conflicts of the previous few years.

In addition, relations with the Dutch were from the start be-devilled by the West Irian problem. A decision on the future of the territory was not reached within the interval of a year provided for in The Hague agreement. The Dutch refused to 'restore' West Irian to Indonesia, and proposed instead that the Papuans should, after a certain lapse of time, be allowed to decided their own future. After the collapse of federalism, they were prepared to transfer sovereignty over West Irian to the Dutch-Indonesian union, which would have meant themselves remaining in *de facto* control. The Indonesian delegation refused these terms, with the result that 'at the first cock-crow' of 1951 West Irian was still firmly under Dutch rule instead of having been 'liberated from colonialism' and 'restored' to the bosom of the Republic, as Sukarno had repeatedly promised. Further negotiations led to a stiffening of attitudes, and in 1956 Indonesia gave notice of the dissolution of the Dutch-Indonesian union. Thereafter the crisis became still more acute. When the United Nations failed to put the matter on its agenda in 1957, violent anti-Dutch demonstrations took place in December of that year, leading to the expropriation of Dutch enterprises and an exodus of the Dutch nationals who were still living in Indonesia.[28]

Indonesia's 'free and active' foreign policy

The independence movement had from its inception aimed at transforming Indonesia into a free member of the international community, and this remained its purpose during the revolutionary period. In the late forties, when the lines of the cold war were being drawn more closely around the USA and the USSR, there seemed to be a danger that Indonesia would be involved in their quarrels. The rebellion led by Musso, who spoke of his 'Gottwald plan' for Indonesia when he arrived from Moscow in 1948, was regarded as an attempt to enrol Indonesia in the Socialist camp, after the model of the East European states. At the same time, the lack of US support for the Republic in its life-and-death struggle against the Dutch was looked on as a consequence of the cold war, since in the Indonesian view the Americans were concerned to avoid giving offence to their European allies. In these circumstances, Indonesia based its foreign policy on the principle of neutrality and declared that, as set forth in the PNI statutes, it would be independent (*bebas*), but also active (*aktip*) in the cause of national interests and world peace. The statutes of most of the other parties contained a similar formula, sometimes with slight modifications: e.g. the Masjumi manifesto declared that 'Indonesia's foreign policy should be based on the maintenance of world peace and the desire for friendship with all peoples, *especially those that believe in God and the principles of democracy.*' At the same time, 'independence' was qualified by the proviso that foreign aid might be accepted so long as it did not involve military obligations or infringe state sovereignty.[29]

As the first governments of the new state were dominated by the Masjumi, it is not surprising that Indonesia at this period leaned towards the West, which professed its faith in God and democracy, and was the only potential source of aid. However, the Natsir government turned a deaf ear to US pressure for the conclusion of Asiatic defence pacts, which became more insistent after the outbreak of the Korean war. The next cabinet under Sukiman took a somewhat more flexible view; its Foreign Minister was Subardjo, who had occupied the same position in Sukarno's first government in 1945, but had not then had a chance to use his diplomatic talents. Being opposed to Sjahrir, he had for a time thrown in his lot with Tan Malaka, but, having a good nose for changes in the internal balance of power, he rallied to the Masjumi in 1948 in the expectation of fresh opportunities. In January 1952, without the knowledge of Parliament or most of his fellow-ministers, he committed the adventurous act of signing a 'mutual security' agreement with the US: his object was to secure economic, technical and military aid, which might however have been available without military commitments.[30] His action was contrary not only to the general objective of independence but even to the Masjumi line, which was relatively favourable to the West. It brought about his resignation and also that of the Sukiman cabinet, and the pro-Western phase in Indonesian foreign policy thus came to an end.

In the next period, attempts were made to strengthen Afro-Asian solidarity. These led, in April 1955, to the celebrated Bandung conference, at which the leaders of nearly thirty independent states met to explore the possibility of a closer union of the 'Third World'. The initiative for this conference, which attracted worldwide attention, came from Ali Sastroamidjojo, the head of the first PNI-dominated government, who wished to stress the 'active' element in foreign policy. He ventilated his idea at the Colombo conference called by Nehru in April 1954, at which the independent

Asian states expressed their attitude towards the Geneva discussions on Indo-China. Nehru and the other Asian statesmen were at first sceptical but finally agreed to the conference, at which the Chinese communist delegates repeated their assurances of peaceful intentions on an international stage.[31] China's attendance was in fact the outstanding feature of the conference, which was hailed as in-augurating a new era, but did not lead to much practical result. The only point on which all the heads of states agreed was the con-demnation of colonialism; but even here there were difficulties of definition. Sukarno exerted his eloquence to secure a consensus (*mufakat*) condemning 'colonialism in all its manifestations', but this typical compromise, achieving unanimity by the use of a vague blanket term, endured no longer than the gathering itself. The Philippine, Turkish and Pakistani leaders who all belonged to the Western system of alliances, declared on their return home that 'colonialism in all its manifestations' included Communism, a view-point which was sharply disputed by Chou En-Lai, the brilliant rep-resentative of China. Any remaining illusions concerning the 'spirit of Bandung' were dispelled by the frontier conflict between India and China in 1959, when force was used to achieve a solution in defiance of the Bandung resolution – one of the few that had been accepted without challenge – that disputes between Asian states should be settled by negotiation.

Indonesia's first major initiative in foreign policy thus ended in failure; but it was not many years before her rulers again attempted to bring about an international alliance.

The army and the state

The revolutionary army (TNI) was from the beginning a unique factor in Indonesian politics. Some of its units were actively involved in Tan Malaka's opposition movement in 1946, and others in the Madiun rebellion; but in both cases their action was ineffective, as the bulk of the army stood loyally behind the Republic. The army's proudest hour was after the occupation of Jogjakarta, when it proved by dint of guerrilla warfare that the Republic, though seemingly extinguished, was still in being. That its forces were disciplined troops and not mere 'terrorist bands' was shown by the fact that Colonels Nasution and Simatupang were able to ensure compliance with the armistice terms when the time came for negotiations. The commander-in-chief, General Sudirman, who was already ill at this time, remained among the guerrillas until the Republic was restored, and died in January 1950.

The large force of over 200,000 men was a financial burden to the new state, and in 1950 plans were revived for its 'rationalization', i.e. transforming the mass army into a well-equipped mobile force, and at the same time disbanding many troops who had deserved well of the Republic. As the Madiun affair had shown, this could easily lead to outbreaks of disorder. In April 1952 the delicate task of reorganization was entrusted to Sultan Hamengkubuwono IX, who was Minister for Defence in the newly-formed Wilopo government. The Sultan was widely popular with the TNI, as had been shown at the first meeting of commanders in November 1945; but, as he stood politically close to the 'administrators' and, especially, Sjahrir's PSI, the anti-demobilization cry was soon raised by his opponents from the ranks of the PNI and PRN, Murba, the PKI, and other parties, who regarded themselves as guardians of the ideals of the revolution, and for whom the State was 'only a means', while a mass army inbued with the correct ideology afforded the best guarantee for the completion of the revolution. These circles attacked the Sultan for his contacts with the Dutch military commission which was still in the country, and accused the Masjumi of complicity with the *Dar-ul-Islam* bands, which were fighting for the establishment of a Muslim state. They also won over some senior officers; in July, for instance, Colonel Bambang Supeno approached the President over the heads of his superiors and complained that the Ministry of Defence, under the influence of Sjahrir's PSI, was destroying the revolutionary spirit in the army. The Sultan thereupon dismissed Supeno from his post as director of an officers' school.

Although the Sultan's policy was supported by the two officers of highest rank – Major-General Simatupang, chief of staff of the armed forces, and Colonel Nasution, the army chief of staff – agitation continued in the next few weeks and there were violent debates in Parliament, which on 16 October adopted by a majority of 91 to 54 a resolution introduced by Manai Sophiaan, calling for a Parliamentary committee of investigation into the army and its leaders and the dismissal of the Dutch military mission.[32]

The army leaders were increasingly resentful of Parliament's interference in their affairs. They had observed with bitterness for some years how ministerial posts were made the object of party horse-trading while corruption spread, and the Parliamentarians, who could argue endlessly over trifles, were at one in their determination to whittle down the armed forces. For this Parliament to presume to decide on the organization and future of the army was more than the senior officers could stand. On 17 October, tanks drew up in front of the President's palace, and a group of officers, including Simatupang and Nasution, went to Sukarno and demanded that he dissolve Parliament. Some of them urged that a directorate be set up, consisting of Sukarno, Hatta, and the Sultan, which should exercise power in agreement with the army.[33]

Sukarno was no friend to the Parliamentary system, but from his point of view the attack on it came from the wrong direction. His intervention was being demanded, not by those who wished to continue the revolution, but by 'administrators' and PSI sympathizers, to whom he had no intention of surrendering. The storm passed over; Nasution took responsibility for the incident and left the service. But repercussions continued. Ali Sastroamidjojo's government tried to exploit the dissension in the army between those who approved and disapproved on the '17 October affair'. The latter were promoted; for instance, Colonel Zulkifli Lubis became deputy to the acting army chief of staff, Bambang Sugeng. Those who had taken part in the coup were isolated; Simatupang was retired at 34 on the ground that the post of chief of staff of the armed forces was being abolished.

In February 1955 a temporary reconciliation took place within the army,[34] when a solemn vow of unity was proclaimed over the graves of Generals Sudirman and Urip Sumodihardjo. The PNI government discovered the consequences of the new spirit when, ignoring military seniority, they attempted to instal Bambang Utojo as army chief of staff in place of Bambang Sugeng. The government's former tool, Zulkifli Lubis, organized a boycott of the installation ceremony on 27 June: he was unanimously supported by the provincial commanders, and the cabinet was forced to resign. In this way, Parliament finally lost control over the army, which became an independent factor of increasing importance.

Internal security: the Darul Islam movement

All these issues, far-reaching as their consequences were to be for the Indonesian state, were overshadowed during its early years by the problem of internal security. In the revolutionary period, bands composed of semi-military units terrorized the rural population, and occasionally ventured into the towns. The greatest threat to security came from the Darul Islam movement for the creation of a Muslim state. Its leader, S. M. Kartosuwirjo, proclaimed the existence of such a state on 7 August 1949 at the *desa* Tjisampah, West Java.

Kartosuwirjo was born in East Java in 1905, and studied medicine at Surabaja, but did not finish the course. He joined Sarekat Islam in 1927, and became its vice-chairman in 1936. At this time he already had a reputation for extreme intransigence, and stood out to the last for a policy of non-cooperation with the Dutch. During the occupation his chief links were with the paramilitary Masjumi units, Hizbullah and the later Sabilillah. After the war he and Natsir founded the new Masjumi, and he became the party's commissar in West Java, where after the Renville Agreement he set about laying the foundations for an Islamic state. He formed units of the irregular Muslim forces into an 'Indonesian Muslim army' (Tentara Islam Indonesia) concentrated around *desa* Tjisampah, which he called the 'Indonesian Medina', and from which they carried out terroristic operations first against the Dutch and later against the Republic. Up till 1955 these accounted in each year for over a thousand deaths, and during the same period there were hundreds of thousands of incidents involving plundering and robbery with violence.[35]

From 1950 onwards the movement also attracted followers in south Sulawesi, where Lieutenant-Colonel Kahar Muzakar, who was in charge of government operations against Soumokil, rebelled on account of the proposed disbandment of his troops under the 'rationalization' programme. At the beginning of 1952 he placed himself under the orders of the 'Imam' Kartosuwirjo, as commander in south Sulawesi, and on 7 August 1953 he proclaimed 'Sulawesi and adjacent territories' to be a part of the Islamic state.[36] Finally, as had been feared for some time, disturbances broke out again in Atjeh: in September 1953, on the orders of Daud Beureueh, government posts were attacked in order to 'free Atjeh from the *pantja sila* régime'. Daud Beureueh, a native Atjehnese born about 1900, was a person of influence and, since the end of colonial times, had been head of the central organization of the *ulamas* of Atjeh (PUSA).[37] The hostility between the *ulamas* and the secular *uleebalangs*, of which we have already spoken, broke out afresh when it became clear that the latter favoured the return of the Dutch. The Republic adopted a cautious policy towards Atjeh, and tried to secure the co-operation of Daud Beureueh, who had been a member of the committee of Masjumi and was a member of the Indonesian parliament. But he remained mistrustful, keeping lines out also to Kartosuwirjo, and, after the formation of Ali Sastroamidjojo's government, he openly supported the Islamic state.

Political fronts

The attempt to resolve these and other problems led to the formation of political fronts which had for some time been foreshadowed but, during the revolutionary period, took second place in the interests of national unity. The parliamentary system brought these antagonisms into the light of day: the *pantja sila* ideology which had been devised as a catalyst was now little but an empty formula which everyone interpreted as he felt inclined, so that confusion was increased rather than allayed.[38]

The main division that now came to be felt was that between the 'ideologists' and 'administrators'. The former comprised the bulk of the PNI, the PKI after it became a 'national' party, and the Murba; also, from opposition to the Masjumi, the PSII and sometimes the Nahdatul Ulama (NU). The second category included the Masjumi, PSI, PIR, and the Christian parties. Of the two sections into which the army was divided, the pro- '17 October' group stood close to the administrators and their opponents to the ideologists. However, conflicts within the army were also affected by other important issues, such as 'bapakism', rationalization, and seniority.

The two fronts extended in practice throughout Indonesian society. The first group accused the second of being tools of imperialism and capitalism, supporting foreign investment interests and advocating *laissez-faire*; nor was it forgotten that the Darul Islam bands occasionally received aid from local Masjumi agencies. The 'administrators' retaliated by accusing the ideologists of being enslaved to outworn theories and using the slogans of class hatred to split society; the West Irian campaign was doing more harm than good to the national interest, and the way to achieve progress was by constructive work, and not by the slogans of *murba* and 'marhaenism'.

Neither of the opposing groups had a firm Parliamentary majority, and, as changes of front on specific points were of common occurrence, no stable government was formed during the period in question. Consequently all the major parties looked to the elections, which had been planned for some time past, for a decisive victory which would enable them to pursue their policies independently of doubtful coalitions.

4 THE GENERAL ELECTION OF 1955

Despite the resignation of Ali Sastroamidjojo's government in July 1955, the first general election in Indonesia's history was held as planned in September of that year.[39] The army, which in its attacks on Parliament had made much of the argument that it was not an expression of the people's will but of political calculations, was itself interested in an early election, and did not for the present try to convert the extra-Parliamentary opposition into a permanent feature of the political scene. On the contrary, Nasution, after resigning his position as chief of staff, had set about organizing a party to represent army interests in Parliament: this was the IPKI (Ikatan Pendukung Kemerdekaan Indonesia: League for the Defence of Indonesian Independence), which took part in the pre-election campaign from 1954 onwards.

A general election in which anyone could vote who was over 18 years old (or younger, if married) was a unique event in Indonesian life. In colonial times, elections to the Volksraad or the regency and municipal councils had always been the privilege of a small group whose noble descent, education, or property raised them high above the 'masses'. Now everyone was entitled to vote, and when a register was taken in May 1954 the total of those inscribed was over 43 million. The population of the country had meanwhile risen to 77 million, two-thirds (51 million) of whom lived in Java.

By introducing party symbols and setting up local election committees, the authorities, in theory at least, made sure that even illiterates were able to vote for the party of their choice. In some *desas* a form of rehearsal took place in which the new principle of the secret ballot was applied to elections for the position of *lurah* (village headman), which had in the past been effected mainly by persuasion, promises and so on. The candidates, displaying their symbols, sat round a table for final identification; behind them the election committee dispensed ballots, and alongside were the cubicles and ballot-boxes, inscribed once more with the appropriate symbols, and with names for such as could read them. After all had voted, the village assembled in more or less full strength to participate in the count, and the new *lurah* was thus elected in democratic fashion, though he had probably taken some care in advance to ensure the result.[40]

The Parliamentary election of 29 September 1955 was doubtless not conducted so impeccably throughout Indonesia, and in the remoter *desas* a good *lurah* could certainly predict the outcome in advance. The *lurahs* were often asked for advice and oftener still told the villagers whom to vote for, so that they had considerable influence on the result. In the more densely populated areas, party representatives toured the villages, and did their best to influence the election by promises and even pressure or threats. As election day approached, rumours and supernatural tales were put about by way of intimating what would happen if the villagers made the wrong choice. Tension subsided on the day itself, when it became clear that no dire consequences were taking place. By the time the next election was held – on 15 December, for the constitutent assembly – these psychological terrors had largely faded away, giving place to a worthy sense of being in some measure responsible for one's own destiny.[41]

The results of the parliamentary election confirmed expectations in some respects, as by showing that the PNI, PKI and Nahdatul Ulama were predominantly 'Javanese' organizations: each of them received over 85 per cent of its support in Java, and by far the greater part of this in the centre and east of the island, whereas the Masjumi depended largely on the outer islands, which provided 50 per cent of the votes cast for it. However, there were also surprises: the unexpectedly good showing of NU at the Masjumi's expense; the remarkable advance of the Communists, who till recently had been proscribed throughout the country; the poor performance of the PSI, which had hitherto played such an important part in politics; and the disappearance of the PIR, the *prijajis'* party, which had split in 1954.

Generally speaking, the results of the parliamentary election were borne out by the subsequent election of 15 December, and in the table below we give the results of the latter along with the official figures for the September election, in respect of the parties to which frequent reference has been made.[42]

Table XI   General elections, 1955

Party	Valid votes received (*29 Sept.*)	Per-centage	Seats in new Parlia-ment	Seats in old Parlia-ment	Votes received (*15 Dec.*)[43]
PNI	8,434,653	22·3	57	42	9,070,218
Masjumi	7,903,886	20·9	57	44	7,789,619
NU	6,955,141	18·4	45	8	6,989,333
PKI	6,176,914	16·4	39	17	6,232,512
PSII	1,091,160	2·9	8	4	1,059,922
Parkindo	1,003,325	2·6	8	5	988,810
Partai Katolik	770,740	2·0	6	8	748,591
PSI	753,191	2·0	5	14	695,932
IPKI	541,306	1·4	4	–	544,803
Perti	483,014	1·3	4	1	465,359
PRN	242,125	0·6	2	13	220,652
Partai Buruh	224,167	0·6	2	6	332,047
Murba	199,588	0·5	2	4	248,633
PIR (Wongso-negoro)	178,481	0·5	1	1	162,420
PIR (Hazairin)	114,644	0·3	1	18	101,509
Others	2,712,964	7·3	16	46	–
Total	37,785,299	100·0	257	233	

From the sociological point of view, the election confirmed the influence on the population of political parties and groups ever since the formation of Sarekat Islam, and more particularly since independence, when they had been free to propagate their views. The three prevailing influences were those Sukarno had singled out as early as 1926: Islam, Marxism, and nationalism. They did not, as he had hoped, constitute a united front, but appeared as rival ideologies, or *aliran*, to use Clifford Geertz's term.[44] *Aliran*, the Indonesian word for 'current' or 'tendency', denotes not only the party in question, but also the organizations more or less closely connected with it. All the major parties had peasants' and workers' associations, women's and youth clubs, and a variety of institutions whose link with the parent body was often tenuous. In 1955, the largest *aliran* complex was that surrounding the PKI, together with the central workers' trade union SOBSI (Sentral Organisasi Buruh Seluruh Indonesia), whose chairman, Njono, joined the PKI in 1954. The PKI was further supported by the powerful peasants' front, the BTI (Barisan Tani Indonesia), and controlled the women's and 'national youth' organizations, Gerwani (Gerakan Wanita Indonesia) and Pemuda Rakjat, as well as many other associations which were often merely of a local character. In the same way, the PNI, Masjumi and NU had their respective *alirans*. The competition of the various associations brought about some modification in the traditional social structure of Java, which at the beginning of the century was still fairly clearly divided between the *prijaji*, *abangan* and *santri* civilizations. Thereafter, the first two of these had drawn closer together to resist the new Islamic offensive, while the *santri* community was split by the reforming activities of the Muhammadijah and the opposition of Nahdatul Ulama. Thus the Javanese society of the 1950s might roughly be divided into four groups: on the one hand reformist and orthodox *santri*, on the other the administrative and peasant *abangan*, corresponding in that order to the four major parties, Masjumi–NU and PNI–PKI.

Within the *santri*, the Masjumi drew most of its support from the cities and the NU from the countryside. In the *abangan* community the situation was less clear-cut. The PNI, thanks to its control of the administration, retained a strong influence in rural areas and was in many places regarded as the '*lurah* party'. The PKI had aimed first and foremost at the *kampongs*, the over-populated settlements fringing the cities, but it was now beginning to appeal to the villages over the heads of the *prijajis*, and to make itself the mouthpiece of peasant demands. In this way it became in time a bitter rival of the PNI. This was seen in 1957 in the regional elections in Java, when the PKI gained two million votes from the PNI and became the strongest party in the island.[45]

The most striking political result of the 1955 election was the equilibrium between Muslim and non-Muslim parties. Since the early fifties, local election results had led many to expect that the Muslims would register a substantial increase, but in fact they did so only in the large outer islands of Sumatra, Kalimantan and Sulawesi. The PNI and PKI were dominant in central Java, and in the Lesser Sunda islands such as Bali and Lombok, while in most other regions the balance of strength between Muslims and others was even, a result due in some cases (e.g. north Sumatra, Menado and the Moluccas) to the adherence of Christian parties.[46]

The chief losers in the election were the Masjumi and PSI. Not only was the former outstripped by the PNI as the largest party in the country, but in many places its strength was surpassed by that of the NU, which had broken away from it in 1952. The remarkable success of the NU, which had been regarded three years before as a mere splinter group, meant that the *kijais* and *ulamas* would be more than ever inclined to go their own way independently of the Masjumi. The fate of the PSI, which shrank to a third of its former strength in the new parliament, showed once again that an élite party could not expect mass support in a young state like Indonesia. Another result of the election was that the outer islands returned fewer members to the new parliament than they had in the old, where, after the absorption of the senate and house of representatives of the USI, they had commanded an absolute majority with 132 members. Under the new rule of one deputy per 300,000 inhabitants, their representation was reduced to one-third of the house.

From the historical point of view, this first general election, which up to the time of writing (December 1968) was also the last, marked the end rather than the beginning of parliamentary life in Indonesia. High hopes had been placed in the election, both by the *desa* population which had so far waited in vain for the blessings of independence, and by the party leaders who had hoped at last to place their power on a stable footing and so avoid the bargaining for ministerial posts which had so discredited the parliamentary system. Just as the proclamation of independence and later the transfer of sovereignty had been regarded as the magic formulae that would bring about prosperity and progress, so now the election had been expected to make all things new, and disappointment was expressed more keenly than before when it was found that fresh difficulties had been added to the old problems. Barely a year after the election, Sukarno was once again openly attacking the system, spoke of the need to 'bury' the political parties, and finally put an end to Indonesian parliamentary democracy.

5   THE ROAD TO CONSTITUTIONAL CRISIS

Ali Sastroamidjojo, who in March 1956 formed his second cabinet which was to hold office for twelve months, endeavoured to secure for it the strongest possible backing in the new Parliament. Besides the PNI, he obtained the support of the Masjumi and NU as well as of middle-of-the-road parties. Except for the PKI and PSI, all parties which were among the ten strongest as a result of the election were represented by one or more ministers in the new government. Its failure was not due to opposition within Parliament but to outside events. The first interference came from the President, who disapproved of the fact that the PKI was excluded although it represented 20 per cent of the electorate (this was the figure for Java), and urged Sastroamidjojo to find room for at least one deputy with PKI sympathies. Sukarno's action in thus overstepping his constitutional powers aroused great indignation among the parties; the deputy whom he had nominated was passed over, and in his place Sastroamidjojo appointed an engineer of no party affiliation named Djuanda. The latter was highly thought of by Sukarno, and it was hoped in this way to save the President's face.[47]

In the case of parties like the Masjumi, hostility to Sukarno's interference in the process of cabinet-formation might be due to concern over his 'incipient pro-Communism';[48] but, in general, what caused alarm was the fact that the supreme authority in the State was beginning to disregard the constitution. During 1956, 'extra-legal activity' in general became more and more widespread. In Sulawesi, the smuggling of goods to and from Singapore and other foreign ports, which had for a long time been carried on in secret, now took place openly and with the support of the army. Ships put in to Menado and unloaded lorries, jeeps, machinery and rice in exchange for copra, without Djakarta being officially informed of these independent supply operations. Soon afterwards the same thing happened in North Sumatra, where the military under Colonel Simbolon began trading in coffee and rubber and using the proceeds to satisfy army needs. Simbolon, a Christian Batak from the Lake Toba region, who had received his military training from the Japanese occupying forces in Sumatra, came to Djakarta in July and defended his action, after which a settlement was reached and, at all events officially, the smuggling ceased.

However, Simbolon's activities led to a new stage in the crisis of

the state, in which Djakarta's authority was flouted to a greater
extent than it had been in the case of Menado. In October 1955,
Simbolon had been the army's strongest candidate, on grounds of
seniority and ability, for the post of chief of staff after Bambang
Utojo was retired by the Burhanuddin government. Other prominent
candidates were Zulkifli Lubis and Gatot Subroto. The cabinet
was unable to decide between them, and finally Nasution, who had
resigned in October 1952, let it be known that he was prepared to
serve, whereupon he was promoted Major-General and appointed
to the post.[49]

Nasution's background was as follows. He was born in 1918 at
Tapanuli in the Batak country. He trained as a teacher and followed
that profession in south Sumatra in 1939–40. In 1940–2 he was a
cadet in the officers' academy at Bandung. During the Japanese
occupation he did not join the Peta, but commanded a Barisan
Pelopor unit. After 1945 he served in the TNI, first as commander
of the Third (Preanger) Division and then of the First (Siliwangi)
Division. He was in charge of the guerrilla warfare against the
Dutch, took a leading part in crushing Tan Malaka's attempted
coup in July 1946 and Musso's in September 1948, and was then
army chief of staff until his resignation in 1952.[50] In 1955 he was
better qualified, by experience and knowledge of strategy, than any
of the other three candidates for the post of chief of staff. Since his
resignation he had devoted himself to military studies, and the
tensions within the army had convinced him that the best way to
restore unity was by means of a common ideology. In this respect,
his views were close to Sukarno's; as a devout Muslim, he
was acceptable to the Masjumi; and thus the choice fell on him.
Simbolon and Zulkifli Lubis, however, who also belonged to the
Batak region, felt aggrieved by Nasution's appointment and har-
boured increasing resentment against him, as well as against
Sukarno, for preferring the 'convert' Nasution to his 'insubordinate'
rivals. When, in February 1956, Nasution announced his intention
of appointing new territorial commanders as had been decided at
the Jogjakarta conference a year earlier, the officers raised a protest.
The 'vow of unity' of February 1955 was already past history, and
the army was once again split into two camps: a pro-government
group formed around Nasution and Gatot Subroto, and another in
opposition around Simbolon and Zulkifli Lubis. Their antagonism
was eventually to lead to open civil war.

After Simbolon's challenge to Djakarta over the smuggling affair, Zulkifli Lubis took the initiative. The name of the Foreign Minister, Ruslan Abdulgani, had been mentioned in connection with a case of corruption, and in August 1956, a few hours before he was due to leave for the Suez Canal conference in London, Lubis attempted to have him arrested. Nasution intervened, whereupon the tension grew stronger. Lubis was made to resign as deputy chief of staff and went to West Java, whence he tried several times in the next few weeks to engineer a coup against the government. But his attempts failed, and by the end of the year Nasution had west Java under control.

The Lubis-Simbolon group was not without friends in political circles. The PSI press, more especially, played up suspicions that Ruslan Abdulgani had taken bribes and committed offences against the currency laws, and suggested that the pro-government wing of the army was supporting a 'corrupt régime'. Ruslan Abdulgani – a prominent member of the PNI who had won international respect as the secretary-general of the Bandung conference – was cleared of the suspicion of corruption by a Parliamentary committee of investigation, and Mohtar Lubis, the editor of *Indonesia Raya*, was brought to trial for libel; but in court he produced photostats showing that Ruslan had in fact violated the currency laws by taking abroad funds belonging to a Chinese business man.[51] Trifling as this offence was compared to other scandals connected with export and import licences, it contributed to undermining the government's prestige. By the end of 1956 the party system had been thrown into hopeless discredit by mutual suspicions and further scandals, accompanied by charges of graft, jobbery and intrigue. The cry went up for a 'business cabinet' under Hatta, and Zulkifli Lubis declared that he would only be answerable to a government of this type. Hatta, who was himself indignant at the lowering of the State's prestige,[52] expressed willingness to form such a government if he were given full powers, and, to free his hands, quitted the Vice-Presidency on 1 December. His withdrawal afforded fresh ammunition to the rebels, who claimed that the government's position must be hopeless if Hatta were leaving it.

During the previous month, at a meeting in West Sumatra of officers and veterans, a Banteng (wild buffalo) council had been formed under the chairmanship of Lieutenant-Colonel Ahmad Husein, commander of the West Sumatra regiment, with the object of ensuring that important official posts were filled by capable and responsible persons, who as far as possible, should be natives of the region in question. Simbolon, who was present at the meeting, went from there to Djakarta, where he was ordered to hand over his command in North Sumatra to Lieut.-Col. Gintings. This, however, he had no intention of doing. On his return from Djakarta he called a meeting of officers which discussed a possible breach with the government. On 20 December Husein took over the powers of the civilian governor of West Sumatra, and two days later Simbolon did the same at Medan. Both officers declared that their action had nothing to do with regional separatism: they had acted, as Simbolon put it, 'to improve the situation of the nation and . . . turn over the reins of government to those national leaders who, with honesty and integrity, can develop the nation, free from a lust for power and self-seeking.'[53] In other words, the government should be entrusted to Hatta. The same demand was now heard at Djakarta, especially as South Sumatra and Atjeh threatened to join the Sumatra insurgents. However, Ali Sastroamidjojo's government refused to relinquish power in this hour of danger. The four Masjumi ministers and the representative of IPKI thereupon resigned, while the rump government sought vainly for a solution. By playing on racial jealousy, it was able to bring about Simbolon's exclusion from North Sumatra, and Nasution conferred with him and Husein to persuade them to desist from rebellion. But neither expedient was successful, and the example of the Banteng council was followed elsewhere by men indignant at the exploitation of their rich provinces by Djakarta, where the money leaked away through channels over which there was no control. The election, they felt, had strengthened 'Javanese imperialism', and they no longer had any influence over Parliament: Hatta was the one hope of salvation for the outer provinces. By the middle of February 1957 councils of officers and veterans on the Banteng model had sprung up in Kalimantan, Sulawesi and the Moluccas, demanding radical reform in Djakarta and threatening that otherwise they would take over the government.

In this emergency, everyone looked towards the President. During 1956 Sukarno had travelled extensively in both Western and Eastern countries, and after his return in October he placed himself at the head of those elements that were hostile to the whole of the existing system. He had always been opposed to parliamentary democracy, and he believed the time had now come to lay every misfortune to its charge. On 21 February he proclaimed his *konsepsi*, or saving formula, in the shape of a *gotong rojong* cabinet representing all the main parties – PNI, Masjumi, NU and PKI – and also the new institution of a National Council (Dewan Nasional) to advise the government. Unlike Parliament, which merely reflected party interests, this body would represent the interests of the people themselves. All the 'functional groups' of society – peasants, students women, artists, the military, etc. – were to find a place in it, as well as the regions, and it was to be guided by the *musjawarah* principle, which was better suited to the Indonesian people than 'ballot-box democracy', with its rule that '50 per cent plus 1 is always right'.[54]

As we have seen, *gotong rojong* and *musjawarah* had always played a dominant role in Sukarno's thinking. When he declared later in 1957 that he had not become a Communist but was 'still the Sukarno of 1927',[55] this was not a mere piece of humbug. Party politics were alien to him, because they followed their own laws. *Musjawarah* on the other hand, left room for manipulation, and *mufakat* was based on the principle of persuasion. In other words, they afforded more scope to agitators and popular tribunes to work on the political situation and reduce the parties' authority.

The party leaders understood this all too well, and with the exception of the PNI and PKI, who saw advantages to themselves in the new system, they hesitated to fall in with it. In particular, they jibbed at the idea of a *gotong rojong* cabinet including the Communists, and were not convinced by Sukarno's comparison of a three-party cabinet with a three-legged horse; if it came to horses, it was rather the Trojan variety that they called to mind. The PKI had so far not been included in any cabinet, and was the only party that had gained directly from the wave of hostility to the parliamentary system: there seemed to be no way of stopping its progress, but its claim to a change of political status was strongly resisted not only by the Masjumi, NU and Christian parties, but also by the military. The outer provinces were also not attracted by Sukarno's ideas. On 2 March the commander in east Indonesia, Lieutenant-Colonel Sumual, read a proclamation at Macassar declaring a state of emergency throughout the area and replacing the civilian governors by military officers. His chief of staff read out a further declaration on the 'common struggle' (Perdjuangan Se-mesta), which gave the name Permesta to the whole insurgent movement. This called for each province to have a five-year plan of its own, 'surplus areas' being allowed to keep 70 per cent of their own revenue. On the national plane, the *gotong rojong* cabinet and the proposed National Council should both be headed by Sukarno and Hatta jointly, and the National Council, 70 per cent of whose members should be drawn from the outer provinces, should in course of time be transformed into a senate.[56]

The 'common struggle', or insurrection, of the outer provinces led to the collapse of parliamentary democracy in Indonesia. Ali Sastroamidjojo's cabinet, weakened as it was by the Masjumi and IPKI resignations, was powerless to resolve the conflict and surrendered its mandate on 14 March. The premier's final act was to sign a decree placing the whole country in a state of emergency and martial law. In this way, the army finally abandoned its role of a dissatisfied onlooker, and for the next few years determined the course of politics. In the outer provinces it had, to all intents and purposes, been doing this for some time; and now party political rule was at an end in Java also. It had lasted approximately eight years – or a *windu*, as a self-contained period of this length is termed in traditional Javanese chronology.

VII

THE ERA OF
GUIDED DEMOCRACY, 1957–65

I CIVIL WAR AND THE RETURN TO THE
1945 CONSTITUTION

In the first few weeks after the state of emergency was proclaimed, it was not as yet apparent that Indonesia's short experience of parliamentary democracy was already at an end. The parties showed no loss of self-confidence in the negotiations with Sukarno's nominee as cabinet *formateur* – Suwirjo, the newly-elected chairman of the PNI – who finally resigned his mandate for lack of support. Sukarno, however, was prompt to take advantage of the situation thus created. He ignored both the Masjumi's claim to form a government and the voices raised on behalf of Hatta, and, in his capacity as President, entrusted 'citizen Sukarno', as he put it, with the task of forming an emergency extra-Parliamentary cabinet.[1]

The Masjumi, PSI and Partai Katolik, who had already expressed strong opposition to the *konsepsi*, regarded Sukarno's action as illegal, and refused to join in the formation of his 'business cabinet' (*kabinet karja*). Sukarno ignored their protest and in April 1957 appointed a government headed by the non-party Djuanda, who had distinguished himself in the revolutionary period by his efficiency and knowledge of affairs, and was respected for his integrity by most of the parties.[2] The deputy Prime Ministers were Hardi (PNI), Idham Chalid (NU) and Leimena (Parkindo). However, from this time on party affiliations played only a secondary role. Two Masjumi ministers retained their posts even after they had been expelled from the party, while important portfolios went to individuals who had played little part in party politics. Dr. Subandrio who had represented Indonesia as ambassador in London and from 1954 onwards in Moscow, became Minister of Foreign Affairs; the Minister for Culture was Professor Prijono of the Murba party, who had received a Stalin prize in 1954 for his work in the Indo-nesian Committee for Peace and in recognition of the pro-Soviet attitude he had displayed from time to time. Even the *pemudas* of 1945 were represented, in the person of Chairul Saleh, who had recently become a supporter of Sukarno's ideas, although, since the transfer of sovereignty, he had accused the Republican leaders of betraying the ideals of independence.

Although Djuanda declared that the government regarded itself as responsible to Parliament in the same way as in the past, it soon became clear that the latter's authority was decisively reduced. In the new era power resided with the President, the army and, as events were to show, the PKI. In May the President passed an emergency law appointing the new National Council; the army, under the state of emergency, assumed control of the provinces, and in June–August, in the last free elections held up to the present time in the provinces of Java, the Communists made such gains that the other parties began to speak of the need for a united anti-Communist front. The following table shows the results of the provincial elections for the four main parties (the figures in brackets give the results for the same area in the election of September 1955).[3]

Table XII   Java provincial elections, June–August 1957

	Djakarta	West Java	Central Java	East Java
Masjumi	153,709	1,841,030	833,707	977,443
	(200,460)	(1,844,442)	(902,387)	(1,109,742)
PNI	124,955	1,055,801	2,400,282	1,899,782
	(152,031)	(1,541,927)	(3,019,568)	(2,257,069)
NU	104,892	597,356	1,865,568	2,999,785
	(120,667)	(673,552)	(1,772,306)	(3,370,554)
PKI	137,305	1,087,269	3,005,150	2,704,523
	(96,363)	(755,634)	(2,326,108)	(2,299,785)

The PKI, whose new strategy had thus, in the space of five years, brought it to the head of all the parties in Java, continued to hold fast to the principle of collaboration with the President. It organized demonstrations in favour of his *konsepsi*, put pressure on members of other parties who rejected it, and took the lead in the 'new life movement' founded during these months, the object of which was to arouse mass support for Indonesia's claim to West Irian, and secure a hearing for it in the United Nations.

The PKI was a more reliable ally for Sukarno than the PNI, whose internal dissensions were accentuated by the electoral defeat. An increasingly strong trend of opinion in the PNI, headed by Hadisubeno, the mayor of Semarang, was in favour of a clear-cut breach with the PKI; this group represented the viewpoint of the national bourgeoisie, which had hitherto been courted by the PKI but now saw its vital interests threatened. The rightward swing of the PNI caused it to be accused of deviating from marhaenism; and the situation was not finally clarified by the splitting-off, in July 1958, of a left wing known as the new Partindo,[4] which at once became involved in ideological quarrels with the PNI, as its sister party had in 1931 with the PNI headed by Sjahrir. Since the PNI was founded in July 1927, it had tried to be all things to all men, and the continuance of tension was now assured by the existence of the right wing under Hadisubeno and Hardi and the formation of a new left wing under Sukarno's old comrades, Surachman and Ali Sastroamidjojo.

The two Muslim parties had also suffered considerably in the election, and their differences for the time being took second place to the need to defend Islam against the rising threat of the PKI. The general situation was a tense one, since the Banteng councils in the outer islands regarded the PKI's success in Java as proof that their challenge to Djakarta was justified. At first it seemed that the National Council, which held its first session in July, might bring some alleviation. Sukarno kept for himself the chairmanship of this body, but the conduct of day-to-day affairs was in the hands of Ruslan Abdulgani, who in the coming months and years assumed the role of chief ideologist of the new policy. The council enjoyed considerable prestige among the public; and among its forty-two members were the chiefs of staff of the army, navy, air force and police (each of these being now an independent body), such dignitaries as the deputy Prime Ministers and the public prosecutor, eminent representatives of the 'functional groups' such as women's associations, artists, religious bodies, journalists, veterans and regional spokesmen.[5] The council was regarded by many as the future senate, and in conformity with the pattern it presented, a general period of *musjawarah*, or free discussion, set in. Delegates from the rebel military commands held conversations with the staff in Djakarta, and officially antagonistic parties such as the Masjumi and PKI discussed the future political shape of the country in the constituent assembly at Bandung, set up in accordance with the election of December 1955. Even Sukarno and Hatta, the estranged members of the erstwhile 'duumvirate' (*dwitunggal*), held a meeting at which they reasserted their adherence to the *pantja sila*, the value of which was increasingly decried by the parties pursuing their respective ideologies.

Nevertheless, as has often been the case in recent Indonesian history, the *musjawarah* brought no clarification of the position. In loyal military circles, protests were raised at the conciliatory attitude adopted towards the dissidents in Sumatra and Sulawesi: among those who thus objected was Colonel Suharto, the Central Java commander, who had not previously taken part in politics, but now pressed for a showdown.[6] In party circles, even the general fear of the PKI's advance did not lead to the formation of any permanent links between anti-Communist organizations. The PKI at this time even made itself the advocate, of the *pantja sila*, which Mohammed Natsir, for example, criticized in November 1957 as an abstract conception devoid of religious content.[7] Meanwhile, the conflict between Sukarno and Hatta remained insoluble.

The dissidents' expressions of sympathy for Hatta placed him in an awkward position. His faith in the efficacy of the parliamentary system for Indonesia had begun to waver; in a lecture to the Universitas Indonesia in June 1957 he declared that there were situations in which a dictatorship was inevitable, though it could only achieve its purpose if it took strict account of society's needs, and was exercised by a man 'of high moral integrity, with the courage to act and assume responsibility, and with an exceptional talent for planning and organization'.[8] This made it clear to all concerned that Hatta did not regard Sukarno as a suitable candidate, since his integrity and powers of organization were generally challenged, either openly or in secret. Hatta himself, the only person who might have filled the bill, had no effective support. He was a declared enemy of the PKI, and the fact that he was popular in the outer islands savoured, at that time, more of treason than anything else.

Thus, in spite of the *musjawarah*, the political fronts became more rather than less sharply divided. Professor Sumitro Djojohadi-kusumo, the PSI's brilliant economics expert, joined the Banteng council in West Sumatra in May 1957 because he felt threatened in Djakarta. Other leading 'administrators' followed suit at the end of the year, being afraid to remain in Java owing to the excesses of the mob stirred up by the PKI. The crisis was already acute when, on 29 November, a motion in the UN Assembly, calling on the Dutch to resume negotiations with Indonesia on the future of West Irian, failed to obtain the necessary two-thirds majority. This gave the signal for outbreaks of violence in the country, which culminated in civil war. On the day after the rebuff in the UN, an attempt was made on Sukarno's life as he was leaving an exhibition at the Tjikini school, at which his children were pupils. Hand grenades thrown into the crowd of spectators killed eleven and wounded over fifty, including many children; Sukarno narrowly escaped.[9] When the suspects were interrogated it came to light that the attempt was perpetrated by adherents of Colonel Zulkifli Lubis. Two days afterwards, acts of robbery and violence began to be committed against the Dutch nationals who were still living in the country. Expropriations of factories and plantations followed, and on 5 December the Ministry of Justice announced the expulsion of 45,000 Dutch residents. The parties protested against the excesses, which were clearly inspired by the authorities; Hatta, the Christian parties, the Masjumi and PSI attacked the government, with the result that they themselves were rated as public enemies and inculpated in the attempt on Sukarno's life. In particular, the Masjumi leaders Mohammed Natsir, Sjafruddin Prawiranegara and Burhanuddin Harahap, fearing for their lives in Djakarta, left the capital at the beginning of January 1958, and placed themselves under the protection of the Banteng council in West Sumatra.

In the meantime, Husein and the other Permesta commanders had repeatedly announced their 'expectations' of the Djakarta régime, the main demands being that Hatta should be included in the government, Nasution and his staff dismissed, and Communism declared illegal. The three Masjumi leaders, on their arrival in West Sumatra, held a discussion with the military commander on the form of an ultimatum to Djakarta. Subsequently, Nasution once again toured Sulawesi and Sumatra in the hope of ensuring the loyalty of those commanders who were still neutral. The crunch came on 10 February, when Padang presented its ultimatum in the following terms: the Djuanda cabinet must resign within five days, Hatta and the Sultan (Hamengkubuwono IX) being designated as the *formateurs* of a new government; Parliament must permit this government to remain in office until fresh elections were held, and Sukarno must for the future confine his activity within constitutional limits.

Sukarno was at this time on holiday in Japan, and was not expected back till 16 February, a fact of which the rebel ultimatum took account. In his absence, the Djakarta cabinet rejected the rebels' terms, dismissed from the army several colonels, including Husein, Lubis, Simbolon and Sumual, and gave orders for their arrest. But the rebels felt strong enough to take the final step, and on the expiry of the ultimatum on 15 February they proclaimed at Padang the Pemerintah Revolusioner Republik Indonesia (Revolutionary Government of the Republic of Indonesia: PRRI), headed by Sjafruddin Prawiranegara, who barely ten years before had set up an emergency government in Sumatra in the name of the Republic instead of, as now, against it. Among the ministers were Simbolon, Burhanuddin Harahap and Dr. Sumitro Djojohadikusumo; another member of the revolutionary group was Assaat, a prominent figure of the early years of independence, who had been acting President of the Republic in the days of USI, and was for a long time chairman of the working committee of the KNIP. On 17 February Somba, the North Sulawesi commander, also declared for the PRRI. It was the most critical moment for the Republic, since the transfer of sovereignty.[10]

The revolutionaries had reason to hope that the Djakarta régime would be unable to reach early agreement on counter-measures. Many adherents of parliamentary democracy might be expected to sympathize with the revolt, and if the government did decide on armed action, a long period of indecisive guerrilla warfare might ensue, such as had been waged for the past decade against Darul Islam. The rebels also hoped for early recognition by the Western world, whose fears of a Communist take-over in Indonesia had been raised to an acute pitch by recent events. In the first few days encouraging statements were in fact made by John Foster Dulles, the US Secretary of state, and arms were shipped to Sumatra from the Western hemisphere. Despite these favourable omens, the rebels' expectations proved false in one decisive respect: the Djakarta government and the army under Nasution were prepared at once to take up the challenge, and by their skill and promptitude had so mastered the situation within a few weeks that the revolt failed to spread as had been feared, and the revolutionary régime was thus doomed to failure.

On 22 February Nasution summoned the army officers to a conference, at which he made a speech indicating clearly that the revolt in Padang went beyond what could be tolerated. He traced the course of events which had led to the revolutionary régime being set up, and dwelt at length on the attempts at reconciliation in the previous year. The government's attitude had been tolerant, and they had even offered a general amnesty to the Permesta Commanders. Some officers might sympathize with Padang's demands, but the rebels' methods were inadmissible, and any who thought otherwise should resign their commissions: from now on, absolute discipline would be demanded.[11] In March the fighting began. In April government troops landed at Padang, which they captured almost unopposed. Bukit Tinggi, the last important town in West Sumatra, fell at the beginning of May, after which the rebel units withdrew into the jungle. In June the PRRI strongholds in north Sulawesi fell into government hands, and the civil war was virtually at an end, the guerrilla activities which lasted some time longer presenting no threat to the government.[12]

It was as though a heavy storm, which had long been gathering on the political horizon, had at last broken and dissipated itself. The event was decisive for Nasution, who had acquitted himself brilliantly as chief of staff, and Sukarno, who saw the way clear to put his plans into action. Everyone could now see, he declared in a speech on 17 August 1958, who were the true leaders of the people, and who the puppets of foreign powers and traitors to the Revolution and its ideals. For the first time, he criticized the slowness of the constituent assembly which had been sitting in Bandung since November 1956. The Indonesian people were fighting to complete the work of the Revolution: the constitution must be a weapon in this fight, and the assembly should not boggle over legalistic scruples, but adapt itself to the needs of the time. The fight could not be stayed. 'It will continue, it will pass over your heads, if you refuse to accept its spirit and the need for haste.' In particular, Sukarno called for the reduction of the 'ultra-multi party system', the revocation of the appeal of November 1945 for the formation of parties, and the introduction of 'guided democracy'. He added a threat. After having crushed the PRRI revolt, the army was determined to prevent a return to earlier conditions, including political excesses, horse-trading for seats in the cabinet, and playing politics with economic questions.[13]

Until the suppression of the PRRI rebellion, scarcely any indication had been given of the exact nature of 'guided democracy', which had been preached as a substitute for the parliamentary kind since the end of 1956. However, hints were dropped from an early stage of a return to the 1945 constitution. Thus, in May 1957 Ruslan Abdulgani, who at that time was very much in Sukarno's confidence, declared in the constituent assembly that they should try to bring the debates to an early conclusion by giving due weight to the basic ideas of the old constitution.[14] After the victory over the PRRI this theme was taken up by Nasution, who, he said, had never quite understood why the 1945 constitution had been abrogated; it provided for strong leadership, and also for the participation of the army in state affairs, e.g. as one of the 'functional groups' which, under its provisions, were to be represented both in Parliament and in the people's congress. Since the suppression of the revolution, it was not difficult for Nasution to claim 'functional' status for the army alongside religious and professional groups, regions, etc. A year earlier, at the time of the national *musjawarah*, the rule had been that officers who wanted to take part in politics had to leave the army. It was now decided that in the new Parliament 35 seats should be allotted to the army out of about 260.[15]

Meanwhile, the constitutional discussion had spread from the assembly to other bodies, such as the national council under Ruslan Abdulgani, Djuanda's cabinet and, after the beginning of 1959, a number of seminars and open discussions held under Sukarno's auspices with parties other than the Masjumi and PSI. In all these debates, a return to the 1945 constitution was advocated more and more frequently as the best solution. A formal proposal to this effect was finally made on 30 January 1959 by IPKI, which stood close to the army. The PNI and PKI were expected to support it in the constituent assembly, while Masjumi, PSI and the Christian parties would probably vote against. The NU was in a decisive position, since its votes would be needed for the necessary two-thirds majority; but the government felt confident of its support, as it possessed evidence on which charges of corruption could be levelled against certain NU leaders. On 19 February the government accordingly decided officially to propose to the constituent assembly the reintroduction of the 1945 constitution,[16] and on 22 April Sukarno made a speech to that body giving reasons for the proposal. Referring, in terms that soon became proverbial, to the 'message of the people's suffering' (*amanat penderitaan rakjat*, or *ampera*), he enlarged on the necessity of finding a suitable political system for the country. It was no use seeking it in textbooks. Montesquieu, Jefferson and Engels had not been concerned with finding solutions for Indonesia. Following their teachings had led to nothing but antagonism: between popular leaders and governments, between those who believed the Revolution to be at an end and those who did not, between those who thought that democracy existed for the people's sake and those who thought the opposite, between advocates of socialism and those of liberal capitalism. All these antagonisms stood in the way of progress, and could only be removed by the 1945 constitution, of which he gave an exhaustive analysis.[17]

Next day Sukarno set off on a world tour, as had by now become his annual custom, expecting that on his return the Presidential constitution would have been readopted by legal means, and that an overwhelming majority of the people would empower him to assume the management of its affairs. But matters turned out otherwise. During his absence the Masjumi succeeded, by playing up the question of Islamic interests, in dissuading the Nahdatul Ulama from voting for the government proposal as it had intended. In an attempt to conciliate the Muslim community, the government had proclaimed its assent to the 'Djakarta charter' of June 1945, which obligated Indonesian Muslims to conform to Islamic law. But the *kijais* and *ulamas* were no more satisfied on this occasion than they had been, over fourteen years earlier, in the constitutional discussions in the BPKI, when they held this compromise formula to be an insufficient safeguard of Muslim interests. Further concessions to the Muslims, on the other hand, were opposed by PNI, PKI, the Christians and the smaller nationalist parties.

When the vote was taken at the end of May and beginning of June, after three attempts it proved impossible to attain anything like the necessary two-thirds majority.[18] Nasution thereupon, under martial law which was still in force, prohibited all political activities, and urged that Sukarno should promulgate the 1945 constitution by means of a decree. This alternative had been discussed before the vote, and would have been acceptable not only to the PNI and PKI but now also to the NU. Having done their duty by standing up for Islam in the assembly, the *kijais* might hope, by supporting the decree, to secure a seat in the cabinet and thus, as Daniel Lev puts it, 'have the best of both worlds'.[19]

Despite the tense situation at home, Sukarno did not cut short his world tour. When he returned at the end of June, he was pressed from every side to issue the decree; but, not content with the unanimous advice of the cabinet, the national council and the army leaders, after conferring with his ministerial staff on 4 July, he insisted on obtaining by telephone the agreement of Nahdatul Ulama and the Partai Katolik.[20] As in the case of the proclamation of independence in 1945, he showed a curious irresolution when it came to finalizing a development which he himself had done most to bring about.

The decree dissolving the constituent assembly and restoring the 1945 constitution – its institutions would be established at an early date – was proclaimed at 5 p.m. on 5 July 1959. It was couched in the style of an old-time imperial edict: 'With the blessing of Almighty God, We, the President and Commander-in-Chief of the armed forces . . .', and so on. The latter of these attributes outweighed the opposition of two hundred elected representatives of the people, over whose heads the measure was enacted, as Sukarno had threatened almost a year earlier.

2 THE IDEOLOGY OF GUIDED DEMOCRACY.
PROGRAMMES, SLOGANS, AND ADJURATIONS

In the early hours of 17 August 1959, cars equipped with loudspeakers patrolled the *kampongs* and outskirts of Djakarta, summoning the people to the palace to hear the President's great speech on this national holiday. Workers, tradesmen, coolies and pedicab drivers emerged from their homes, some of which were tumbledown huts, and flocked to the huge Merdeka Square in front of the great white palace that shone like an island of promise amid the poverty that crept up to its very walls. Party delegations and youth groups, bands of schoolchildren and columns of troops marched up from all directions; there were flags, banners and portraits – in short, the usual picture of independence celebrations, though this year expectations were greater, as a change for the better seemed at last to be in sight.

Sukarno's speech was concerned with the 'rediscovery' of the Revolution.[21] As usual, he began with a review of the past, which he divided into periods: that of 'physical revolution' (1945–50), that of 'survival' (1950–5), and finally that of reorganization, which had culminated in the return to the 1945 constitution, a measure that the experience of liberalism had shown to be necessary. Once again he emphasized the antagonisms for which guided democracy was to provide a cure. He compared the path trodden by the Indonesian people with Dante's journey from the Inferno to Paradise. The present stage was one of purification, of casting out the ten devils whom the country knew only too well: individualism, liberalism, federalism, the selfishness of races and groups, deviationists and adventurers, corruption, rebellion and the domination of parties. The time had come to return to Indonesia's old ways of *musjawarah* and *mufakat*, with leadership exercised by older persons who would not dictate but guide, as had been the practice in all the indigenous Asian democracies.

The most important task was that of 'retooling', or reorganization – a general shake-up in every sphere that had been affected by the 'poison of liberalism'. 'Understand this,' Sukarno cried. 'Everything must be retooled, turned inside out, and set to rights – and this work has already begun.' Parliamentary institutions and the party system, the armed forces, and all other bodies and associations must once more become instruments of the revolution, to enable it to fulfil its old aims of social justice and welfare. The new government had set itself three main objectives: to provide the population with food and clothing (*sandang-pangan*), to restore public security, and to continue the fight against political and economic imperialism. These were the first steps towards making Indonesian socialism a reality. The whole people must help the government in its task, and therefore, besides the parties which were willing to co-operate, popular representatives were to be appointed to the functional groups. A national planning council had already been set up to work out a detailed economic plan, and a national front would be formed to aid in the completion of the revolution. Its main tasks were to be:

1 To establish a democratic unitary state from Sabang of north Sumatra to Merauke in West Irian.
2 To build a social order based on justice and prosperity, both in the material sphere and in things of the mind.
3 To promote friendly relations between Indonesia and all states in the world, especially those of Asia and Africa, so as to bring about a new world free from imperialism and colonialism.

Sukarno went on to announce that in future foreign enterprises would only be tolerated in Indonesia if they conformed to the government's orders: from now on, no foreigner had any rights over Indonesian soil. He also threw down the gauntlet to cultural imperialism. The government would make it its business to foster a national culture which would truly reflect the Indonesian way of life. The revolution was a complex process, involving simultaneous action in many spheres. Success would not come overnight; the difficulties would take time to overcome, but the country was now back on the path from which it had strayed. He concluded by invoking the threefold aim which he had formulated during the fight for independence. The national spirit must be set aflame in order to forge the national will which would assert itself in national deeds. Only so could obstacles to progress be removed and the revolution completed.

In essence, Sukarno's speech contained no new ideas: there was nothing in it that he had not been preaching for years and decades past. His thinking had remained static or, if the term be preferred, consistent. The state, the constitution, parties, tradition and culture – all these were only means towards the realization of his revolutionary dreams, which he boldly identified with those of the whole people. At this time he made the boastful remark: 'Why is it that the masses beg me to speak to them? Because they want to hear their own thoughts, which they cannot yet formulate themselves.'[22]

In September the Supreme Advisory Council (Dewan Pertimbangan Agung), as the National Council of 1957 was now called, resolved to adopt Sukarno's speech of 17 August as the official programme of the revolution under the title Manipol (political manifesto). Since the speech which had thus become so important had lasted at least two hours and it was difficult for the public to remember all its points, Sukarno was asked to summarize them, which he did at a youth congress at Bandung in the following terms:

Undang Undang Dasar 1945 (the 1945 constitution)
Sosialisme Indonesia (Indonesian socialism)
Demokrasi terpimpin (guided democracy)
Ekonomi terpimpin (guided economy)
Kepribadian Indonesia (Indonesian identity)

From these five principles a West Javanese politician coined the word usdek, and thus the formula 'Manipol-Usdek' was born. Its chief interpreter was Ruslan Abdulgani, who later declared that it 'flew on the wings of Garuda (the legendary bird and national emblem) from village to village, and from city to city, over mountains, rivers, and seas throughout the archipelago, where it entered the hearts of all our people'.[23] Manipol-Usdek thus joined the *pantja sila*, which were restored to honour with the reintroduction of the 1945 constitution; and year by year fresh slogans were coined, generally in the form of sonorous abbreviations of the titles of Sukarno's national day speeches, for example:

1960, Djarek (*Djalan Revolusi Kita*: the path of our revolution)
1961, Resopim (*Revolusi, Sosialisme, Pimpinan*: revolution, socialism, leadership)
1964, Trisakti Tavip (the 'three principles', in the year of 'dangerous living')
1965, Berdikari (*Berdiri diatas kaki sendiri*: standing on one's own feet)

All these coinages were in fact repetitions of Manipol-Usdek and paraphrases of the *pantja sila*. The 'three principles' of 1964 consisted of political, economic and cultural independence, and the slogan was thus identical with that of 1965.[24] The most important slogan, however, was 'Nasakom', the title of the national front which had been officially talked of since 1957, and was at last formed in January 1961 by the ten parties that were then still legal (see below). Nasakom represented the initial syllables of the words for nationalism, religion (*agama*) and Communism. This was a revival of the idea Sukarno had put forward in his series of articles in 1926, that the nationalists, Muslims, and other religious groups should combine with the Marxists in a united front to complete the revolution in the spirit of *gotong rojong*, or mutual help.

The history of the independence movement, and especially that of the Republic, had shown that ideological differences tended to deepen rather than bridge the gulf between the respective *aliran*. It had been hoped in 1945 that the *pantja sila* would overcome this tendency; but it had become clear from the time of the constituent assembly's debates that neither the Muslims nor the Communists embraced the 'five principles' for their own sake, but only as a cover for the pursuit of sectional ends. Nevertheless, Sukarno still maintained his faith in the magic formula, which he extolled in 1958 as the 'static basis' or true image of social conditions and the 'dynamic lodestar' for the achievement of socialism.[25] The logical consequence of the *pantja sila*, it was now proclaimed, was the uniting of all revolutionary forces, whether nationalist, religious or Marxist. It was wrong to suppose that the proletariat was the only revolutionary class. The whole of Indonesian society had been exploited by imperialism: peasants and workers, traders and employees, scholars, and pedicab drivers had all experienced the process of degradation at first hand, and were, by the same token, anti-imperialistic and revolutionary, for 'anyone is a revolutionary who fights imperialism'. The uniting of revolutionary forces was, for Sukarno, identical with the union of Communist, religious and nationalistic elements, which he himself had claimed to embody as far back as 1941. Now as in 1926, he held that Marxism, being historical materialism, had nothing to do with philosophical materialism. Now as then, he believed in God as the creator of the world: God had existed for ever, though men's ideas about Him might change.[26]

Sukarno put forward such thoughts as these not only at courses for those trained to interpret the *pantja sila*, but also in discussion with the parties. Thus, at the sixth PKI congress in September 1959, he declared that he rejected philosophical materialism but accepted historical materialism. His personal philosophy was a mixture of nationalism, Islam and Marxism, and if the Communists doubted the possibility of this, they should remember their historical materialism, since he himself was a product of history. Furthermore, they should respect the fact that nationalism and religion were living forces in Indonesia. Anyone who denied this could not be a Communist, since he would be shutting his eyes to objective facts.[27]

In the same way as Sukarno used Marxist texts to win over the PKI to join the national front, he approached the Nahdatul Ulama with quotations from the Koran and Hadith, the foundations of the Islamic faith, on which Tjokroaminoto had once based his arguments in favour of socialism.[28] With his old comrades on the nationalist front, he had least difficulty from the ideological point of view in gaining support for the united front, except in so far as he had to warn them against 'rightist deviation'. In July 1960 he complained of a wave of anti-Communism, and took issue with the view that the PNI was a party of the centre. Anyone who believed in marhaenism was *ipso facto* a man of the left: 'Take care', he adjured them, 'that you do not abandon the leftward path.'[29]

As an institution, Nasakom never attained any great importance.

Despite Sukarno's persuasion, the parties never genuinely collaborated with one another, and the five-point programme announced in 1963 as a kind of revolutionary gymnastic for the '20 million members' of the united front was as empty and meaningless as the front itself.[30] But the idea of Nasakom was to play an important part in the next few years. It was advocated indefatigably by the PKI, which saw in the slogan 'Nasakom in all fields' a chance of improving its position and, above all, securing ministerial office.

Like the *pantja sila*, Manipol-Usdek, Djarek, Resopim, and the rest, Nasakom was an important component of the process known as *indoktrinasi*. The task of reviving the revolutionary spirit was entrusted to a special committee under Ruslan Abdulgani, the vice-chairman of the national council. After the sudden death of Muhammad Yamin in November 1962, Ruslan took his place as Minister of Information, and thus possessed the means to carry on a national campaign of indoctrination with a zeal reminiscent of Dr. Goebbels. Ruslan, however, was a man of a different stamp. While eloquent and a shrewd manipulator of effects, he was not, like the Nazi demagogue, imbued with contempt for his fellow-men: he was a friend to everyone and believed in the truth of what he preached. Armed with the *pantja sila*, Manipol, and so on, he travelled from meeting to meeting and from island to island, visiting the jungle dwellers of South Borneo and the West Irian Papuans. He addressed students and professors, journalists, diplomats and soldiers, party and religious groups, proclaiming the importance of the Indonesian revolution, not only to the nation itself, but to the whole world. In a speech on the holiday commemorating the birth of the Prophet, he expressed his ideas as follows. Standing with a pointer in front of two maps, one of the world and one of Indonesia, he explained that, towards the end of the Roman era, the civilized world around the Mediterranean was divided into two powerful and hostile blocs, consisting of the Roman (Byzantine) and the Persian empires. War between the two was inevitable, but in this situation Allah revealed His message of salvation to the Prophet in the obscure desert country of Arabia, and thus started Islam on its incomparable career of victory. Since those days, fresh antagonisms had arisen in the world, culminating in the modern rivalry between East and West and the irreconcilable opposition between the adherents of liberalism and those of the Communist manifesto. In this situation and in the unknown land of Indonesia, 'Bung' (comrade) Karno, as Sukarno was familiarly called, had been inspired to formulate the *pantja sila*, which pointed the way to a new happy future for mankind, and by obedience to which all conflicts in the contemporary world could speedily be resolved.[31]

The theme of Indonesia's message of salvation was proclaimed to the world by Sukarno in a speech to the United Nations in New York on 30 September 1960, when he assured the fellow-delegates that the only way to put a stop to the cold war was to embody the *pantja sila* in the UN Charter. It was the 'five principles', he emphasized, which guaranteed the success of the Indonesian example of peaceful co-existence between Communists and the adherents of various religions, affirming, as they did belief, in God and in social justice.[32] In his eyes they were the coping-stone of all revolutionary programmes and, as he also said at this time, made good the deficiencies of the Declaration of Human Rights, which ignored social justice, and the Communist manifesto, which ignored belief in God. Only the *pantja sila* provided a comprehensive statement of human ideals.[33]

The same facile optimism, which events had so far done nothing to justify, pervaded the eight-year plan put forward in 1960. Soon after the issue of the constitutional decree, Sukarno had set up a national planning commission, which held its first meeting on 28 August 1959. Its chairman, Professor Muhammad Yamin, was a West Sumatran who had come to school in Java at an early age and had become a leader of the youth movement Indonesia Muda. After completing his law studies, he joined Partindo and Gerindo, and during the occupation he served in the Japanese propaganda department. Towards the end of the war he was a member of the committees concerned with preparing for independence, in which he made long speeches of doubtful historical accuracy extolling the greatness of Indonesia's past. Later he became a follower of Tan Malaka, whom he proclaimed in a short biography to be greater than Plato or George Washington. In short, both Yamin's historical disquisitions and his political activity had about them a streak of exaggeration which hardly marked him out as the ideal chairman of an economic planning commission. But, like most other members of the Dewan Perantjang Nasional (or Depernas), he had been appointed not so much for his professional expertise as for his determination to 'complete' the revolution. This was the grave error of Sukarno, who, tired of the 'administrators' with their everlasting criticism, began to seek collaborators who could build castles in the air and, at all events on paper, bring his ideas to rapid and impressive fulfilment. In a speech to the commission, he warned it not to follow the example of the constituent assembly but to lead the country, as soon as might be, out of the Inferno into Paradise. Its planning was to embrace every domain – not only economics but culture, attitudes to life and so on – and he presented the delegates with an exhaustive programme containing suggestions for increasing production, improving distribution, solving the land question, etc.[34]

The plan, which was duly compiled by the appointed date of 17 August 1960, was divided into two sets of projects, A and B. The former, of which there were 355 in all (under the headings of culture, education and research, food and clothing, industry, pharmacy, distribution, social welfare, administration and defence), were regarded as objectives to be financed by the state's principal sources of revenue as enumerated under B, viz. oil, tin, rubber, copra, timber, aluminium, fisheries and tourism. Many of the ideas in the plan were divorced from reality: for example, the B projects, which were expected to yield 2,500 million US dollars in the eight-year period, were treated purely from the point of view of exploitation, regardless of the initial need for investment. The annual revenue from fisheries alone was estimated at 500 million dollars, an illusory figure which Djuanda, with his experience of planning, soon afterwards reduced to 1·5 million dollars.[35] Thus the eight-year plan, like the united front, remained a pious wish and was more important as a symbol than as an expression of reality. As if appreciating this, the planning commission divided it into seventeen parts, eight chapters, and 1,945 paragraphs, thus aptly recalling the date of the declaration of independence and setting the plan on a level with the other magic formulae – *pantja sila*, Nasakom, Manipol-Usdek, Trisakti-Tavip and Berdikari – which Sukarno was to designate in 1965 as the Pantja Azimat Revolusi, or 'five talismans of the revolution'.[36] Not to be outdone in symbolism, Sukarno inaugurated the plan on the first day of 1961 in a solemn ceremony at which he laid the foundation stone of an exhibition building, which was eventually to house artistic representations of the successive phases of the plan leading to Indonesian socialism. The stone was laid on the very spot where he had proclaimed the country's independence on 17 August 1945, and which was now to mark the beginning of the crowning stage of the revolution.[37]

3 GUIDED DEMOCRACY IN ACTION.
DECREES, REGIMENTATION AND OPPOSITION

While Sukarno was the unchallenged master in the field of ideology, the executive was dominated by the military. Since the proclamation of the state of emergency in March 1957 the army had established itself as the power responsible for law and order and administration, more especially in the outer provinces, but also in Java, where its influence was all-pervasive, although it interfered less in administrative matters. The army exercised press censorship, set limits to the activity of the parties, and suspended their organs of opinion at will, and it was not only PKI circles that complained that colonialism had been replaced by 'colonelism'. In July 1959, twelve of the forty-three cabinet posts in Sukarno's new government were filled by officers: Nasution, now promoted to Lieutenant-General, became Minister for Defence and Security, and the important Ministry of Production went to Colonel Suprajogi. As Sukarno was himself Prime Minister under the new constitution, Djuanda became his deputy, or 'first minister', and also took over the portfolio of Finance. Dr. Subandrio remained Foreign Minister; Dr. Leimena became Minister for Distribution, Ipik Gandamana for Home Affairs, and Muljadi Djojomartono for Social Welfare. These so-called 'key ministries' composed the inner cabinet; each was surrounded by a group of 'junior ministries', allotted irrespective of party. Within a few weeks, ministers of both categories who belonged to any political party were in fact directed to resign from it.[38]

The cabinet's chief task was to stabilize the economy, which had recently got into a disordered state. In the first years after the transfer of sovereignty, the balance between revenue and expenditure had been held fairly even, thanks to the retention of the colonial economic system and the continued employment of many Dutch experts, as well as the raw materials boom due to the Korean war.[39] From 1952 onwards, the large profits from the export of rubber encouraged the authorities to budget more ambitiously. But at this very time export prices began to drop, and the state fell more and more deeply into debt. Larger amounts of money were put into circulation, and the cost-of-living index rose by about 10 per cent annually. Burhanuddin Harahap's government (1955-6) tried to check this development, and its measures of economy and stabilization had some success, as there was at this time a slight rise in the price of the country's main exports (rubber, oil, tin, copra, coffee, tea and tobacco). In 1956 actual expenditure fell short of that estimated for the first time since 1951.

Then, however, misfortune supervened. A fresh rapid decline in export prices (except for petroleum and tobacco),[40] the expropriation of Dutch concerns, and the resulting stagnation of inter-island trade, the growth of smuggling in the outer provinces, the civil war of 1958, the defection to the rebels of financial and economic experts such as Professor Sumitro Djojohadikusumo, Sjarifuddin Prawiranegara and Burhanuddin Harahap, and the President's annual world tours, with their attendant expense – all these factors combined to bring about the inflation and economic catastrophe of 1958–9. Before long, while wages remained fixed, the prices of staple foods such as rice, fish and meat doubled, as did those of textiles; the cost-of-living index rose by 25·2 per cent in 1957, 53·2 per cent in 1958, and 32·9 per cent in the first seven months of 1959.[41] Bank reserves dwindled to almost zero, and the black market rate for the US dollar – always a faithful reflection of economic conditions – soared between 1956 and 1959 from three to eleven times the official rate of 11·4 rupiahs.

A week after Sukarno's speech of 17 August 1959 announcing a 'general shake-up', the first drastic measures were taken. On 25 August all 500 and 1,000-rupiah banknotes were reduced to a tenth of their value; and all bank credits over 25,000 rupiahs were 'frozen' to 90 per cent of their value and treated as long-term loans to the state. These draconic measures checked the inflationary rise in prices, but did not achieve the hoped-for stabilization. The public flocked to withdraw their deposits of up to 25,000 rupiahs in small amounts, and many banks were obliged to stop payment. Bankruptcy was also the fate of many medium-sized firms which could not meet their current salary and wage bills.[42] The government's next measure, which showed greater realism, was to raise the official dollar rate from 11·4 to 45 rupiahs; but they then proceeded to a step which once more caused the exchange rate to get out of control. This was the notorious Decree No. 10 of 16 November 1959, whereby Sukarno confirmed a government decision of 23 May forbidding foreigners, as from the end of the year, to trade in the rural parts of Indonesia. By 'foreigners' was meant the Chinese, who had always been the mainstay of commercial life in country areas, and had succeeded in excluding native competition. This state of affairs had remained unchanged since the early days of Sarekat Islam, which, it will be remembered, was founded in order to counter the Chinese monopoly. Anti-Chinese excesses were frequent in times of crisis, and bitterness between the races had increased in the revolutionary period, as the nationalists accused the Chinese of being pro-Dutch and hostile to the cause of Indonesia.[43] In the case of many of the Chinese traders, this charge was justified. Four hundred thousand of them took advantage of the provisions of The Hague agreement of 1949 in order formally to reject Indonesian citizenship, which became theirs automatically by the transfer of sovereignty. Together with later immigrants and others who had never been Dutch nationals, they formed a 'foreign' community comprising about half of the two and a half million Chinese living in Indonesia in the 1950s. The new decree, however, affected not only these, but also the remainder of the Chinese population, i.e. those born in Indonesia (*Peranakan Tionghoa*) who for the time being possessed both Indonesian and Chinese nationality. An agreement concluded with Chou En-Lai at the Bandung conference of 1955, but not ratified till 1960, provided that such people were to opt within two years for one nationality or the other.

The expulsion and resettlement of the Chinese traders was carried out in a harsh fashion by the army. This led to an acrimonious exchange of notes and strained diplomatic relations with the Chinese People's Republic. It also upset the distribution of goods in rural areas, since the Indonesian co-operatives who took over the shops had neither the capital nor the trade connections of the former owners. In the next few years, many of the Chinese who were thus evicted migrated to China. Before leaving the country they endeavoured to convert their bank holdings and the sums they had received in compensation into hard currency: the black market was thus again flooded with rupiahs, and this contributed to a further rapid rise in the dollar rate, from 250 rupiahs in 1960 to 300 in 1961 and 1,100 in 1962.

A further decree (no. 6 of 1959) was issued with the object of tightening Djakarta's control over the provinces by curbing the authority of provincial councils and transferring the real power to governors appointed by the President.[44] This aroused violent protests from the parties, including the PKI, which saw in the new measure a threat to nullify its success at the last election, and feared the total loss of its influence on the rural population, which had already been curtailed by the military. But the protests were without avail. Shortly afterwards, it was made clear to the parties in a decree of January 1960 that they had the choice of toeing the government line or being banned. Among the conditions for their continued existence were acceptance of the *pantja sila* as the state ideology and of the 1945 constitution, limitation of the number of their branches throughout the country, and the relinquishment of aid from abroad. Sukarno reserved the right to dissolve such parties as had e.g. sympathized with the PRRI: an unmistakable warning to the Masjumi and PSI, which had from the start opposed 'guided democracy' and continued to make no secret of their hostility to it. Parliamentary opposition, led by these two parties, to the policy of government by decree was met by Sukarno with the retort that under the 1945 constitution he was responsible only to the proposed People's Congress. In the spring of 1960 Parliament, which for some time had been balked of its legislative functions, took the opportunity of a budget debate to criticize the government's financial planning. The right to reject the budget belonged to Parliament, even under the 1945 constitution, and when it seemed likely that this right would be exercised, Sukarno issued a decree on 5 March dissolving the last body which owed its existence to popular election. The ostensible ground was that the deputies had not justified the hope, expressed in Manipol, of mutual co-operation between the government and the people's representatives. The fault, it was declared, lay in the structure of Parliament, which jeopardized the unity of the state and prevented the achievement of revolutionary ideals.[45]

In the next two or three weeks Sukarno negotiated with the leaders of various parties, excluding the Masjumi and PSI, and on 27 March he announced the composition of a new popular assembly known as the *gotong rojong* parliament (Dewan Perwakilan Rakjat – Gotong Rojong: DPR-GR). As in the other governing bodies – Depernas, the planning commission or the national council, now called Dewan Pertimbangan Agung (DPA) – the DPR-GR, which numbered 262 deputies, was composed half of representatives of groups and half of the members of such parties as were regarded as loyal (see Table XIII): the choice of individuals in this category was, however, reserved to Sukarno.

On 9 March an attack was made on Sukarno's life. A pilot who was well acquainted with the layout of the palaces at Bogor and Djakarta machine-gunned them from a low-flying MIG-17, aiming at points where the President might be expected to be. The investigation led to the discovery of a conspiracy to murder both Sukarno and Nasution.[46] Not long afterwards, Sukarno set off on another world tour, and the parties which had been excluded from the DPR-GR – Masjumi, PSI and IPKI – seized the opportunity to form a 'democratic league' against the growing Communist influence. Although the PKI itself had only 30 seats in the DPR-GR, it also enjoyed the support of a majority of the representatives of workers' and peasants' groups. The league to restore democracy attracted some members of the PNI, NU and Christian parties in the DPR-GR, but its main hopes were placed in the army, with its traditional hostility to Communism. The politicians hoped to bring about a coup in Sukarno's absence, but their plans were frustrated by the prestige of Nasution, who was responsible with Sukarno for the new order, and by the fact that the army preferred to rely on its own strength and, moreover, stood to gain by the principles of 'guided democracy',[47] since, in fact, they gave them the leadership in the provinces.

In this situation, Hatta once again came to the fore. His resignation from the Vice-Presidency in December 1956 had been partly due to his wish to be eligible under the constitution for the office of Prime Minister, which many people hoped he would assume. Before the reintroduction of the 1945 constitution, a proposal was made in the constituent assembly that Hatta should first be reappointed Vice-President, to which Djuanda replied that the government had tried many times to persuade him to return, but without success.[48] This, however, was not true. Hatta was perfectly prepared to give his services under the 1945 constitution, which allowed the Vice-President to play a political role, and he had made this plain to the government. The fact that Djuanda, who was in other respects a man of integrity, actually repeated his statement at a reception in Hatta's presence[49] showed that the dictator who now occupied the presidency was glad of a pretext to disencumber himself of his awkward second-in-command.

After the foundation of the Democratic League, Hatta wrote a series of articles in *Pandji Masjarakat*, the burden of which was that Sukarno's measures marked a step towards dictatorship. However, world history had repeatedly shown that dictatorships based on the authority of a single man collapsed on his death like a house of cards, and Sukarno's régime would be no exception. The groups which he had succeeded in temporarily uniting were a mixed collection of natural enemies rather than allies, and if they achieved a *musjawarah*, it was only because Sukarno was there to tell them what to think. All that democrats could do in these circumstances was to wait and see how Sukarno's *konsepsi* developed. No basic change could take place as long as he was supported by the armed forces and the mass parties; since the suppression of the provincial revolts, the country was being run in a totalitarian fashion. Hatta did not dispute that Sukarno was a patriot and wanted what was best for his country and people. But his nature and temperament were such that he could only apprehend broad ideas and paid no attention to details, vital though they might be. As a result, he often achieved the exact opposite of what he intended; and 'the dictatorial system that he has introduced under the name of guided democracy will involve him in situations contrary to his ideals'.[50]

In conclusion, Hatta spoke of the Democratic League; he expressed sympathy with its views, but was doubtful of its prospects. The parties which belonged to it were united, at bottom, only in disliking the *gotong rojong* parliament; but an alliance could not be built on negatives. They should seek to work out positive aims, develop a sense of responsibility and be guided by the maxim 'the right man in the right place'.

The Democratic League was in fact of no lasting importance. After his return in June, Sukarno ordered the army to desist from supporting it in various parts of the country. At the same time he took action to meet the fears of communist influence expressed by the Nahdatul Ulama and other parties by nominating 21 new members of the DPR-GR, most of whom belonged to authoritative Muslim groups. The body's total membership was thus 283. The table on p. 203 shows its party composition in comparison with that of the parliament returned by the election of September 1955.

To these, in the DPR-GR, should be added the following 153 members of functional groups: army 15, navy 7, air force 7, police 5, workers 26, peasants 25, Muslim authorities 24, youth 9, women's organizations 8, intellectuals 5, others 22.

In August 1960 the Masjumi and PSI were officially prohibited, not only, as the official explanation had it, because they had supported the PRRI, but because they had been Sukarno's adversaries from the word go, had rejected all attempts to form a united front, and in his opinion were largely to blame for the 'antagonisms' that beset

Indonesian politics. The differences between Sukarno, Sjahrir and Natsir, with their respective following, dated back for decades, and were unbridgeable. In January 1962, when another attempt on Sukarno's life was made by fanatical Muslims at Macassar, the Masjumi and PSI leaders – including Sjahrir and Natsir, who had been powerless against Sukarno's popular appeal – were taken to East Java in 'protective custody'.

Table XIII Parliamentary representation of the principal parties, before and after the introduction of guided democracy[51]

Party	August 1956	July 1960
Masjumi	57	–
PNI	57	44
NU	45	36
PKI	32	30
PSII	8	5
Parkindo	8	6
Partai Katolik	7	5
PSI	5	–
Perti	4	2
IPKI	4	–
Murba	2	1
Partindo (1958–)	–	1
Others	31	–
Total for all parties	260	130

From 1960 onwards, Hatta remained under unobtrusive supervision in Djakarta, where he watched the gradual fulfilment of his prophecies. At first it did not appear as though Sukarno's system would involve him in contradiction with his own ideals. Soon after the ban on the Masjumi and PSI, the Provisional People's Consultative Congress (Madjelis Permusjawaratan Rakjat Sementara: MPRS) was established as the sovereign authority of the State. It comprised the members of the DPR-GR, the Planning Commission and the former National Council, and its numbers were swelled to 609 by the addition, chiefly, of 'functional' representatives. The parties as such composed less than a quarter of the new body, and their influence was thus decisively reduced.

As all the members of the MPRS were Sukarno's nominees, there was little danger of its challenging his decisions. At its three sessions during the period of guided democracy (November 1960, May 1963, and April 1965) it confined itself to rubber-stamping his policies and honouring him with sonorous titles, particularly that of 'great leader of the revolution' (Pemimpin Besar Revolusi) in November 1960. In May 1963 it conferred on him the presidency for life.

The régime of guided democracy was at pains to act in a magnanimous fashion. Nasution succeeded in putting down the PRRI-Permesta rebellion in the outer provinces by inviting the insurgents to come back 'under the wing of the Republic'; and in the course of 1961 large numbers of them took advantage of the amnesty.[52] Efforts were made to persuade the press to help in the completion of the revolution, and Ruslan Abdulgani urged its representatives to be 'Manipolists first and journalists second'. As they failed to respond, the press law was tightened up in the spring of 1963. Nevertheless, in August of that year Ruslan complained to journalists that the press was still introducing discords into the 'great symphony of the Revolution', based on the theme of *pantja sila*, and with Manipol-Usdek as its key signature.[53] However, the government's most difficult task was to 'manipolize' and 'usdekize' – as Sukarno put it in his speech on 17 August 1960 – the universities which had sprung up all over the country during the fifties.

Hatta's lecture to the Universitas Indonesia on 11 June 1957, concerning the moral responsibility of the intelligentsia, did not go unheeded in academic circles. Invoking Julien Benda and his *trahison des clercs*, he asserted that scholars who sold themselves to the great ones of this world were betrayers of their trust.[54] The government, however, was able by degrees to stifle criticism of guided democracy, which was at first outspoken, by appointing 'usdekists' as university principals, with instructions to report on the rest of the faculty. The latter's behaviour then became more or less similar to that of the German professors under Hitler. Some emigrated in the early days of the threat to academic freedom, such as the philologist Takdir Alisjahbana, who took up a post at the university of Kuala Lumpur after the dissolution of the constituent assembly, of which he was a member; he was joined there, after the suppression of the PRRI rebellion, by Dr. Sumitro Djojohadikusumo. Some paid for their liberal attitude by long periods of arrest – this applied particularly to members of the PSI – or were suspended from teaching, like the jurist Professor Riekerk, who dared to criticize the *pantja sila* in his lectures at the University of Macassar. Others, like Slamet Santoso at the Universitas Indonesia, were subject to permanent mistrust. Most of the academics, however, fearing that any criticism would be reported to 'certain quarters', held their peace.[55] There is, to date, no evidence of any significant resistance movement at the universities, devoted to planning the overthrow of the Sukarno régime. Although the reaction in student circles after the '30 September movement' in 1965 indicates the continuance of a critical attitude towards the state, it was not till some time after the attempted coup of that date that the intelligentsia formed a united front known as KASI (Kesatuan Aksi Sardjana Indonesia), which, however, then called for the demise of the Sukarno government in no uncertain terms.

4 THE FIGHT AGAINST IMPERIALISM. CONFERENCES AND CONFRONTATION

The fight against imperialism, which Sukarno pursued on a grand scale, acted as a relief to the internal tensions brought about by guided democracy; but it would be a mistake to regard his aggressive foreign policy as dictated merely by the need to divert attention from the growth of economic distress or of friction between the army and the PKI. Sukarno's anti-imperialism was sincerely felt. His campaigns against the 'demon with ten heads', as he called it in the 1920s, dated as far back as his appeals for unity on the home front: indeed, the two were intimately connected, since, then as later, anti-imperialism was the only real link between the various trends of native opinion. In Sukarno's view, imperialism was an international conspiracy and must be fought by international means. In 1926, therefore, he had been a champion of pan-Asianism and had called for unity among all nations threatened or injured by imperialism, from Egypt to China.[56] One of his motives for collaborating with the Japanese had been the hope that the Pacific War would deal the final blow to Western imperialism in Asia. However, he realized at the end of the war that the Western position was not yet broken, and he again made use of every opportunity to call for a united front, for instance at the Bandung conference of 1955. His hopes of mobilizing the 'third world' were, before long, disappointed by the conflict between India and China, and he grew increasingly convinced that there were in reality only two camps, the imperialist and the anti-imperialist. Under guided democracy, this view became the keynote of his foreign policy.[57] In his speech at UN headquarters in September 1960, he urged that, the fight against Fascism being over, the Charter should proclaim the battle against imperialism. True, unbridled imperialism was also a thing of the past; but he continued: 'Mark my words: imperialism in its death-throes is dangerous, like a wounded tiger in the jungle.'[58]

In the next few years, Sukarno yielded to none in his efforts to exterminate the 'wounded tiger'. In a speech at the first conference of non-aligned states at Belgrade in September 1961, he divided the world into 'Old Established Forces' (Oldefos) and 'New Established Forces' (Nefos): this led to the plan of a large-scale Nefo conference (Conefo), to be held at Djakarta in 1966. The Nefos included all the young independent countries of Asia, Africa and Latin America, the Socialist world and 'progressive forces' in the capitalist states. As before, the world was divided into two camps only, and this dichotomy was even reflected in sport matters: Israel and Nationalist China, being 'hangers-on of imperialism', received no invitation to the Fourth Asian Games at Djakarta in September 1962. When Indonesia, in return, was excluded from the Olympic Games at Tokyo, Sukarno retaliated against the 'pro-imperialist' International Olympic Committee by organizing the Games of the New Emerging Forces (Ganefo) in November 1963 at the Bung Karno stadium presented to Djakarta by the USSR.

Thereafter came a long series of conferences at which Sukarno pleaded for unity against the 'common enemy': the Afro-Asian journalists' conference at Djakarta in April 1963, the second conference of non-aligned states at Cairo in October 1964, an Afro-Asian Muslim gathering at Bandung in March 1965, and, soon afterwards, the tenth anniversary of the Bandung conference of 1955, celebrated in Djakarta, where Sukarno laid the foundation stone of the complex of buildings designed for Conefo (Congress of the New Emerging Forces) in the presence of representatives of thirty-six states. On this as on the previous occasions he emphasized that the world was divided into two irreconcilable blocs, Oldefo and Nefo: the latter were determined to create a new world free from exploitation, however much the old, saturated powers might seek to prevent them.[59]

Conefo – the projected conference which never took place – had, in Sukarno's imagination, a still wider role to perform: it was to embody on the international plane Indonesia's 'message to the world', the co-operation of religious, national and communist organizations – in fact, a Nasakom International.[60] There was also much talk at this time of Conefo as a rival to the UN, from which Sukarno withdrew his country on 7 January 1965, in protest at Malaysia's admission to membership of the Security Council, which he regarded as a fresh proof of imperialistic intrigue. In this way, Sukarno's resolve to free the world from the evils of imperialism and to go down in history as a saviour of mankind had, in a few brief years, driven Indonesia into a dangerous isolation. Even such 'third world' centres as New Delhi, Belgrade or Cairo urged him to reconsider his decision to leave the United Nations. The only capital to applaud his action was Peking, which lavished praise on the 'revolutionary spirit' of the Indonesian dictator who, with his home-made ideology, had put his shoulder to the wheel of genuine world revolution.

The picture which Sukarno thus painted over and over again of the threat to the political and economic independence of the new states by the neo-colonialist and imperialist powers – known as Nekolim in the acronymic zoo – was one in which he had believed from his earliest years. All international conflicts, from the Dutch refusal to give up West Irian to the US intervention in Vietnam, from events in the Congo to disturbances in Latin America, were in his opinion due to Nekolim cupidity and intrigue.

In interpreting Indonesian foreign policy in the era of guided democracy, these convictions of his must be taken into account. Prejudiced and over-simplified as they were, his attempts to give effect to them on the national and international plane show him as a man consistent to the point of obstinacy – a far cry from the un-principled, incalculable adventurer so often depicted in the press, perhaps on account of the vagaries of his private life.

West Irian

After the proclamation of the state of emergency in 1957, the first theme to be inflamed to fever pitch was the 'liberation of West Irian'. We have already described the expropriation and expulsion of Dutch nationals in December of that year. A law for the nationaliz-ation of the last Dutch enterprises was passed at the end of 1958. In the Manipol speech, Sukarno served notice of the termination of the last Dutch rights of ownership over Indonesian soil, and a year later, in 1960, he announced in his national day speech the breaking-off of diplomatic relations with the Netherlands.

The Dutch, who maintained their unwillingness to negotiate over West Irian, had meanwhile set about strengthening their military position there, and in May 1960 sent the aircraft carrier *Karel Doorman* to south-east Asia. This was regarded in Indonesia as a direct challenge, and the cry was raised for a full-scale war of liberation. The forces that had put down the rebels and irregular bands had been mainly equipped with small arms, but the demand was now for warships tanks and aircraft, to take possession of the territory by force if need be. Encouragement was forthcoming from the USSR, where, in the course of 1961, Nasution purchased arms to the total value of a thousand million US dollars. The Soviet government having thus made plain its attitude in the increasingly tense situation, Dutch opinion was alarmed by the refusal of the US to endorse the setting up, in April 1961, of a Papuan council at Hollandia which was to prepare the way for West Irian independence.

The Dutch felt isolated, and some quarters began to favour yielding to Indonesian demands. Sukarno and Nasution appealed to the Dutch people to remember its noble tradition of resistance to oppression and wrong, and to behave in such a way that the transfer of West Irian to Indonesian sovereignty could be achieved by peaceful means. These appeals were not without effect on the Dutch public, but the government were obdurate. The speech from the throne on 19 September 1961 declared that there was no possibility of talks with Indonesia on the future of West New Guinea, as the Indonesian conditions were contrary to the right of national self-determination. The Foreign Minister, Luns, took a similar line shortly afterwards at the UN, but added that his government were prepared to share with the UN the task of training the Papuans to to govern themselves.[61] The Indonesians, however, opposed the 'self-determination trick', and Subandrio, their Foreign Minister, led a delegation to New York 'with the sole purpose of defeating the Dutch proposal for the self-determination of West Irian'. In this they were successful: the Dutch motion fell through, but a pro-Indonesian resolution also failed to gain the necessary two-thirds majority.[62]

The voting at the UN took place at the end of November, and

thereafter Sukarno took prompt action. At Jogjakarta on 19 December – the place and date recalling the last Dutch assault on the Republic – he proclaimed the 'people's three commands' (*tri komando rakjat*, or *trikora*): the Dutch were to be prevented from setting up a puppet state, the red and white flag was to fly over West Irian; and the Indonesian people were to hold themselves ready for general mobilization. A special military command (Mandala) was set up at Macassar under Suharto, promoted to Major-General, to plan the necessary operations. Suharto was not an independent agent but was subordinate to Sukarno, who had declared himself commander-in-chief of the special liberation forces. He hoped in fact to achieve the transfer of sovereignty by diplomatic means, so that the military should not have all the kudos of recovering the territory after all the years of dispute. One of his first secret instructions to Suharto ran: 'Military plans are to be geared to the diplomatic battle.'[63] In speeches during the next few months he repeated again and again that the door stood open for negotiations with the Dutch, but only on the basis of a transfer of sovereignty; Indonesia was not prepared to negotiate 'in the air'. From 23 March 1962 onwards, small marine and parachute units were landed from time to time in West Irian for guerrilla operations against the Dutch troops stationed there, as a means of pressure on the Dutch government to accept the compromise proposals worked out by the US diplomat Ellsworth Bunker. These provided that the Dutch would make over the territory to the UN for an interregnum period, following which it would be administered by Indonesia. After a further length of time to be specified, the Papuans were then to decide their own future by means of free elections.

Conversations on the basis of this plan were held in Washington between the Dutch ambassador van Roijen and Adam Malik, then Indonesian ambassador to the USSR, who had been one of the *pemuda* leaders of 1945, and subsequently a follower of Tan Malaka and member of the Murba party. In July the Dutch finally agreed to accept the plan in principle. The negotiations were then taken over by Subandrio, who made it his chief object to shorten the interregnum period, originally set at several years. He was helped, perhaps decisively, by the plan of operations worked out by Suharto's command, entitled Djajawidjaja, under which, if the Dutch refused to agree to a short time-limit, a full-scale attack was to be launched, involving some 75,000 troops.[64]

By the treaty signed on 15 August, the Dutch were to transfer sovereignty over West Irian to the UN on 1 October 1962 and the interregnum was to last till 30 April 1963; Indonesia was to take over the administration on the following day, and the plebiscite was to be held in 1969. Sukarno's repeated demand for the transfer of sovereignty to Indonesia 'before the first cock-crow of 1963' was met by a symbolic compromise: up to the end of 1962 the Nether-lands tricolour was to fly alongside the United Nations flag, and on 1 January 1963 the Indonesian flag was to take its place.

Sukarno thus had every right, in his national day speech on 17 August, to proclaim 1962 as a year of triumph. Not only had the West Irian problem been solved, but internal security had once more been restored. The Darul Islam leader Kartosuwirjo had been tracked down and arrested in June, and his followers had then surrendered. In a tone of challenging superiority, Sukarno invited his critics 'who themselves have always shirked responsibility' to say whether he had or had not been right in treating West Irian and the security and unity of the state as more urgent problems than the improvement of economic conditions. History, he said, would give the answer to this question; and a few moments later he added: 'We acted in accordance with history, and that is why we have won.'[65]

Sukarno had in fact triumphed, for the time being at any rate, in another respect also – over the army in general, and over Nasution in particular. From the outset he had aimed to free himself from dependence on the 'king-maker', and had chafed at Nasution's incursions into the political field. The latter's mistrust of Commun-ism – he had not forgotten the Madiun revolt, and from time to time warned against 'foreign ideologies' – was in Sukarno's eyes a potential threat to the concept of Nasakom; and, desiring as he did to govern the course of political events himself, the President took a still more unfavourable view of the army's claim, since the pro-clamation of martial law, to act as the guardian of the state. Regard-ing himself as the Sun Yat-Sen of Indonesia, Sukarno had no intention of tolerating a Chiang Kai-Shek. He was in addition displeased by Nasution's action in offering an amnesty to the PRRI rebels behind his (Sukarno's) back, while at the same time refusing to dismiss anti-Communist commanders in South Sumatra, South Kalimantan and South Sulawesi who, in August 1960, had banned on their own authority the PKI in their respective areas.[66]

On 23 June 1962, when victory in the West Irian crisis was in sight, Nasution was transferred from the post of army chief of staff to that of chief of staff of the armed forces, which had been vacant since the retirement of Major-General Simatupang. The object of the move was to separate Nasution from his main base of support. He was succeeded as army chief of staff by Major-General Yani, who had commanded operations against the PRRI in Sumatra and had hitherto shown no sign of wishing to take an independent line in politics: his motto was expressed by himself in the English words: 'There is no reason for a "why"; you have to do it or to die.'[67] He was regarded as a faithful adherent of Sukarno's ideology, Nasakom included, and one of his first acts was to remove the local commanders who had taken independent action against the PKI.

Malaysia

After the events of mid-1962, plans began to be discussed in the army for the detachment of special units for civil operations (*operasi bhakti*), as a contribution to the task of building up the state. However, Sukarno declared on armed forces day (5 October) that the overriding need was for vigilance, since 'the imperialists are still attempting to encircle the Indonesian republic'.[68] By these words he drew attention to developments in the north. In his view, imperialism had been weakened but not defeated by the West Irian victory, and the proposed Malaysian federation was intended to provide it with a new base of operations. On 27 May 1961 Tunku Abdul Rahman, the Prime Minister of Malaya, had unfolded to a meeting of foreign journalists the plan for a political and economic federation of Malaya, Singapore, and the British territories of Sarawak, and North Borneo (Sabah). The Tunku had previously been opposed to federation between Malaya and Singapore, because the resulting population would have been preponderantly Chinese, but this was now offset by the North Borneo territories. In November 1961 the Tunku and the British Premier, Harold Macmillan, announced that the peoples concerned would be consulted on the proposal. The Indonesians knew that there was a desire for independence in the Borneo territories, and had done their best to stimulate it. As soon as the agreement with the Dutch over West Irian was secured, Subandrio declared that Indonesia could not acquiesce in the plan for Malaysia, which the PKI, at its congress in April 1962, had already denounced as a neo-colonial stratagem.[69]

Overt hostility to the Malaysia plan broke out when, in the early hours of 8 December at Brunei, a rebel group proclaimed the independence of Kalimantan Utara (northern Borneo). After the rebellion was suppressed, a propaganda campaign was unleashed in Indonesia, where the plan was described as nothing but an attempt by British imperialism to secure its future supplies of oil, tin, rubber and copra. Opposition also came from the Philippines, which revived old claims to Sabah on the ground that it had formed part of the sultanate of Sulu, now part of Philippine territory. The Philippine government sought a diplomatic solution, and in June 1963 a conference took place at Manila between the Foreign Ministers of Malaya, the Philippines and Indonesia. Here it was proposed that the three nations of Malay race, collectively termed Maphilindo, should meet regularly for a *musjawarah*, at which they would seek closer political and economic co-operation. It was also agreed that the heads of the three states would meet at the beginning of August to settle the Malaysia dispute. However, in the intervening period the Tunku went to London, and signed declarations according to which Malaysia would come into being on 31 August. The Philippines and Indonesia regarded this as a breach of faith, and little hope was entertained of the success of the summit conference. This, nevertheless, appeared to bring positive results: the Tunku agreed that before Malaysia was proclaimed, a UN referendum should be held in Sabah and Sarawak, to which Indonesian and Philippine delegations would be admitted as observers. The UN Michelmore Commission accordingly began its work in mid-August, but the observers were not admitted till the beginning of September and could therefore witness only part of the referendum. Both the Philippines and the Indonesians objected that it had been accompanied by pressure and threats,[70] but the Tunku nevertheless proclaimed the state of Malaysia on 16 September.

Djakarta's reaction was violent. Youth groups, mobilized by the PKI, stormed the British embassy, since Britain was regarded as the main instigator of the 'imperialist plot'. In a second assault the embassy was set on fire, trade unions took over British factories, and British subjects were evacuated from the capital. London threatened to break off diplomatic relations, and calm was restored only with difficulty. The unbridled régime of the 'ideologists' began to bear fruit. Guided democracy became a hotbed of emotion and hysteria.

This was in no small degree Sukarno's own doing; at this time he again made crusading speeches throughout the country, the watchword being 'Smash Malaysia!' (*ganjang Malaysia*). The British and Malaysian press labelled him an 'inveterate trouble-maker' and 'the Hitler of Asia' – descriptions which he quoted in his own speeches, indignant that his fight against imperialism could be so misunderstood. It was not a question of aggrandizement, he protested – Indonesia was large enough already; it was a question of principle and the right to fashion one's own life. Those who called him 'incalculable' were wide of the mark: he had been guided by the same principles ever since he was a young man.[71]

The army, for its part, welcomed the new campaign and endorsed Sukarno's ideological pleadings. The West Irian operation had brought its total strength to some 280,000 men, who were virtually idle now that the Darul Islam movement had been crushed. The 'civic mission' of building roads and bridges, helping on the land and in fisheries, was slow in getting under way, as the soldiers did not care for the role of workers and peasants. Moreover, the 'threat from the north' was not wholly fictitious, as far as the army was concerned. The Permesta rebels had carried on their smuggling trade with Singapore, and the PRRI got its weapons through Singapore and Malaya. Finally, the devotees of Socialism in Indonesia were perhaps not wrong in feeling threatened by the creation of a model capitalist state to the northward.[72]

Indonesia sent volunteers to Borneo; the British concentrated troops along the straits of Malacca; and as the world press began to report the first armed clashes, the US government once more attempted to resolve the conflict. Robert F. Kennedy was sent to south-east Asia as a mediator, and succeeded in arranging an armistice which came into force on 25 January 1964. At the same time he endeavoured to induce the antagonists to resume negotiations. The Tunku stipulated that all Indonesian troops must first be withdrawn from northern Borneo, and the preliminary conference at Bangkok in February and March broke down on this demand; the Tunku was not satisfied with Indonesia's 'willingness in principle' to withdraw the troops, but insisted on 'substantial withdrawal'. A compromise was eventually reached whereby Indonesia undertook to 'begin' withdrawing the troops. On 20 June 1964 the three heads of state – Abdul Rahman, Macapagal and Sukarno – again met briefly in Tokyo. Macapagal proposed that an Afro-Asian commission should be invited to work out proposals for a settlement; the others agreed, but the Tunku maintained his demand for the withdrawal of all Indonesian troops from Malaysian territory. Next day, however, it became known that the British intended to reinforce their troops in northern Borneo, and the laborious edifice of agreement once more collapsed.[73]

Unlike the West Irian campaign, Indonesia's opposition to Malaysia excited the hostility and not the support of world opinion. Even the neutrals showed little sympathy for Sukarno's demands. At the second conference of non-aligned states in Cairo in October 1964, his efforts failed to secure the endorsement of Indonesia's complaint: the conference condemned imperialist designs in Vietnam, Aden, Angola and Cuba, but said no word of Malaysia.[74] Indonesia's only remaining ally was the Chinese People's Republic, as shortly became clear after her withdrawal from the UN. On 16 October China exploded her first atomic bomb, and this aroused Indonesian hopes of effective aid against any 'imperialist' attack. In January 1965, on one of Subandrio's many visits to China, which earned him the sobriquet of *hadji Peking*, he received an assurance that in such an event China 'would not stand idly by'. Sukarno for his part showed his confidence in his Chinese comrades at the end of 1964 by allowing a Chinese team of doctors to treat him for a chronic kidney disorder. There was much talk in the press of the 'Peking-Djakarta axis', and trips to and from China grew more frequent: Peking had in fact become the Mecca of Indonesia's 'progressive' forces.[75]

As the undeclared war with Malaysia continued, Indonesian volunteers infiltrated across the land frontier, and occasionally into the Malay peninsula. In May 1964, Sukarno, after the analogy of the final phase of the West Irian conflict, had proclaimed the 'people's two commands' (*Dwikora*): support for the peoples of Malaysia in their fight for independence, and the strengthening of Indonesia's defences. These commands were reinforced in practice by demonstrations in front of 'imperialist' embassies, the expropriation of any concerns still in private hands – including American ones after the beginning of 1965 – the burning of books written by enemies of the revolution, and the display of hoardings and banners showing the imperialists being trampled down by the heroes of the 'new emerging forces'. Anti-imperialism had reached the stage of organized hysteria.

5   THE ROAD TOWARDS A PEOPLE'S DEMOCRACY.
ECONOMIC CRISIS, LAND PROBLEMS AND THE
RENEWED SUCCESS OF THE PKI

Most of these activities were organized by the PKI, whose star had
risen rapidly since the introduction of guided democracy. At the
outset, it had appeared as though the PKI would be the chief victim
of the new régime: it had suffered most from the censorship and
security measures imposed by the military under the state of
emergency, and it was also more prejudiced than other parties by
the constant postponement of new general elections, since the
results of 1955 and 1957 had shown that it could look forward to
attaining a parliamentary majority. Its criticisms of the introduction
of guided democracy were held against it more than was the case
with other parties, and its organ *Harian Rakjat* was often banned for
weeks on end. In July 1960, almost the whole *politburo* was arrested
for a time, after the party had dared to sum up the government's
record for the first twelve months of guided democracy and to deal
out black marks to certain ministers. A month later, when Sukarno
banned the Masjumi and PSI, the commanders of South Sumatra,
South Sulawesi and South Kalimantan, as we have seen, outlawed
the PKI as well, and refused for months to revoke their action, even
after Sukarno had intervened in its favour.[76]

Without Sukarno's help, as the Communists well knew, the days
of the PKI were numbered. Accordingly they rallied more and more
to the President's cause. In the early sixties, Aidit no longer spoke
of a simultaneous struggle against foreign imperialists and native
feudal lords, but emphasized, in language almost identical with
Sukarno's, that the phase of national revolution must be concluded
before that of social revolution, with the class struggle and the
building of Socialism, could begin. The PKI put its money on
national unity, the *pantja sila*, Manipol-Usdek, Nasakom and all the
other movements launched by Sukarno, simply because it had no
other choice. Nor did its support go unrewarded. In the *gotong
rojong* parliament, the planning commission, the people's congress
and the united front, the PKI secured a substantial number of
seats and was always represented in the presidium. The only point in
which Sukarno was unable to prevail over military opposition was
the participation of PKI in the government. In March 1962, the
PKI leaders attained ministerial rank by the appointment of Aidit

and Lukman as third Vice-Chairmen of the people's congress and the *gotong rojong* parliament respectively, but, as the cabinet now comprised fifty-seven ministers, this did not mean much. The PKI was not given any single department of state to administer, though its leaders pressed for this from 1963 onwards, invoking the slogan of 'Nasakom in every domain'.

It was open to question, however, whether the PKI really wished to join the government, or whether it did not prefer to make popular capital out of its constant rejection. So far, the fact that it had not been in control of any ministry had redounded to its advantage, as it was immune from charges of corruption, maladministration or incompetence. In 1963, it was still the case that it could not hope for much kudos from participating in the government. The drastic financial measures of August 1959 had failed to put the country's economy to rights. The former Dutch enterprises, nationalized at the beginning of 1958, were incompetently run, and no longer yielded a profit; transport and distribution, especially as between the different islands, had virtually collapsed with the expulsion of the Dutch shipping company (KPM). Supplies in rural areas had been jeopardized by the eviction of the Chinese. Inflation, which had been stemmed with difficulty, set in once more, despite frequent recourse to credits, owing to the need for special measures to procure food and clothing for the population, high expenditure on armaments, the President's costly foreign tours, and elaborate conferences at home. The dollar rate, fixed officially at 45 rupiahs in 1959, rose to 250 rupiahs on the black market in 1960, 300 in 1961, 1,100 in 1962 and 1,500 in 1963, or thirty to forty times its official value. The prices of basic foodstuffs rose equally rapidly. In Djakarta, a litre of rice cost 6·61 rupiahs at the beginning of 1961, 48·75 at the end of that year, and at the beginning of 1963, 80 rupiahs on the free market. Meanwhile wages and salaries remained at the same level; in 1961, the average worker received 6–10 rupiahs a day in cash, plus an equal amount in kind. To avoid chaos the government was forced to provide rice gratis to workers, employees and officials, and to distribute textiles, also free of charge, to the peasants to induce them to part with their crops. The burden was increased by the upkeep of the armed forces, which had from the beginning accounted for a third of the state budget. The afflux of volunteers had brought the army's strength up to 350,000, and that of the navy, air force and police up to 150,000. The slough of debt seemed almost bottomless, and at the beginning of 1963 Indonesia owed to foreign creditors a total of some 2,500 million US dollars.[77]

Even Sukarno, who was in general quite unconcerned by economic problems, was forced by this ruinous situation to give some thought to the question of remedies. On 1 April 1963 he issued an economic declaration (*Deklarasi ekonomi*, or Dekon) recommending decentralization and private initiative and calling on the national front to organize a short-term supply policy concentrating on raising production and solving the food and clothing problem.[78] The government, still headed by Djuanda, went a step further, and sought new loans from the USA and the International Monetary Fund, for which purpose they commissioned an American team of experts to draw up a plan of financial reform. This recommended a further substantial devaluation of the rupiah to an official rate of 315 to the dollar, and preferential treatment for imports and exports; luxury goods were to be imported at the more realistic rate of 815 rupiahs to the dollar, while the official rate was to apply to imports of essential commodities. At the same time, wages and salaries were raised by between 50 and 150 per cent.[79] In practice, however, these measures, known as the 'regulations of 26 May', failed to improve the situation. Prices at once multiplied (e.g. the cost of public transport by 500 per cent) and distress was in general rather increased than alleviated. The Communists raised a hue and cry against 'imperialist dictation', and the hoped-for credits of hundreds of millions of US dollars failed to materialize owing to the confrontation of Malaysia.

To sum up, the year 1963 had for a time offered the prospect of stabilization. West Irian came under Indonesian administration, and the Darul Islam movement, which had for so long threatened internal security, was suppressed, except for Kahar Muzakar's guerrillas in south Sulawesi, which were active till 1965. The PRRI-Permesta rebellion was at an end, and economic reform was at least being seriously discussed. But then came the Malaysian crisis and, in November, the sudden death of Djuanda, whose ambitious successor, Subandrio, unlike him, did not have the courage to stand up to Sukarno; he became a willing tool in the hands of the President, who, giddy from his early successes, tended more and more to assume airs of infallibility.

The year 1963 also saw the termination of the state of emergency and of military domination, at all events in Java. This in turn gave the signal for a fresh offensive by the PKI. Despite all the setbacks of the past few years, the membership of the party and its affiliated bodies had continued to grow steadily. The PKI itself claimed 2 million members in 1963; SOBSI, the trade union centre, 3·8 million; BTI, the peasants' organization, 5 million in 1964; the Pemuda Rakjat, 1·5 million; and Gerwani, the women's movement, 750,000 in 1962.[80] The chief reason why the Communist organizations gained ground while all the other parties stagnated or declined was the appalling economic situation, for which only the PKI claimed to offer a remedy: it took up the cry for rice and clothing, dared to criticize the mismanagement of state enterprises, and castigated the military who chiefly benefited therefrom, as the new exploiter class and representatives of 'capitalist bureaucracy' (*kabir*). In addition, the PKI began to concentrate its attention on Sukarno's promised land reform, especially in Java, where the rapid growth of population had made this a burning question.

Table XIV   Ownership of sawah land in Java, 1960[81]

Size of farm (hectares)	Number of owners	Percentage of total owners
0·5 and below	7,143,938	78·03
0·6–1	1,074,286	11·74
1·1–2	624,321	6·82
2·1–5	274,406	3·00
5·1–10	32,334	0·35
over 10	6,084	0·06
Total	9,155,369	100

The population of Java at this time had risen to 63 million, of which, according to government figures, 24 million persons, or 3·4 million peasant families, were landless.[82] But even those families which owned half a hectare or less could only live for about six months of the year on the produce of their land, and for the rest of the time had to hire themselves out as day-labourers or seek other employment. These were classed by the PKI as 'poor peasants' (*tani miskin*). The 'middle peasants' (*tani sedang*), owning up to about 2 hectares, were, according to the PKI analysis, able to subsist, but not to afford the purchase of better means of production, and were thus, like the poor peasants, largely dependent on money-lenders, local traders, and speculators who bought up the rice crop in advance. The 'rich peasants' (*tani kaja*) were those who owned over 2 hectares of rice-fields, which they cultivated themselves. In so far as they possessed more land than they could cultivate, they were regarded as sharing in the exploitation of the rural proletariat (*buruh tani*), who had no land of their own, and whose conditions of labour the Communists likened to slavery. The next group, from about 5 hectares upwards, were the big landowners (*tuan tanah*), who often lived in the cities on the revenue from their lands and had always been the Communists' sworn enemies.[83]

Well knowing that the land question offered it its main chance of success, the PKI at its fifth national congress in 1954 demanded that the big landowners, both native and foreign, should be expropriated without compensation, and their land distributed to the *buruh tani* and *tani miskin*. At its sixth congress, five years later, it resolved to investigate land ownership conditions, and instructed its cadres to go into the *desas* and work, eat and live with the peasants, so as to acquire a thorough knowledge of their wants and grievances.[84] However, after the introduction of guided democracy, Communists were frequently treated as agitators by local military commanders, and expelled from the villages. Under reform laws which came into force in 1960, private ownership of *sawah* land in Java was restricted to 5–7 hectares, any excess being distributed to landless peasants against compensation. Reforms in the system of land tenure were also projected, and land reform committees were set up to regulate the detailed application of the law.[85]

At first these measures were put into effect very hesitantly. However, at the end of 1963, after the state of emergency was lifted, the PKI, aided by the BTI, began its so-called 'unilateral action' (*aksi sepihak*). If agreement was not reached with the landowners, the rents and delivery quotas were unilaterally reduced by the peasants, and land in excess of 7 hectares was distributed. This marked the beginning of the class struggle in Java. At the same time the PKI, in anticipation of new elections, endeavoured to influence the composition of the *lurah* class by urging the villagers to depose anti-Communist headmen and elect others. Finally, the PKI lost no opportunity of denouncing the 'bogus' co-operatives and trade unions set up during the state of emergency with the approval of the military or even under their leadership, like the SOKSI trade union formed as a rival to SOBSI.

The PKI's mistrust, however, was especially directed at the *pembina* system operated by the Siliwangi division in West Java. The *pembinas* ('instructors') were, as Aidit complained at the beginning of 1964, agents sent by the 'capitalist bureaucrats into the villages after the end of the state of emergency, for the purpose of continuing to watch the *desas* on behalf of the military, preventing unilateral action against big landlords etc.' This, Aidit contended, was quite unauthorized, and it would be a calamity for peasant and democratic interests if the rest of the country followed the example of West Java.[86]

The PKI's new offensive was not confined to extending its influence in the countryside. Given the army's latent hostility, the party leaders judged it still more important to infiltrate the armed forces and so improve their chances in the event of a showdown.[87] Their main efforts were directed towards the younger officers, since they knew that for the time being, at any rate, there was little hope with the higher command. Apart from some exceptions like Brigadier Supardjo, who had been close to the PKI for years past, most of the generals viewed its activity with growing mistrust, and this situation was not altered by General Yani's appointment as chief of staff. The memory of Madiun was still fresh, and many senior officers who had studied at Western academies took a different view of 'Western imperialism' than Aidit or Sukarno; in such circles, the President's policy was from time to time openly criticized. Meanwhile, Aidit used the opportunity offered to him in 1963 to preach Communist aims to younger officers and cadets of the army, air force, navy and police. In order to conquer their prejudices against the PKI, he urged that the armed forces, which were mainly recruited from workers' and peasants' families, ought to identify themselves with the people's wishes. 'Any elements in the forces' – he declared in June 1963 at Bandung to the military academy of the land forces (SESKOAD) – 'which are not imbued with popular feeling are nothing but foreign bodies. It is the duty of all soldiers to fight loyally on the people's side and combat all attempts at counter-revolution.'[88]

Those of the young officers, who were won over by these and similar means to sympathize with Communism, were subjected to further attention from the ideological point of view. A special party bureau (Biro Chusus) was set up for this purpose: information about it, partly contradictory, came to light as a result of trials in later years. The head of the bureau in the early sixties seems to have been one Sjam or Kamaruzaman, who was not a member of the party's central committee or *politburo*: he may have been chosen because he also functioned at times as an agent for army affairs.[89] According to his own evidence, given in February 1968, the bureau was not set up till 1964: he himself was in charge of the indoctrination of army officers, while Walujo looked after the air force and Pono the navy and police. By 1965, he stated, agencies of the bureau had been set up in West, Central and East Java, and north, west and south Sumatra. The bureau itself co-ordinated their work and maintained contact with party headquarters.[90]

In these ways, the PKI hoped to secure long-term advantages which would turn the scale in its favour in the event of a general election or a contest with the army for Sukarno's political heritage. As for Sukarno himself, he regarded the party as an advance guard in the battle for Indonesian Socialism, and its leaders felt able to rely fully on his support. Their only problem was to ensure that he was consistent in his attitude, and to convince him that the revolution could only succeed if the advance guard were not hampered by counter-revolutionary elements. At the end of 1964, such elements seemed to be on the increase. In September, some members of the Murba party had founded an Association of Followers of Sukarnoism (Badan Pendukung Sukarnoisme: BPS), which sought to emphasize the national and religious components of Nasakom, and prevent its slipping under Communist control. The leaders of this movement were Sukarni, Adam Malik and Chairul Saleh, who were all prominent in the 1945 *pemuda* group. In December, however, Sukarno yielded to Communist pressure and banned the BPS. In January 1965 the Murba party itself was banned, thus paying with temporary extinction for its temerity in challenging its old enemy of revolutionary days. Soon afterwards, twenty-one newspapers which had supported the BPS were deprived of their licence to print, and pro-Murba correspondents of the Antara news agency were compulsorily retired,[91] thus leaving the apparatus of public information in the hands of the PKI. The ban on Murba was a warning to the other parties that were still licensed and had joined with it in December in the Bogor Declaration supporting Sukarno's policy and ideology; these were the PNI, NU, Parkindo, PSII, Perti, Partindo, IPKI and Partai Katolik, who thus were given a demonstration of the strength of Communist influence. In some parties there were elements prepared to co-operate with the PKI; this was per-haps chiefly true of the PNI, where Sukarno's constant appeals to overcome 'anti-Communist phobia' had strengthened the revo-lutionary wing under Ali Sastroamidjojo and Surachman, while the Hardi-Hadisubeno group were accused of betraying marhaenism. But other parties continued to make no secret of their distrust of Communism, such as the Nahdatul Ulama, which was reinforced by elements of the banned Masjumi, and whose youth organization, Pemuda Ansor, sometimes engaged in street battles with the Communist Pemuda Rakjat. However, the PKI's *bête noire* was the Muslim students' organization HMI (Himpunan Mahasiswa Islam), which acted as an anti-Communist mouthpiece and which Sukarno, despite PKI pressure, was not prepared to dissolve, as to do so would have compromised the Nasakom ideology: he was prepared, within that ideology, to allow the Communists pride of place, but not to eliminate one of its main components.

The PKI leaders were thus some distance away from their objec-tive of turning Indonesia into a people's republic of the approved pattern, but they believed they were on the right road. They gave a tangible demonstration of optimism in May 1965, when they celebrated the forty-fifth anniversary of the party's existence on a scale without precedent in Indonesia's history: unending processions and parades by various organizations, a sea of red flags mingled with the national red-and-white, huge portraits of Marx, Lenin, Stalin, Mao, Aidit and Sukarno (who had for some time been admitted to the Communist pantheon), and ecstatic speeches elaborating on the party's new slogan, adopted on 11 May at the fourth plenum of the central committee: 'Strengthen the revolutionary offensive on all fronts!' Such was the pattern in all the larger cities of the country. Sukarno, who was the guest of honour on this occasion, as he had been at all PKI congresses since 1959, referred to the Communists as his 'blood-brothers and the most powerful force dedicated to the completion of the revolution'. Why, he asked in a speech on 23 May to a huge audience in the Bung Karno stadium, did the PKI now have over three million members, while more than twenty million sympathized with its programme? Because it had remained pro-gressive and revolutionary through thick and thin; because it firmly supported Nasakom, without which the revolution could not be brought to its consummation. He prayed to God that the party might continue to flourish.

Aidit, the architect of the PKI's progress, also spoke of Nasakom. It was, he declared, 'the *key* to progress and to the Indonesian people's contribution to the fight of the new emerging forces against imperialism'.[92] Aidit, who had made a name for himself in the international Communist movement by adapting Marxism-Leninism to Indonesian conditions, naturally regarded Nasakom as a means towards the creation of a people's democracy, not an end in itself as did Sukarno with his pious wishes for the success of Communism. In an analysis intended for party consumption at the end of 1963, Nasakom had been described as 'the illusion of a man of flexible principles, and the point at which the class struggle must be sacrificed'.[93] This contemptuous estimation was of course unknown to Sukarno in May 1965, as he stood arm in arm with Aidit receiving the people's plaudits in honour of their President and prophet of Indonesian socialism. But in less than six months, Nasakom was in truth to be revealed as a hollow illusion.

VIII

THE END OF SUKARNO'S REIGN

I   THE MOVEMENT OF 30 SEPTEMBER

The celebrations of the PKI's forty-fifth anniversary lasted a whole week. They were still in progress on 26 May 1965, when Subandrio, who had become an increasingly close confidant of the President's – he was not only Foreign Minister and deputy Prime Minister, but also head of BPI (Badan Pusat Intelligensi: the state security office) – called on Sukarno to show him an ominous document which had reached the BPI by post. This purported to be a letter from Sir Andrew Gilchrist, the British ambassador, to the Foreign Office in London, and contained the passage: 'It would be as well to emphasize once more to our local friends in the army that the strictest caution, discipline and co-ordination are essential to the success of the enterprise.'[1]

The Gilchrist document, whose authenticity is subject to dispute,[2] added fuel to Sukarno's distrust of 'counter-revolutionary elements' in the army. Rumours had been going about since February that a *dewan djenderal*, or 'council of generals', had been formed to plot Sukarno's overthrow. The high command, it was said, disapproved of his leftist policy, looked askance at the progress of Communism and the ban on the BPS and Murba, and were opposed to Indonesia's withdrawal from the United Nations. Moreover, they were unanimously hostile to Sukarno's plan, announced on 11 February 1965, to save the revolution in case of need by arming the workers and peasants as a fifth defence force alongside the army, navy, air force and police. The military knew this to be no idle threat; when Subandrio visited Peking on 25 January, Chou En-Lai had promised him 100,000 small arms. Even General Yani, on whom Sukarno had thought he could rely, made no secret of his dislike of the plan, and when an NCO named Sujono was murdered in North Sumatra by members of the BTI, in connection with a dispute over land confiscation, Yani spoke openly of the dangers of arming workers and peasants.[3]

On receiving the Gilchrist document, Sukarno summoned the commanders of the four defence forces to the palace, read it to them, and asked Yani if it was true that there were friends of imperialism in the army. Yani denied this emphatically, and Sukarno then asked whether there was a 'council of generals' that presumed to criticize his policy. Yani denied this also: there was a council of generals, but its only function was to decide on promotions and transfers of senior officers. When Sukarno pressed the question whether officers had not criticized his policies, Yani finally replied: 'Yes, Bapak, there used to be something of the kind, but it is over. I have them all in my hand, and you can trust them implicitly.'[4] Sukarno, however, remained suspicious. The rumours about the council of generals persisted and were reinforced by other signs, such as the army's continued opposition to the arming of workers and peasants and to the bestowal of any important ministry on the PKI; in addition, Yani sought in June 1965 to persuade the PNI to collaborate more closely with the army in fighting Communism.[5] The overthrow of Sukarno's friend Ben Bella, the President of Algeria, by Boumedienne on 19 June, which led to the postponement of the second Afro-Asian summit conference, still further heightened Sukarno's distrust of the 'green shirts', as the military were sometimes disparagingly called.

The air force (Angkatan Udara Republik Indonesia, or AURI) was in a different position. Having, unlike the army, no 'revolutionary past', it sought to make up for this by revolutionary zeal in the present. Its commander-in-chief from January 1962 onwards, Air Vice-Marshal Omar Dhani, was no less pro-Communist than his predecessor, Air Marshal Suryadarma. He had warmly supported Nasakom, and in 1965 repeatedly declared that in the event of a showdown between the army and the PKI, the air force would side with the latter for the salvation of the revolution.[6]

At the end of July, Sukarno became seriously ill. A disease of the kidneys gave him more trouble than usual, and a team of doctors summoned from China detected, as they thought, signs of cerebral haemorrhage. Aidit, who returned at the beginning of August from Peking, was told by the Chinese that, if Sukarno suffered another attack, the result could only be death or paralysis.[7] His illness, which reached its climax about 4 August, touched off the sequence of events which had been generally expected to take place after his death, viz. a contest for the political succession between the two major powers in the state, the army and the PKI. In both camps, deliberations had taken place as to what should happen when Sukarno died. In the army's case, these were perhaps of a routine character, since the army would continue to be in possession of the weapons that would decide the conflict. The PKI leaders, of course, knew this, and the possibility of their patron's premature death now confronted them with an acute problem.

Shortly after his return from China on 7 August, and after visiting Sukarno's sick-bed in Bogor, on the 12th Aidit contacted Kamaruzaman (Sjam), the head of the special bureau for the infiltration of the armed forces, and discussed with him the likelihood that the council of generals would attempt a coup in the event of Sukarno's death. At this interview Sjam may have been instructed to sound 'progressive officers' with a view to anticipating the generals' action.[8] On 15 August, a meeting took place between some of the younger officers, who had been subjected to indoctrination by the bureau and were no doubt regarded as specially reliable by Sjam and his colleagues Supono and Walujo. The chief of these was Lieutenant-Colonel Untung of the Tjakrabirawa regiment, the commander of the President's guard. He had been the head of a parachute unit which was dropped in West Irian in 1962, and later commanded a battalion of the Diponegoro division in Central Java; he may have been won over by Sjam's agents even before his appointment to command the palace guard in January 1965.[9] Others concerned were Colonel Latief, of the first infantry brigade at Djakarta, and Major Sujono, of the air force. The officers discussed with Sjam and Supono the President's illness and the possibility of a generals' coup,[10] which they were clearly determined to prevent.

A few days later (about 19 August) Aidit reported at a session of the *politburo* that certain 'progressive officers' were prepared to forestall a coup by the council of generals, and had asked what the PKI's position would be. Aidit urged that the party should support the plan, as it was better to anticipate (*mendahului*) than be overtaken by events (*didahului*): if the generals took over power, it would mean the annihilation of the party which had been built up with such effort. The *politburo*, recognizing that the question was of crucial importance, was unable to resolve on a course of action and left the responsibility of decision to the central committee. The die was cast at a closed meeting about ten days later. What took place is still a matter of dispute, as Njono, the chairman of SOBSI and a member of the central committee, made statements under preliminary investigation which he later retracted. According to his first version, the central committee decided in favour of a military operation for the purpose of forming a revolutionary council. Aidit was said to have been responsible for military planning and for fixing the time of the outbreak, while such matters as the composition of the council were left to the *politburo*. About 2,000 young men and women belonging to Communist organizations such as SOBSI, Gerwani and Pemuda Rakjat were to be trained for a short period in the air force manoeuvre area, the public pretext being the need for defence against a possible imperialist aggression.[11]

Njono's circumstantial account, which would place on the PKI the main responsibility for the events which ensued, contained a number of demonstrably false statements which throw doubt on the remainder.[12] However, it appears from the testimony of Peris Pardede, a member of the enlarged *politburo*, at Njono's trial, and of Sudisman, a member of the central committee, at later trials,[13] that a decision was taken in favour of supporting the 'progressive officers'' plans for a coup against the generals; this seems to be borne out by the fact that the conspirators began to hold regular meetings after the central committee session, at the beginning of September. This leaves open the question what form the PKI's support was to take. The party could not have ventured, in the short time available, to mobilize its millions of followers for an open revolt: this would have been no less risky than to do nothing and wait for the army to seize power, on the assumption that the 'generals' council' existed as the PKI seems to have believed. Either course might be tantamount to suicide. In these circumstances an 'internal army purge' appeared the best solution, and this may have been what Aidit had in mind when he consulted Sjam in the first place. But nothing in the way the attempted coup was planned pointed to such unity of command and sense of purpose as might have been expected if Communist headquarters were really in charge. On the other hand, there is evidence that Sjam met Aidit from time to time and modified the plans on his instructions. The possibility cannot be ruled out that there were disagreements, if not an actual split, in the central committee over the question of participating in the officers' coup.

Sjam, whose links with the PKI were at that time well concealed, was from the outset the ruling spirit of the group of conspirators, known as the 'Movement of 30 September'. During the month they held about eight further meetings to discuss military plans and the details of the operation.[14] They made contact with units in Central Java (no. 454 battalion of the Diponegoro division, under Major Sukirno) and East Java (no. 530 battalion of the Brawidjaja division, under Major Bambang Supeno), which were due to appear in Djakarta for the army day parade on 5 October, and were now ordered to advance their arrival. In Djakarta itself there were units of the Tjakrabirawa regiment under Untung and the first infantry brigade under Latief, and support was also expected from an armoured company at Bandung. The Halim air base outside Djakarta was chosen for the operation; in the adjoining area of Lubang Buaja (Crocodile Hole) volunteers from various youth units had received military training during August and September under the supervision of Major Sujono. According to the plan, the units were to be divided into three groups, whose names and duties were as follows:

1   Pasopati: to kidnap Generals Nasution, Yani, S. Parman, Suprapto, Harjono, Pandjaitan, Sutojo and Sukendro from their houses, and bring them to Lubang Buaja, dead or alive.
2   Bhimasakti: to blockade or occupy strategic objectives in Djakarta such as the President's palace, the radio station and the post and telegraph office.
3   Gatotkatja: to settle accounts with the generals brought to Lubang Buaja as 'lackeys of imperialism', and thereafter to act as a reserve.

Arms, vehicles and other equipment were furnished by the air force, whose base served as headquarters for the rebel central command (Senko); accommodation was also provided there for Aidit, Sukarno and other political leaders. At an early stage in the discussions with the officers, Sjam had been asked what would happen if Sukarno refused his support, and had replied that in that event he would have to be pushed aside. When Untung and Sujono protested at this, Sjam promised to discuss the matter once more with the chairman. He was able to calm the officers' misgivings only by arguing that the operation was in the spirit of Nasakom, and was necessary to safeguard the President's life and doctrines.

Originally the list of those to be kidnapped had included Hatta and Chairul Saleh. The latter had been advanced to the rank of second deputy to Sukarno (after Subandrio); he was chairman of the provisional people's congress and Minister for Basic Industry, and was sometimes referred to in PKI circles as the 'Chiang Kai-Shek of Indonesia'. Another name that had figured on the list was that of Sukarni, the chairman of Murba. However, Sjam, possibly on Aidit's instructions, deleted the civilians' names, and that of Brigadier Sukendro was also removed at the last moment, as he had gone to Peking on a delegation to celebrate the anniversary of the Chinese People's Republic on 1 October. Air Marshal Omar Dhani was also in Peking during the later stage of the planning: he was sent there by Sukarno, behind the back of Nasution, who was Minister for Security, to negotiate for the arms promised by the Chinese, and returned home about a week before the coup.[15]

Sukarno, meanwhile, had recovered, and on 17 August was able to deliver his customary national day speech; on this occasion, long passages of it were drafted by Njoto, Aidit's second-in-command in the PKI.[16] The President's distrust of the military was expressed in forceful terms: he complained that there were still groups in society that wanted to play the boss, regarded themselves as 'directors of the Republic' and were not prepared to take orders. He then went on: 'Even though a man was a brave general in 1945, if he now starts to destroy revolutionary national unity, to stir up trouble in the Nasakom front and to oppose the principles of the revolution, he is nothing but a champion of reaction.' Speaking of the arming of workers and peasants, 'which has recently been so much argued about', Sukarno said that under the constitution every citizen had the right and duty to help defend the motherland. For this reason he had often told the armed forces to 'live amongst the people as a fish in water' – and they should remember that a fish cannot do without water, though the water can do without fish. The defence of the State included the defence of the people's interests, and therefore he would not hesitate to arm the workers and peasants if it should prove necessary to do so.[17]

The fact that Sukarno sent Omar Dhani to Peking in September on a secret mission to arrange the delivery of arms indicates that he was prepared to carry out his threat. It also strengthens the view that he knew nothing of the plans for the coup, which were by then well advanced. Much as he distrusted certain generals who opposed the Nasakom policy, it was not in his style to resort to a massacre such as was now being planned by the conspirators. He may have been assured, for instance by Omar Dhani, who at this time possessed his full confidence, that they intended to prevent a coup by the army generals. Dhani was at the palace on 29 September when he reported the arrival in Djakarta of General Supardjo, whom Sjam had summoned from his post in North Kalimantan by means of a cypher telegram without the knowledge of the army command. Sukarno thereupon indicated that he wished to see Supardjo at the palace on 3 October.[18] If the conspirators had been in direct contact with the President, or actually under his orders, he would presumably have seen Supardjo at once. There is thus no sign that Sukarno was informed in advance of the conspirators' plans.

The arrival of Supardjo, who had been Sudirman's aide-de-camp during the revolution and later belonged to the small circle of PKI sympathizers in the TNI, constituted one of the final preparations for the coup. The troops from Central and East Java had meanwhile entered the capital, and on 29 and 30 September the last discussions were held between their commanders and Supardjo on the one hand and, on the other, Sjam with his confederates Supono, Untung, Latief and Sujono. Untung, whom Sjam had appointed leader of the group, accompanied Sukarno on the evening of 30 September, in his capacity as commander of the President's bodyguard, to the stadium at Senayan, where Sukarno was to address a meeting of technicians. Untung left Senayan after 11 p.m. and told an officer friend that he intended that night to arrest the 'council of generals' who were plotting against the President.[19] He then went to Sjam's house, where the latter, Supono and Supardjo were awaiting him; they went together to fetch Latief, and all proceeded to the headquarters at Halim. Previously, Sujono (as he stated at Njono's trial) had driven Aidit from Sjam's house to Halim in the company of Major-General Pranoto Reksosamudro, who had not taken part in the preparations for the coup but was, like Supardjo, regarded as sympathetic to the PKI. Aidit had asked Sujono – still according to the latter's story – whether Latief had succeeded in bringing up armoured troops and whether Latief, Supardjo and Untung were already at Halim.[20] Thus, if Sujono's evidence is to be believed, Aidit was well acquainted with the group's plans, yet at the same time apparently not in charge of the operation.

2 THE ABORTIVE COUP OF I OCTOBER

Shortly after midnight,[21] the Pasopati units at Lubang Buaja were assembled, and received final instructions from First-Lieutenant Dul Arief, a direct subordinate of Untung's in the Tjakrabirawa regiment, who told them that the generals who were in collusion with the American secret service must be brought to the base alive or dead. Seven commandos were formed, the leaders of which had on the previous day reconnoitred the homes of the prospective victims. The commandos left the base after 2 a.m. The generals, awakened by clamour in front of their houses, were told that they had been summoned by the President. Three of them – Yani, Pandjaitan and Harjono – became suspicious when the intruders refused to allow them to dress properly: they attempted self-defence, and were shot down before their families' eyes. Others – Suprapto, Parman and Sutojo – apparently believed the message, having recognized the uniform of the palace guard: they opened their doors and were overpowered without difficulty. All six generals, living or dead, were removed in lorries by the troops, who returned to Lubang Buaja. Only in Nasution's case were the assassins unsuccessful: he was hidden by his wife in a back room and escaped over a wall into the adjoining grounds of the Iraqi embassy, injuring his foot in the process. His suspicions of the troops' intentions had been confirmed by an outbreak of shots inside the house, one of which wounded his five-year-old daughter. He remained for hours hiding in the embassy grounds, not revealing his presence even to friends whom he saw pass by. In his place the murderers abducted his aide-de-camp, Lieutenant Tendean, whom they may have mistaken for him in the dark. The sentry guarding the next-door house of Dr. Leimena, one of the deputy premiers, was shot in the course of the raid, but no attempt was made to kidnap Leimena himself.

At Lubang Buaja the captives, who were identified merely as 'servants of imperialism', were, according to one version, handed over to frenzied members of youth organizations who tortured them to death. Other reports say that, on Sjam's orders, the three living generals were first shot before being dismembered and thrown into a disused well some thirty feet deep.[22] The mutilated bodies were discovered two or three days later.

Meanwhile operation Bhimasakti had begun: the units involved, consisting chiefly of battalions 454 and 530 from Central and East

Java, had surrounded the palace and occupied the radio and telegraph centre. At 7.10, after the morning news, Radio Djakarta
broadcast a statement which Sjam had handed shortly before to
Untung, who in turn passed it to Captain Suradi, who was in charge
of the station. In this statement the public for the first time was
informed of what was going on. It was told that the movement of 30
September had prevented a coup which the council of generals, in
concert with the CIA, had planned to carry out on armed forces day,
5 October. The statement added that a revolutionary council (*dewan
revolusi*) would shortly be proclaimed. It would conform to existing
policy directives and to the decisions of the MPRS (provisional
people's congress), DPR-GR (*gotong rojong* parliament) and DPA
(national council). Finally, an appeal was addressed to officers
throughout the army to eradicate the influence of the generals'
council. Power-hungry generals, who no longer cared for their
troops, but lived a life of luxury, dishonouring women and embezzling public funds, must, the statement declared, be driven out
of the army and punished.[23]

The statement also alleged that Sukarno had been taken under the
protection of the Movement of 30 September. This, however, was
not so. General Supardjo, accompanied by the commanders of the
units involved in the coup – Lieutenant-Colonel Heru Atmodjo, of
the air force; Major Bambang Supeno, of the Brawidjaja division;
and Major Sukirno, of the Diponegoro division – had left headquarters early in the morning to inform the President of what had
happened, and take him back with them to Halim, but they found
that he was not in the palace.[24] He had returned there about midnight from the technicians' congress, but had left again soon after for
Slipi, the home of his Japanese wife Ratna Dewi. His aides did not
know this, and in the morning tried to reach him at Grogol, the
home of another of his wives, Haryati. Finding that he was not there,
they made contact by radio with his car, which was on the way from
Slipi to the palace, and told the driver to make instead for Grogol, as
the palace was surrounded by unidentified troops. It was thus at
Grogol, about 7.30 a.m., that Sukarno learnt from his staff, as far
as they themselves knew the facts, what had happened in the small
hours of that morning. The question then arose where he should go.
He finally decided for Halim, as an aircraft was kept in readiness
there and he could thus leave at any time the capital. His decision
was evidently taken after learning of Nasution's escape, which made

it likely that the military would attempt an immediate counter-stroke.[25]

Sukarno arrived at Halim about 8.30 and was met by Omar Dhani. When the latter asked him if he should support the Movement of 30 September, Sukarno replied '*Terserah*', signifying that he should decide for himself. Soon afterwards Supardjo returned from his fruitless mission to the palace, and reported to Sukarno. The latter's question as to where the kidnapped generals were was met with silence; whereupon Sukarno, who knew that they were dead, observed, 'Such things can happen in a revolution', and enjoined Supardjo to see that further bloodshed was prevented. He also asked why Untung had been chosen as leader, to which Supardjo replied that he was considered the ablest. Sukarno then directed that the navy and police commanders should be brought to Halim, together with the Djakarta commandant, Major-General Umar Wirahadikusuma, and Leimena (Subandrio, the first deputy Prime Minister, was at this time in North Sumatra).[26] It thus appears that Sukarno, after the first shock, was trying to regain the initiative and that he was helped in this during 1 October by Supardjo. But on that day, as Supardjo later said when brought to trial, there were three governments in being. To begin with, there was Sukarno's own régime, and secondly that of Sjam and Untung, who issued a 'Decree No. 1' at 11 a.m. This stated that, until a people's congress could be elected, authority would reside exclusively in the revolutionary council, which had still to be appointed. Day-to-day business would be conducted by its presidium, which was identical with the leadership of the Movement of 30 September. The former cabinet was thus automatically deprived of its functions. Until a new council of ministers could be formed, the members of the late government could carry on routine activity, but they would be answerable for their acts to the revolutionary council.[27]

This announcement made it finally clear to the 'third government' of 1 October that a coup had taken place against the legitimate state authority. This third government consisted of Major-General Suharto and Kostrad – the command of the army's strategic reserve. Suharto[28] had been aroused by a neighbour at about 5.30 and been told of the shooting and abduction of his fellow-generals. He realized that the army commanders and their immediate deputies had been put out of action, and, as it was customary for him to take over General Yani's functions in the latter's absence, even if Yani's deputies – who were in fact victims of the coup – were available, he now decided to assume provisional command of the army. He made his way to Kostrad headquarters near the palace and *en route* saw troops in green berets, indicating that their normal station was not in Djakarta. It did not take him long to find out that they had come from East and Central Java for the armed forces day celebration, and that battalions 530 and 454 were 'missing' from their garrisons. He thus discovered relatively soon the identity of some of the rebel troops. In order to find out their total strength, he arranged with General Umar, the city commandant, that all troops under the latter's command would remain in barracks; the navy and police agreed to do likewise, each sending a liaison officer to Kostrad. When the air force made difficulties, Suharto began to suspect that they were in the rebel camp, and this was borne out by independent intelligence. It became clear beyond doubt at 3.30 p.m., when the radio broadcast an order of the day drawn up in the forenoon by Omar Dhani but so far kept secret, to the effect that the air force supported the Movement of 30 September.

Suharto, as he declared a few days later, had surmised as soon as he heard the Untung group's announcement that they were acting, not to prevent a coup, but to achieve one of their own. The tale of a pro-imperialist 'council of generals' was absurd. He himself was represented in almost all the senior military bodies, and knew that there was a council dealing with promotions between the ranks of colonel and brigadier: he was in fact deputy chairman of this body, but it never discussed politics, and he was equally certain that there was no conspiracy in the general staff under Yani. However, by his own account he was not certain that Untung – whom he had known well in Central Java – was attempting a coup until he heard Decree No. 1, which spoke of the supreme authority of the revolutionary council and the ouster of the former cabinet, but did not say a word about the President. At the same time, it may be doubted whether Suharto would have given up his plans for counter-action if the Movement of 30 September had professed loyalty to Sukarno. When, towards noon, Sukarno's aides, Sumirat and Bambang Widjanarko, had come to Kostrad headquarters to summon Umar to confer with the President, Suharto had told Umar to stay where he was; and when the aides made it clear that they were not disclosing Sukarno's whereabouts, Suharto told them that if the President wished to discuss army matters, he (Suharto) was the person to whom he should apply.[29]

The two aides thus returned empty-handed to Halim at about noon; by this time Leimena and the navy and police commanders had arrived there. The news that Kostrad was beginning to emerge as the centre of opposition to the coup may have caused Sukarno to feel alarmed.[30] To prevent a military counterstroke, he sought to appoint a new commander-in-chief, but after much discussion no suitable candidate had been found. Through Supardjo, he consulted with the rebel command, but the latter meanwhile had apparently become divided on the question of its attitude towards the President. At 1 p.m. it was announced on the radio that the President was in good health, and was still at the head of affairs; but there was no mention of him an hour later, when the composition of the forty-five-man revolutionary council was broadcast. The list of names had obviously been drawn up in a hurry, and gave no clue as to any political tendency; when Sukarno heard it, he is said to have exclaimed: 'That is not a PKI list.'[31]

Soon afterwards, Sukarno announced his decision to entrust the leadership of the army to Major-General Pranoto Reksosamudro: the Untung-Sjam group were evidently in agreement,[32] but the question was how Kostrad and especially Suharto would take the appointment. Suharto had also been suggested as a 'caretaker' commander-in-chief, but Sukarno had ruled him out as 'too stubborn' (*koppig*); he wished to retain effective control of the army while the crisis lasted, and this seemed likely to be easier with Pranoto than with Suharto. The latter, however, refused to budge from the position of power he had acquired during the previous few hours. He had by this time a clear idea of the strength of the rebel forces, and had ordered the commanders of battalions 454 and 530, which had been surrounding the palace, to report to Kostrad headquarters. There he made clear to them that they had been used by a group of conspirators, whose object was to overthrow the Sukarno régime: the President had not even been mentioned as a member of the revolutionary council. He ordered them to come over to Kostrad, failing which they would be attacked by his troops. At about 4.30 p.m., battalion 530 (from East Java) placed itself under Kostrad's orders; however, battalion 454 withdrew to Halim after the expiry of the time-limit fixed by Suharto.

The latter's next objective was to free the radio station; in this he succeeded, again without bloodshed, at about 7 p.m. Around this time Widjanarko, the President's aide, came to Kostrad to summon

Pranoto to Halim. He arrived in time to witness the scene in which Martadinata, the navy commander who had also come from Halim, announced Pranoto's appointment as 'caretaker' to Suharto and Nasution, the latter having meanwhile reached Kostrad head-quarters. The two army generals received the news angrily and accused Martadinata of meddling in the affairs of a service other than his own. Turning to Widjanarko, Suharto declared that Pranoto would not go to Halim: he, Suharto, had taken over temporary command of the army, and Sukarno should apply to him if he wanted anything from it. He added: 'Tell Bapak to leave Halim. Tell him it is very important that he should get away from there as soon as possible.'[33] Sukarno's aide understood the message, and reported to the President at about 9 p.m. that Suharto meant to attack Halim. This caused panic among the rebels, who realized that they had lost the day: they had counted on surprise and general confusion, but Suharto's cool-headed action had thwarted their plans. The fact that they let their troops stand idle throughout the day in front of the empty palace, instead of attacking Kostrad, a few hundred yards away, when it became clear in the early morning that this was their adversary, shows how feebly the whole plot was organized. Its amateurishness was also shown by the evident differences of opinion among the conspirators as to how they should treat Sukarno when he began to take an independent line; in doing this he was supported by Supardjo, who in this way began to draw away from the main rebel group.

Meanwhile, it was clear to Sukarno that the army was now openly disregarding his orders, and that this fateful day had dealt a decisive blow to his authority. Unable to make up his mind whether to accept the challenge and withdraw to Central or East Java, he finally took Leimena's advice, and was brought to his palace at Bogor.

About midnight, when the army's paratroop regiment (RPKAD) was already nearing Halim, Aidit also left there in an aircraft placed at his disposal by Omar Dhani. It is not clear what he did during the twenty-four hours he spent at Halim. It is hard to suppose that he, the brilliant PKI theoretician, took a major part in planning the clumsy and abortive coup; but the party was to suffer bitterly for the ineffective support of the 'progressive officers'. In the next few days Aidit made a hasty tour of Central Java, apparently in order to prevent further support being rendered to the Movement of 30 September; but his efforts bore no fruit, and Sukarno's authority was no longer strong enough to avert the outbreak of mass indignation.

3 THE BREAKING OF SUKARNO'S POWER

The PKI's direct responsibility for the coup was proved to the army's satisfaction by the fact that Pemuda Rakjat bands were sent from Halim to Djakarta on 1 October to reinforce the Bhimasakti troops, and that the Communist press (*Warta Bhakti* on the afternoon of the 1st, and *Harian Rakjat* on the morning of the 2nd) came out in support of the rebellion. The PKI propaganda campaign of the past weeks, calling for the strengthening of the revolution in all fields; Aidit's appeals to Communist youth to be bold in action as well as in thought; the words of other Communist leaders such as Anwar Sanusi, to the effect that Mother Indonesia was in her birth-pangs, and that the long-awaited baby would soon see the light of day[34] – all this took on additional significance in the army leaders' eyes after the events of 1 October.

On the 2nd, Sukarno held a conference at Bogor at which Suharto, who arrived several hours late, demanded and obtained a mandate to restore law and order, having threatened that he would otherwise rescind all the measures he had so far taken,[35] thus indicating to the public that the President and the army leaders were in open conflict. In this way Suharto retained the substance of power, although Sukarno's nominee Pranoto held the appointment of 'caretaker' from 1 to 14 October, and political developments followed the army's wishes and not the President's. The Communist press was banned, the army newspapers carried the first charges against the Communists as instigators of the coup, and the hue and cry against the PKI leaders began.

The first crisis of popular feeling came on 4 October, when the shamefully mutilated bodies of the six murdered generals were recovered from the well at Lubang Buaja. They were buried next day in the heroes' cemetery of Kalibata outside Djakarta. Hundreds of thousands attended the ceremony: it was Armed Forces Day, which was to have been celebrated with especial pomp, as it was the twentieth anniversary of the TNI. Nasution, leaning on crutches, made a speech in honour of the dead, declaring that they had done their duty loyally, and had been the victims of unadulterated slander. His own small daughter meanwhile had died of the injury she received in the shooting affray, and his speech lent force to the cry for revenge upon the criminals of Lubang Buaja.[36] The army-controlled press and the television network continued to show pictures of the mutilated generals; the first confessions of Communist youths began to appear, and a wave of anti-Communism broke loose. The PKI headquarters were stormed, well-known Communists began to be murdered in the *kampongs*, and, as often in times of crisis, there were riots against the Chinese, who in the last few years had openly supported the PKI-Peking axis. Petitions poured into the palace begging Sukarno to ban the PKI on account of its evident complicity with the 'Gestapu' – as the Movement of 30 September was now opprobriously called. But Sukarno had no intention of sacrificing Nasakom to the anti-Communist frenzy. He regretted and condemned the events of 1 October, but held that their importance should not be exaggerated. The incident was a 'wave in the ocean of revolution', and it was wrong to give way to emotion, let alone stir it up by false reports. He demanded proof that the PKI had initiated the movement, and pointed out that nothing could suit the book of the imperialists, the true enemies of the Indonesian revolution, better than a split in the nation's ranks. Therefore he continued to call for unswerving loyalty to Nasakom as the only sound policy.[37]

But Sukarno's sermons were no longer heeded. Army circles were dominated by the cry for revenge, and when Sukarno refused to ban the PKI, the army took the law into its own hands. Since coups by 'progressive officers' had been attempted at Solo, Jogjakarta and other cities of Central Java in connection with the Djakarta events, and the remnants of the '30 September' leaders had withdrawn from Halim to that area, the RPKAD paratroopers under Colonel Sarwo Edhie were despatched there to carry out a purge. They were joined by anti-Communist groups, such as Ansor, the NU youth organization, who were given a short period of training with RPKAD, and the hue and cry soon became a holy war. Although Central Java was traditionally the main base of support for the PKI, the 'Nekolim army' – as the RPKAD was called by its opponents – met with little organized resistance: only the *pemuda* units hit back. The terror raged for weeks, and in Central Java alone there were soon tens of thousands of victims, including Aidit himself, who was tracked down by agents on 22 November.[38]

From Central Java the wave of murders spread to East Java, Bali and other provinces. Both suspects and innocents were slaughtered; the whole of Indonesia was in the grip of terror, and by the end of the year more than 200,000 had perished.[39] Sukarno vainly attempted to put an end to the carnage: he demanded loyalty to Nasakom, and insisted that his ministers do likewise,[40] not realizing that it was precisely Nasakom that had brought tension to this pitch; the creation of an artificial united front had not lessened but increased the mutual distrust of the religious and Communist bodies. Nasakom might be the objective reflection of Indonesian society, as Sukarno was fond of saying, but it was of no use as a programme for the revolution, since all the ideologies pulled against one another. Sukarno's personal synthesis of nationalism, Islam and Marxism was an illusion, as far as the respective parties were concerned. For such as Nasution, who had all along criticized the Nasakom policy, the Movement of 30 September was a final proof that it must be thrown over. In November, while the slaughter was still at its height, Nasution asked a group of students whether, in view of Communist terror and treachery, this foreign ideology could still be tolerated in Indonesia. His audience answered, with one accord, 'No'.[41] At this time, and against Sukarno's will, the army leaders issued directives for a 'purge of personnel' in the armed forces and the public service, designed to eliminate adherents of the Nasakom policy.[42] Sukarno, however, did not yet give way. In a speech on 10 November he said: 'I shall oppose anyone who wishes to betray the revolution or to alter its course. I do not know who will win the fight. I really do not know – God knows. But I will do my duty without fear of consequences. I know there are people who are not satisfied with my leadership. But I consider it my duty none the less to see that the revolution holds on its course and does not collapse.'[43]

Such appeals on Sukarno's part were still not without effect. The navy and police commanders at this time made official statements in support of Nasakom.[44] In the air force, as recent events had shown, Sukarno had a strong following, and in the army too there were some who backed his policy, such as General Adjie, commanding the Siliwangi division at Bandung, and especially local commanders in East and Central Java. At the end of 1965 the outcome of the 'fight', as Sukarno called it, indeed appeared to be uncertain. It was, however, decided in the course of 1966 by the nation's students. Under guided democracy, the students had been courted as the 'élite of the

nation', and in March 1964 representatives of their various organizations had jointly taken a solemn oath (*ikrar bersama*) to support
with all their power the doctrines of the Great Leader of the
Revolution.[45] At the same time, as among the political parties, there
were frequent disputes, particularly between the Muslim HMI and
student groups from the 'people's universities' run by the PKI,
which sometimes led to street fighting. Those of the students who
had hitherto considered Nasakom a workable policy reacted to the
'Communist betrayal' more sharply, if anything, than the already
hostile religious groups. In the first days of October the students
took part in anti-PKI demonstrations, and on the 25th they founded
an 'Action Front' known as Kami (Kesatuan Aksi Mahasiswa
Indonesia), with the objective of helping the army to eradicate the
'Gestapu' and all who held with it.[46]

The first action of this group was to address an open letter to the
President on 3 November, calling for the disolution of the PKI. In
the next few weeks there was growing indignation in Kami circles
at the fact that Sukarno paid no attention to this demand and
continued to allow 'Gestapu adherents' to occupy important positions
in his government, while seeking to gloss over the events of 1
October by claiming that the PKI's guilt had not been proved
beyond doubt. Student discontent was increased in December by
the sudden devaluation of the rupiah to one-hundredth of its
former value and the accompanying sharp rise in prices: many
could not even afford public transport. Such was the introduction to
1966, which was to be 'the students' year'. On 10 January the
People's Three Demands (Tri Tuntutan Rakjat, or Tritura) were
formulated at a mass meeting at the Universitas Indonesia: dissolution of the PKI, reduction of prices, and purge of Gestapu
elements from the cabinet. Stirred up by a fiery address from Colonel
Sarwo Edhie, who had led the RPKAD commandos against the
Communists, the students marched on the palace, and demanded to
be received by a minister to whom they could hand their manifesto.
They blocked the streets, and traffic was nearly paralysed until
Chairul Saleh finally acceded to their request.

In the next few days Kami's action was followed up; the hundreds
of demonstrators had now turned into thousands, who, adopting the
methods they had been taught by the PKI, carried their demands
about the streets in the form of banners, or painted them on the walls
of houses. Their first success was that, on 13 January, bus fares

were reduced to their previous level: this enhanced Kami's confidence and brought it the applause of the general public. Sukarno, however, did not at first seem much impressed by the new element in Indonesian politics. On 15 January he invited a Kami delegation to attend a cabinet meeting at Bogor, and on the 18th he received some of its leaders for what he called a 'fatherly' talk, admonishing them not to go too far, and to see to it that the revolution was not deflected from its course. Subandrio, on the other hand, took the students seriously: in a speech on 15 January, he asked whether their activities, 'which really exceeded all measure', were not stimulated by payment from foreign sources, that is to say the CIA. From this moment on, Subandrio became the students' Enemy No. 1: indignant demonstrators picketed his office and residence, demanding that he withdraw the accusation. Subandrio, however, appealed for a counter-movement among students, a 'Sukarno front' which he hoped might be formed from the Ali Surachman wing of the PNI, Partindo and the associations formerly under PKI control. This actually came about, and a period of banner warfare ensued in which one side accused Kami of being an imperialist agency and the other denounced Subandrio as a protector of the Gestapu.

In army circles the student agitation was looked on with favour, but there was some hesitation as to the right attitude to adopt towards the Father of the Nation and mandatory of the provisional People's Congress. Deep indignation at Sukarno's treatment of the Gestapu revolt conflicted with loyalty to the constitution, which the officers had sworn to respect; and their anger, like that of the students, was directed in the first instance at Subandrio, who had been detested by the army ever since he had claimed the transfer of West Irian as a triumph for his diplomatic powers. As Nasution said publicly at the time, 'The Foreign Minister may be very clever, but his speeches would not have achieved anything if he had not had a strong armed force behind him.'[47] Moreover, the army blamed Subandrio more than anyone else for the worsening of the situation in 1965. He had truckled to the PKI and, it was later alleged, himself put about rumours concerning the generals' council. During Sukarno's illness he had made enquiries about precisely those generals who had afterwards been murdered, and had been at pains to find out how much support Nasution still enjoyed in the Siliwangi division that he had formerly commanded.[48] For all these reasons, the army was not long in concluding that Subandrio had played a key part in the Gestapu conspiracy. The fact that he was in north Sumatra when it broke out, and did not return to Djakarta as soon as events there became known, seemed to confirm his guilt. At all events, the call for his overthrow was heard as early as October 1965.[49]

Kami's campaign against Subandrio was thus assured of strong support. Meanwhile, the struggle for power in Djakarta came to a head at the middle of February. In a speech on the 13th, Sukarno warned 'certain groups' against warping the course of the revolution in a rightist direction, and called for a strengthening of the 'Sukarno front'. Next day Cosmas Batubara, the chairman of Kami, issued a manifesto, in which he declared that the students would not budge a millimetre from the people's demands; tactics might change, but the three aims remained the same. Subandrio's response was to call a meeting of the pro-Sukarno groups, and urge them to form brigades, a hundred men strong, for the purpose of fighting Kami detachments.

On 21 February, Sukarno announced the long-awaited reform of his government. Kami's indignation knew no bounds when they learnt that, instead of dismissing PKI and Gestapu sympathizers, he had removed Nasution from his post as Minister of Defence. Next day a demonstration was held against the 'Gestapu cabinet', at which, for the first time, people were injured; but the students' main protest was scheduled for 24 February, when the members of the new cabinet were to take the oath.[50] In the early hours of the morning the students blocked the streets leading to the palace, making barricades of commandeered motor vehicles to prevent the new ministers from attending the ceremony. Some of the latter reached the palace by helicopter, whereupon the students and school pupils advanced on the building, and chanted demands for the cabinet's dismissal. When ordered to disperse, they paid no attention, and some tried to enter the palace itself. The guards opened fire. Arief Rachman Hakim, of the medical faculty at the Universitas Indonesia was shot dead, and many others were wounded. A yellow jacket, stained with blood, was hoisted on a mast in front of the palace, as a sign to all that the first martyr had given his life for the students' movement.

Hakim was buried next day, mourned by the entire city. The days of Sukarno's exclusive power were numbered; it had in any case been non-existent for some months past. By dismissing Nasution, he had overstepped the liberty which the army were still prepared to allow him. The military now openly supported Kami, and the President's attempt to ban the latter on 25 February was ineffectual. The students re-formed under the banner of Kappi, the high school organization (Kesatuan Aksi Peladjar-Peladjar Indonesia). When the press was forbidden to report their activities, news of them was given from the 28th onwards through a secret transmitter. Reinforcements arrived from Bandung, and street battles took place between Kami troops, now organized in a 'Hakim regiment', and 'Sukarno brigades', mobilized by Sjafeij, the new Minister for Security. Attacks took place on Subandrio's Foreign Ministry and Sumardjo's Ministry of Education, the Chinese information bureau and consulate and, by way of retaliation from the other side, the US embassy building.

The country seemed on the road to chaos. On 10 March Sukarno summoned the leaders of the political parties to a conference at the palace, where he called on them to sign a statement that the student's acts were counter-revolutionary, staged by the imperialists and paid for by the CIA. Later he declared that he had proof that the green and yellow jackets worn by the high school and university students, which they could hardly have afforded to buy, had been smuggled into the country by the imperialists, and that members of the American embassy had provided the demonstrators with food.[51] In this way Sukarno sought to evade the truth of his former saying that 'whoever has youth has the future'.[52] Nevertheless, these words were truer than ever before: Sukarno had lost command of the future.

Next morning, on 11 March, a message was passed to him during a cabinet meeting. It was from the colonel of the Tjakrabirawa regiment, and stated that unidentified troops were advancing on the palace. A few moments later Sukarno, followed by Subandrio and Chairul Saleh, had left the palace and were on the way to Bogor in the President's helicopter, which was kept in constant readiness. Their haste was justified; the troops belonged to Sarwo Edhie's RPKAD, and had orders to arrest Subandrio. During that afternoon, three generals – Basuki Rahmat, Amir Mahmud and Mohammed Yusuf – appeared at Bogor and presented Sukarno with a demand that Suharto should be placed in charge of the government and the restoration of public security. Sukarno gave in, and signed the full powers in favour of Suharto, who in return promised to safeguard the President's authority and personal safety and to govern in accordance with his doctrine.[53] The 'fight' of which Sukarno had spoken at the end of the previous year was thus brought to a conclusion.

4 THE BEGINNINGS OF THE NEW ORDER

The first measure announced by Suharto 'in the President's name' was the outlawing of the PKI on 12 March. The preamble to the decree stated that 'the subversive activity of the counter-revolutionary movement of 30 September and of the PKI' had of late increased, and that by fomenting slander and suspicion they were attempting once again to endanger public safety and national unity. In order to implement the revolution, continue the struggle against feudalism, capitalism and imperialism, and bring about a just social order on the basis of the *pantja sila*, it was necessary to take firm measures against the PKI, which was accordingly banned, together with the mass organizations under its control. In the next few days, members of the PKI were summoned, on pain of heavy penalties, to declare themselves to competent authorities, and other parties were forbidden to accept them as members.[54]

These measures, which Suharto enacted in the President's name, but against his will, and 'at the risk of being hanged for them',[55] illustrate the tactics and methods pursued during the next few months by what was called the 'new order' (*orde baru*) in Indonesia. While the language and slogans of the old order were preserved for external purposes, the policy was exactly the reverse, as was sharply evident from the phrase quoted above: the PKI was banned as a means of continuing the fight against feudalism. Similar developments followed in the realm of foreign affairs. While the struggle against imperialism was still stressed for external consumption, the new Foreign Minister, Adam Malik, began to establish secret contacts with the officially non-existent Malaysia. A good-will mission was sent to Kuala Lumpur in May, and at the same time peace talks were begun at Bangkok between Adam Malik and Abdul Razak, leading to the formal conclusion of peace at Djakarta on 11 August.

The first two demands put forward by the students, who rightly regarded the transfer of power to Suharto as a victory for their cause, were soon satisfied. The banning of the PKI was followed on

18 March by the arrest of fifteen ministers, including four to whom the students particularly objected, viz. Subandrio (Foreign Affairs), Sumardjo (Education), Sjafeij (Security) and Jusuf Muda Dalam, the chairman of the national bank. Another of those arrested was Chairul Saleh, the third deputy premier, Minister for Basic Industries and chairman of the MPRS. He was among the *pemuda* leaders of 1945 who pressed the hesitant Sukarno to issue the proclamation of independence, but later succumbed to the temptations of office, and was said to have salted away hundreds of thousands of dollars in foreign banks. Other revolutionary veterans, however, played an important part in the 'new order'. Besides Adam Malik, the chief of these were Sultan Hamengkubuwono IX and B. M. Diah. The Sultan, who had been minister of defence in the Wilopo cabinet of 1952, joined Sukarno's team in 1964 and became Minister for Development Co-ordination in the reshuffle of February 1966. Under Suharto he was made responsible for economy and development. Diah, who had been ambassador in London and Bangkok, succeeded Ruslan Abdulgani as Minister of Information in July 1966.

The students, however, were not content with Suharto's refashioned cabinet of 28 March. After the fall of Subandrio, their criticism was directed against Sukarno himself. They found an ally in the Action Front of intellectuals (KASI: Kesatuan Aksi Sardjana Indonesia) formed at Bandung on 24 February. At the beginning of March, the students protested that the political climate was becoming reminiscent of that before 1 October 1965, with the moral terrorization of all who opposed the *pantja sila*.[56]

The *pantja sila*, indeed, survived the deposition of their inventor. When Sukarno declared in December 1965 that they involved the acceptance of a leftward course in politics, Hatta, who had been for so long condemned to silence, protested (in January) that they were neither rightist nor leftist in themselves, but could only be effectual on a basis of mutual support. In the past they had been the object of lip-service, especially from the PKI, and this had helped to bring about the catastrophe of 1 October. The Communists could not be Marxist-Leninists, unless they aimed at world revolution; but the philosophy of the *pantja sila* was contrary to this, and to materialism altogether.[57] This interpretation by the old theoretician of the revolution was widely adopted by the 'new order'. At the beginning of May a symposium was held by Kami and Kasi at the Universitas

Indonesia on the theme 'The rise of the generation of 1966: the search for new ways', and the central topic of discussion was 'the return to the *pantja sila*'.[58] In contradiction to Sukarno's doctrine, it was contended that only uncritical thinking could lead to the view 'that Nasakom was implicit in the *pantja sila*, let alone identical with them', and Sukarno's idea of a fusion of ideologies was also harshly criticized.[59]

In general, Indonesia's intellectual life began to revive. There were animated discussions of subjects that had for years been taboo, and the cry was raised for an extraordinary session of the MPRS. When this body convened for its fourth session on 20 June, the organizations that had meanwhile come into existence had whole programmes ready for discussion. Kami demanded the application of the 1945 constitution without the modifications that the MPRS had introduced under guided democracy, such as the appointment of Sukarno as life President; further, an end to the harmful confrontation with Malaysia, return to the United Nations, and a new government composed of reliable adherents of the new order, which would give absolute priority to the solution of economic problems.[60] These demands were expressed in moderate terms, as it was known that Sukarno's followers still had a majority in the MPRS, even though the 120 members representing the PKI and related organizations had been either killed or arrested.[61] Among the resolutions finally adopted was one providing that, within two years, general elections would be held for a genuine people's congress – up till now, the supreme body in the state had consisted purely of appointed members. Sukarno's life Presidency, voted on 18 May 1963, was rescinded, with expressions of regret, as being contrary to the 1945 constitution; he was to remain in office till 1968, when the elections were to be held, but at the same time the MPRS approved the transfer of governmental power to Suharto, so that Sukarno could not, as he had threatened, revoke this measure at any time. A new cabinet, which would give priority to economic questions, was to be formed by 17 August. Foreign policy was to be 'active and independent' – a formula which could be interpreted in any way one chose. Finally the MPRS, which elected Nasution as its new chairman, confirmed all the measures taken by Suharto, endorsed the ban on the PKI, and forbade the dissemination of Marxist-Leninist doctrine in Indonesia.[62]

Sukarno, as the inaugurator of the MPRS, delivered a speech on

22 June: it was awaited with some degree of suspense, being his first utterance since Suharto's take-over. It was, however, a disappointment to those who had hoped that he would render an account of his stewardship. Instead, he repeated his statements and theories of former years, particularly those that had been endorsed by the MPRS. He expatiated on the theme 'Service to freedom cannot die': a man might be imprisoned, shot or physically destroyed, but his service to freedom was immune from death or torture.[63] Sukarno's hearers were left to guess whether he was referring to his own services or to those of the PKI, which he had always extolled for its devotion to the country's freedom. For the rest, Sukarno had no intention of playing the generals' game by becoming merely a representative head of state with no further direct interest in politics. This was made clear in his speech on 17 August 1966, when he enunciated various conditions for Indonesia's return to the UN, which was then the object of the new régime's policy; he also criticized the conduct of the peace negotiations with Malaysia and urged that Conefo (the Conference of the New Emerging Forces) should be held at an early date, although the government had postponed it indefinitely on grounds of expense.

Sentiments such as these were met by student groups with boos and cat-calls, which had never happened at the Independence Day celebrations of the two previous decades. As John Hughes observes, Sukarno might have seen from this how wide a gulf separated him from the 'new emerging forces' of his own country. The title of his speech, 'Do not forsake the path of history' (*Djangan sekali meninggalkan sedjarah*), was irreverently abbreviated to '*Djas merah*', i.e. 'Red jacket', as it contained a profession of Marxist faith in spite of the MPRS's ban. Renewed student demonstrations broke out, and at Bandung there were riots between supporters and opponents of Sukarno, in which another student, Julius Usman, was killed.

Thus the dualism of Indonesian politics was not removed by the transfer of power. Sukarno's criticisms were especially irksome to the country's present rulers because they were hoping to gain international sympathy and financial credits for the new Indonesia. The country's indebtedness had soared to a figure of 2,500 million dollars, but Sukarno was still talking of building the 'biggest mosque in the world' at Djakarta, the 'biggest bridge in the world' between Sumatra and Java, and the 'longest motorway in the world' from North Sumatra to West Irian – which prompted Adinegoro, the veteran head of the Indonesian press service, to remark that the President was afflicted with megalomania.

As far as the outside world was concerned, the architects of the new order did their best to ignore Sukarno's attempts to struggle out of the mesh in which he was confined. The Minister of Information, B. M. Diah, told correspondents in August that whatever the President said would not affect government decisions. On 19 September, by way of confirmation, Adam Malik announced Indonesia's return to the UN. But the functions remaining to Sukarno, such as the formal reception of new ambassadors, afforded him many opportunities of hinting to foreigners that the new order was not so stable as it appeared. Attention was paid to the strength of Sukarno's following in Central and East Java and several branches of the armed forces, e.g. the navy's Korps Komando Operasi (KKO). Major-General Dharsono, who was known for his critical attitude towards Sukarno, and who in August replaced the pro-Sukarno Ibrahim Adjie as commander of the Siliwangi division, remarked in public after the Bandung disturbances that a man like Sukarno could not simply be dismissed like a servant. Nevertheless, the new rulers had already begun decisively to undermine Sukarno's influence on the home front. Many of his followers in the army command were transferred to other duties. Adjie, for instance, was appointed ambassador in London.

At the end of August there began to be held in Djakarta a series of trials of Sukarno's closest collaborators, which was bound to diminish his standing with the general public. The first of these involved the bank president and former minister, Jusuf Muda Dalam, who was charged *inter alia* with embezzlement of public funds, traffic in import licences, and the secret purchase of arms. However, what aroused indignation, and once more brought the students out to the barricades, was the *dolce vita* of the accused, his orgies and the many women he had presented with cars and houses.[64] Sukarno's own name came up from time to time at Dalam's trial, which strengthened the impression that the leaders of guided democracy had enjoyed a dissipated life at the starving people's expense. This charge was levelled at Sukarno, together with that of having flouted the moral sense of the Indonesian people, when Dalam was condemned to death at the middle of September. As a further attack on Sukarno's prestige, the students planned to invade the palace gardens on the anniversary of the 1965 coup, seize the statues, which were mostly female nudes, and parade them through the town. To prevent this, a ban on demonstrations was issued. Nevertheless, on 3 October, the students, some in disguise, assembled in front of the palace. They were driven away by soldiers with fixed bayonets, and fifty of them had to be treated in hospital for slight injuries.

Subandrio's trial began on 1 October, the anniversary of the coup. He, Sukarno's closest associate, was accused of having known of the conspiracy in advance and supported it; his trip to Sumatra at the end of September had been for the purpose of setting up a revolutionary council there. He was further charged with having exacerbated unrest at the beginning of 1966 by creating the 'Sukarno front', and at the same time salted away public funds.[65] The trial was conducted impartially by a special military court, and Subandrio was given a fair chance to rebut the several charges. He declared that it was absurd to accuse him of playing the Communists' game: if they had come to power he would now be answering to them, for Indonesia had till the last pursued an independent foreign policy. Despite a mass of witnesses, the testimony failed to show that Subandrio was guilty as charged. One of his lawyers pleaded that, to prove to the world that the new order was based on law, the court should deliver judgement in accordance with the evidence, which could only mean an acquittal.[66]

Nevertheless, on 26 October Subandrio was condemned to death. The judgement was a political, not a legal one. Subandrio was the victim of pressure by the mob, which he had himself excited in the first months of the year by unproven accusations that the students were tools of the CIA. In early 1970 the death sentence was commuted into life imprisonment by the then President Suharto.

In the next trial, that of ex-Air Marshal Omar Dhani in December,[67] the legal situation was clearer. There was no getting round his order dated 1 October 1965, according to which the air force supported the coup. Yet, although the death sentence was certain, excitement was if anything greater at the beginning of his trial than at Subandrio's. The public hoped that it would at last throw light on the role that the President had played at Halim on the fateful day, and whether he was an accomplice or even the instigator of the generals' murder, as the student press and some Muslim organs had alleged for weeks past. However, Dhani's trial lent no further weight to these speculations. None of the evidence implied that Sukarno knew of the intended coup before 1 October; on the other hand, it became

clear that when he learnt of it, he took no steps to arrest the conspirators or their middleman, Supardjo. Moreover, the fact that in
the ensuing weeks he had, directly or indirectly, sought to protect
individuals associated with the Gestapu could now be laid to his
charge as a crime against the state.

Thanks to the trials, Sukarno's prestige had dwindled to zero in a
matter of months. Even before Dhani was sentenced to death on 24
December, the chiefs of the army, air force, navy and police issued a
joint statement on the 21st that they would in future take action
'without respect of persons' against any who disregarded resolutions
of the people's congress.[68] This was a final warning to Sukarno that
the days of his presidency were numbered unless he conformed
to the new order. The generals intimated that they expected him
to follow up his June speech to the MPRS by rendering an account
of the events for which he was held responsible. But Sukarno did not
comply. As a head of state who still commanded respect, he had
ignored invitations to collaborate with the new order, and he had no
intention now of yielding to pressure. When, on 10 January 1967, he
issued the expected supplement to his speech,[69] it was not a declaration of repentance but a disclaimer of sole responsibility for the
mistakes and setbacks of the past few years. He repeated that, as he
had stated in connection with Subandrio's trial, the coup had come as
an absolute surprise to him. It was due, he contended, to irrespon-
sible persons, imperialist intrigue and the adoption of a wrong
course by the Communists. The blame for it might as well be laid on
Nasution, then Minister for Security, as on himself. As regards the
economic situation, he as an individual accepted no responsibility for
its shortcomings, any more than for the moral decline of a whole
nation. Then he took the offensive. Who would admit responsibility
for the seven attacks on his own life, the Muslim rebellions, or the
revolutionary government in Sumatra, where certain groups had not
shrunk from co-operating with the imperialists to bring about his
overthrow?

This apologia by one who had directed the country's policy for
nearly a decade – subject, it is true, to the need for frequent compromise, as he had no domestic force on which he could rely without
question – provoked universal anger and led to the adoption of direct
measures for his deposition. The initiative came from the *gotong
rojong* parliament, to which Sukarno had in the past assigned purely
advisory functions, and which was on 27 January enlarged by 108

new members to a total of 360. On 5 February Nuddin Lubis proposed a resolution recommending to the MPRS, which was to meet again in March, that Sukarno should be removed from office on the ground of misgovernment, and that a court should investigate the charges brought against him in connection with the Movement of 30 September. A few days later, a supplementary resolution was moved for the appointment of Suharto as acting president until the next general election.[70]

Before the opening of the MPRS session which was to terminate Sukarno's political career, the events which had led to his deposition and fall once more became topical in connection with the trial, which began on 23 February, of Supardjo, tracked down and arrested in the previous month. Again many witnesses were called, but fresh condemnatory material did not come to light, as Sukarno's enemies had hoped. Supardjo, for his part, made bold to accuse the 'new order' of rebellion against the legitimate régime and of responsibility for the death of 'five hundred thousand Indonesians'.[71]

The special session of the MPRS was fixed for 7–11 March. The new régime was no less attached to symbolism than the old, and it was the intention to strip Sukarno of the presidential title on the anniversary of Suharto's assumption of power. However, the deposition in fact took place on the 12th. The choice of the formula to be used was again the subject of debate. On 11 March Suharto spoke against the idea of bringing Sukarno to trial, declaring that there was no evidence that he had been the mind behind the Movement of 30 September, or even one of its chief members; he even spoke of a need to allow Sukarno to remain in office as President.[72]

Suharto, though he had withdrawn his support from Sukarno after 1 October 1965 and was now regarded as the wielder of responsible power (*wahju tjakraningrat*), did not want to appear in the light of a usurper. In 1966, when the students pressed for Sukarno's immediate deposition, he had repeatedly indicated that Indonesia would abide strictly by constitutional methods. Now that the time had come to get rid of Sukarno, he did not want him kicked out of the house like a dog, as many people were demanding who had forgotten that the house was largely of Sukarno's building. Although the President had of late years been carried away by egotism and dazzled by his own ideas, he had resisted all enticement and pressure to join the new order,[73] and, in spite of criticism, remained loyal to his ideas till the end. In the past years and decades,

Sukarno had often enough quoted Krishna's injunction to Arjuna in the Bhagavadgita, to do his duty without thought of loss or gain.[74] Suharto knew this, and perhaps admired as a Javanese what he was obliged to condemn as a statesman.

IX

THE NEW ORDER AT WORK

I CONSOLIDATION OF SUHARTO'S POWERS

The political storm that swept Indonesia in the middle sixties has now died away. On 27 March 1968 General Suharto, who had been acting President since March 1967, was officially installed as the second President of Indonesia by the People's Provisional Consultative Assembly (MPRS) for an initial term of five years. The new régime thus finally achieved the constitutional legitimacy for which Suharto had been striving since he took power from Sukarno on 11 March 1966. The steady but gradual consolidation of the new order clearly reflects the style of the new President, who studies the power situation in a spirit of calm calculation and then advances with determination on what he judges to be the right path. The MPRS had in fact offered him little resistance since Sukarno's downfall: ever since the introduction of guided democracy the supreme legislative body, as the constitution calls it, had been obedient to every wish of the man in power, who dismissed or appointed its members with this end in view. Suharto, for his part, took more account of power groups outside parliament, which he succeeded by degrees in dominating until, at the end of the sixties, his position was inherently so strong that the MPRS decision merely reflected the actual state of political power.

Suharto had to take account of regional and personal rivalries in the army (where from time to time there was open talk of cliques favouring either Suharto or Nasution) and of tension between different branches of the armed forces, especially the air force, formerly looked on as 'progressive', and the anti-Communist army. The naval and police units were divided amongst themselves and constituted a factor of uncertainty. Besides Suharto's skill in judging the power situation, his instant action against potentially rebellious elements and his judicious appointments policy, he was aided in consolidating his power by the danger, to which he made frequent reference, of a revolt by adherents of Sukarno and by the millions of members of the dissolved communist mass organizations (see section 4 below). In this way Suharto was able, towards the end of 1969, to complete the reorganization of the armed forces which he had begun in 1967, the key posts now being occupied by his own followers.

On 10 November 1969 it was announced[1] that the separate posts of commanders-in-chief of the army, navy and air force, the holders of which had been more or less independent of one another, had been done away with and replaced by chiefs of staff on the Pentagon model, subordinate to a deputy chief of the armed forces whose nomination would be announced shortly. As in the USA, the President was to be commander-in-chief of the armed forces, and Suharto also kept for himself the Ministries of Defence and Security. His nominee as deputy chief of the armed forces was General Maraden Panggabean, a Christian from the Batak country in Sumatra, who had risen in barely five years from a brigadier to a four-star general. At the time of the attempted coup he had been in command of units on the Kalimantan front, and had hastened to Suharto's aid, for which he was rewarded with the post of army chief of staff. His successor in this capacity was Lieutenant-General Umar Wirahadikusumah, who had been the city commandant of Djakarta in September 1965 and aided Suharto at the latter's headquarters (Kostrad) in his first measures against the 30 September movement.

New appointments were made in the navy and air force, where the posts of chief of staff were filled by two young officers who had taken little part in politics, Rear-Admiral Sudomo and Air Vice-Marshal Suwoto Sukendar. Their predecessors, Admiral Muljadi and Air Marshal Rusmin Nurjadin, were to be appointed ambassadors. The police force is officially no longer to be reckoned as a branch of the armed forces, though its commander enjoys equal rank to the military chiefs of staff.

At the same time six territorial commands were created for Sumatra, Java, Kalimantan (Borneo), Sulawesi (Celebes), Nusa Tenggara (the Lesser Sunda Islands) and the Moluccas including West Irian: this replaces the former system of commands based largely on the boundaries of provinces. In addition there are supraregional commands like the powerful Command for Restoration of Peace and Security (Kopkamtib) under Lieutenant-General Sumitro, and a new department of Civic Mission Affairs has been set up in the Defence Ministry under Major-General Darjatmo. According to a statement by Suharto on 5 October 1969, special attention is to be devoted in future to the army's 'civic mission', a ten-year-old cause to which Nasution pledged himself but which had not hitherto got beyond the stage of plans and experiments. General A. H. Nasution no longer figures in the new command structure, but he is still president of the People's Assembly and is occasionally mentioned in connection with plans to complete the staffing of the Bandung Military Academy.

By taking over control of the armed forces and by creating the six territorial commands, Suharto has placed himself in a position of strength without precedent in the twenty-five years of Indonesia's history. What use does he intend to make of it?

2 THE NEW GOVERNMENT'S PLANS

On 6 June 1968 Suharto announced the formation of a new government known as the 'development (*pembangunan*) cabinet', with the main task of stabilizing the country's affairs and promoting economic recovery. This aim was emphasized by the recall of Dr. Sumitro Djojohadikusumo, economic expert and the decided opponent of Sukarno in the fifties and sixties, who joined the PRRI rebellion in protest against Sukarno's policy and afterwards defied him by taking refuge in Malaysia. He became Minister of Trade in the new cabinet, which also included several other prominent experts, so that Indonesia may have some hope of a gradual improvement in its economic situation.[2]

The government's internal policy is based on the five-year plan announced at the beginning of 1969 and known as Repelita, i.e. Rentjana Pembangunan Lima Tahun or Five-Year Construction Plan: the country has not yet broken free from the spell of acronymic titles. It represents a modest programme compared with the eight-year plan drawn up at the outset of Sukarno's 'guided democracy'. First priority is given to developing agriculture in order to make the country self-sufficient in food by 1974: at present Indonesia is still obliged, as in the past, to buy a hundred million dollars' worth of rice a year abroad. The plan also provides for rebuilding and enlarging the system of roads and dams, creating an efficient communications network, building more houses and providing increased employment.[3] A total budget of $2,600 million is involved, but foreign aid and private investments are relied on for 80 per cent of this, a dangerously high proportion. The first results, however, have been encouraging: up to the end of 1969, 175 investment projects were put into effect, the total value being $1,000 million. Nothing could more clearly mark the contrast with the Sukarno era than this 'invitation to the imperialist wolves' – as *New China* called it[4] – to set the Indonesian economy on its feet again. The renewed flow of dollars is a sign that international finance has confidence in the new régime, even though it is as yet unable to pay off the debts of the Sukarno period which amount to $2,500 million. At the time of writing (April 1970) Indonesia's efforts are bent on securing the acceptance by its creditors throughout the world of a plan worked out by the German banker J. H. Abs, whereby the interest would be cancelled and the remaining $1,800 million repaid over the next thirty years. The strongest argument of Suharto's régime in favour of the plan is that the currency has been placed on a sound footing in the last few years and that the tremendous rate of inflation – 650 per cent in 1966 – fell to 120 per cent in 1967, 80 per cent in 1968 and in 1969 to a respectable 10 per cent. The government can also point to a modest rise in exports (from $876 million in 1968 to $1,015 million in 1969) and to the fact that the state banks, for the first time in the country's history, have been able to grant medium-term loans of moderate size to enable native investors to start up new industries: the total of these since 1968 is about $36·8 million.[5]

In order to continue balancing its budget the government has done its best, through its able Foreign Minister Malik, to obtain new credits throughout the world. For 1970 alone it needs $600 million to balance a budget of twice that sum, an increase of 30 per cent on the budget for 1969.[6] As has been the case almost continuously since the early fifties, the lion's share of the state revenue is consumed by the armed forces, whose total strength at present is in the vicinity of 600,000 men. The item 'routine expenses for armed forces' is estimated at $292 million. In addition a 50 per cent salary increase is contemplated for all employees of the state, a category in which the armed forces are included. Up to now, officials and employees of the Civil Service received on the average less than $10 a month plus an equivalent amount of rice. Finally, a sum of $25 million is allocated to meet the expenses of preparing for a general election, postponed in 1968 by the MPRS to July 1971: this is further discussed in section 5 below.

3 THE 'ACT OF FREE CHOICE' IN WEST IRIAN, 1969

The new Suharto government had scarcely taken up the reins of power in mid-1968 when the West Irian question again came to the forefront. Under the New York agreement of 1962 which envisaged the transfer of the territory to Indonesia by the United Nations in 1963, a plebiscite was to be held under UN auspices before the end of 1969 to determine whether the inhabitants wished to stay under Indonesian rule or to become independent. Suharto's government, anxious to show the world that it could be relied on to respect international treaties, expressed readiness to arrange for the plebiscite, and in August 1968 the UN sent the Bolivian diplomat Ortiz-Sanz to Indonesia to superintend the arrangements and the vote itself. Before this, Suharto sent Brigadier-General Sarwo Edhie to West Irian as military commander; he had earned his promotion by the bloody suppression of the 30 September movement in Central Java. Edhie's task was to put down certain rebellious tribes and counter the influence of the Freedom Committee of West Papua (OPM), an exiled body operating from the Netherlands. He had some success in this and in giving himself a new image in West Irian as a 'gentle persuader'.[7] By dint of offering amnesties and distributing gifts of axes, saws and hoes he was able to induce some thousands of rebels to lay down their arms by the end of 1968. His success seemed to be complete when, at the beginning of January 1969, Lodewijk Mandatjan, the chief of the Arfak tribes, appeared at Djakarta in the new uniform of an Indonesian army officer and presented Suharto with a symbolic bow and arrow in token of his readiness to co-operate in furthering the interests of West Irian.[8]

Suharto's reply on this as on other occasions was to declare emphatically that he would regard a vote by the Papuans to break away from Indonesia as an act of treason and would 'at whatever sacrifice' defend Indonesian sovereignty over the territory.[9] In February 1969 his government further declared that it was not prepared to allow the plebiscite to be carried out on the basis of 'one man one vote', but that the Indonesian *musjawarah* principle must be applied. This meant that only the members of the eight regency councils of West Irian, whom the Indonesians had appointed during the past years, should be consulted on the future of the territory, as the mass of the Papuans were allegedly too backward to take such an important decision.[10]

This one-sided interpretation of the New York agreement provoked an outburst of activity by the OPM, which calculated that a
'one man one vote' consultation of the 800,000 Papuans would
result in a decisive defeat for the Indonesians. When the Regency
Council met in April at Djajapura (the capital of the territory,
formerly known as Hollandia and later Sukarnopura), some 200
Papuans demonstrated and demanded the retention of the 'one man
one vote' principle. In an attempt to mediate, Ortiz-Sanz proposed
that 'one man one vote' should apply in the more developed coastal
districts and the *musjawarah* proceeding in the interior.[11] But the
Indonesians insisted on the exclusive application of the latter, which,
as we have several times had occasion to show, amounts in practice
to the stronger over-persuading the weaker, and therefore in this
case was certain to turn out to Indonesia's advantage.

The result was that a fresh revolt broke out in West Irian at the
beginning of May 1969. Using primitive agricultural implements,
the rebels put several airfields out of action; they also attacked
Indonesian patrols and fired on the aircraft in which Sarwo Edhie
was carrying out a reconnaissance flight. The Indonesians, to whom
the revolt was particularly inopportune at this time, reacted fiercely.
Another five hundred parachutists were despatched to the territory,
and journalists and diplomats were barred from it. The UN commission was detained at Djakarta while the rebellion was being
crushed, and the Indonesian government refused Ortiz-Sanz's
request that a fresh amnesty be granted.[12] Meanwhile the Freedom
Committee leaders made frantic efforts in London, Washington and
New York, and even at a conference of African states at Addis
Ababa, to obtain international support for their 'one man one vote'
demand. The lead was taken by Marcus Kasiepo and Nicholas
Jouwe, the prospective President and Prime Minister of a free
Papuan state; but they found no power prepared to challenge Indonesia or to give them diplomatic support, though the foreign press
reported their charges to the effect that the Indonesians had 68,000
men in West Irian and not only 9,000 as they officially claimed, and
that this force was engaged in stifling opposition, making a free vote
impossible and drowning in blood the resistance of 10,000 freedom
fighters. It must also be said that Marcus Kasiepo and Nicholas
Jouwe, who had held important office in the New Guinea Council set
up in the time of Dutch rule, refused an invitation to take part in a
'unity conference', though this was proposed from the Indonesian

side by their own brothers, Frans Kasiepo and Lucas Jouwe – the former being governor of West Irian and the latter, a Protestant pastor, his closest adviser.[13] This family quarrel is in itself an illustration of how small the number of Papuan politicians is at present.

A week or so later, on 14 May 1969, conditions in West Irian had ostensibly returned to normal, and no further obstacle stood in the way of the vote being carried out in the manner desired by the Indonesians. On 15 July the first regency council, that of Merauke, voted unanimously to remain under the Indonesian flag: the proceedings were witnessed by Ortiz-Sanz and other diplomatic representatives. Other regency councils followed suit, also unanimously, the last, on 2 August, being Djajapura, where most of the opponents to Indonesian rule were to be found. In this way General Suharto, the former leader of the commando for the liberation of West Irian, was able on August 17 – the choice of a symbolic date is as important for him as it was formerly for Sukarno – to proclaim the final union of West Irian with Indonesia.

4 INTERNAL SECURITY AND THE PROBLEM OF PRISONERS

Whatever may be said against Sukarno's use of political power – and certainly there was much in it to criticize, especially his gross neglect of economic problems for the sake of an increasingly fantastic ideology – it must be admitted that in his time, after the suppression of the Darul Islam and PRRI revolts, there was no serious internal security problem and the only political prisoners were a few irreconcilable enemies who spurned his attempts at compromise. Whatever may be said in favour of Suharto's use of power – and there is much in it to praise, such as his efforts to stabilize the economy and his sense of political reality – it remains true that the new order has a grave security problem on its hands and the country's prisons are full to bursting.

When, in October 1965, Suharto pressed Sukarno to ban the Communist party, the latter replied that it was not to his interest to do so and be faced with a guerrilla war.[14] In taking this line Sukarno may have been primarily concerned to defend his Nasakom policy, but what he said was justified by events, even though it at first appeared, after the persecution of communists and mass arrests in

1965-6, as though the PKI was down and out for an indefinite period. At this time it was only in west Kalimantan that the troops of the new order encountered organized and continued resistance; but at the beginning of 1968 *New China* was able to report as follows on the struggle in Indonesia:

'The Indonesian communists moved from the cities to the countryside and are arousing the masses of the peasants, building up revolutionary armed forces, establishing Red bases and thereby preparing themselves to persevere in long-term armed struggle. A revolutionary high tide against the Suharto-Nasution Fascist régime is bound to come . . . The Indonesian people's revolutionary struggle has just begun.'[15]

Before many months were out, the military rulers of Indonesia were able to see that these words were not merely a piece of dialectical self-deception. Between July and September 1968 regular engagements took place between government troops and communist units in the inaccessible region of Blitar in East Java. The Communist forces were led by Hutapea and Tjugito, two members of the old PKI *politburo* who were high on the army's 'wanted' list. Hutapea was killed in action and Tjugito taken prisoner. The commander in East Java, Lieutenant-General Jassin, afterwards declared that if the Communist bases had not been discovered so promptly they would have been hard to capture: they were modelled on the Vietcong bases in south Vietnam.[16] It was later reported that Moscow-line Communists had put the military on the track of the Peking-oriented guerrillas.[17] A message of greeting from the Maoist wing of the PKI, addressed to Peking on the twentieth anniversary of Communist China, contained a bitter attack on 'Indonesian revisionists and renegades' who, at Moscow's bidding, 'spread the poison of opposing the people's struggle for resistance'.[18]

After the Blitar rebellion, further mass arrests took place among Indonesian civilians and in the army, including the corps of generals. Suharto ceased to maintain friendly relations with Sukarno, who was regarded as a rallying-point for the rebels and may have been in touch with them from his palace at Bogor. Thereafter he was put under close supervision and later moved to Djakarta, where he spent the rest of his days (he died in June, 1970) under house arrest in the country home of his Japanese wife Ratna Dewi. No such luxury was in store for the mass of political prisoners whose number was increased to well over a hundred thousand by the latest arrests: the total is hard to estimate, official data for the whole country varying from 70,000 to 160,000.[19] They are divided into four categories: A. Communist leaders and persons who took an active part in the 30 September movement; B. Communist cadres who cannot be proved to have taken part in subversive activity; C. fellow-travellers and sympathizers with the PKI; D. those as yet unclassified, who probably for the most part belong to category C. The following figures were published in October 1969 by, respectively, the Procurator-General, Sugih Arto, and a spokesman for the army, which is responsible for the custody of the prisoners:[20]

	Procurator-General	*Army*
Category A	5,000	4,668
Category B	10–11,000	15,988
Category C	26,000	29,124
Category D	27,000	22,114

These varying estimates are not calculated to dispel international fears that the Indonesian government is not treating the problem with due concern. The International Commission of Jurists stated in a protest dated December 1969 that 120,000 prisoners were still being held 'in deplorable conditions' in 350 military detention camps throughout Indonesia, without having been indicted or brought to trial. It was further stated that local commanders often deliberately shut their eyes to acts of terror by anti-Communists.[21] Earlier it had been charged that communist internees in Central Java had been ill-treated in camps and massacred by the hundred. After appointing a commission to investigate these charges Suharto rejected them as unfounded.[22]

The fate of the prisoners is in many respects an embarrassing problem for the new régime in Indonesia: it is a blemish on the country's international good name, and the prisoners' keep costs the government $20,000 a day. But it would be too great a security risk to set free the mass of prisoners who may originally have been only fellow-travellers but have now had time to become thoroughly indoctrinated. Moreover, not a few of them would fall victims to anti-Communist terror outside the camps as soon as they were released. For reasons of this sort, plans to set the prisoners free *en*

History of Indonesia

masse have so far come to nothing. In any case it is not proposed to allow those in categories A and B to return to society. The former are to be brought to trial by degrees; since there is no evidence against the latter, a plan was mooted at the beginning of 1969 to deport them to a remote island in the Moluccas. In August 1969 a first batch of 500 was shipped off to the island of Buru, about the size of Bali, which though almost uninhabited is capable of economic development, and further groups followed between then and the end of the year. Three sets of barracks – Tefaat I–III – were constructed on the island, and there the prisoners, whose only crime is that they were members of a party that was both legal and popular up to the end of the Sukarno era, are to do their best to make themselves self-supporting within a period of eight months. At the end of that time they may be joined by their families from Java and build themselves small dwellings near the barracks but outside the barbed-wire enclosure.[23] History repeats itself: forty years ago the Dutch colonial power dealt in the same way with the Communists, who were deported to West Irian. In those days, however, the deportees had at least been convicted of subversive action, unlike the prospective inhabitants of Buru.

5 TOWARDS GENERAL ELECTIONS

Tough as the new régime has shown itself in security matters, it has also been at pains to preserve a democratic image and is, within limits, prepared to accept criticism. This was shown, for instance, in January 1970, when a rise in the price of petroleum products led, as in 1966, to student demonstrations calling for their reduction. The demonstrators had, however, additional grievance, namely corruption at even the highest levels of government. The campaign against this was led by the intrepid journalist Mohtar Lubis, editor of *Indonesia Raya*, who had in the past paid with years of imprisonment for his attacks on Sukarno. In an open letter to Suharto at the beginning of 1970 he said *inter alia*: 'We have proof that the assistants around you have done things which are not in line with your policies.'[24]

The student demonstrators in Djakarta demanded that the 'corrupt generals' should sell their luxury cars instead of trying to wipe out the state deficit by raising prices. The chief target of their indignation was General Ibnu Sutowo, an associate of Suharto's who, as director of the state oil company Pertamina, was said to have handed over only 60 per cent of the profits to the government and smuggled the rest away for the benefit of the army.[25] As in 1966, the demonstrations suddenly spread to the other islands. On 22 January, after a protest march on the palace by students and school pupils, Suharto categorically declared that the prices would not be reduced and that the demonstrations must stop – an order which was duly enforced by troops armed with automatic weapons. However, Suharto did not ignore the students' major complaint: he set up a Committee for Combating Corruption, whose members were respected older politicians belonging to the Supreme Advisory Council (Dewan Pertimbangan Agung), and promised it the full support of the military and civil authorities. The members were J. J. Kasimo, I. Johannes, Anwar Tjokroaminoto and Wilopo; Mohammed Hatta, the veteran Vice-President of Indonesia, was attached to the committee as an adviser.[26]

Suharto has thus shown himself concerned to balance the interests of groups which adopt a favourable attitude towards his régime, and to remove the fears of non-military elements that they will receive less consideration in the 'new order'. Preparations for the elections, postponed by the MPRS to 1971, led almost at once to a tussle between party politicians and army elements, the former being charged by their opponents with placing party interests above the state and the latter with seeking to perpetuate the régime. The immediate cause of conflict was the army's claim that the government should have the right to nominate over a third of the delegates to the new Parliament – which would mean that their nominees could in future block any amendment to the constitution, for which a two-thirds majority of the People's Congress (MPR) is required. It looked more than once as though no agreement could be reached and the election would have to be postponed further. An electoral law was, however, passed in November 1969; in appearance a compromise, it actually represented a victory for the military. The latter agreed that the Indonesian parliament (DPR), which was to consist of 460 members, should include only 100 government nominees (about 22 per cent of the total); but in the more important body, the People's Congress (MPR), the nominees were to number 307 out of 920, or $33\frac{1}{3}$ per cent. In return, the army were prepared to hold aloof from the elections and leave a clear field to the parties and functional groups of a professional or regional character. The civilian politicians fear that military influence will in fact make itself felt, especially in the choice of 'functional' candidates in provincial areas.[27]

The nine surviving parties have thus good reason to put up a strong fight for every single seat if their influence, already small, is not to be further reduced. The first party to be noticed is the Partai Nasional Indonesia (PNI), whose leadership in the post-Sukarno era passed to its anti-Communist wing under Osa Maliki, so that Sukarno's Marxist-tinged ideology of Marhaenism and Nasakom is for the time being in eclipse. At its fourth plenary consultative assembly, held at Djakarta in April 1969, the party endorsed the army's double role as a military and socio-political force and thus made itself acceptable to the régime.[28] So far, Suharto has shown less benevolence as regards lifting the ban imposed by Sukarno in 1960 on the Masjumi party and the Partai Sosialis Indonesia (PSI): he appears unconvinced of their loyalty to the new order. In summer 1968, however, he gave permission for the foundation of a new Partai Muslimin Indonesia, evidently hoping that this would content the adherents of Masjumi. In addition the old Muslim organizations continue to exist – Partai Sarekat Islam Indonesia (PSII), Nahdatul Ulama (NU) and Perti, which was formerly confined to West Sumatra. The remaining parties consist, firstly, of Murba, originally founded by Tan Malaka and tolerated by the present régime chiefly, no doubt, because of its hostility to the PKI; the League for the Defence of Indonesian Independence (IPKI), founded in 1954 to represent the interests of army veterans; and finally the two Christian parties, Parkindo and Partai Katolik. No further parties are to be authorized in the pre-election period: Suharto, like Sukarno before him, has in fact repeatedly spoken of the need to simplify the party system. In February 1970 he advised the party leaders and representatives of functional groups to unite in three larger formations 'so that Indonesian democracy may be viable and capable of action'. He envisaged these as being respectively 'national' (later amended to 'material'), 'spiritual' and 'functional' in character.[29] The parties' reaction to this idea is not clear at the time of writing.

Members of the organizations banned after the attempted coup in 1965 are deprived of the right to vote or be elected, as are all political prisoners including, up to his death, Sukarno. On the establishment of the General Election Committee in January Suharto declared that the result of the election 'should unequivocally reaffirm the *pantjasila* as the State's ideology'; he added that during the campaign period, the length of which would be limited to six months, the constitution (of 1945) must not be called in question and foreign governments must not be 'slandered'.[30]

It is clear from these various 'expectations', prescriptions and reservations that the second general election in Indonesia's history will not be a free one in the Western sense. The new rulers are anxious to appear democratic but have at the same time taken good care that, whatever the upshot of the elections, their hold on power will not be relaxed for the present.

NOTES

I INDONESIA AT THE TURN OF THE CENTURY

1 Bastian, Adolf, *Indonesien oder die Inseln des malaiischen Archipels* [Indonesia or the Islands of the Malay Archipelago], Berlin, Ferdinand Dümmler, 1884–94. It is not clear whether Bastian, who was regarded until 1927 as the coiner of the name 'Indonesia', was influenced by G. W. Earl, who before 1850 considered using 'Indunesians' but rejected it in favour of 'Malayunesians', or by J. R. Logan, who wrote in 1850 in his *Journal of the Indian Archipelago and Eastern Asia*, vol. IV, p. 254n.: 'I prefer the purely geographical term Indonesia, which is merely a shorter synonym for the Indian islands or the Indian archipelago. We thus get Indonesian for Indian archipelagian or archipelagic, and Indonesians for Indian archipelagians or Indian islanders.' I am obliged to J. Noorduyn of Leiden for drawing my attention to this passage.

2 Cf. Hatta, Mohammed, *Verspreide Geschriften* [Miscellaneous Writings], Djakarta-Amsterdam-Surabaja, 1952, pp. 343ff. In a non-political sense the term Indonesia had meanwhile been used frequently by Dutch scholars (Snouck Hurgronje, N. Adriani, C. van Vollenhoven). In 1921 D. van Hinloopen-Labberton urged in the Volksraad that the archipelago should be officially named Indonesia, instead of Nederlandsch-Indië. As far as can be ascertained, 'Indonesia' was first used as a political term by Indonesian students in Holland in 1918, as the name 'Indians' which they had used for themselves had created confusion. See Sosrokartono, Notosuroto and Surjaningrat, Suardi, *Soembangsih. Gedenkboek Boedi-Oetomo 1908 – 20 May 1918*, Amsterdam, 1918, p. 138.

3 Yamin, Muhammad, *Gadjah Mada*, 6th edn; Djakarta, 1960, pp. 89ff.

4 See Muhammed Yamin's speech of May 1945 to the Committee for the Investigation of Questions of Indonesian Independence (Badan Penjelidikan Kemerdekaan Indonesia), in M. Yamin, *Naskah Persiapan Undang-Undang Dasar 1945* [Documents preparatory to the 1945 Constitution], vol. 1: Jajasan Prapantja, pp. 90, 103.

5 Cf. Soedjatmoko, M. Ali, Resink, G. J., and Kahin, G. McT., (eds), *An Introduction to Indonesian Historiography*, Ithaca, N.Y., 1965, especially the article by C. C. Berg, 'The Javanese Picture of the Past,' pp. 87–117.

Notes

6 See Jack-Hinton, Colin, 'Marco Polo in Southeast Asia', *Journal o, South-East Asian Studies*, vol. V, no. 2, pp. 43ff.

7 Ibid.

8 See Bastian, vol. V, p. 13, n. 3. The Buginese also gave the name 'Djawa-Djawa' to the slaves, whom they procured from the eastern part of Celebes, so that the expression took on a connotation of barbarism. (Information from J. Noorduyn, Feb. 1968.)

9 See the full description of the 'Djawah' colony in C. Snouck Hurgronje, *Mekka in the latter part of the 19th century*, Leiden and London, 1931, pp. 213-92.

10 For the importance of Indonesian trade, see: van Leur, J. C., *Indonesian Trade and Society*, The Hague and Bandung, 1956; Meilink Roelofz, M. A. P., *Asian Trade and European Influence in the Indonesian Archipelago between 1500 and about 1630*, The Hague, 1962; and Wolters, O. W., *Early Indonesian Commerce: a Study of the Origins of Srividjaja*. Ithaca, N.Y., 1967.

11 Cf. Wolters, p. 151.

12 See C. C. Berg in Soedjatmoko *et al.*, pp. 98ff.

13 See Meilink Roelofz, pp. 136ff.

14 *Babad Tanah Djawi* [The Chronicle of Java], Dutch trans. by W. L. Olthof, The Hague, 1941, p. 140.

15 Snouck Hurgronje, *Mekka*, pp. 260ff.

16 By B. Schrieke; cf. Anthony Reid, 'Nineteenth-Century Pan-Islam in Indonesia and Malaysia', *Journal of Asian Studies*, vol. XXVI, no. 2 (Feb. 1967), p. 272.

17 For further information on the Padri war, see Radjab, M., *Perang Paderi di Sumatera Barat 1803-38* [The Padri war in West Sumatra, 1803-38], Djakarta, 1954, pp. 8ff. On the importance of the war in the history of Indonesian Islam, see Benda, Harry J., *The Crescent and the Rising Sun*, The Hague and Bandung, 1958, p. 18, and A. Reid, loc. cit.

18 Cf. Reid, pp. 274ff.

19 See, e.g., de Graaf, H. J., *Geschiedenis van Indonesië* [History of Indonesia], The Hague and Bandung, 1949, p. 454.

20 For a fictional account of these events, ostensibly based on diaries of the time, see Baum, Vicky, *The Tale of Bali* (trans. from German: New York, 1938).

21 See Stöhr, W., and Zoetmulder, P. J., *Die Religionen Indonesiens*, Stuttgart, 1965.

22 For *adat* law, see van Vollenhoven, C., *Het Adatrecht van Nederlandsch-Indië*, 3 vols., Leiden, 1931-3. A brief account is given in ter Haar, B., *Adat Law in Indonesia* (trans. from Dutch), New York, 1948.

23 Schrieke, B., *Indonesian Sociological Studies*, part I, The Hague and Bandung, 1955, p. 180. For the *desa*, see also, Adam, L., De Autonomie Van het Indonesische Dorp, Amersfoort, 1924; Wertheim, W. F., *Indonesian Society in Transition*, The Hague and Bandung, 1956, pp. 132ff.; van Niel, R., *The Emergence of the Modern Indonesian Élite*, The Hague and Bandung, 1960, pp. 16ff.; ter Haar, pp. 71ff.; and the instructive study by Sartono Kartodirdjo, *The Peasants' Revolt of Banten in 1888*, The Hague, 1966, chap. 2: The Socio-Economic Background, pp. 29–67.

24 For details, see Haga, B. J., *Indonesische en Indische Democratie*, The Hague, 1924, pp. 126ff.

25 For the texts of such agreements see Filet, P. W., *De Verhouding der Vorsten op Java tot de Nederlandsch-Indische Regeering* [The Attitude of the Java Princes to the East Indian Government], The Hague, 1895, pp. 257ff.

26 Cf. Schrieke, vol. I, pp. 201–21 (The position of the regents from the days of the Dutch East India Company to the constitutional regulation of 1854).

27 Except where otherwise indicated, all dates and statistics are taken from the annual *Regeeringsalmanak voor Nederlandsch-Indië*. This figure is based on a district to district count, *Regeeringsalmanak* 1887, pp. 84–94. For several regions no exact data were available. It should be noted in this connection that the number of villages in Java and Madura was later considerably reduced as a result of resettlements. It was 23,024 in 1920 and even less in later years, Cf. Adams, *Autonomie* pp. 10 and 21ff.

28 Furnivall, J. S., *Colonial Policy and Practice : a Comparative Study of Burma and Netherlands India*, Cambridge, 1948, pp. 439, 447, 474f., 538. Furnivall discusses also the disadvantages and dangers of indirect rule; cf. pp. 427ff.

29 Cf. Djajadiningrat, A., *Herinneringen* [Memoirs], Amsterdam and Batavia, 1936, pp. 182ff.

30 See Kartodirdjo, p. 332.

31 Cf. Djajadiningrat, pp. 20ff., and Kartodirdjo, pp. 154ff. The former passage is based largely on its author's contribution of 1908 to the *Tijdschrift voor het Binnenlandsch Bestuur*, 34. Deel, pp. 1–22, entitled 'Het leven in een pesantren' [Life in a *pesantren*], which shows clearly the rivalry between Islam and the *prijajis* on account of the latter's close links with the colonial rulers.

32 For the development of the pilgrimage to Mecca, see in general Vredenbregt, J., 'The Haddj', in *Bijdragen tot de Taal-, Land- en Volkenkunde* [Linguistic, Geographical and Ethnographic Studies], Deel 118 (1962), pp. 91–154. However, Vredenbregt's figures, based

on the official data issued by the colonial government, are considerably lower than those furnished by the consulate at Jeddah – see e.g. the *Indische Gids*, 1899, vol. I, p. 560. This shows that large numbers of the population went to Mecca without the knowledge of the colonial government.

33 Details in Reid, pp. 277ff.

34 See Drewes, G. W. J., 'The Struggle between Javanism and Islam as illustrated by the Serat Dermagandul', in *Bijdragen tot de Taal-, Land- en Volkenkunde* (1966), pp. 309ff.

35 See n. 27.

36 Blumberger, J. Th. Petrus, *De Indo-Europeesche Beweging in Neder-landsch-Indië* [The Eurasian Movement in the Dutch East Indies], Haarlem, 1939, pp. 13ff.

37 'Het onderwijs der Javanen' [Education in Java], unsigned article in *Tijdschrift van Nederlandsch-Indië*, year 14 (1852), part 2, p. 210.

38 Quarles van Ufford, K. W., 'Het onderwijs in Nederlandsch-Indië', loc cit., pp. 146ff.

39 Ibid., p. 204.

40 Details in the article 'Onderwijs' in *Encyclopaedie van Nederlandsch Oost-Indië* (henceforth cited as ENI), vol. III (1919), pp. 114ff.

41 Hadiningrat, R. M. A. A., 'De achteruitgang van het prestige der Inlandsche Hoofden en de middelen om daarin verbetering te brengen' [The decline in the prestige of native rulers and ways of improving the situation], in *Tijdschrift voor het Binnenlandsch Bestuur*, 17. Deel (1899), pp. 371, 380.

42 For a detailed analysis, see Kartodirdjo, S., *The Peasants' Revolt in Banten 1888*, The Hague, 1966.

43 For the Ratu Adil movements, see Dahm, B., *Sukarno and the Struggle for Indonesian Independence*, Ithaca (N.Y.), Cornell University Press, 1969, chap. 1.

44 For the Samin movement, see Blumberger, J. Th. Petrus, *De nationalistische Beweging in Nederlandsch-Indië*, Haarlem, 1931, pp. 9ff.; Mangunkusumo, Tjipto, *Het Saminisme*, Semarang, 1918; and, more recently, Benda, Harry J., and Castles, Lance, 'The Samin Movement', in *Bijdragen*, Deel 125 (1969), pp. 207–40.

45 Van Deventer attached to his article statistical data based on government information. The article is reproduced in, among other works, Colenbrander, H. T., and Stokvis, J. E., *Leven en Werk van Mr. C. Th. van Deventer*, Amsterdam, 1916, vol. II, pp. 1–47.

46 Cf. Brooshooft, P., *De ethische koers in de koloniale politiek*, Amsterdam, 1901, chaps. 2 and 3. It was this pamphlet that gave the 'ethical' policy its name.

47 The most vigorous advocate of this idea was Snouck Hurgronje,

who had meanwhile become the Dutch Government's adviser on Islamic and Arab matters. See, e.g., his series of lectures, *Nederland en de Islam*, Leiden, 1911, where he expressed the hope (p. 83) that the problem of Islam could likewise be solved by 'association'. For a discussion of 'association', see van Niel, R., *The Emergence of the modern Indonesian Élite*, The Hague and Bandung, 1960, pp. 36ff.

48 In an article, 'Het Imperialisme van Nederland', in *Indische Gids* (1902), I, p. 41.

49 From van Deventer's essay 'Indië en de Democratie' (1902), quoted here from Colenbrander and Stokvis, vol. II, p. 89.

50 Ibid., p. 93.

51 Compiled from data in the *Regeeringsalmanak voor Nederlandsch-Indië* for 1903.

52 Cf. van der Wal, S. L., *Het Onderwijsbeleid in Nederlandsch-Indië 1900–1940* [Educational Policy in the Dutch East Indies, 1900–1940], Groningen, 1963, pp. 5ff.

53 Ibid., pp. 57ff.

54 Ibid., p. 22, n. 1.

55 Ibid., p. 109.

56 Compiled from data in van der Wal, p. 108, n. 2, and Hinloopen Labberton, D. van, *Handboek van Insulinde*, Amsterdam, 1910, p. 186.

57 In 1905 the native Christians in Java and Madura numbered 24,663, and in the outer islands 433,131, out of a total population of about 37 million: see article *Bevolking* in ENI, vol. I, p. 299.

58 Cf. van der Wal, pp. 87ff., 96, 108ff. and 188ff. For a general work on the development of education (van der Wal is a compilation of original sources), see also Brugmans, I. J., *Geschiedenis van het onderwijs in Nederlandsch-Indië*, Groningen, 1938.

59 From the article '*Onderwijs*', in ENI, vol. III, pp. 103ff. and 114f.

60 See Hinloopen Labberton, p. 211.

61 Cf. Kartini's letter of 24 July 1903 in Raden Adjeng Kartini, *Door Duisternis tot Licht* [Through Darkness to Light], Amsterdam, 1911. Further information on Salim in Gunseikanbu [Japanese military government], ed.: *Orang Indonesia jang terkemuka di Djawa* (Prominent Indonesian Personalities in Java), Djakarta 2604 [i.e., 1944], p. 461.

II THE BEGINNINGS OF INDONESIAN NATIONALISM

1 See Hatta, B. Mohammed, *Verspreide Geschriften*, pp. 161ff., 355ff., 509. Van Deventer had already drawn attention to the influence of

events in other Asian states: see Colenbrander and Stokvis, vol. II,
p. 208.

2 Kartini, R. A., *Letters of a Javanese Princess*, trans. from the Dutch
by A. L. Symmers, ed. by Hildred Geertz, New York, Norton,
1964, p. 31.

3 Ibid., p. 61 (letter of January 1900).

4 Ibid., p. 44 (letter of November 1899).

5 The first edition of Kartini's letters, edited by J. H. Abendanon
(Kartini, R. A., *Door Duisternis tot Licht*, Amsterdam, 1911) was
followed by numerous further editions and translations. A good
introduction to Kartini's ideas, with some further information, is
provided by H. Bouman in *Meer Licht over Kartini*, Amsterdam,
1954. The only full commentary on her letters that has so far been
published is in Indonesian: see Toer, Pramoedya Ananta, *Panggil aku
Kartini* [Call me simply Kartini], Djakarta, 1962, 2 vols.

6 Djajadiningrat, A., *Herinneringen*, pp. 226ff.

7 Hadiningrat, R. M. A. A., 'De achteruitgnang van het prestige der
Inlandsche Hoofden en de middelen, om daarin verbetering te
brengen', in *Tijdschrift voor het Binnenlandsch Bestuur*, 17. Deel
(1899), pp. 367–85.

8 Cf. Toer, p. 131. Toer has evidently confused Van Deventer's
essay on the Indies and democracy with Hadiningrat's report.

9 Hadiningrat, p. 377.

10 For the 'Mindere Welvaartscommissie (Commission on Lack of
Welfare), which functioned from 1902 to 1907, but did not meet
after the latter year and was dissolved in 1914, see the article
'Welvaartsonderzoek', in ENI, vol. IV, pp. 751–8.

11 At the turn of the century the *bupatis* received the considerable sum
of 12,000 guilders a year, *wedanas* 2,500 and assistant *wedanas* 1,200
guilders. See, e.g., Day, Clive, *The Policy and Administration of the
Dutch in Java*, London, 1904, p. 418.

12 According to Tehupeiroy, W. K., 'Iets over de Inlandsche genees-
kundigen', in *Indisch Genootschap* (28 January 1908), pp. 101–34,
and the same author's 'Reorganisatie van het onderwijs aan de
School tot Opleiding van Inlandsche Artsen te Weltevreden', *Indische
Gids* (1909), pp. 922–33.

13 See Gunawan Mangunkusumo's contribution to the memorial
volume commemorating the first ten years of Budi Utomo in
Soembangsih (1918), quoted by Akira Nagazumi in *The origin and
the earlier years of the Budi Utomo, 1908–18* (typescript dissertation,
Ithaca (New York), Cornell University, 1967), p. 57.

14 *Herinneringen*, p. 272.

15 According to Balfas, M., *Tjipto Mangunkusumo, Demokrat sedjati*

[T. M., a Genuine Democrat], Djakarta-Amsterdam, 1952 and 1957, and A. Djajadiningrat, *Herinneringen*, p. 278.

16 See Tehupeiroy, W. K. (1908), pp. 105ff.

17 Cf. Balfas, pp. 18 and 33.

18 See *Indische Gids* (1902), II, pp. 730ff.

19 Cf. van Niel, pp. 49ff.

20 For further details, see Nagazumi, pp. 50ff.

21 Ibid., pp. 43 and 56ff.

22 Full text ibid., Appendix I, pp. 332–6.

23 Ibid., Appendix II, pp. 337–9.

24 Cf. Gunawan Mangunkusumo's reminiscences in *Soembangsih*, pp. 11–12, quoted in Nagazumi, p. 65.

25 There were also passages in the first statements which referred to the necessity of a renewal of Javanese culture. This would not necessarily contradict the Indonesian idea. The students might have thought that in developing the country the leadership would fall to the Javanese and that they should therefore have a distinctive outlook of their own. But there could, of course, have been a division among the students in the question of whether the Indonesian or the Javanese idea should predominate.

26 *Herinneringen*, pp. 236ff.

27 *Indisch Genootschap*, 1907, p. 197.

28 Ariokoesoemo di Poetro, R. M., 'Bestuursonthouding of en Bestuursbemoeienis', *Tijdschrift voor het Binnenlandsch Bestuur* (hereinafter T.B.B.), Deel 26 (1904), pp. 351ff.

29 Koesoemodikdo, 'Soewatoe timbangan jang tiada diminta' [Unsought Advice), T.B.B., Deel 30 (1906), pp. 34–45.

30 Tjokroadikoesoemo, R. M. T., 'Pengatoeran boeat menambahi kemadjoean bagei orang Djawa' [Measures to Promote the Progress of the Javanese], T.B.B., Deel 33 (1907), pp. 454–64.

31 Cf. Nagazumi, pp. 146ff.

32 Ibid., pp. 79ff.

33 Ibid., pp. 83ff., and Eyken, A. J. H., 'De Jong Javaansche Beweging' [The Young Javanese Movement], in *Berichten en Mededeelingen van de Vereeniging van Ambtenaren bij het Binnenlands Bestuur in Nederlandsch-Indië*, no. 3 (1909), p. 40, also *Indische Gids* (1909), I, p. 102.

34 For the composition of the committee, see Nagazumi, p. 104, n. 304.

35 *Indische Gids* (1909), I, p. 102.

36 For a different view of the regents' league see Nagazumi, pp. 138ff., where its opposition to Budi Utomo is contested.

37 Nagazumi, pp. 143ff.

38 Ibid., pp. 108ff.

39 Ibid., pp. 115ff.
40 Van Niel, p. 60.
41 Mangunkusumo, Tjipto, 'De Wajang', *Indische Gids* (1914), i. p. 533.
42 Koch, D. M. G., *Verantwoording. Een halve eeuw in Indonesië*, The Hague and Bandung, 1956, pp. 42ff.
43 See, e.g., the introductory chapters of Douwes Dekker, E. F. E., *Indië. Handboek voor den Indischen Nationalist*, Batavia, 1921.
44 Blumberger, J. Th. Petrus, *De Indo-Europeesche Beweging in Nederlandsch-Indië*, Haarlem, 1939, pp. 35ff.
45 Koch, *Verantwoording*, p. 60.
46 Djajadiningrat, *Herinneringen*, p. 278.
47 Idema, *Parlementaire Geschiedenis van Nederlandsch-Indië 1891–1918*, The Hague, 1924, p. 289.
48 Djajadiningrat, *Herinneringen*, p. 282.
49 Blumberger, p. 37.
50 *Ons standpunt. Verslag van de Deputatie uit het Hoofdbestuur der Vormaalige Indische Partij naar den Gouverneur-Generaal van Nederlandsch-Indië op 13 Maart 1913*, The Hague, 1913, pp. 3–9.
51 Ibid., pp. 10–15.
52 Ibid., p. 42.
53 Ibid., pp. 20 and 39.
54 *Indische Gids* (1913), I, pp. 241ff.
55 According to Pranata, *Ki Hadjar Dewantoro*, Djakarta, 1959, pp. 32ff.
56 Reproduced in Balfas, *Tjipto Mangunkusumo*, pp. 11ff.
57 Douwes Dekker, E. F. E., Mangunkusumo, Tjipto and Surjaningrat, Suardi, *Onze Verbanning* [Our Banishment], Schiedam, 1913, p. 77.

III THE STRENGTH AND WEAKNESS
OF THE INDEPENDENCE MOVEMENT

1 Cf. the article 'Chineezen', in ENI, vol. I, pp. 480ff.
2 See Van Niel, p. 88.
3 Cf. Toer, P. A., *Sedjarah Modern Indonesia* [Modern History of Indonesia], typescript, Djakarta, 1964, pp. 28ff.
4 Tur (Indonesian spelling: the Dutch 'oe' is retained only in bibliographical references) involves himself in many contradictions here. He describes in his *Sedjarah* how Tirtoadisurjo attended the STOVIA, whereas in his book on Kartini (cf. note 5 to Chapter II) he identifies T. with the young Javanese of whom Kartini writes in her letter of 12 January 1900, and who, after attending the HBS, was moved

about several times by the authorities until he was engaged as a teacher of Javanese at the school controllers in Batavia: see Toer, *Panggil aku Kartini*, pp. 127ff. and 132. Tur furnishes no evidence of Tirtoadisurjo's early political activity other than the fact that he worked for several newspapers. According to Van Niel (pp. 89ff.) he attended neither the STOVIA nor the HBS, but the OSVIA, which seems more probable in view of his contacts with former OSVIA pupils.

5 See Amelz, ed.: *H.O.S. Tjokroaminoto : Hidup dan Perdjuangannja* [Hadji Umar Said T.: His life and Fight], Djakarta, n.d. [1951], p. 89.

6 Ibid., pp. 48ff. and 93ff.; also Van Niel, p. 92.

7 Cf. ENI, vol. III, p. 695.

8 For the evidence of SI membership, see Dahm, B., *Sukarno*, pp. 12ff.

9 See ENI, vol. III, p. 695.

10 See Geertz, Clifford, *The Religion of Java*, Glencoe (Ill.) 1960. In this study he distinguishes and analyses the *santri*, *abangan* and *prijaji* civilizations.

11 According to Vredenbregt, 'The Haddj', in BKI (*Bijdragen tot de Taal-, Land- en Volkenkunde*, Koninklijk Instituut), Leiden, 1962, pp. 142ff. and 149.

12 For further details see Drewes, G. W. J., *Drie Javaansche Goeroes : Hun Leven, Onderricht en Messiasprediking* [Three Javanese *gurus*: Their Lives, Doctrines and Messianic Preaching], Leiden, 1924; also Dahm, *Sukarno*, chap. 1, and van der Kroef, Justus M., 'Javanese Messianic Expectations: Their Origin and Cultural Context', in *Comparative Studies in Society and History*, 1959, pp. 299–323.

13 Dahm, pp. 15ff.

14 Raffles, Stamford, *The History of Java*, vol. II, London, 1817, p. 70.

15 See e.g. *Indische Gids*, 1913, II, pp. 949ff.

16 ENI, vol. III, p. 696.

17 Van Niel, pp. 96ff.

18 Balfas, *Tjipto Mangunkusumo*, p. 16.

19 Van Niel, pp. 118ff.

20 See van der Wal, S. L., *De Volksraad en de Staatkundige Ontwikkeling van Nederlandsch-Indië, Eerstes Stuk 1891–1926* [The Volksraad and the Political Development of the Dutch East Indies, part I, 1891–1926], a source publication of the Dutch Historical Society (Historisch Genootschap), hereinafter referred to as *Volksraad* I. According to p. 165, note 1, the breakdown of SI members in 1916

was as follows: Java and Madura 277,377, Sumatra 75,849, Borneo 5,574, Bali 1,064 and Celebes 599.

21 Ibid., p. 164.
22 Ibid., p. 180.
23 Ibid., p. 147.
24 Hatta, Mohammed, *Verspreide Geschriften*, pp. 226, 300 and 376.
25 Van der Wal, *Volksraad* I, pp. 1–26.
26 Ibid., pp. 109ff.
27 Ibid., pp. 146ff.
28 For details, see the article 'Volksraad' in ENI, vol. IV, pp. 612ff.
29 *Volksraad* I, pp. 193ff.
30 For further details of the elections and nominations see ibid., pp. 221ff.
31 Ibid., p. 604.
32 Ibid., pp. 274ff.
33 Ibid., p. 264.
34 Colijn, H., *Staatskundige Hervormingen in Nederlandsch-Indië* [Political Reform in Netherlands India], Kampen, 1918; see also Van der Wal, *Volksraad* I, pp. 225 and 249ff.
35 *Volksraad* I, p. 299.
36 Ibid., p. 292.
37 Ibid., p. 325.
38 McVey, Ruth, *The Rise of Indonesian Communism*, Ithaca (N.Y.), 1965, p. 19.
39 Dahm, p. 33.
40 For details, see Blumberger, J. Th. Petrus, *De Communistische Beweging in Nederlandsch-Indië*, Haarlem, 1935, pp. 4ff.
41 McVey, pp. 44ff.
42 For references, see Dahm, p. 19.
43 Koch, D. M. G., 'Marxisme in Europa en hier' [Marxism in Europe and Here], in *Koloniale Vraagstucken* [Colonial Problems], Weltevreden, 1919, pp. 48ff.
44 At the 9th party congress. See McVey, p. 193.
45 Ibid., pp. 57ff.
46 Dahm, pp. 37f., and McVey, p. 93.
47 McVey, p. 279.
48 Ibid., pp. 273ff. and 311ff.
49 Ibid., pp. 317ff. For Tan Malaka's background, see ibid., pp. 116–23.
50 Ibid., p. 298.
51 Ibid., pp. 320ff. and 334ff.
52 On the Communist revolt in west Java and west Sumatra, see the exhaustive reports drawn up on the instructions of the colonial government: (i) the Bantam Report (*Rapport van de commissie voor*

*het onderzoek naar de oorzaken van de zich in de maand November
1926 in verscheidene gedeelten van de residentie Bantam voorgedaan
hebbende ongeregelheden, ingesteld bij Gouvernementsbesluit van Januari
1927* [Report of the commission of investigation, appointed by
government decision No. 1 of January 1927, into the causes of the
disturbances which took place in November 1926 in various parts
of the Bantam residency]), Weltevreden, 1928; and (ii) the West
Coast Report (*Rapport van de commissie van onderzoek, ingesteld bij
Gouvernementsbesluit van 13 Februari 1927 No. 1a*, Deel i–iv [Report
of the commission of investigation appointed by government
decision No. 1a of 13 February 1927, parts i–iv]), Weltevreden, 1928.
Extracts from these reports have been published in English in
Benda, Harry J., and McVey, Ruth, *The Communist Uprisings of
1926–1927 in Indonesia* (Key Documents, Modern Indonesia Project,
Translation Series, Cornell University, Southeast Asia Program),
Ithaca (N.Y.), 1960.

53 On the Taman Siswa schools, see now McVey, Ruth, 'Taman
Siswa and the Indonesian national awakening', in *Indonesia*, no. 4,
October 1967 (Modern Indonesia Project, Cornell University, pp.
128–49); also the Eng. trans. of Ki Hadjar Dewantoro's article of
1935 on the national educational system and the Taman Siswa
Institute at Jogjakarta (ibid., pp. 150–68). According to the figures
appended to this, there were in 1938 (1933 in brackets): 190 (170)
sections with 225 (208) Taman Siswa schools. 147 (145) of the
sections were in Java and Madura, 57 (25) in Sumatra, 4 (3) in Borneo
1 (1) in Celebes and 1(1) in Bali. The teachers numbered 700,
including 100 women, and the pupils 17,000, including 4,000 girls.

54 Blumberger, J. Th. Petrus, *De nationalistische beweging in Nederlandsch-Indië*, Haarlem, 1931, p. 183. For the development of the
association as related by itself, see also *Gedenkboek Indonesische
Vereeniging 1908–1923*, The Hague, 1924.

55 *Volksraad* I, p. 262, note 3.

56 For details of these, see Blumberger, *De nationalistische beweging*,
pp. 38ff.

57 *Overzicht van de inlandsche en maleiisch-chineesche pers* [Review of
the Native and Malay-Chinese press], ed. by Bureau voor de Volks-
lectuur, afdeeling pers, Weltevreden, no. 14 of 1925, pp. 22ff.

58 Cf. Dahm, *Sukarno*, pp. 23–56.

59 Ibid., pp. 6of.

60 The article is reproduced in Ir. [Engineer] Sukarno, *Dibawah
Bendera Revolusi* [Under the Flag of the Revolution], vol. 1, Djakarta,
1963, pp. 1–23. It is now available in English, published by the
Modern Indonesian Project at Cornell University, 1970.

Notes

61 *Islam dan Sosialisme* [Islam and Socialism], which appeared in 1924, and was republished at Djakarta in 1950 by his sons, Harsono and Anwar.

62 Dahm, pp. 77ff.

63 Blumberger, *De nationalistische beweging*, pp. 390ff.

64 Colijn, H., *Koloniale Vraagstukken van heden en morgen* [Colonial Questions of Today and Tomorrow], Amsterdam, 1928, pp. 59ff.

65 Cf. Sutan Sjahrir, *Pikiran dan Perdjuangan* [Theory and Battle], Djakarta, 1947; a collection of Sjahrir's articles of the early thirties.

66 For 'marhaenism', see further Dahm, pp. 143ff.

67 Koch, D. M. G., *Om de Vrijheid* [For Liberty], Djakarta, 1950, p. 114.

68 It may have been regarded as an extenuating circumstance in Sukarno's case that, while still under interrogation arrest, he announced his withdrawal from Partindo and abandonment of the principle of non-cooperation, which he had till then ardently defended (Dahm, pp. 172f.), whereas Hatta and Sjahrir did not recant after their arrest. Hatta has recently ascribed to Sukarno's 'defection' the fact that he was sent to Endeh in Flores instead of to Boven Digul: see *Harian Kami*, 16 February 1968, p. 4.

69 On the extension of the Volksraad's powers, see ENI, vol. VI (1932), pp. 438ff.

70 E.g. on the ground of urgency, necessary secrecy, or the Governor-General's power as crown representative, to arbitrate disputes.

71 Cf. Samkalden, I., *Het college van gedelegeerden uit den volksraad*, Leiden, 1938, pp. 200ff. This states that the first interpellation took place only in 1930, and that the right of initiative was not exercised till 1936.

72 According to van der Wal, S. L., *De Volksraad en de Staatkundige Ontwikkeling in Nederlands-Indië, Tweede Stuk 1927–1942*, Groningen, 1965 (hereinafter referred to as *Volksraad* II), pp. 122 and 190, and Samkalden, I., p. 216.

73 *Volksraad* II, pp. 46 and 94.

74 Koch, *Om de Vrijheid*, p. 115.

75 Cf. Pluvier, J. M., *Overzicht van de ontwikkeling der nationalistische beweging in Indonesië in de jaren 1930–1942*, The Hague, 1953, p. 57; also, with references to Volksraad debates, *Volksraad* II, p. 136.

76 On the Wilde Scholen Ordonnantie, see Pluvier, pp. 54–7.

77 For details of the Sutardjo petition, see Pluvier, pp. 118ff., and *Volksraad* II, pp. 219ff. (documents).

78 Colijn, H., *Koloniale Vraagstukken*, pp. 49ff.

79 *Volksraad* II, p. 392.

80 Ibid., pp. 396ff.

81 Ibid., pp. 410ff.
82 Ibid., p. 486.
83 Ibid., pp. 443ff.
84 On the reorganization of the nationalist movement, see Pluvier, pp. 94ff.
85 On the history of the religious organizations, see Blumberger, *De nationalistische beweging*, pp. 90ff., and especially the thorough study by Benda, Harry J., *The Crescent and the Rising Sun*, The Hague and Bandung, 1958, chaps. 2 and 3 ('The Renaissance of Indonesian Islam', and 'Challenge and Response: Indonesian Islam in the closing years of Dutch rule').
86 *Volksraad* II, p. 415.
87 McVey, *Rise of Indonesian Communism*, p. 35.
88 Dahm, *Sukarno*, p. 110.
89 Van der Wal, *Volksraad* II, pp. 593ff. The membership figures are as given by an Indonesian lawyer (Sastromuljono?) who was clearly well acquainted with conditions in the movement. In some cases the parties themselves gave higher figures, e.g. the PSII claimed 25,000, of whom 5,000 were said to have joined in 1939 alone: ibid., p. 515.
90 According to *Indisch Verslag 1939* II, *Statistisch Jaaroverzicht van Nederlandsch-Indië over het jaar 1938*, Batavia, 1939, especially tables 58 and 67.
91 For a review of the attitudes of the various Indonesian parties after the occupation of the Netherlands, see *Volksraad* II, pp. 572ff., and Pluvier, pp. 167ff. As regards Tjipto, see Sutan Sjahrir, *Out of Exile*, New York, 1948, p. 220, and Dahm, p. 213.
92 *Volksraad* II, p. 551, note 4.
93 Ibid., pp. 680ff.
94 Pluvier, pp. 181ff.
95 *Verslag van de Commissie tot Bestudeering van Staatsrechtelijke Hervormingen*, Deel I en II [Report of the Commission for the Study of Political Reforms, parts I and II], Batavia, 1941, especially part II, pp. 373ff.
96 For further details, see van Mook, H. J., *The Netherlands Indies and Japan. Battle on Paper 1940-41*, New York, 1944.
97 Dahm, *Sukarno*, pp. 111-15, 217-20.
98 Van der Wal, p. 590, and Pluvier, pp. 183ff.
99 Pluvier, pp. 186-8; for the Comité Indië Weerbar see Nagazumi, *Budi Utomo*, pp. 200ff. and 230-9.
100 *Volksraad* II, pp. 699ff. Extracts from the Queen's speeches, ibid., pp. 604 and 689ff.
101 Pluvier, p. 190.

Notes

102 *Volksraad* II, pp. 651ff.

103 Ibid., pp. 657ff.

104 For details see Piekaar, A. J., *Atjeh en de oorlog met Japan* [Atjeh and the war with Japan], The Hague and Bandung, 1949, pp. 57ff.

IV THE JAPANESE INTERREGNUM, 1942–45

1 Cf. (with further references) Benda, H. J., 'The Beginnings of the Japanese Occupation of Java', *Far Eastern Quarterly*, vol. XV, no. 4 (1956); also Nishijima, Shigetada, and Kishi, Koichi (eds.), *Japanese Military Administration in Indonesia*, Washington, Joint Publications Research Service, 1963, pp. 132ff. and 330ff.; also Sutan Sjahrir, *Out of Exile*, pp. 237ff., and Dahm, *Sukarno*, pp. 164ff.

2 Nishijima and Kishi, pp. 342ff.

3 For the military government's first orders, see the booklet issued in 1942: *Undang-Undang dari Pembesar Balatentara Dai Nippon nos. 1–20* [Regulations of the Japanese commander-in-chief, nos. 1–20].

4 On Japanese plans for Indonesia, see Nishijima and Kishi, pp. 103ff.; also Benda, H. J., Irikura, James K., and Kishi, Koichi, *Japanese Military Administration in Indonesia : Selected Documents* (Translation Series no. 6, Southeast Asia Studies), Yale University (New Haven), 1965; also Elsbree, W. H., *Japan's Role in Southeast Asia Movements, 1940–45*, Cambridge (Mass.), 1953, pp. 13ff., and Aziz, M. A., *Japan's Colonialism in Indonesia*, The Hague, 1955, pp. 99ff.

5 Cf. *Indisch Verslag* 1939, II, pp. 2 and 13–16 for figures.

6 Nishijima and Kishi, pp. 106–8.

7 Ibid., p. 334.

8 Cf. also Kahin, G. McT., *Nationalism and Revolution in Indonesia*, Ithaca (N.Y.), 1958, p. 103.

9 Sutan Sjahrir, pp. 225ff. In Sjahrir's memoirs Tjipto Mangunkusumo is referred to as Dr. Suribno, Amir Sjarifuddin as Siregar, and Mohammed Hatta as Hafil.

10 Cf. Dahm, *Sukarno*, pp. 226f.

11 Ibid., pp. 115–17, 121f.

12 Sjahrir, p. 242.

13 Dahm, pp. 232f.

14 Nishijima and Kishi, pp. 410ff.

15 Ibid., p. 349.

16 Dahm, pp. 245f.

17 Nishijima and Kishi, p. 358.
18 Ibid., p. 124.
19 Dahm, p. 246.
20 Nishijima and Kishi, p. 405.
21 Ibid., p. 359.
22 *Asia Raya*, 2 August 2603 [i.e., 1943].
23 For details, see Benda, H. J., *The Crescent and the Rising Sun*, pp. 111ff.
24 Ibid., p. 148.
25 On the Ahmadijah in Indonesia see Pijper, G. F., 'De Ahmadijah in Indonesië', in *Bingkisan Budi: Een Bundel Opstellen aan Dr. Ph. S. van Ronkel* [Collection of Papers], Leiden, 1950, pp. 247–54.
26 Ibid., p. 248.
27 Benda, *Crescent*, p. 160.
28 *Asia Raya*, 2 December 2603 [i.e., 1943]. For relations between the Japanese occupation authorities and the sultanate of Jogjakarta, see Selosoemardjan, *Social Changes in Jogjakarta*, Ithaca (N.Y.), 1962, chapter 3 (The Japanese occupation period), pp. 41–58.
29 For the establishment of *tonari gumi*, see Benda, *Crescent*, pp. 154ff.
30 Mangkupradja, Gatot, 'The Peta and my Relations with the Japanese: A Correction of Sukarno's Autobiography', in *Indonesia*, Ithaca (N.Y.), no. 5, Cornell University, 1968, pp. 105–34.
31 On the genesis of Peta, see ibid.; also Pauker, G. J., *The Role of the Military in Underdeveloped Countries*, Princeton, 1962, pp. 185ff.; Benda, *Crescent*, pp. 138ff.; Nishijima and Kishi, pp. 192ff.; and Aziz, *Japan's Colonialism*, pp. 225ff.
32 Dahm, pp. 271ff.
33 Ibid.
34 For events leading up to the Tokyo promise, cf. Benda, Irikura and Kishi, *Selected Documents*, nos. 64–72, and Nishijima and Kishi, pp. 413ff. and 373ff.
35 *Asia Raya*, 12 September 2604 [i.e., 1944], p. 2.
36 *Asia Raya*, 17 November 2604 [1944], p. 1.
37 Dahm, pp. 283ff.
38 For the Blitar incident, see Anderson, B. R. O'G., *Some Aspects of Indonesian Politics under the Japanese Occupation 1944–45* (Modern Indonesia Project, Interim Report Series), Ithaca (N.Y.), Cornell University, 1961, pp. 46ff.; also Nishijima and Kishi, pp. 250ff.
39 Nishijima and Kishi, pp. 105ff.
40 For the different *pemuda* groups, cf. Anderson, pp. 48ff., and Dimyati, M., *Sedjarah Perdjuangan Indonesia* (History of the Indonesian Struggle), Djakarta, 1951, pp. 91ff.
41 See Anderson, pp. 51ff., and the account by a participant, Sidik

Notes

Kertapati, *Sekitar Proklamasi 17 Augustus 1945* [About the Proclamation of 17 August 1945], Djakarta, 1964, pp. 76ff.

42 A complete list of members and the groups to which they belonged is given in Anderson, pp. 18ff.

43 According to Ichibangase, the Japanese deputy chairman of BPKI, in a subsequent interrogation: see Dahm, p. 296; also, as regards the hope of gaining time, Nishijima and Kishi, pp. 423ff.

44 Anderson takes a different view, seeing in the small number of Muslims an affront by the occupying power to Indonesian Islam. Cf. also Benda, H. J., *Crescent*, p. 187.

45 For analyses of the *pantja sila* speech, an English version of which was published at Djakarta in 1952 by the Indonesian ministry of information, see Kahin, pp. 122–7, Anderson, pp. 24–6, and Dahm, pp. 336–43. A critique of the *pantja sila* as a political ideology will be found in J. M. van der Kroef, *Indonesia in the Modern World*, vol. II, Bandung, 1956, pp. 198–252.

46 Dahm, p. 200.

47 Anderson, pp. 57ff.

48 What follows is based on Yamin, Muhammed, *Naskah Persiapan Undang-Undang Dasar 1945* [Documents on the Preparation of the 1945 Constitution], vol. I, Djakarta, 1959. For the voting, see p. 184.

49 Ibid., p. 214.

50 Ibid., pp. 287ff.

51 Ibid., pp. 299ff.

52 Anderson, pp. 26ff.

53 Yamin, *Naskah*, pp. 371ff.

54 Thus in a directive of 3 August 1945; see Nishijima and Kishi, pp. 432ff.

55 Ibid., pp. 207ff.

56 For details on Sumatra, especially Atjeh, see Piekaar, *Atjeh en de oorlog med Japan*, esp. pp. 220ff., 233ff., 244 and 362.

57 Nishijima and Kishi, pp. 172ff.

58 Cf. Anderson, p. 63, n. 183.

V   THE INDONESIAN REVOLUTION

1 Sjahrir, *Out of Exile*, pp. 253ff.

2 Ibid., p. 255.

3 Hatta, Mohammed, 'Legende en realiteit rondom de proclamatie van 17 Agustus', in *Verspreide Geschriften*, pp. 338ff.

4 Dahm, *Sukarno*, pp. 313f.

5 Cf. Anderson, *Some Aspects*, pp. 105ff.; Yamin, *Naskah*, pp. 399ff.; Nishijima and Kishi, pp. 514ff.; and Adam Malik, *Riwajat dan perdjuangan sekitar proklamasi kemerdekaan Indonesia* [History and Battle for the Proclamation of Indonesian Independence], Djakarta, 1956, p. 61.

6 According to Nishijima and Kishi, p. 515, Sukarno was nominated for the Presidency by Latuharhary, the representative of the Moluccas. It appears, however, from Yamin, *Naskah*, p. 427 that it was Oto Iskandar Dinata who proposed that Sukarno and Hatta should be chosen by acclamation as President and Vice-President respectively.

7 For text, see Dimyati, *Sedjarah perdjuangan Indonesia* [History of the Indonesian Struggle], Djakarta, 1951, pp. 95–7.

8 Dahm, pp. 319ff.

9 For further details, see Pauker, G. J., 'The Role of the Military in Indonesia', loc. cit., pp. 190ff. A. H. Nasution (*TNI—Tentara Nasional Indonesia* [The Indonesian National Army], Bandung-Djakarta, 1963, p. 155) estimates the number of trained troops at 150,000 for Java and Sumatra, plus 'hundreds of thousands' of partially trained men.

10 Anderson, p. 118.

11 Wolf, Charles, jr., *The Indonesian Story*, New York, 1948, p. 21.

12 Nasution, *TNI*, p. 165. Elsewhere (p. 154) Nasution expresses the opinion that there were enough arms to equip a hundred infantry battalions.

13 Ibid., pp. 120ff., and Simatupang, T. B., *Laporan dari Banaran* [Report from Banaran], Djakarta, 1961, pp. 196ff.

14 *TNI*, pp. 224ff.

15 Ibid., p. 138.

16 Ibid., pp. 226–8 and 244ff.; also Simatupang, *Laporan*, pp. 198ff.

17 Anderson, pp. 112ff. For the composition of Indonesian cabinets from 1945 to 1965, see Finch, S., and Lev, Dan S., *Republic of Indonesia Cabinets, 1945–65* (Modern Indonesia Project), Ithaca (N.Y.), Cornell University, 1965.

18 Kahin, *Nationalism and Revolution in Indonesia*, pp. 85ff.

19 Ibid., pp. 118ff., and Anderson, pp. 103ff. Tan Malaka's reappearance in the movement is described by Malik, A., *Riwajat*, pp. 48ff., and in his autobiography *Dari pendjara ke pendjara* [From Prison to Prison], vol. III, Djakarta, n.d., pp. 55ff.

20 Yamin, Muhammad, *Tan Malaka. Bapak Republik Indonesia*, 'Ost-java' [East Java], 1946.

21 *Riwajat*, pp. 76ff.; cf. also Anderson, pp. 123ff., and Kertapati, S., *Sekitar Proklamasi 17 Agustus*, pp. 138ff.

Notes

22 Anderson, pp. 120ff. Full text in Raliby, Osman (ed.), *Documenta Historica* I. *Sedjarah documenter dari pertumbuhan dan perdjuangan Negara Republik Indonesia* [Documentary History of the Origins and Struggle of the Indonesian Republic], Djakarta, 1953, p. 47.

23 Kahin, pp. 151ff.; Dahm, pp. 326ff.

24 Text in Nasution, *TNI*, pp. 180ff. For the battle for Surabaja, see ibid., pp. 182ff.

25 See, e.g., his diary, written in exile and published under the pseudonym 'Sjahrazad', *Indonesische Overpeinzingen* [Indonesian Reflections], Amsterdam, 1945, An English translation by C. Wolf, jr., with a supplementary passage on the Japanese occupation, was published as: Sjahrir, Sutan, *Out of Exile*, New York, 1949.

26 Eng. trans. of the pamphlet, with a detailed elaboration, by Anderson, B. R. O'G., Modern Indonesian Project, Cornell University, Ithaca (N.Y.), 1968.

27 For the composition of Sjahrir's first cabinet, see Finch and Lev, *Cabinets*, p. 4.

28 For the different strands of opinion in Masjumi, see Kahin, pp. 156–8.

29 Ibid., pp. 173ff., and Nasution, *TNI*, pp. 232ff.

30 Nasution, *TNI*, chap. 4 ('Politik kurang memperhitungkan strategi' ['Politics take too little account of strategy']), pp. 169–98, 231ff., (where he expresses sympathy for Tan Malaka's viewpoint).

31 Dimyati, *Sedjarah*, p. 117.

32 Kahin, pp. 177ff.

33 Ibid., pp. 189ff.

34 For details, see Wolf, C., *The Indonesian Story*, pp. 33ff.

35 Ibid., pp. 43ff.

36 Kahin, p. 201.

37 For the names and party affiliations of members of the Working Committee, see ibid., pp. 204ff.

38 Wolf, p. 122.

39 Kahin, pp. 208ff. (also for the composition of the Sjarifuddin cabinet).

40 Ibid., p. 226.

41 Ibid., p. 228.

42 Ibid., pp. 259ff.

43 Brackman, A. C., *Indonesian Communism: A History*, New York, 1963, pp. 64ff.

44 For this and what follows, see ibid., pp. 80ff., and Kahin, pp. 272ff.

45 Kahin, p. 276.

46 Ibid., pp. 292ff.

47 Aidit, D. N., *Konfrontasi Peristiwa Madiun 1948—Peristiwa Sumatera 1956* [Comparison of Events at Madiun in 1948 and in Sumatra in 1956], Djakarta, 1957.

48 This appears clearly from the documentation in Kahin, op. cit., pp. 271–303. Kahin was in Indonesia during the revolutionary period, on which his book is a mine of information. Cf. also Brackman (who was also in Indonesia at the time), pp. 100ff., where he quotes from Suripno's memoirs.

49 Kahin, p. 295.

50 Ibid., pp. 334ff.

51 For the text of Sjafruddin's mandate, see Finch and Lev, *Cabinets*, p. 17. It appears, however, that he was not aware of the measure until months afterwards, and that he exercised his own initiative in forming the emergency government soon after the occupation of Jogjakarta; see Baharuddin, R. E., 'Tjerita tentang pemerintah darurat Sjafruddin di Sumatera Tengah' ['An Account of Sjafruddin's emergency government in Central Sumatra'], in Marpaung, D., (ed.), *Bingkisan Nasional. Kenangan 10 Tahun Revolusi Indonesia* [A National Gift. Commemorating Ten Years of the Indonesian Revolution], Djakarta, 1955, pp. 115–19.

52 Simatupang, *Laporan*, pp. 17ff.

53 Brackman, p. 109.

54 Kahin, pp. 313ff.

55 Brackman, pp. 109ff. and 117.

56 For an account, based on diaries, of the beginnings and development of the guerrilla forces, see Simatupang, *Laporan*, pp. 25ff. An English translation of his 'Report from Banaran' is in preparation (Cornell University). Nasution, who was in command of the troops in Java at this time, published important documents in his later military writings, especially in *Pokok-Pokok Gerilja*, Djakarta, 1954, pp. 126ff. (Eng. trans.: Naustion, A. H., *Fundamentals of Guerilla Warfare*, New York, Praeger, 1965.)

57 Kahin, p. 401.

58 Brackman, p. 118, quoting a 'Tan Malaka pamphlet'.

59 Nasution, *TNI*, p. 32.

60 Brackman, p. 118.

61 The Dutch initials stand for *Bijeenkomst van Federaal Overleg*.

62 For details see Kahin, pp. 403ff.

63 Ibid., pp. 423ff.

64 Ibid., pp. 433–45.

Notes

1 Cf. *Asia Raya* for 8 November 2604 [i.e., 1944], p. 3.
2 See Piekaar, A. J., *Atjeh en de oorlog met Japan* [Atjeh and the War with Japan], The Hague – Bandung, 1949.
3 On this, see Schiller, A. A., *The Formation of Federal Indonesia*, The Hague – Bandung, 1955, chap. iii ('Local Government'), pp. 8off.
4 For an analysis of the constitution of the USI, see Kahin, *Nationalism*, pp. 446ff. The full text may be found in Engelbrecht, W. A. (ed.), *Kitab² Undang², Undang² dan Peraturan² Serta Undang² Dasar Sementara Republik Indonesia* [Law Codes, Laws and Decrees, together with the provisional Constitution of the Republic of Indonesia], Leiden, 1954, pp. 17–25. This provides Dutch translations, and also includes the codes of laws belonging to the colonial period.
5 A provisional government of the Republic under Susanto Tirtoprodjo held office from December 1949 to January 1950. For its composition and that of the Halim cabinet, see Finch and Lev, pp. 2off.
6 Westerling, Raymond, *Challenge to Terror*, London, 1952, p. 110.
7 Supomo, R., *The Provisional Constitution of the Republic of Indonesia*, trans. Jones, G. N. (Modern Indonesia Project, Translation Series), Ithaca (N.Y.), Cornell University, 1964.
8 Cf. Sukarno's speech of 17 August 1950, in Sukarno, *Dari Proklamasi sampai Gesuri* [National Day speeches, 1945–63], Djakarta, 1963, pp. 81ff.; quotations, pp. 120 and 123ff.
9 Dahm, *Sukarno*, pp. 145ff. and 200ff.
10 Compiled from Feith, H., *The Decline of Constitutional Democracy in Indonesia*, Ithaca (N.Y.), 1962, pp. 128ff. Further data on the history, statutes and programmes of the respective parties and their representation in parliament are given in the handbook issued by the Ministry of Information, *Kepartaian dan Parlamentaria Indonesia*, Djakarta, 1954.
11 A collection of Natsir's articles was published in Natsir, M., *Capita Selecta*, Bandung – The Hague, 1955, 2 vols.
12 Dahm, *Sukarno*, pp. 185ff.
13 Feith, *Decline*, pp. 113ff.
14 *Kepartaian*, p. 460.
15 Cf. Kahin, *Nationalism*, pp. 309ff.
16 Cf. *Kepartaian*, p. 462: 'The government offers to the Indonesian middle class, a group of social and political importance, opportunities to develop and consolidate its position in society.'
17 Ibid., pp. 412ff.

18 See Geertz, C., *The Religion of Java*, Glencoe (Ill.), 1960, and also the exhaustive sociological analysis of the rural santri and abangan cultures in Jay, R., *Religion and Politics in Rural Central Java*, (Southeast Asia Studies), New Haven, Yale University, 1963.

19 See *Kepartaian*, pp. 42ff. and 50ff.

20 Ibid., pp. 301ff. and 313. On the problem of the integration of Eurasians in the Indonesian state, see van der Kroef, J. M., 'The Eurasian Dilemma', in his *Indonesia in the Modern World*, part I, Bandung, 1954, pp. 257–308.

21 For the PIR, see *Kepartaian*, pp. 213ff.

22 For the PSI, see ibid., pp. 525ff. (ideology) and 535ff. (action programme).

23 For the Murba, see Feith, *Decline*, pp. 131ff., and *Kepartaian*, pp. 545ff.

24 For the PKI, see van der Kroef, J. M., *The Communist Party of Indonesia*, Vancouver (B.C.), 1965, pp. 44ff.; Hindley, D., *The Communist Party of Indonesia, 1951–1963*, Berkeley (Calif.), 1964, pp. 29ff.; and Brackman, A., *Indonesian Communism*, New York, 1963, pp. 137ff.

25 For the Christian parties, see *Kepartaian*, pp. 387ff. (Partai Katolik) and 469ff. (Parkindo).

26 The fortunes of the successive cabinets are traced in detail in Feith, *Decline*.

27 Figures from *Indisch Verslag 1939*. II, *Statistisch Jaaroverzicht van Nederlandsch-Indië*, Batavia, 1939, pp. 97 and 102.

28 For the course of the negotiations over West Irian, see Duynstee, J. F. M., *Nieuw Guinea als schakel tussen Nederland en Indonesië* [New Guinea as a Link between the Netherlands and Indonesia], Amsterdam, 1961, and Lijphart, A., *The Trauma of Decolonization: The Dutch and West New Guinea*, New Haven and London, 1966.

29 *Kepartaian*, p. 465; emphasis added.

30 Cf. Feith, *Decline*, pp. 198ff.

31 On the Bandung conference see ibid., pp. 384ff., and Kahin, G. McT., *The Asian-African Conference, Bandung, Indonesia, 1955*, Ithaca (N.Y.), 1956.

32 Van der Kroef, J. M., 'The Present Political Crisis', in *Indonesia in the Modern World*, part II, pp. 312ff.

33 Ibid. Also Feith, *Decline*, pp. 246ff., and Pauker, G. J., 'The Role of the Military in Indonesia', in Johnson, John J. (ed.), *The Role of the Military in Underdeveloped Countries*, Princeton, 1967, p. 207.

34 See Feith, *Decline*, pp. 394ff.

35 On Kartosuwirjo, see Pinardi, *S. M. Kartosuwirjo*, Djakarta, 1964.

Notes

For data concerning the victims of the Darul Islam movement, see ibid., p. 179.

36 On K. Muzakar, see Djarwadi, R., *Kisah Kahar Muzakar* [K. M.'s Story], Surabaja, n.d. [1963].

37 Cf. Piekaar, A. J., *Atjeh*, pp. 18ff. PUSA stands for Persatuan Ulama Seluruh Atjeh (All-Atjeh Ulama Union).

38 For a criticism of the *pantja sila* at this time, see van der Kroef, 'Pantjasila', in *Indonesia in the Modern World*, part II, pp. 198–261.

39 For details, see Feith, H., *The Indonesian Elections of 1955* (Modern Indonesia Project, Interim Report Series), Ithaca (N.Y.), Cornell University, 1957.

40 For a lively description of such an election in 1954 as a sociological case-study, see Geertz, C., *The Social History of an Indonesian Town*, Cambridge (Mass.), 1965, pp. 155ff.

41 Cf. Feith, *Elections*, pp. 43ff.

42 Ibid., pp. 58ff. and 65.

43 See Feith, *Elections*, p. 65n.

44 Cf. Geertz, *Social History*, pp. 127–9 and *passim*. Apart from Geertz's stimulating works on the social structure of modern Indonesia – in addition to *Social History* and *The Religion of Java*, these include *Peddlers and Princes*, Chicago, 1963, and *Agricultural Involution*, Berkeley, 1963 – the theme of social change in Indonesia is treated in the classic study by Wertheim, W. F., *Indonesian Society in Transition*, The Hague and Bandung, 1959.

45 See Table XII below, also Lev, Daniel S., *The Transition to Guided Democracy : Indonesian Politics, 1957–59*, Modern Indonesia Project, Monograph Series, Cornell University, Ithaca (N.Y.), 1965, pp. 84ff.

46 Cf. Feith, *Elections*, table 5, p. 81.

47 Feith, *Decline*, pp. 468ff.

48 Mohammed Natsir in conversation with the author at Djakarta, October 1966.

49 Cf. Feith, *Decline*, pp. 440ff.

50 Dates from Nasution, A. H., *Mengamankan Pandji² Revolusi* [Protect the Banner of the Revolution], Djakarta, 1964, pp. 290ff.

51 See Feith, *Decline*, pp. 503ff. and 510.

52 See e.g. his speech on receiving an honorary doctorate at Jogjakarta in November 1956, Hatta, Mohammed, *Past and Future*, Modern Indonesia Project, Translation Series, Ithaca (N.Y.), Cornell University, 1960.

53 Feith, *Decline*, p. 527.

54 Ibid., pp. 541ff., and Lev, D. S., *Transition*, pp. 16ff.

55 See his speech on the anniversary of the foundation of the PNI, 3 July 1957, in Sukarno, *Marhaen and Proletarian*, Modern Indonesia

Project, Translation Series, Iathaca (N.Y.), Cornell University, 1960, p. 27.

56 Cf. Feith, *Decline*, pp. 544ff., and Lev, *Transition*, p. 15.

VII THE ERA OF GUIDED DEMOCRACY, 1957–65

1 See Lev, D., *Transition*, pp. 19ff.
2 On Djuanda see, e.g., Tjiptoning, *Apa dan Siapa* [Who and What], Jogjakarta, 1951, pp. 107–17.
3 Compiled from Lev, *Transition*, pp. 90–5.
4 For details, see ibid., pp. 105ff. and 160ff.
5 For individual names, see ibid., pp. 26–7.
6 Ibid., p. 29.
7 Abdulgani, Roeslan, *Pantjasila, The Prime Mover of the Indonesian Revolution*, Djakarta, 1964, p. 95. For a general discussion of the status of Islam and the *pantja sila*, see Lev, *Transition*, pp. 123ff.
8 Hatta, Mohammed, *Tanggung Djawab Moril Kaum Intelligentsia* [The Moral Responsibility of the Intelligentsia], Bandung, 1966 reprint, p. 18, supplemented by a conversation between Hatta and the author at Djakarta on 29 June 1966. On the relations between Sukarno and Hatta at this time cf. also van der Kroef, J. M., 'Sukarno and Hatta. The great Debate in Indonesia', *Political Quarterly*, vol. XXIX (1958), pp. 238–50.
9 Cf. Sukarno's description of the attack in Sukarno, *An Autobiography as Told to Cindy Adams*, New York, 1965, pp. 272–3.
10 See Lev, *Transition*, pp. 28–39, and Feith, *Decline*, pp. 585–8.
11 Nasution, A. H., *Menudju Tentara Rakjat* [On the Way to a People's Army], Djakarta, n.d. (1964), pp. 23–37.
12 For a description of the fighting in Sumatra, see, e.g., Mossman, James, *Rebels in Paradise, Indonesian Civil War*, London, Cape, 1961.
13 Sukarno, 'Tahun Tantangan' [The Year of Challenges], in *Dari Proklamasi sampai Gesuri*, pp. 371ff.
14 Abdulgani, R., *Pantjasila*, pp. 76ff.
15 See Lev, *Transition*, pp. 207, 224–8 and 241; also Nasution, *Menudju*, pp. 26–7.
16 See Lev, *Transition*, pp. 235–51.
17 Sukarno's speech was published in Indonesian and English by the Ministry of Information under the title *Res Publica. Sekali Lagi Res Publica* [The State, and yet again the State]. It is reproduced in Yamin, M., *Naskah*, pp. 653–702.
18 The results of the successive votes are given as follows in Lev, pp.

Notes

267–8. Public vote on 30 May 1959: 269 for the 1945 constitution, 199 against. Secret vote on 1 June: 264 ayes, 204 noes. Public vote on 2 June: 263 ayes, 203 noes.

19 Lev, *Transition*, p. 273.

20 R. Abdulgani, in a conversation with the author at New Haven, Conn., on 21 July 1968.

21 The speech was provisionally entitled 'The Rediscovery of our Revolution' (Penemuan Kembali Revolusi Kita), and was published in *Dibawah Bendera Revolusi* II, Djakarta, 1966, pp. 351–91, and elsewhere. For an English translation see Sukarno, *Towards the Freedom and Dignity of Man*, Djakarta, 1961, pp. 39–76 ('The Rediscovery of our Revolution').

22 Hannah, Wilfried A., *Bung Karno's Indonesia: A Collection of 25 Reports for the American Universities Field Staff*, New York, 1960, report 13, p. 3.

23 Abdulgani, R., *Pantjasila*, pp. 218ff.

24 For a full interpretation of developments only touched on here, see Weatherbee, D. E., *Ideology in Indonesia: Sukarno's Indonesian Revolution* (Southeast Asia Studies, Monograph Series no. 8), New Haven, Yale University, 1966.

25 Sukarno, *Pantjasila sebagai Dasar Negra* [The Pantja Sila as the Basis of the State], Djakarta, n.d. (1961), pp. 24ff.

26 Ibid., pp. 6off. and 84. For Sukarno's earlier utterances, see above, Chapter III, section 4.

27 Notosutardjo, H. A. (ed.), *Kepribadian Revolusi Bangsa Indonesia* [The Independence of the Indonesian People's Revolution], Djakarta, 1964, pp. 135ff.

28 Notosutardjo, H. A. (ed.), *Bung Karno mentjari dan menemukan Tuhan* [Sukarno seeks God and finds Him], Djakarta, 1965, pp. 139ff.; also Salam, Solichin, *Bung Karno dan Kehidupan Berpikir dalam Islam* [Sukarno and living Islamic Thought], Djakarta, 1964, pp. 6off. and 77ff.

29 Sukarno, *Shaping dan Reshaping*, ed. by Partai Nasional Indonesia, Djakarta, 1964, pp. 56 and 68.

30 The five points were: (i) consolidation of successes in the field of internal security, (ii) overcoming economic difficulties by increasing production, (iii) continuing the fight against imperialism and neo-colonialism while strengthening the mutual support of all national revolutionary groups, (iv) propagating ideology and (v) retooling the apparatus of state. See Sukarno, *Dibawah Bendera Revolusi* II, pp. 538ff. Branches of Nasakom were to be established even in the villages, but collaboration there was if anything less of a reality than at the centre, where fear of Sukarno's displeasure had its effect.

History of Indonesia

31 Quoted from notes by the author, who listened to some of Abdulgani's propaganda speeches in 1966. The latter's interpretations of the *pantja sila* may be studied in Abdulgani, R., *Pantjasila* (speeches etc., down to 1964) and in his other collections of speeches to various audiences, e.g. (to journalists) *Pantjaran Api* [The Fire Spreads], Djakarta, 1963; (to students) *Dihadapan Tunas Bangsa* [To the Élite of the Nation], Djakarta, 1964; (to Muslims) *Api Islam dalam Kobaran Api Revolusi Indonesia* [The Fire of Islam in the Blaze of the Indonesian Revolution], Djakarta, 1966.

32 Sukarno, *To Build the World Anew*, Djakarta, 1960, pp. 29ff.

33 *Dibawah Bendera Revolusi (DBR)* II, p. 433.

34 Sukarno, *Amanat Pembangun Presiden* [The President's Message on Development], Djakarta, n.d. [1962], pp. 64–126. This contains the text of his speech and instructions to the commission.

35 For criticism of the eight-year plan, see Paauw, D. S., 'From Colonial to Guided Economy' in McVey, R., (ed.), *Indonesia*, New Haven, H.R.A.F., 1963, pp. 222–31; also Pauker, G. J., 'Indonesia's Eight Year Development Plan', *Pacific Affairs*, Summer 1961, pp. 115–30, and Humphrey, D. D., 'Indonesia's Plan for National Development', *Asian Survey*, Dec. 1962, pp. 12–21.

36 *DBR* II, pp. 664ff. and 681ff. (speech of 17 August 1965).

37 On symbolism in Indonesian politics see also Feith, H., 'Indonesia's political Symbols and their Wielders', *World Politics*, Oct. 1963, pp. 79–97.

38 Cf. Finch and Lev, *Indonesian Cabinets*, pp. 40–2.

39 On economic development from 1949 onwards see Paauw, D. S., *Financing Economic Development: The Indonesian Case*, Glencoe (Ill.), 1960, and his article cited in note 35 above. For the period of parliamentary democracy, see also Higgins, B., *Indonesia's Economic Stabilization and Development*, New York, 1957, and Sutter, J. O., *Indonesianisasi: Politics in a Changing Economy, 1940–55* (Southeast Asia Program), Ithaca (N.Y.), Cornell University, 1959, 4 vols. For the early days of the Indonesian republic, there is an interesting study by Dr. Sumitro Djojohadikusumo, *Persoalan Ekonomi Di Indonesia*, Djakarta, 1953.

40 Cf. Paauw's table 'Value of Exports', in *Financing*, pp. 450ff.

41 Paauw, 'From Colonial to Guided Democracy', in McVey, R., (ed.), *Indonesia*, pp. 204ff. For the rise in prices cf. Brackman, A., *Indonesian Communism*, p. 266.

42 *Asian Recorder*, New Delhi, 1959, p. 2906.

43 The Chinese problem is dealt with more fully by Skinner, G. W., in 'The Chinese Minority', in McVey, R., (ed.), *Indonesia*, pp. 97–117. As regards the Peranakan see Somers, M. F., *Peranakan*

Chinese Politics in Indonesia, Southeast Asia Program, Ithaca (N.Y.), Cornell University, 1964.

44 See Legge, J. D., *Central Authority and Regional Autonomy in Indonesia : A Study in Local Administration 1950–60*, Ithaca (N.Y.), 1961, pp. 209–29.

45 *Asian Recorder*, 1960, p. 3230.

46 Van der Kroef, *The Communist Party of Indonesia*, p. 115.

47 Cf. Feith, H., 'Dynamics of Guided Democracy', by McVey, R., (ed.), *Indonesia*, pp. 343–4, and Lev, D. S., 'The Political Role of the Army in Indonesia', *Pacific Affairs*, Winter 1963/4, pp. 357–8.

48 Notosutardjo, H. A., *Proses Kembali Kepada Djiwa Proklamasi 1945* [Return to the Spirit of the 1945 Proclamation Era], Djakarta, 1964, pp. 489–90.

49 Conversation between Hatta and the author at Djakarta, 29 June 1966.

50 Hatta, Mohammed, *Demokrasi Kita* [Our Democracy] (reprint of his series of articles of May 1960), Djakarta, 1966, pp. 18ff.

51 Compiled from Feith, 'Dynamics', loc. cit., p. 345.

52 For the later course and suppression of the rebellion, see Feith H., and Lev, D. S., 'The End of the Indonesian Rebellion', *Pacific Affairs*, Spring 1963, pp. 32–46.

53 Abdulgani, Ruslan, *Pantjaran Api*, p. 189.

54 Hatta, M., *Tanggung Djawab*, p. 28.

55 Cf. the speech delivered on 6 May 1966 by S. H. Mashuri, director of higher education, at the opening of a symposium at the Universitas Indonesia, and reproduced in *Kebangkitan Semangat 66. Mendjeladja Tracee Baru* [The Spirit of 1966 in the Ascendant: the Search for new Ways], typescript, Djakarta, 1966, where Mashuri also refers to the *trahison des clercs*.

56 Dahm, *Sukarno*, pp. 115–17.

57 For further details see Weatherbee, *Ideology*, pp. 57ff.

58 Sukarno, *To Build the World Anew*, p. 13.

59 English translations of Sukarno's speeches to international bodies were published by the Ministry of Information. For a chonology and further bibliographical details, see Weatherbee, pp. 106–10.

60 See, e.g., Sukarno's speech of 1 May 1965, *Conefo—suatu Nasakom Internasional*, Djakarta, 1965; also speeches of this period on Nasakom such as those of 1 June, *Nasakom adalah benar* [Nasakom is truth], and 25 July, *Nasakom, Djiwaku* [Nasakom is my soul], both Djakarta, 1965.

61 Cf. Duynstee, *Nieuw-Guinea als Schakel tussen Nederland en Indonesië*, Amsterdam, 1963, pp. 416ff.

62 Baharuddin Lopa, *Djalannja Revolusi Indonesia membebaskan Irian*

Barat [The Indonesian Revolution and the Liberation of West Irian], Djakarta, 1963, p. 94.

63 Ibid., pp. 195ff.

64 Ibid., pp. 118ff.

65 *DBR* II, p. 509.

66 For Nasution's political attitude at this time see his speeches: English version, *Towards a People's Army*, Djakarta, 1964. On Sukarno's rivalry with the army see Feith, 'Dynamics', pp. 336ff., and Kahin's essay in Kahin, G. McT., (ed.), *Major Governments in Asia*, Ithaca (N.Y.), 1965, pp. 655ff.

67 Suhardiman, *Kesetiaan Pahlawan Revolusi Yani kepada Revolusi, Pemimpin Besar Revolusi dan Adjaran² Bung Karno* [The Loyalty of Yani, Hero of the Revolution, to the Revolution, its Great Leader and the Teachings of Bung Karno], Djakarta, 1966, p. 29.

68 Sukarno, *Message and Order of the Day*, Djakarta, 1962, p. 8.

69 On the conflict between Indonesia and Malaysia, see Pluvier, J. M., *Confrontations: A Study in Indonesian Politics*, Kuala Lumpur, 1965; also Kahin, G. McT., 'Malaysia and Indonesia', *Pacific Affairs*, Autumn 1964, pp. 253–70, and Mackie, J. A. C., 'Indonesia. A Background to Confrontation', *World Today*, vol. xx, April 1964. For the Indonesian viewpoint see the Foreign Ministry's White Book *Why Indonesia opposes British-made Malaysia*, Djakarta, 1964.

70 For text of protests, see *Why Indonesia Opposes*, pp. 137ff.

71 See Sukarno's speeches of 25 Sep. and 5 Oct. 1963, also those of 23 Jan., 20 Feb., 16 March, 13 April, 3 and 20 May 1964, in *Gelora Konfrontasi Megganjang Malaysia* [Confrontation sweeps to destroy Malaysia], Djakarta, 1964, pp. 287ff.

72 Cf. van der Kroef, *Communist Party*, pp. 271ff.

73 *Why Indonesia Opposes*, pp. 42ff.

74 Cf. *Masa Konfrontasi* [The Time of Confrontation], speeches delivered and resolutions adopted at the Cairo conference, Djakarta, Ministry of Foreign Affairs, 1965.

75 For delegations to and from Peking at this time, see summaries in *Pantjasila. A monthly Magazine on Indonesian Politics and Culture*, vol. II (1964–5).

76 On the development of the PKI under guided democracy see van der Kroef, *Communist Party*, pp. 104ff. and 227ff., also Hindley, D., *The Communist Party of Indonesia, 1951–1963*, pp. 263ff. and 286ff.

77 On the rise in prices, see, e.g., *Far Eastern Economic Review*, Hong Kong, 11 April 1963: 'Money Magic in Indonesia'. The development of wages is analysed by E. D. Hawkins in 'Labor in Transition', in McVey, R., (ed.), *Indonesia*, p. 262. On Indonesia's indebtedness

Notes

see Hindley, D., 'Foreign Aid to Indonesia and its Political Implications', *Pacific Affairs*, Summer 1963, pp. 107–19.

78 *Deklarasi Ekonomi*, Djakarta, 1963; summarized in *Asian Recorder*, 1963, p. 5343.

79 See *Far Eastern Economic Review* for 6 and 13 June 1963.

80 For the different organizations, see van der Kroef, *Communist Party*, Chap. 5, 'Party Organization, Program and Front Groups'.

81 From Pelzer, K. J., 'The Agricultural Foundation', in McVey, R., (ed.), *Indonesia*, p. 127, where the data are classified according to regions.

82 Gunawan, B., *Kudeta: Staatsgreep in Djakarta* [Coup d'état in Djakarta], Meppel (Drenthe), 1968, p. 94. For details of the position outlined here see ibid., chap. 6, 'Van Zuilenverbond naar Klassenstrijd' ('From *aliran* to class-struggle'), pp. 91–110.

83 Cf. Aidit, D. N., *Kaum Tani menggangjang Setan² Desa* [The Peasants destroy the Devils of the Desa], Djakarta, 1964, pp. 20ff. Aidit's classification by size of holdings is not consistent: at one point he reckons three-hectare peasants among the *tuan tanah*.

84 Ibid., p. 11.

85 Cf. Pelzer, K., loc. cit., pp. 129ff. and 499ff.; also Gunawan, pp. 92ff.

86 Aidit, D. N., *Kaum Tani*, pp. 48ff.

87 *Fakta² Persoalan Sekitar Gerakan 30 September* [Facts and Recollections concerning the Movement of 30 September], Army press office, Djakarta, 1966, pp. 437ff.

88 Aidit, D. N., *PKI dan Angkatan Darat* [The PKI and the Army], Djakarta, 1963, p. 30. For relations between the PKI and the navy, see Aidit's lecture of 16 July 1963 *PKI dan Alri*, Djakarta, 1963; for the police, *PKI dan Polisi* (three lectures by Aidit), Djakarta, 1963; for the air force, his lecture of March 1964 *Revolusi, Angkatan Bersendjata dan Partai Komunis (PKI dan AURI)*, Dkajarta, 1964.

89 *Sinar Harapan* for 13 March 1967, p. 1.

90 *Harian Kami* for 21 Feb. 1968, pp. 1 and 4; *Sinar Harapan* for 20 Feb. 1968, p. 1.

91 *Pantjasila* II, no. 14, p. 9; no. 15, pp. 10, 13 and 30.

92 The texts of Sukarno's and Aidit's speeches of 23 May 1965 are given in Antara bulletins of the 24th, nos. 2/Mo 5/18/119 and 4/Mo 5/22/134. Emphasis added.

93 See *Fakta*,² p. 392.

VIII   THE END OF SUKARNO'S REIGN

1   For the text, see Gunawan, *Kudeta* [Coup d'état], p. 138.
2   Subandrio stated in October 1966 that the document was found in the house of a British subject named Bill Palmer: the latter denied this. As the document was unsigned, and printed stationery of the British embassy fell into Communist hands during the looting in September 1963, the possibility cannot be ruled out that it was forged in order to discredit the army with the President. Subandrio as former head of the BPI, was accused at his trial of having fabricated it for this purpose in his 'slander factory'. (Note by the author, who attended the trial as a spectator.) However, much of the evidence advanced at the various trials is itself of questionable authenticity. In the present chapter, the author has been obliged to rely in part on this evidence, and, while adopting a critical attitude towards the documents published by the army, is well aware that his judgements must be regarded as provisional.
3   Untung stated that he knew of a 'generals' council' as early as February 1965; see *Fakta*[2], p. 318. In that month, Sukarno announced his intention of arming the workers and peasants in case of need. See *Pantjasila* II, no. 15, p. 30. For Yani's opposition, see the Indonesian weekly *Selecta*, no. 263, of 3 Oct. 1966, p. 30. The fact that Yani repeatedly spoke of Sujono's murder as a warning was brought to the author's attention by R. Howland, then a member of the US embassy at Djakarta. Details of Chou En-Lai's offer of arms to Subandrio were revealed at the trials of Subandrio, Omar Dhani and Supardjo: see, e.g., *Angkatan Bersendjata* for 15 Feb. 1967, p. 2. Peking's offer of military aid was not announced in Indonesia at the time (see *Pantjasila* II, no. 15, p. 33) but became known from Hsinhua bulletins.
4   Sukarno in conversation with the author at Djakarta, 24 Oct. 1966. Cf. also Gunawan, *Kudeta*, pp. 139ff.
5   Cf. Njono's statement in his defence speech on 19 Feb. 1966, in *G–30–S Dihadapan Mahmillub I : Perkara Njono* [The Movement of 30 September on trial before Special Military Court no. 1: defendant Njono], Djakarta, 1966, p. 277.
6   Cf. Commodore Susanto's evidence at Dhani's trial, *Sinar Harapan*, 8 Dec. 1966, p. 1. See also Harahap, Harif, *Omar Dhani, Dalang G–30–S* [Omar Dhani, the Master Mind of the 30 September Movement], Palembang, 1967, p. 17.
7   *Perkara Njono*, p. 131; see also Gunawan, pp. 134ff.
8   Cf. Sjam's statements at his trial in *Harian Kami*, 21 Feb. 1968, p. 1.

9   *Fakta²*, p. 317.

10   Gunawan, p. 145, following Untung's statement at his trial: see
     G–30–S Dihadapan Mahmillub II : Perkara Untung, Djakarta, 1966,
     p. 35.

11   From *Fakta²*, pp. 258ff. (Njono), and *Perkara Njono*, pp. 130ff.
     (Peris Pardede).

12   Njono stated, for instance, that the secret *politburo* sessions took
     place under Aidit's chairmanship in mid-July, whereas Aidit did
     not return to Indonesia till 7 August. Aidit was at no time in charge
     of the 'military planning' of the 30 September Movement; not only
     Communist bodies received training in the air force area, but also
     groups from the left wing of the PNI, Partindo, etc.

13   For Sudisman's statements, see *Kompas*, 28 Feb. 1967, p. 1, and
     Antara reports of his trial in July 1967. Peris Perdede's statements
     are also reproduced in Gunawan, pp. 141–4.

14   For detailed accounts of the conspirators' meetings, see, e.g.,
     Aktivitas Intern PKI Kearah Kup 1 Oktober 1965 [The Internal
     Activity of the PKI in Preparation for the Coup of 1 October 1965];
     typescript of Untung's, Latief's and Sujono's testimony in the
     preliminary investigations in October and November 1965, pp.
     52ff.; *Fakta²*, pp. 320ff.; and *40 Hari Kegagalan G–30–S* [Forty
     Days after the Defeat of the 30 September Movement], Djakarta,
     1965, pp. 11ff.

15   For details, see *Sinar Harapan*, 6 Dec. 1966, p. 2, and 8 Dec. 1966,
     p. 1.

16   Sukarno himself stated this in his written testimony, read out at the
     Subandrio trial on 8 Oct. 1966 as an explanation of why Njoto, who
     was in Moscow at the beginning of August 1965, was recalled to
     Djakarta.

17   *DBR* II, pp. 663 and 677ff.

18   See *Kompas*, 24 Feb. 1967.

19   Suwarno's testimony at the trial of Supardjo: see *Berita Yudha*, 27
     Feb. 1967.

20   Sujono's testimony at Njono's trial: see *Perkara Njono*, pp. 218ff.,
     also *Perkara Untung*, pp. 95ff. and 115. Sujono stated that at the
     preliminary investigation he had not mentioned the fact that Pranoto
     was brought to Halim in order not to compromise the President,
     who had appointed Pranoto commander-in-chief. However, on 1
     October Sukarno's aide-de-camp, Bambang Widjanarko, came to
     Kostrad in search of Pranoto, and was told by Suharto that Pranoto
     would not go to Halim: cf. below, note 33. It thus appears doubtful
     whether Pranoto did go to Halim with Aidit. On Sujono's evidence,
     see also Gunawan, pp. 154ff.

21 *Aktivitas Intern*, pp. 103ff.
22 For details see *Selecta*, special number of 3 Oct. 1966 entitled *Pahlawan Revolusi*. Gunawan, p. 157, speaks of an attempt to kidnap Leimena also. In fact, however, the assailants merely wanted to safeguard their rear while breaking into Nasution's house, and made no attempt to enter Leimena's. (Author's conversation with Leimena at Djakarta, 17 Oct. 1966.)

Sukarno later stated that medical examination had shown that the generals were shot before being mutilated. Cf. Sjam's statement that he 'agreed' to the shooting of the three generals who were still alive (*Sinar Harapan*, 22 Feb. 1968, p. 1).
23 Eng. trans. in *Indonesia* 1 (April 1966), Ithaca (N.Y.), Cornell University, pp. 134ff.
24 See Supardjo's testimony, *Kompas*, 25 Feb. 1967, p. 2.
25 These details were first revealed in the trials of Omar Dhani and Supardjo: cf. the evidence of Saelan, Suwarno, Sumirat, Widjanarko, Sabur, Sunarjo and others, collected in Gunawan, pp. 159ff.
26 Ibid., pp. 163ff.
27 Text in *Indonesia* 1, pp. 136ff., where the time is wrongly given as 2 p.m. It was in fact 11 a.m.; see *Tjatatan Kronologis Disekitar Gerakan 30 September* [30 September Movement: Chronology of Events], Djakarta, Information Department of KOTI (Komando Operasi Tertinggi), 1965 (23 Oct.), p. 5, no. 18.
28 What follows is based on Suharto's speech to the National Front on 15 Oct. 1965, reproduced in *Indonesia* 1, pp. 160–78.
29 Bambang Widjanarko's evidence at Supardjo's trial, *Kompas*, 28 Feb. 1967, p. 1.
30 Dr. Leimena told the author on 17 Oct. 1966 that Sukarno was much agitated at the time when he (Leimena) reached Halim, i.e. about noon.
31 Leimena's evidence at the trial of Omar Dhani (*Sinar Harapan*, 6 Dec. 1966, p. 1).
32 Cf. Gunawan, pp. 172ff.
33 Widjanarko's evidence at Supardjo's trial (*Kompas*, 28 Feb. 1967, p. 1). For Suharto's own account, see *Indonesia* 1, p. 171.
34 For a chronology of such statements, see *Aktivitas Intern*, pp. 27ff.
35 *Indonesia* 1, p. 174.
36 *Rangkaian Pidato dan Pernjataan² Resmi Disekitar Peristiwa Gerakan 30 September* [Collection of Speeches and official statements on the 30 September Movement], Djakarta, KOTI, 1965, no. 17.
37 See Sukarno's speeches of 23 and 27 October and 6, 10 and 20 November 1965, reproduced verbatim ibid., nos. 26, 33, 34, 35 and 44.

Notes

38 For details, see e.g. Rosamona, *Matinja Aidit* [Aidit's Death] Djakarta, 1967. Aidit remained at Solo till 20 November and then withdrew to the *kampong* of Sambeng Gede. Here he was captured by the RPKAD, after his hiding-place had been betrayed by an agent who had been with him for some time. For Aidit's alleged confession, made shortly before his death, admitting primary responsibility for the 30 September Movement, see Hughes, John, *Indonesian Upheaval*, New York, 1967, pp. 168–72.

39 There is no exact estimate of the number killed. Towards the end of 1965, Sukarno spoke of 87,000, but much higher figures have been given since. At an address to the Congress of World Affairs at San Francisco on 5 October 1966, Adam Malik estimated the number of dead at 100–250,000. Cf. also Hughes, pp. 184–9, where estimates are quoted ranging from 60,000 to 1,000,000.

40 Cf. *Rangkaian Pidato*, nos. 26, 33, 34, 35 and 44 (Sukarno), 27 (Subandrio) and 28 (Leimena); also Abdulgani, R., *Dengan Pantjasila Berdjiwa Nasakom menumpas G–30–S* [With the *Pantja Sila* and the Nasakom Spirit against the 30 September Movement], Djakarta, 1966 (seven speeches delivered in Oct.–Nov. 1965).

41 *Indonesia* I; Nasution's speech of 12 Nov. 1965, pp. 182ff.

42 Cf. the instructions of the supreme command of the armed forces (KOTI) dated 12 and 15 Nov. 1965 (*Rangkaian Pidato*, nos. 40–2).

43 Ibid., no. 35, pp. 19ff.

44 Ibid., nos. 37 (Admiral Martadinata on Heroes' Day 10 Nov. 1965) and 38 (General Sutjipto Judodihardjo, police commandant, on the same occasion).

45 Text in Abdulgani, R., *Dihadapan Tunas Bangsa*, pp. 451ff.

46 What follows is based on the author's conversations with various student leaders during 1966. Cf. also Imawan, S. J., *KAMI. Kebangkitan Angkatan '66* [KAMI, the Rise of the 1966 Generation], Padang, 1966.

47 Lopa, B., *Djalannja Revolusi*, p. 153.

48 Testimony of Generals Sukendro and Suhartono at Subandrio's trial: see *Kompas*, 3 Oct. 1966, p. 2. Subandrio denied these allegations.

49 According to Subandrio himself in a speech of 23 Oct. 1965 (*Rangkaian Pidato*, no. 27, p. 8).

50 For an eye-witness account, see Hughes, *Indonesian Upheaval*, pp. 212ff.

51 Sukarno himself told the author this on 24 October 1966; however, the 'proofs' turned out to be merely suspicions.

52 Cf. Dahm, *Sukarno*, pp. 305f.

53 For text see *Hakekat Ketetapan MPRS No.* IX *Tgl. 21 Djuni 196*

Surat Perintah Presiden Tgl. 11 Maret 1966 [Background to MPRS
Resolution No. 9 of 21 June 1966. The President's Order of 11
March 1966], Djakarta, 1966, document 1. For the events of 11
March, see Hughes, pp. 233ff.

54 *Hakekat*, documents nos. 4–7.

55 Ibid., document 12; Suharto's speech of 18 March 1966.

56 *Pernjataan KASI dan Civitas Academica Universitas Padjajaran
Bandung* [Declaration by KASI and the Civitas Academica of the
Padjajaran University, Bandung], Bandung, 3 March 1966.

57 Hatta, M., *Pantjasila. Djalan Lurus* [*Pantja Sila*, the True Way],
Bandung (Angkasa), 1966.

58 *Symposium Kebangkitan Semangat '66 : Mendjeladjah Tracee Baru*
[Symposium on the Flowering of the 1966 Spirit: the Search for
New Ways], *Indonesia*, unpaginated typescript, Djakarta, Fakultas
Ekonomi, Universitas Indonesia, 1966.

59 Ibid., 'Bidang Ideologi: Kembali Ke Rel Pantjasila' [Ideology:
Back to the *Pantja Sila*], esp. contributions by Drijarkara and
Timur Djaelani.

60 Quoted from the pamphlet *Sidang MPRA membuka Halman jang
baru* [The Session of the MPRS opens a New Era], 10 June 1966.

61 Ibid., under the heading 'Relative Strengths'. Of the 480 deputies
expected to attend the session, 320 were believed to be adherents
of Sukarno.

62 For texts, see *Hasil-Hasil Sidang Umum MPRS Ke-IV* [Results of
the Fourth Session of the MPRS], Bandung, 1966.

63 Sukarno, *Nawa Aksara* [Nine Teachings], Djakarta, 1966, especially
pp. 11ff.

64 *Proses Jusuf Muda Dalam*, (Pembimbing Masa) Djakarta, 1967,
esp. pp. 172ff. (testimony by his wives and mistresses).

65 For Subandrio's trial, see *G–30–S Dihadapan Mahmillub III. Proses
Subandrio* [The 30 September Movement on trial before Special
Military Court No. III. Trial of Subandrio], Djakarta, 1967; this
includes the indictment, testimony and speeches for the prosecution
and defence.

66 Speech by Yap Thiam Hien, 17 October 1966.

67 The record of Dhani's trial is to be published as Part IV of the series,
the first three comprising the trials of Njono, Untung and Subandrio
respectively. It was not available to the author at the time of writing,
and therefore the account is based on newspaper reports, as are
those of the trials of Supardjo, Sudisman and Sjam.

68 See *Kompas*, 22 Dec. 1966, p. 1.

69 'Pelengkap Nawaksara' [Supplement to *Nawa Aksara*'], *Sinar
Harapan*, 11 Jan. 1967.

Notes

70 *Sinar Harapan*, 6 and 15 Feb. 1967. See also, ibid., a list of fourteen points on which Sukarno was to answer before a court of law.

71 See *Kompas*, 24 and 25 Feb. 1967. The only statement publicly known at that time which suggests that Sukarno was informed of the intended coup before 30 September is not to be found in the testimony at the Supardjo trial, but consists of a statement by Brigadier R. H. Sugandhi, quoted in a broadcast by Nasution on 13 February (see van der Kroef, J. M., 'Sukarno's Fall', *Orbis*, vol. XI (Summer 1967), no. 2, p. 496), and published on the 15th by nearly all Indonesian newspapers. Sugandhi said that, shortly before the coup, Aidit came to him, informed him of the plan, and sought his cooperation. Sugandhi thereupon told the President of the Communists' plans, but for his pains was told not to fall a victim to 'anti-Communist phobia'. Sukarno is said to have added that in a revolution, 'even a father might devour his children'. The present author hesitates to treat this belated testimony as documentary evidence. Why, for instance, did Sugandhi not warn his fellow-generals of Aidit's alleged communication?

72 See *Berita Yudha*, 13 March 1967. Cf. also Suharto's words of 7 March, quoted in van der Kroef, 'Sukarno's Fall', pp. 496ff.; cf. p. 492, note 3.

73 Cf. Mashuri's remarks of 22 Feb. 1967, in *Kompas*, 25 Feb. 1967, p. 2.

74 During the quarrel with the generals, most extensively in his speech of 10 Nov. 1965: *Rangkaian Pidato*, no. 35, pp. 19ff. Also in earlier critical periods. See Dahm, Sukarno, pp. 102 (1927) and 280 (1944).

IX THE NEW ORDER AT WORK

1 On the reorganization of the armed forces see articles by O. G. Roeder in the *Neue Zürcher Zeitung* for 25 October and 27 November 1969; also reports in *Straits Times* for 11 November 1969, *Japan Times* of the same date and *Hsinhua* for 14 November 1969 (no. 111316).

2 The following is the composition of the 'Pembangunan cabinet' at the time of writing, as communicated by the Indonesian embassy in London: defence and security, General Suharto; home affairs, Major-General Amir Mahmud; foreign affairs, Adam Malik; justice, Professor Oemar Seno Adji; information, Air Vice-Marshal Budiardjo; finance, Professor Ali Wardhana; trade, Professor Sumitro

Djojohadikusumo; agriculture, Professor Tojib Hadiwidjaja; industry, Major-General Mohammad Jusuf; mining, Professor Sumantri Brodjonegoro; public works and electricity, Dr. Sutami; communications, Dr. Frans Seda; education and culture, Mr. Mashuri; health, Professor G. A. Siwabessy; religious affairs; Kijai Hadji Mohammad Dahlan; manpower, Rear-Admiral Mursalin; social affairs, Dr. A. M. Tambunan; 'transmigration' and co-operatives, Lieutenant-General M. Sarbini. Ministers without portfolio: Sultan Hamengku Buwono IX, Kijai Hadji Dr. Idham Chalid, Harsono Tjokroaminoto, Professor Soenawar Soekowati, M. Mintaredja.

3 *New York Times*, 19 February 1969; *Asia Magazine*, 1 June 1969.
4 *Hsinhua*, 28 March 1970 (no. 032627).
5 *New York Times*, 19 January and 6 February 1970.
6 For details of the Indonesian budget for 1970, see *Japan Times* for 3, 6 and 7 January 1970.
7 *Christian Science Monitor*, 8 May 1969, and *Frankfurter Allgemeine Zeitung*, 5 May 1969.
8 *Japan Times*, 8 January 1969; *Straits Times*, 13 January 1969.
9 *Straits Times*, 4 February and 13 March 1969.
10 *Japan Times*, 15 and 27 February 1969.
11 *Observer* Foreign News Service, 29 April 1969: 'Anxiety over West Irian Referendum'.
12 *New York Times*, 7 and 11 May 1969; *Guardian*, 7 and 9 May 1969; *Christian Science Monitor*, 8 May 1969; *Daily Telegraph*, 8 May 1969.
13 *The Times* (London), 14 May 1969; *Financial Times*, 27 May 1969; *Frankfurter Allgemeine Zeitung*, 28 May 1969.
14 Sukarno to the writer in October 1966, at Djakarta.
15 *Hsinhua* for 14 January 1968 (no. 011302): '*Peoples Daily*' greets beginning of armed struggle in Indonesia'.
16 *New York Times*, 13 February 1969, Philip Shabecoff: 'Indonesia is still purging Reds 3 years after coup'.
17 Ibid.
18 *Hsinhua* for 11 October 1969 (no. 101003): 'Delegation of Central Committee of Indonesian Communist Party issues statement greeting Chinese national day'.
19 For figures of 150–160,000 prisoners, see *New York Times* for 13 February 1969 and *Guardian*, 1 November 1969. For a figure of 120,000 see *Japan Times* for 18 October 1969 and *Le Monde* for 19 December 1969. For 70,000 see *Neue Zürcher Zeitung* for 25 October 1969.
20 *Neue Zürcher Zeitung*, 25 October 1969.
21 *Le Monde*, 19 December 1969.

Notes

22 *Le Monde*, 28 February 1969; *Neue Zürcher Zeitung*, 13 and 21 March 1969; *New York Times*, 22 March 1969.
23 *Christian Science Monitor*, 16 December 1969; *Neue Zürcher Zeitung*, 7 January 1970.
24 *Japan Times*, 4 January 1970.
25 *Frankfurter Allgemeine Zeitung*, 27 January 1970.
26 *Indonesian News* (London Embassy), vol. 1, no. 2 (Feb. 1970), pp. 7–8.
27 *Neue Zürcher Zeitung*, 14 March 1970.
28 Ibid., 25 April 1969.
29 Ibid., 14 March 1970.
30 *Indonesian News*, vol. 1, no. 2, p. 6.

SELECT BIBLIOGRAPHY

See Notes for additional titles and special references

I HISTORY AND POLITICS

Anderson, B. R. O-G., *Some Aspects of Indonesian Politics under the Japanese Occupation 1944–1945*. Ithaca: Cornell University–Modern Indonesia Project, 1961.

—— *The Pemuda Revolution*. Ph.D. Dissertation, Cornell University, 1967.

Arx, A. von, *L'evolution politique en Indonésie de 1900–1942*. Fribourg: Artigianelli-Monza, 1949.

Benda, H. J., *The Crescent and the Rising Sun*. The Hague and Bandung: W. van Hoeve, 1958.

—— 'The Pattern of Administrative Reforms in the Closing Years of Dutch Rule in Indonesia' in *Journal of Asian Studies*, Vol. xxv, 1966, pp. 589–605.

—— and Irikura, J. K., Koichi Kishi. *Japanese Military Administration in Indonesia. Selected Documents*. New Haven: Yale University–Southeast Asia Studies, 1965.

—— and McVey, R., *The Communist Uprisings in Indonesia 1926–1927. Key Documents*. Ithaca: Cornell University–Modern Indonesia Project, 1960.

Blumberger, J. Th. Petrus, *De nationalistische beweging in Nederlandsch-Indië*. Haarlem: Tjeenk Willink en Zoon, 1931.

Bousquet, G.-H., *La politique musulmane et coloniale de Pays-Bas*. Paris: Paul Hartman, 1938.

Brackman, A. C., *Communist Collapse in Indonesia*. New York: Norton Library, 1969.

—— *Indonesian Communism: A History*. New York: Praeger, 1963.

Dahm, B., *Sukarno and the Struggle for Indonesian Independence*. (Transl. from the German.) Ithaca: Cornell University Press, 1969.

Day, C., *The Policy and Administration of the Dutch in Java*. New York: Macmillan, 1904. Reprinted Kuala Lumpur: Oxford University Press, 1967.

Feith, H., *The Decline of Constitutional Democracy in Indonesia*. Ithaca: Cornell University Press, 1962.

Select Bibliography

—— 'Dynamics of Guided Democracy' in R. McVey (ed.). *Indonesia.* New Haven: HRAF, 1963, pp. 309–409.

—— and Castles, L., (eds.), *Indonesian Political Thinking 1945–1946.* Ithaca: Cornell University Press, 1970.

Furnivall, J. S., *Colonial Policy and Practice : A Comparative Study of Burma and Netherlands India.* Cambridge: Cambridge University Press, 1948.

Graaf, H. J. de, *Geschiedenis van Indonesië.* The Hague and Bandung: W. van Hoeve, 1949.

Gunawan, B., *Kudeta. Staatsgreep in Djakarta.* Meppel: J. A. Boom en Zoon, 1968.

Hatta, M., *Verspreide Geschriften.* Djakarta, Amsterdam, Surabaja: v. d. Peet, 1952.

Hindley, D., *The Communist Party of Indonesia 1951–1963.* Berkeley and Los Angeles: The University of California Press, 1964.

Kahin, G. McT., *Nationalism and Revolution in Indonesia.* Ithaca: Cornell University Press, 1952.

Kartodirdjo, S., *The Peasants' Revolt of Banten in 1888.* The Hague: H. L. Smits, 1966.

Kroef, J. M. van der, *The Communist Party of Indonesia.* Vancouver, B.C.: University of British Columbia Press, 1965.

Legge, J. D., *Central Authority and Regional Autonomy in Indonesia : A Study in Local Administration 1950–1960.* Ithaca: Cornell University Press, 1961.

Lev, D. S., *The Transition to Guided Democracy : Indonesian Politics 1957–1959.* Ithaca: Cornell University–Modern Indonesia Project, 1965.

McVey, R., *The Rise of Indonesian Communism.* Ithaca: Cornell University Press, 1965.

McVey, R., (ed.), *Indonesia.* New Haven: Human Relations Area Files (HRAF), 1963.

Nagazumi, A., *The Origin and the Earlier Years of Budi Utomo 1908–1918.* Ph.D. Dissertation, Cornell University, 1967.

Nasution, A. H., *Fundamentals of Guerilla Warfare.* New York: Praeger, 1965.

—— *Towards a Peoples Army.* Djakarta: C. V. Delegasi, 1964.

Nishijima, Shigetada, Koichi Kishi, *Japanese Military Administration in Indonesia.* Washington: U.S. Department of Commerce, Joint Publications Research Service, 1963.

Palmier, L. H., *Indonesia and the Dutch..* London and New York: Oxford University Press 1962.

Pauker, G. J., 'The Role of the Military in Indonesia' in J. J. Johnson (ed.). *The Role of the Military in Underdeveloped Countries.* Princeton: Princeton University Press, 1962, pp. 185–230.

Pluvier, J. M., *Confrontations: A Study in Indonesian Politics.* New York and Kuala Lumpur: Oxford University Press, 1965.
—— *Overzicht van de ontwikkeling der nationalistische beweging in Indonesië in de jaren 1930 tot 1942.* The Hague and Bandung: W. van Hoeve, 1953.
Raffles, Sir T. S., *The History of Java.* 2 vols London: Black Parbury, Allen and J. Murray, 1817; New York: Oxford University Press, 1965.
Skinner, G. W., 'The Chinese Minority' in McVey (ed.), *Indonesia,* pp. 97–111.
Soedjatmoko, M. Ali, Resink, G. J., and Kahin, G. McT., (eds.), *An Introduction to Indonesian Historiography.* Ithaca: Cornell University Press, 1965.
Sukarno, *An Autobiography as Told to Cindy Adams.* Indianapolis: Bobbs Merrill and Co., 1965.
—— *Nationalism, Islam and Marxism.* (Transl. from the Indonesian.) Ithaca: Cornell University–Modern Indonesia Project, 1970.
Taylor, A. M., *Indonesian Independence and the United Nations.* Ithaca: Cornell University Press, 1960.
Van Niel, R., *The Emergence of the Modern Indonesian Elite.* The Hague and Bandung: W. van Hoeve, 1960.
—— 'The Course of Indonesian History' in R. McVey (ed.), *Indonesia,* pp. 272–308.
Veur, P. W. van der, 'The Eurasians of Indonesia' in *Journal of Southeast Asian History,* vol. IX, 1968, pp. 191–207.
Vlekke, B. H. M., *Nusantara. A History of Indonesia.* The Hague and Bandung: W. van Hoeve, 1959.
Wal, S. L. van der, (ed.), *De Volksraad en de staatkundige ontwikkeling van Nederlands-Indië.* 2 vols. Groningen: J. B. Wolters, 1964 and 1965.
Wal, S. L. van der, (ed.), *De opkomst van de nationalistische beweging in Nederlands-Indië.* Groningen: J. B. Wolters, 1967.
Weatherbee, D. E., *Ideology in Indonesia: Sukarno's Indonesian Revolution.* New Haven: Yale University–Southeast Asia Studies, 1966.
Willmot, D. E., *The National Status of the Chinese in Indonesia 1900–1958.* Ithaca: Cornell University–Modern Indonesia Project, 1961.
Wolters, O. W., *Early Indonesian Commerce: A Study of the Origins of Sriwidjaja.* Ithaca: Cornell University Press, 1967.
Woodman, D., *The Republic of Indonesia.* London: The Cresset Press, 1955.
Zainu'ddin, A., *A Short History of Indonesia.* New York: Praeger, 1970; Melbourne: Cassell Australia Ltd.

Select Bibliography

2 CULTURAL FOUNDATION, SOCIAL CHANGE AND ECONOMIC DEVELOPMENT

Alisjahbana, S. T., *Indonesia. Social and Cultural Revolution.* New York and Kuala Lumpur: Oxford University Press, 1966.

Anderson, B. R. O'G., *Mythology and the Tolerance of the Javanese.* Ithaca: Cornell University-Modern Indonesia Project, 1965.

Bodenstedt, A. A., *Sprache und Politik in Indonesien. Entwicklung und Funktionen einer neuen Nationalsprache.* Heidelberg: Südasieninstitut der Universität Heidelberg, 1967.

Brugmans, I. J., *Geschiedenis van het onderwijs in Nederlandsch-Indië.* Groningen: J. B. Wolters, 1938.

Castles, I., *Religion, Politics and Economic Behaviour in Java. The Kudus Cigarette Industry.* New Haven: Yale University–Southeast Asia Studies, 1967.

Furnivall, J. S., *Netherlands India : A Study in Plural Economy.* Cambridge: Cambridge University Press, 1939 and 1967.

Geertz, C., *Agricultural Involution. The Processes of Ecological Change in Indonesia.* Berkeley and Los Angeles: The University of California Press, 1963.

—— *Peddlers and Princes. Social Change and Economic Development in Two Indonesian Towns.* Chicago and London: The University of Chicago Press, 1963.

—— *The Religion of Java.* New York: The Free Press of Glencoe, 1960.

—— *The Social History of an Indonesian Town.* Cambridge, Maas.: M.I.T.-Press, 1965.

Geertz, H., *The Javanese Family. A Study of Kinship and Socialization.* New York: The Free Press of Glencoe, 1961.

—— 'Indonesian Cultures and Communities' in R. McVey (ed.), *Indonesia,* pp. 24–96.

Haar, B. Ter., *Adat Law in Indonesia.* (Transl. from the Dutch.) New York: Institute of Pacific Relations, 1948.

Hawkins, E. D., 'Labor in Transition' in R. McVey (ed.), *Indonesia,* pp. 248–271.

Hicks, G. L. and McNicoll, G., *The Indonesian Economy 1950–1965: A Bibliography.* New Haven: Yale University–Southeast Asia Studies, 1967.

—— *The Indonesian Economy 1950–1967: Bibliographic Supplement.* New Haven: Yale University–Southeast Asia Studies, 1968.

Higgins, B., *Indonesian Economic Stabilization and Development.* New York: Institute of Pacific Relations, 1957.

Holt, C., *Art in Indonesia. Continuities and Change*. Ithaca: Cornell University Press, 1967.

Hood, M., 'The Enduring Tradition: Music and Theatre in Java and Bali' in R. McVey (ed.), *Indonesia*, pp. 438–471.

Jay, R. R., *Religion and Politics in Rural Central Java*. New Haven: Yale University–Southeast Asia Studies, 1963.

Johns, A. H., 'Genesis of a Modern Literature' in R. McVey (ed.), *Indonesia*, pp. 410–437.

Josselin de Jong, P. E., *Minangkabau and Negri Sembilan. Socio-Political Structure in Indonesia*. Leiden: E. Ijdo, 1950.

Kartini, R. A., *Letters of a Javanese Princess*. New York: The Norton Library, 1964.

Koentjaraningrat (ed.), *Villages in Indonesia*. Ithaca: Cornell University Press, 1967.

Kroef, J. M. van der, *Indonesia in the Modern World*. 2 vols. Bandung: Masa Baru, 1954 and 1956.

—— *Indonesian Social Evolution*. Amsterdam: v. d. Peet, 1958.

Legge, J. D., *Indonesia*. Englewood Cliffs, N. J.: Prentice-Hall, 1964.

Leur, J. C. van, *Indonesian Trade and Society*. The Hague and Bandung: W. van Hoeve, 1955.

Mackie, J. A. C., *Problems of Indonesian Inflation*. Ithaca: Cornell University–Modern Indonesia Project, 1967.

—— 'Indonesian Government Estates and Their Masters' in *Pacific Affairs*, vol. XXXIV, 1961, pp. 337–360.

Paauw, D. S., *Financing Economic Development: The Indonesian Case*. New York: The Free Press of Glencoe, 1960.

—— 'From Colonial to Guided Economy' in R. McVey (ed.), *Indonesia*, pp. 155–247.

Palmier, L. H., *Social Status and Power in Java*. New York: Humanities Press, 1960; London: The Athlone Press, University of London, 1960 and 1969.

Pelzer, K. J., 'Physical and Human Resource Patterns' and 'The Agricultural Foundation' both in R. McVey (ed.), *Indonesia*, pp. 1–23 and 118–154 respectively.

Schrieke, B., *Indonesian Sociological Studies*. 2 vols. The Hague and Bandung: W. van Hoeve, 1955.

Schrieke, B., (ed.), *The Effect of Western Influence on Native Civilizations in the Malay Archipelago*. Batavia: G. Kolff and Co., 1929.

Selosoemardjan, *Social Changes in Jogjakarta*. Ithaca: Cornell University Press, 1962.

Stöhr, W. and Zoetmulder, P., *Die Religionen Indonesiens*. Stuttgart: W. Kohlhammer, 1967.

Sutter, J. O., *Indonesianisasi: Politics in a Changing Economy 1940–1955*.

Select Bibliography

Ithaca: Cornell University–Southeast Asia Program, Data Paper No. 36, 4 vols., 1959.

Wal, S. L. van der, (ed.), *Het onderwijsbeleid in Nederlands-Indië 1900–1940*. Groningen: J. B. Wolters, 1963.

Wertheim, W. F., *Indonesian Society in Transition*. The Hague and Bandung: W. van Hoeve, 1956 and 1959.

INDEX

Index

Index

Cosmas Batubara, 242
Cultivation system (Cultuurstelsel, 1830–
60), 10, 12–13
Curaçao, 77

Dalam, Jusuf Muda, 245, 248
Dahlan, Kijai Ahmad, 75
Darjatmo, Major-General, 255
Darsono (Communist leader), 52–3, 55, 57–8
Darul Islam movement, 166–8, 217
Datuk (Communist leader), 57
Daud Beureueh, 167–8
Decentralization Law (1903), 46
Dekon (*Deklarasi ekonomi*), 217
Democratic Fraction, 156
Democratic League, 201, 202
Democratic People's Front. *See* FDR
Desas (village communities), 7–10 *et passim*; for the mid-fifties, 169–73; for the mid-sixties, 218–20
Deventer, C. Th. van, 13–14, 20, 22
Dewan djenderal (council of generals), 224–7
Dewan Perantjang Nasional or Depernas (National Planning Council), 195, 200, 203
Dewan Perwakilan Rakjat. *See* Parliament
Dewan Perwakilan Rakjat—Gotong Ro-jong. *See* DPR-GR
Dhani, Air Vice-Marshal Omar, 225, 229–30, 233, 236, 249–50
Dharsono, Major-General, 248
Diah, B. M., 99, 104, 110, 118, 245, 248
Dinata, Oto Iskandar, 101, 108, 114; Minister without Portfolio, 118
Diponegoro rebellion, 4, 5
Djajadiningrat, A., 25, 29, 47–9
Djajadiningrat, Hussein, 61, 87, 98, 101
Djakarta, Java, 66, 129 147, 157, 216; Putera bureau, 88; religious affairs bureau, 91; Fourth Asian Games at, 206; Ganefo, 206; Afro-Asian journalists' conference, 206
Djakarta charter, 106, 188
Djawa Hokokai (Javanese People's Loyalty Movement), 93, 95–6, 98, 103, 115
Djojobojo-Prophecies, 42–3, 79, 82, 147
Djojohadikusomo, Dr. Sumitro, 157, 183, 185, 198, 204, 255
Djojomartono, Muljadi, Minister for Social Welfare, 197

Djojosukarto, Sidik, 155
Djuanda, 184, 187, 196, 217; Minister of Economic Affairs, 146–7; in Sastro-amidjo's cabinet, 174; forms a cabinet, 180; deputy premier, 197; death, 217
Dokter djawa school. *See* Stovia
Douwes Dekker ('Multatuli'), *Max Havelaar*, 33, 38
Douwes Dekker, E. F. E., 11, 33–7, 51, 56, 60, 62–3, 79, 108, 112
DPA (Dewan Pertimbangan Agung—Supreme Advisory Council), 105, 191, 200, 232, 263
DPR-GR (Dewan Perwakilan Rakjat—gotong rojong parliament), 200–3, 216, 232, 250–1
Dulles, John Foster, 185
Dutch, the. *See* Netherlands
Dutch East India Company, 4, 8, 10

East Indonesia, 148
East Java, 148, 238–9, 248
East Sumatra, 130, 148
Economic blockade, 130
Economic development, 197–9, 216–17, 240, 256; Eight-Year-Plan (1960), 196; Five-Year-Plan (1969), 255–6
Edhie, Colonel (later Brigadier-General) Sarwo, 240, 243, 257–8
Education: early schools, 12; demand for, and the school system, 15–19; western teaching the common bond of unity, 21; Dutch-Chinese schools, 38; Taman Siswa schools, 60, 71; general situation at end of colonial period, 161
ELS (*Europeesche Lagere School*—European primary school), 16–19
Empat Serangkai, 87
Ethical party and policy, 16, 19, 35–6, 51
Eurasians, 11, 34, 51, 156; their status, 38
Expres, De, 34

FDR (Front Demokrasi Rakjat), 131–3
Five duties. See *Pantja dharma*
Flores, Lesser Sundas, 2, 4, 6, 159
Fock, Dirk (Governor-General), 50–1, 59
Foreign policy: in the 1950's, 162–4; in the 1960's, 205–14, 244, 246, 248

Gabungan Politik Indonesia. *See* Gapi
Gandamma, Ipik, Home Affairs Minister, 197
Gani, A. K., 74, 155

Index

Index

Index

rank, 215–16; increase of membership, 217–18; and land reform, 218–19; and the Army, 219–21, 225; Biro Chusus bureau, 220, 226; Movement of Sept. 30 and coup of Oct. 1, 226–30, 237; their press banned, 237; public feeling against, 238–42; their 'people's universities', 240; outlawed, 244; revolt in Blitar, 260

Planning Commission (1959–60), 195–6, 200, 203

PNI (Partai Nasional Indonesia), 65–8, 70, 74, 122–4, 126, 129, 134, 154–6, 160, 163, 168, 170–4, 178, 181–2, 187–8, 201, 203, 221, 225, 241, 264; a new party formed (1945), 115

PNI-Baru (Pendidikan Nasional Indonesia – Indonesia National Education), 68–9, 74

Police (AKRI), 233, 234, 239, 253–4

PP (Persatuan Perdjuangan), 122–3, 157

PPPKI (Permufakatan Perhimpunan Politiek Kebangsaan Indonesia – Union of Indonesian Political Organizations), 65–66, 73, 114, 155

Prambanan conference of PKI, 57

Pranoto Reksosomudro, Major-General, 230, 235–7

Prawiranegara, Sjafruddin. See Sjafruddin

Prijajis (later known as Pamong pradja —administrative corps, lesser nobility), 8, 10, 13, 18, 23–4, 27, 29–31 38, 40, 71, 92–3, 94, 101, 154, 156, 172; their association, 80

Prijono, Professor, Minister for Culture, 180–1

Prisoners, problem of, 260–2

Provinces: republican governments set up, 114; governors appointed, 114; central control increased, 199–200

Provisional People's Consultative Congress. See MPRS

PRRI (Pemerintah Revolusioner Republik Indonesia – Revolutionary Government of the Republic of Indonesia), 185, 213

PRRI–Permesta rebellion, 184–7, 202, 204, 217

PSI (Partai Sosialis Indonesia), 131, 156, 160, 165, 166, 168, 171, 173–4, 180, 187, 201–3, 216, 264

PSII (Partai Sarekat Islam Indonesia). See SI

Pudja, I. Gusti Ketat, 108
Purbatjaraka, Professor, 87
PUSA (central organization of the ulamas of Atjeh), 81, 167
Putera (Pusat Tenaga Rakjat – Centre of People's Power), 87–9, 92, 96

Radical Concentration, 56
Radjiman Wedioningrat, Dr., 30, 48, 101, 108
Raffles, Sir Stamford, 5
Rahmat, General Basuki, 243
Ratu Adil (Righteous Prince) movements, 13, 42–3, 53–4; Forces of the Ratu Adil, 147
Razak, Abdul, 244
Regencies. See Kabupatens
Regents. See Bupatis
Renville Agreement, 130–3, 140, 157
Repeliita (Rentjana Pembangunan Lima Tahun – Five-Year Construction Plan), 255
Republik Malaku Selatan (RMS – Republic of the South Moluccas), 148
Rice: cultivation, 7; price 198, 216
Riekerk, Professor, 204–5
Rivai, Abdul, 26, 48
Roijen, van (Dutch ambassador), 140–1, 209
RPKAD (paratroop regiment), 236, 238, 240, 243
Rum–Van Roijen Agreement, 140–1

Sabilillah (paramilitary Masjumi unit), 167
Salim, Hadji Agus, 19, 22, 44, 52, 54–5, 75–6, 91, 101, 104, 106, 124, 144; Vice-Minister (later Minister) of Foreign Affairs, 128, 137
Samanhudi, Hadji, 39–40, 44
Samin, Surontiko, 13; his movement, 13
Samsudin, Raden, 84, 101
Santri civilization, 41–2, 153, 172
Sanusi, Anwar, 101, 237
Sardjono (chairman of PKI up to 1948), 132, 134
Sarekat Dagang Islamijah (Association of Muslim Traders), 39
Sarekat Islam. See SI
Sarekat Rakjat (People's Associations), 57
Sartono (founder member of PNI), 65, 68, 101, 154–5; Minister without Portfolio, 118

317

Index

Sasanka Purnama, 29–31
Sastrawidagda, Dr. Samsi: Finance Minister, 117–18; Education Minister, 137
Sastroamidjojo, Ali, 65, 154–5, 163, 182, 222; Prime Minister, 166, 168; second term, 174, 177
Sastrowidogdo, Dr. Samsi, 65
Sawah land, 7, 218–19
Sedio Mulo (*bupati*-organization), 32
Seinendan (paramilitary body), 94, 99
Semaun (Communist leader), 52–3, 55, 57–9
Sentral Organisasi Buruh Seluruh Indonesia. *See* SOBSI
Serikat Kerakjatan Indonesia (Indonesian People's Association), 156
SESKOAD (Military Academy of the Army), 220, 225
Sestiadjit (leader of Labour party), 133
Sewojo, Dwidjo, 48
Shumubu (office for religious affairs), 98
SI (Sarekat Islam, full title after 1929 Partai Sarekat Islam Indonesia – Muslim Association), 40–8, 51–2, 54–7, 60, 62–5, 67, 74–6, 91, 143, 154, 167, 171, 203, 221, 264; Semarang branch (left wing), 52–3, 56; Jogjakarta branch (right wing), 52, 56; changes name, 66
Siang Hwee (Chinese trading association), 38–9
Sidik Djojosukarto, 155–6
Simatupang, Colonel (later Major-General), T. B., 94, 132, 137, 144, 164–6, 211
Simbolon, Colonel, 174–5, 177, 185
Sinar Hindia (Light of the Indies), 55
Singa Mangaradja XII, priest-king of the Bataks, 5
Singodimedjo, Kasman, 94, 113
Sjafeij, Minister of Security, 243, 245
Sjafruddin Prawiranegra, 184, 198; Finance Minister, 137, 146; forms emergency government, 139, 141; political faith, 153; leads PRRI revolt, 185
Sjahrir, Sutan, 67–70, 75, 77, 85–6, 93, 99, 110, 112, 117, 136, 140, 144, 150, 156–7, 160, 163, 165, 182, 203; supports republican cause, 119–20; forms government, 120–1; attacks collaborationists, 121; his following, 122; second government, and opposition to his policies, 123–4; negotiates with the Dutch, 124–125, 128–9; third government, 124; at,

New Delhi Inter-Asian Conference 128; resigns, 129; forms the PSI, 131; arrested by the Dutch, 137
Sjam or Kamaruzaman (head of Biro Chusus), 221, 226–9, 232–3, 235
Sjarifuddin, Amir, 74, 82, 85, 93, 122, 124, 132, 136, 144; Information Minister, 117–18; Defence Minister, 121–2; forms a government, 129; fall of, 131; announces his membership of PKI, 133–4; arrested, 135; executed, 137
Sneevliet, Hendrik, 51, 53–5, 57
SOBSI (Sentral Organisasi Buruh Seluruh Indonesia – All Indonesian union federation), 131, 172, 218, 219, 227
Socialist parties, 156–9
Soumokil (Minister of Justice), 148
Spoor (Dutch commander-in-chief), 139
Starkenborgh-Stachouwer, Tjarda van (Governor-General), 73, 78–9
Stovia (school for the training of native doctors), 18, 24–8, 30
Students: their 'Action Front' against PKI, 240–3; re-form under Kappi, 243; ment), 134, 157, 227; object to certain ministers, 245; opposition to Sukarno, 245–7; plan to invade Sukarno's palace gardens, 248–9; and corrupt generals, 262–3
Suadi, Lieut.-Colonel, 134
Suardi Surjaningrat, 36–7, 39, 44, 52, 56, 60–1, 112; takes name of Ki Hadjar Dewantoro (*q.v.*), 60
Subandrio, Dr.: Foreign Minister, 180, 197, 208–9, 214, 217, 224, 233, 241–2, 243; Deputy premier and head of BPI, 224; arrested, 245; imprisoned, 249
Subardjo, 100–1, 111, 113; Foreign Minister, 117, 163
Sudarsono, Major-General, 124
Sudirman, General, 115, 117, 124, 134, 137, 167, 230
Sudisman (head of PKI defence department), 134, 157, 227
Sudomo, Rear-Admiral, 254
Suharto, 183, 209, 233, 251, 260, 262; and the coup of Oct. 1, 234; self-appointed commander of the army, 236; demands mandate from Sukarno, 237; granted full powers, 243–4; outlaws PKI, 244; protects Sukarno, 251–2; consolidates his powers, 253–5; forms 'development

Index

Index

Suprajogi, Colonel, Minister of Production, 197
Suprapto, General, 228, 231
Supratman, W. R., 66
Supreme Advisory Council. *See* DPA
Suprijadi, Lieut., 98, 116
Surabaja, Java, 11, 18, 129; Indonesia Study Club, 63; the 'battle' at, 121, 155
Surachman, Ali, 118, 155, 182, 222, 241
Suradi, Captain, 232
Surinam, 77, 79
Suripno (PKI leader), 133–5
Surjohamidjojo, 108
Surjaningrat, Suardi. *See* Suardi
Surjopranoto, 52
Suroso, R. P., 155
Suryadarma, Air Marshal, 225
Sutardjo, Kartohadikusomo, 72, 81, 87, 94, 104, 156
Sutojo, General, 228, 231
Sutomo, Dr. Raden, 27, 63, 65–6, 85
Sutomo (Bung Tomo), 121, 155
Sutowo, General Ibnu, 262
Suwirjo (chairman of PNI), 180

Talma, Mr., 49
Taman Siswa schools, 60, 71
Tan Ling Djie, 157
Tan Malaka, 57, 59, 61, 132, 134, 139, 144, 157, 163–4, 175, 195, 209, 264; biography, 58; ideal of 'Aslia', 118; bids for power, 118, 137–8; joined by ousted ministers, 121; founds PP, and his demands popularly acclaimed, 122–3; aims to overthrow Sjahrir and Sukarno, 123; pardoned, 133; forms Murba party, 138; death, 139–40
Tasikmalaja rebellion, 92
Tendean, Lieut., 231
Tentara Islam Indonesia (Indonesian Muslim army), 167
Tentara Republik Indonesia. *See* Army
Terauchi, Marshal, 108, 110
Thamrin, Mohammed Husni, 71–2, 79, 85, 108
Tiga A (Three A's) movement, 84–5, 91
Tidschrift, Het, 29, 34
Timor, Lesser Sundas, 4, 159
Tirtoadisurjo, R. M., 39, 41, 44
Tirtoprodjo, Susanto, 155
Tjipto Mangunkusumo (father of the Independence movement), 25–7, 31–7,

39, 44, 47–9, 51, 56, 59–60, 63, 77, 85, 112
Tjokroadikusumo, regent of Temanggung, 29–30
Tjokroadisurjo, Iskaq, 63, 65, 74, 115, 154–5
Tjokroaminoto, Anwar, 263
Tjokroaminoto, Umar Said, 39–40, 42–5, 47–9, 52–6, 63–4, 68, 74, 85, 144, 193
Tjokrosujoso, Abikusno. *See* Abikusno
Tjugito (member of the PKI Politburo), 260
Tjuo Sangi-In (Central Advisory Committee), 90–1, 93, 95–8, 103, 107
TNI (Tentara Negara Indonesia). *See* Army
Tojo (Japanese Prime Minister), 88–9, 95, 107
Totoks (full blooded Europeans), 11
Trade union federation. *See* SOBSI
Trade union of the army (SOKSI), 219
Trading associations, 38–9

Ulamas (religious scholars), 6, 75, 81, 91, 106, 114, 145, 153, 167, 173, 188. *See also* Nahdatul Ulama (NU)
Uleebalangs, 6, 20, 145, 168
Umar, Teuku, 6
Umar Wirahadikusuma, Major-General, 233–4, 254
United Nations, 129–30, 139, 162, 182, 184, 195, 206–10, 214, 247, 257–8; Committee of Good Offices (*see* CGO); Michelmore Commission, 212; Indonesia withdraws from 224; Indonesia rejoins, 248
United States, 129–30, 132–3, 136, 141, 162, 207–8, 213, 217
Universitas Indonesia, 24, 60, 99, 183, 204–5, 240, 245–6
Untung, Lieut.-Colonel, 226–7, 230–5
Urip Sumohardjo, General, 94, 166; army chief of staff, 116–17, 137
USDEK, 191
Usman, Julius, 247
USSR, 133, 162, 208
Utojo, Kusumo, 48
Utusan Hindia (The Indian Messenger), 53

Village communities. See *Desas*
Village headman. See *Lurah*
Visman, Dr. F. H., 78

320

Index

Volksraad (Colonial Council), 44–52, 56, 65, 67, 70–2, 77–8, 80–1, 91, 159, 169; composition 1927–38, 71; Council of Delegates in the Volksraad, 70

Volunteer army. *See* Peta

Vriji Woord, Het (ISDV organ), 53

Wahhabi movement, 4–5

Wahidin Sudirohusodo, Dr., 26, 30, 112

Walujo, 226

Wajang – play, 32, 37, 39

Wedanas (district administrators), 9

Wedioningrat, Dr. Radjiman. *See* Radjiman

Welter, Charles J. I. M. (Colonial Minister), 72, 80

West Irian (New Guinea), 142, 158, 162, 168, 182, 207–11, 217, 254, 257–9, 262

Westerling, 'Turk', 147–8

Widjanarko, Bambang, 234–6

Wikana, of Pesindo, 103, 110–11, 115, 118, 134

Wilopo (PNI leader), 155, 160, 263; Prime Minister, 165

Wirjopranoto, Sukardjo, 80, 85, 101

Wirnata Kusuma, R. A. A. (regent of Bandung), 72, 101, 103, 113, 117; Minister for Home Affairs, 117

Wiwoho Purbohadijojo, 75, 77–8

Women, emancipation of, 22

Wongsongnegoro (leader of PIR), 156

Yamin, Muhammad, 74, 99, 101, 104, 106, 118, 123–4, 144, 195–6

Yani, Major-General (army chief of staff), 211, 220, 224–5, 228, 231, 233–4

Yusuf, General Mohammed, 243

Zainuddin (Communist politician), 57

Zeven Provinciën mutiny, 71

Zhdanov, 132